The FAST-CHANGING
ARCTIC

NORTHERN LIGHTS SERIES

COPUBLISHED WITH THE ARCTIC INSTITUTE OF NORTH AMERICA
ISSN 1701-0004 (PRINT) ISSN 1925-2943 (ONLINE)

This series takes up the geographical region of the North (circumpolar regions within the zone of discontinuous permafrost) and publishes works from all areas of northern scholarship, including natural sciences, social sciences, earth sciences, and the humanities.

The FAST-CHANGING
ARCTIC

RETHINKING ARCTIC SECURITY
FOR A WARMER WORLD

Edited by Barry Scott Zellen

UNIVERSITY OF
CALGARY
PRESS

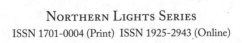

Northern Lights Series
ISSN 1701-0004 (Print) ISSN 1925-2943 (Online)

University of Calgary Press
2500 University Drive NW
Calgary, Alberta
Canada T2N 1N4
www.uofcpress.com

LIBRARY AND ARCHIVES CANADA CATALOGUING IN PUBLICATION

The fast-changing Arctic : rethinking Arctic security for a warmer world / edited by Barry Scott Zellen.

(Northern lights series, ISSN 1701-0004 ; 15)
Includes bibliographical references and index.
Issued also in electronic formats.
Co-published by: Arctic Institute of North America.
ISBN 978-1-55238-646-0

1. Security, International—Arctic regions. 2. Arctic regions—Military policy. 3. Arctic regions—Strategic aspects. 4. Arctic regions—Foreign relations. 5. Global warming—Arctic regions. I. Zellen, Barry Scott, 1963- II. Arctic Institute of North America III. Series: Northern lights series ; 15

UA880.F38 2013   355'.0335113   C2013-900291-X

The University of Calgary Press acknowledges the support of the Government of Alberta through the Alberta Multimedia Development Fund for our publications. We acknowledge the financial support of the Government of Canada through the Canada Book Fund for our publishing activities. We acknowledge the financial support of the Canada Council for the Arts for our publishing program.

Government
of Alberta ▓   Canada   Canada Council   Conseil des Arts
                                                         for the Arts   du Canada

Printed and bound in Canada by Houghton Boston
♻ This book is printed on Enviro 100 paper

Cover photo by westphalia (istockphoto.com)
Cover design, page design, and typesetting by Melina Cusano

Contents

REGIONAL PERSPECTIVES

EUROPE AND THE HIGH NORTH ATLANTIC

NORTH AMERICA

Foreword:
Witnessing an Arctic Renaissance

Mead Treadwell, Lieutenant Governor, State of Alaska

Long famed for its inaccessibility, the Arctic Ocean is rapidly becoming accessible – with a rising tide of trade, commerce and resource development fostered by unprecedented seasonal sea ice retreats.[1]

For Arctic states across the globe, the accessible Arctic Ocean presents opportunities of a lifetime. Consider the following: The U.S. Geological Survey estimates that 13 per cent of the world's undiscovered oil and 23 per cent of its undiscovered gas will be found in the Arctic, and six of the eight Arctic nations are already engaging in offshore energy exploration. Sea ice retreat has beckoned major new shipping in the North, and Russia will have sent as many as eighteen vessels via the Northern Sea Route in 2011 – including a giant gas condensate tanker, which transited the route in a record eight days.

The Arctic's energy resources, minerals, tourism, and shipping potential make this increasingly accessible region a classic emerging market. Billions of public and private dollars will be invested in its development. New infrastructure will increase our physical access to the Arctic, and commercial expansion will follow.

We are witnessing an exciting Arctic renaissance. Just as the International Polar Year 2007–9 revealed that the Arctic is not static but is constantly changing, Arctic borders are likewise on the move. Lingering border disputes, issues regarding new territory, and implementation of the Law of the Sea Treaty are among the sovereign challenges we're working to resolve in the region. Among Arctic neighbors, it's an ongoing balancing act between competition and cooperation.

But I'm most excited about the cooperation. Through my participation in meetings of the U.S. Arctic Research Commission, the Russian Geographical Society, the Northern Forum, the Northern Research Forum, the Arctic Council and its predecessor, the Arctic Environmental Protection Strategy – whose record of circumpolar cooperation has spanned twenty years and counting – I've been privileged to see us build a real neighborhood at the top of the world.

The Arctic needs outside partners who share our vision of opportunity and respect for the people and critters that have always lived here. The best partners favor cooperation, transparency, and respect as we engage in the rulemaking and resource development of our region, and they bring science and investment to the table. One cooperative effort that I'm especially proud of is the Arctic Council's Arctic Marine Shipping Assessment (AMSA) – which the U.S. Arctic Research Commission sponsored during my chairmanship, and, in which – for the first time – eight Arctic nations gathered to discuss cooperation on safe shipping their region. As a result, further cooperation is taking place among Arctic partners on multiple fronts to implement the recommendations of AMSA:

- A historic search and rescue agreement was signed at the 7th Annual Arctic Council Ministerial in Nuuk, Greenland, in May 2011, and the first implementation meeting was a Canadian-led search and rescue exercise that took place just several months following. Such exercises expose our deficiencies in equipment, mapping, ice forecasting, ports and other aids to navigation, and help our militaries and civil responders "play well" together.

- Arctic partners have advocated that the International Maritime Organization adopt a mandatory polar code to set minimum standards for ships operating in polar waters.

- The Arctic Council is negotiating an international agreement on Arctic marine oil pollution and response.

- Joint discussions on the development and upgrades of common Arctic security infrastructure – including deep-water ports, vessel-tracking systems, Polar-class icebreakers, telecommunications, and high-resolution mapping and ice imagery – are underway.

Let us hope that these developments lead to the kind of coordinated investment that is the hallmark of the St. Lawrence Seaway system – a model established between the United States and Canada for that shared waterway on our common border.

Diligent scientific monitoring has been the keystone of Arctic cooperation and negotiation so far. The Arctic Council's sponsorship of a Sustained Arctic Observing Network (SAON) is another deliverable of our successful cooperation, and the best International Polar Year legacy we can leave behind. If we do SAON right, our research will support sustainable Arctic energy; safe, secure, and reliable shipping; successful search and rescue operations; more advanced oil-spill prevention and response techniques; better knowledge of how to protect and manage our species populations in the region; and increased data for modeling to produce more accurate and timely forecasts. All told, it will help us predict changing climate conditions, guard against ocean acidification, and monitor moving fish stocks and changing populations of seals, walrus, polar bear and birdlife.

Over the next few years, we must see even more cooperation across the Arctic neighborhood. The following chapters make clear that an understanding of energy, shipping, sovereignty, and climate are key to our successful collaboration.

Note

1   On September 16, 2012, Arctic sea ice extent fell to a record low of 1.32 million square miles. As National Snow and Ice Data Center (NSIDC) director Mark Serreze observed: "While lots of people talk about opening of the Northwest Passage through the Canadian Arctic islands and the Northern Sea Route along the Russian coast, twenty years from now in August you might be able to take a ship right across the Arctic Ocean." National Snow and Ice Data Center, "Press Release: Arctic sea ice reaches lowest extent for the year and the satellite record," September 19, 2012, http://nsidc.org/news/press/2012_seaiceminimum.html.

ARCTIC CLIMATE CHANGE: STRATEGIC CHALLENGES AND OPPORTUNITIES

1. The Fast-Changing Maritime Arctic[1]

Lawson W. Brigham

The maritime Arctic continues to experience a steady pace of development and expansion of marine operations. In recent times, a record number of vessels have transited the Northwest Passage, and several milestone operations have occurred in the Russian Arctic. Affecting all commercial and naval operations, and of particular importance to planners of future ventures, is the recently observed decline of the Arctic Ocean's sea-ice cover, as well as its year-to-year variability. While this historic retreat and climate-change impacts on the Arctic received global attention, the realities of the region's natural-resource development and greater commercial use have gained higher profiles in political discussions.

Sea Ice Changes

NASA researchers and the National Snow and Ice Data Center, University of Colorado at Boulder, reported that the area of the Arctic Ocean covered by sea ice on September 12, 2009, was the third lowest since satellite measurements began in 1979. While this area was larger than the record minimum coverage observed in 2007 and the minimum area for 2008, it represents one of the smallest areas on record. Arctic sea-ice coverage has declined by nearly 12 per cent each of the past three decades, for a remarkable total decrease of 34 per cent.[2]

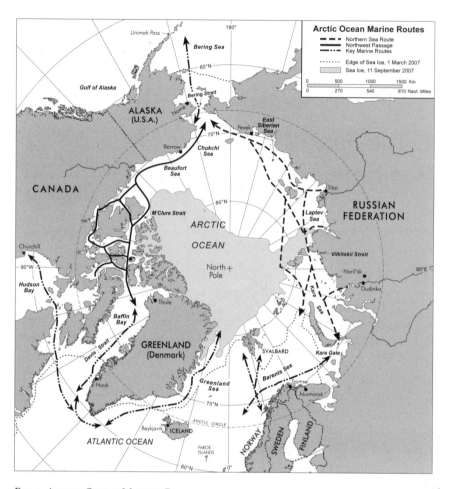

Arctic Ocean Marine Routes

- ▬ ▬ Northern Sea Route
- ▬▬ Northwest Passage
- ▬ ·▬ Key Marine Routes
- · · · · · Edge of Sea Ice, 1 March 2007
- ▢ Sea Ice, 11 September 2007

| 0 | 500 | 1000 | 1500 Km |
| 0 | 270 | 540 | 810 Naut. Miles |

Fig. 1. Arctic Ocean Marine Routes.

Despite this extraordinary change in coverage and observed thinning of sea ice (estimated from recent satellite measurements compared with declassified sonar measurements from U.S. Navy submarines), much of the Arctic Ocean today remains fully or partially ice-covered for most of the year. This is a significant factor when considering new regulatory requirements for polar-class ships and potential operational restrictions for non-icecapable naval and commercial ships.

Much speculation has also continued about what year the entire Arctic Ocean might be essentially ice-free for a short period in summer. It is plausible that this could happen by 2030, according to recent simulations of sea-ice models driven by global climate change. From a practical maritime perspective, the significance of this physical change in the Arctic Ocean will be the disappearance of multiyear ice, ice that survives the summer melt for one year or longer. It is this older sea ice that is more difficult to break, and its presence makes it more challenging to operate in the Arctic offshore. Its potential disappearance could in future decades make this ocean significantly more navigable.

Increasing Activity

During August and September 2009, two German merchant ships, the heavy-lift vessels *Beluga Fraternity* and *Beluga Foresight*, sailed from Ulsan, Korea, to the Atlantic Ocean along the northern coast of Eurasia. The voyages captured global media attention and represent a significant new maritime linkage of Asian suppliers to the Russian Arctic. The primary task of the two ice-strengthened ships (built in 2008) was to deliver forty-four heavy plant modules to barges on the Ob River in western Siberia; additional cargo was reported to have been carried in October from Archangel, on the White Sea, to Nigeria.[3]

Along the Northern Sea Route, defined in Russian law as the sailing routes between Bering Strait west to Kara Gate at the southern end of Novaya Zemlya, ice conditions were very light. However, convoy escort was still provided by the Russian nuclear-powered icebreakers *50 Let Pobedy* and *Rossiya*. Significantly, details of the fees paid for the icebreaker escort services and Russian pilots were not reported. Earlier in the summer, the *50 Let Pobedy* carried tourists on two voyages to the North Pole.

Sweden's non-nuclear-powered icebreaker *Oden*, on a scientific voyage, also reached the Pole on August 23, its sixth visit there since 1991. The ship conducted scientific operations north of Greenland along the Lomonosov Ridge, July 31 though September 10, for the Danish Continental Shelf Project and the Swedish Polar Research Secretariat.

Two year-round Arctic marine transportation systems were fully operational during 2009 in the Barents and Kara seas. Three icebreaking tankers operated by Sovcomflot shuttled oil from the offshore Varendey terminal in the Pechora Sea to Murmansk. A five-ship fleet of new icebreaking

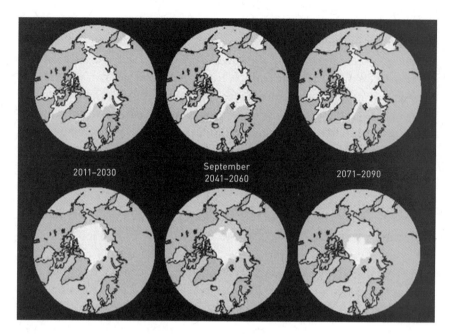

Fig. 2. Projected Sea-Ice Extent from 2004 Arctic Climate Impact Assessment. In 2004, the Arctic Climate Impact Assessment projected that year-round sea ice could disappear by century's end. Some experts now believe this could happen as early as 2030, if not sooner, making the Arctic Ocean significantly more navigable. (Source: Arctic Climate Impact Assessment.)

containerships carried nickel plates from the port of Dudinka on the Yenisey River (it services the mining and smelting complex in Norilsk) to Murmansk, an operation that has been year-round for three decades. The commercial ice-breaking ships used in both of these systems are designed to operate without icebreaker escort. The year 2009 also marked the fiftieth anniversary of the operation of the first nuclear-powered surface ship, Russia's icebreaker *Lenin*, now a museum ship in Murmansk.

In the Canadian Arctic, thirteen vessels – eleven yachts and two ice-strengthened tour ships, the Bahamian-flagged *Bremen* and *Hanseatic* – sailed the routes of the Northwest Passage in east and west directions between the Pacific and Atlantic oceans. Of the 135 full transits of the various routes of the Passage since Roald Amundsen's historic voyage in 1903–6 (60 voyages since 2000), the thirteen vessels represent the highest number of full transits in a single summer season.[4]

Three notable scientific expeditions were conducted in the central Arctic Ocean, two of which were primarily related to gathering data to support the extended continental shelf claims of several Arctic nations. The *Oden*'s voyage for Denmark and Sweden is described previously. Additionally, the U.S.–Canada Arctic Continental Shelf Survey was conducted August 7 to September 16, 2009, using the U.S. Coast Guard icebreaker *Healy* (WAGB-20) and Canadian Coast Guard icebreaker *Louis S. St-Laurent*, operating in and near Canada Basin within the central Arctic Ocean.

And the Russian research vessel Professor Khromov was used to support a joint Russia–U.S. expedition named the Russian–American Long-term Census of the Arctic. The National Oceanic and Atmospheric Administration and Russian Academy of Sciences team collected oceanographic data and conducted biological surveys in the East Siberian and Chukchi seas as far north as 70 degrees. The bilateral nature of these three operations in the Arctic Ocean shows the levels of successful international collaboration that can be achieved today in Arctic science and affairs.

Agreements and Cooperation

At the April 29, 2009, Arctic Council Ministerial Meeting in Tromsö, Norway, the Arctic Marine Shipping Assessment 2009 Report (AMSA) was approved and released. This comprehensive study outlines a framework for protecting the region's people and marine environment. Led by Canada, Finland, and the United States since 2005 under the council's working group on Protection of the Arctic Marine Environment, AMSA focuses on marine safety and environmental protection.

The assessment can now be considered a baseline (relying on a historic snapshot of Arctic marine activity collected for 2004), a strategic guide for many stakeholders involved in future uses of this ocean, and a policy document of the Arctic Council. The report was negotiated and represents a consensus document of the eight Arctic states. AMSA reaffirms the Arctic state view that the United Nations Convention on the Law of the Sea (UNCLOS) remains the legal framework that influences and guides current and future governance of the Arctic Ocean. AMSA also acknowledges that the International Maritime Organization (IMO) is the lead and appropriate UN body that can

- Develop a comprehensive, multination Arctic SAR agreement.

- Update and mandatorily apply relevant parts of IMO's Guidelines for Ships Operating in Arctic Ice-Covered Waters.

- Augment global IMO ship safety and pollution prevention conventions with specific mandatory Arctic requirements or other provisions for ship construction, design, equipment, crewing, training, and operations.

- Explore the possible harmonization of Arctic marine shipping regulatory regimes, including measures to protect the central Arctic Ocean, consistent with UNCLOS.

- Consider surveys of indigenous Arctic marine use.

- Identify areas of heightened ecological and cultural significance, and explore the need for specially designated marine areas for environmental protection.

- Increase cooperation in oil spill prevention and continue to develop circumpolar pollution response capabilities.

- Continue to develop a comprehensive marine traffic awareness system to improve monitoring and tracking of marine activity, enhance data sharing in near real-time, and augment vessel management services.

- Engage Arctic states with relevant international organizations to further assess the effects on marine mammals of ship noise, disturbance, and ship strikes in Arctic waters.

- Invest in hydrographic, meteorological, and oceanographic data in support of safe navigation and voyage planning in Arctic waters in Ilulissat, where a declaration was signed reaffirming the importance of UNCLOS as the legal framework for addressing issues in the Arctic Ocean.

focus on marine-safety and environmental-protection measures for the global maritime industry, including operations in the Arctic.

The study also, importantly, included the concerns and perspectives of the region's indigenous residents. One of the key AMSA findings noted as a serious concern was the lack of basic marine infrastructure in the Arctic (such as charts, communications, search and rescue, ports, salvage, environmental response, and more), except for the Norwegian coast and coastal northwest Russia. A number of the AMSA recommendations (see box) show the breadth of issues addressed by this study and its clear message by the Arctic Council to the global community.

The council also approved formation of a task force to address the development of an Arctic search and rescue agreement. The U.S. Coast Guard and Department of State hosted the first meeting of this task force in December 2009 to begin the process. During the year, IMO held significant discussions on Arctic marine safety. The organization developed a plan for ship-construction standards and ice-navigator qualifications to be implemented as early as 2014. The Swedish shipping company Rederi AB TransAtlantic formed an International Ice Advisory Board, a group of ice-navigation experts, to facilitate the dialogue and dissemination of operation information to global maritime interests. Meetings of the Ice Board have been held in Lulea and Kalmar, two of Sweden's coastal cities.

Diplomacy and Strategic Interests

Canada has received media attention recently for publishing new rules regulating domestic and foreign ship traffic in Arctic waters. The plan calls for a new Northern Canada Vessel Traffic Services Zone that would require registration of ships 300 tons or greater, tugs with a two-ship tonnage of 500 tons or more, and any vessel carrying dangerous goods or potential pollutants.

The announcement of the new regulations noted that the rules were "consistent with international law regarding ice-covered areas," in reference to Arctic 234 of UNCLOS. This allows coastal states to adopt and enforce non-discriminatory regulations for the prevention, reduction, and control of marine pollution in ice-covered waters within the exclusive economic zone.

There have been few reports on the status of Canada's planned army training center in Resolute and refurbishment of a deepwater port in Nanisivik.

Both Arctic facilities were announced in August 2007 by Prime Minister Stephen Harper as measures to boost Canada's sovereignty in the region. The Arctic/Offshore Patrol Ship project (six to eight ice-capable, armed patrol ships), announced in 2007, continues with a planned first ship delivery in 2014.

Canada also held a second ministerial meeting of the five Arctic Ocean coastal states (Canada, Denmark, Norway, Russia, and the United States, which border the Arctic Ocean) on March 29, 2010. Discussions were held on the need for deepening cooperation as seabed claims are submitted, and the importance of addressing the many challenges of greater Arctic Ocean accessibility.[5] Concern was expressed outside and within the group that missing from the meeting were Iceland, Finland, Sweden, and representatives of the Arctic's indigenous peoples. Denmark had hosted the first meeting of this group in May 2008.

In October 2009, the United States took action in closing off more than 150,000 square nautical miles of U.S. Arctic waters (north of Bering Strait in the Chukchi and Beaufort seas) to commercial fishing. U.S. Commerce Secretary Gary Locke, who has authority over North Pacific Fisheries Management Council decisions, noted that this was a precautionary measure pending further study of the region, which is undergoing significant Arctic environmental change.[6] One of the diplomatic complications of this closure is that among the areas in which the United States suspended fishing is the disputed zone in the Beaufort Sea, which is on the border with Canada. In November 2009 Vice Chief of Naval Operations Admiral Jonathan W. Greenert released to the public a U.S. Navy Arctic Roadmap, a thirty-three-page strategic plan developed by the Navy's Task Force Climate Change and led by Oceanographer of the Navy Rear Admiral David Titley. This roadmap notes the changing Arctic environment and focuses on several objectives, including the development of strong cooperative partnerships, assessing fleet readiness and mission requirements, and improving environmental prediction in the region.

Soon after this Navy initiative, Senator Lisa Murkowski (R-AK) and Congressman Don Young (R-AK) submitted bills to study the possibility of building a deepwater port in the U.S. Arctic. Issues to be assessed include the location and strategic capabilities for such a port. Replacement of the aging Polar-class icebreakers and continued lack of coastal icebreaking assets in the

U.S Arctic remain challenging tasks, given the ongoing replacement of U.S. Coast Guard cutters and aircraft in the lengthy Deepwater program.

The Stockholm International Peace Research Institute's March 2010 release of a report titled China Prepares for an Ice-free Arctic received global media attention. This report reviews China's expanding polar research capabilities, describes its commercial interests in summertime trans-Arctic voyages, and comments on the nation's diverse views on engagement with the Arctic states.[7] Many others see China's real interests in terms of access to the region's immense natural-resource wealth.

The Arctic has been a strategic waterway for submarines during the past half-century, a legacy that continues. In March 2009 an ice exercise was held in the central Arctic Ocean involving the USS Annapolis (SSN-760) and USS Helena (SSN-725). Less well known is the number of surface ships that have voyaged to the North Pole and crossed the Arctic Ocean.

There have been eighty icebreaker voyages to the North Pole during 1977–2009, twenty in support of science and the remaining sixty for marine tourism on board Russian icebreakers. Icebreakers from Sweden, Germany, the United States, Canada, and Norway have also reached the North Pole. Only one was not conducted during the summer season, when the sea ice is at its minimal extent and thickness. The voyages' dates indicate a short summer navigation season of ten weeks (July through mid-September).

The first surface ship to reach the North Pole was the Soviet nuclear-powered icebreaker Arktika on August 17, 1977. The ship sailed along a track from Murmansk east to the Laptev Sea and then north to the Pole. She returned on a direct route to homeport. The distance covered was 3,852 nautical miles, sailed in fourteen days at a remarkable speed of 11.5 knots.[8]

The Soviet icebreaker Sibir reached the North Pole on May 25, 1987, navigating in near-maximum thickness of Arctic sea ice. This ship rescued personnel from the Soviet North Pole Drift Station 27 and also established the new Drift Station 29 in the northern Laptev Sea, during a demanding voyage in the central Arctic Ocean from May 8 to June 19, 1987.[9]

Seven of the voyages that reached the North Pole were also trans-Arctic, or complete crossings of the ocean for tourism and scientific research: In August 1991, the Soviet nuclear icebreaker Sovetskiy Soyuz carried tourists across the central Arctic Ocean. During July and August, 1994, the Canadian Coast Guard's Louis S. St-Laurent and U.S. Coast Guard's Polar Sea (WAGB-11) conducted the first scientific transect of the Arctic Ocean by surface ship. The icebreakers sailed from Bering Strait to the North Pole and out of the Arctic through Fram Strait (between Greenland and Svalbard), a voyage of some 2,200 nautical miles directly across the central Arctic Ocean. The Russian nuclear-powered icebreaker *Yamal* sailed on two trans-Arctic voyages with tourists during the summer of 1996. And a second scientific transect of the Arctic Ocean by icebreaker was accomplished in summer 2005 by Sweden's *Oden* and the U.S. Coast Guard's *Healy*.

These trans-Arctic voyages indicate that marine access throughout the entire Arctic Ocean in summer has been achieved by highly capable nuclear- and non-nuclear-powered polar icebreakers.

Continuing Operations

Shell Oil should gain approval to conduct drilling on its lease sites on the seabed of the Chukchi Sea, off northwest Alaska. Operations during summer 2012 in this relatively remote region will require a sizable fleet of on-scene icebreakers and support vessels. Cairn Energy, which commenced drilling off Greenland's west coast near Disko Island in 2010 and 2011, is poised to drill again in 2012. A 60,000-ton drillship, the UK-flag Stena Forth, was chartered to conduct these challenging offshore operations. Built in Korea, the ship and an ice-management team of icebreakers have contended with drifting icebergs in this operational area of Baffin Bay.[10] Finding substantial oil or gas at one or both of the lease sites will generate significant international interest and potential Arctic investment.

In addition to offshore drilling, experimental voyages along Russia's Northern Sea Route will continue during summer 2012. Sovcomflot, Russia's largest shipping company, has indicated plans for 2012 to conduct continued experimental voyages of an oil tanker sailing from the Varendey offshore terminal east along the Northern Sea Route to Asia.[11] One of Sovcomflot's 70,000-deadweight-ton shuttle tankers normally carrying oil to Murmansk will be used for these international voyages.[12] Trial voyages of liquid natural gas ships from western Siberia to Asia may also occur.

The technical and operational challenges posed by these voyages have been known for some time and largely overcome in recent years. However, what remains unclear is the overall economic viability of such Arctic voyages, given the costs of icebreaker escort, whether necessary for passage or not, as well as other service fees along the route. These voyages are primary examples of future linkages of Russian Arctic natural resources to global markets. Further, this flurry of marine activity is indicative of continued investment in Arctic marine operations despite the current global economic situation.

Globalization, climate change, and geopolitics continue to shape the future of the maritime Arctic. International bodies such as the Arctic Council and International Maritime Organization have awakened to the urgent need to protect Arctic people and the marine environment. They must also address the key issue of inadequate marine infrastructure in much of the region. Many wildcard issues remain to play out, such as the future of Greenland, strategic interests of new stakeholders, future oil and gas discoveries, the plausible loss of multiyear Arctic sea ice, emerging seasonal shipping routes, and much more. Nevertheless, one thing is certain: The Arctic Ocean will be a busier and more complex place.

U.S. Coast Guard Must Enhance its Polar Roles in a Fast-Changing Arctic[13]

The U.S. Coast Guard led the U.S. delegation during the negotiations of new Arctic search-and-rescue (SAR) agreement among the eight Arctic states that was signed in May 2011. Coast Guard experts have also been members of delegations addressing Antarctic SAR and tourism. These are excellent and appropriate initiatives, given the service's federal responsibilities in maritime SAR and safety in both polar regions.

But the timely actions are not enough. The Coast Guard must be more proactive and engaged to ensure that our many polar maritime interests are given proper attention. Importantly, what needs to be accomplished does not need to be directly linked to the justification and acquisition of polar icebreakers. The following modest plan would energize and enhance the service's key roles in polar affairs:

- *Arctic Council Involvement:* The Coast Guard must be a regular member of the U.S. delegation to the Arctic Council to provide broad maritime expertise. This intergovernmental forum is an evolving policy body that will continue to address emerging marine issues.

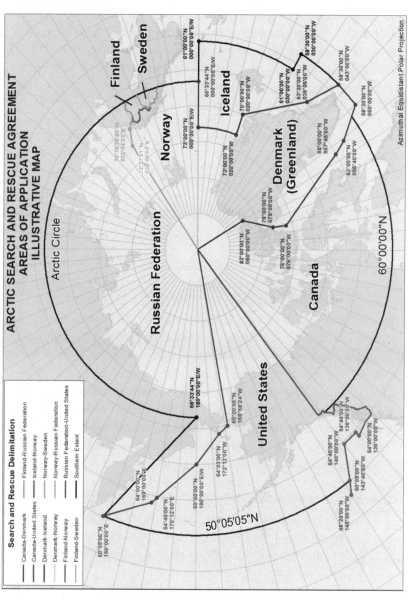

FIG. 3. ARCTIC SEARCH AND RESCUE AGREEMENT AREAS OF APPLICATION.

ARCTIC SEARCH AND RESCUE AGREEMENT
AREAS OF APPLICATION
ILLUSTRATIVE MAP

Azimuthal Equidistant Polar Projection

Search and Rescue Delimitation

Canada-Denmark
Canada-United States
Denmark-Iceland
Denmark-Norway
Finland-Norway
Finland-Sweden

Finland-Russian Federation
Iceland-Norway
Norway-Sweden
Norway-Russian Federation
Russian Federation-United States
Southern Extent

- *Arctic Emergencies Forum:* The Coast Guard should assume the role of U.S. representative to the Arctic Council's working group on Emergency Prevention, Preparedness, and Response, now chaired by the United States. Officials at the Department of Energy staff both the chair and a lead U.S. representative position. The Coast Guard can contribute maritime expertise, particularly in marine-pollution response.

- *Arctic Ocean Protection:* The service must be a regular member of the U.S. delegation to the Arctic Council's working group on Protection of the Arctic Marine Environment, which conducts assessments and drafts policy strategies for the Arctic ministers. The Arctic Marine Shipping Assessment (AMSA) was conducted under its auspices, and Coast Guard experts contributed extensively to the study. An Arctic Ocean Review is ongoing in the group, and the Coast Guard must participate in its development.

- *AMSA Implementation Plan:* AMSA was released in 2009, and the Coast Guard has smartly developed an internal tracking system to facilitate implementation of its seventeen recommendations. A publicly released implementation plan would be an important next step, similar to the U.S. Navy Arctic Roadmap of late 2009 and NOAA's Arctic Vision and Strategy to be released later in 2010.

- *U.S. Delegation to the International Maritime Organization (IMO):* The Coast Guard should strengthen the polar maritime expertise of the U.S. delegation to the IMO, which it leads. The IMO is developing a mandatory code for polar ships and is beginning to address safety and environmental protection issues unique to the Arctic. This requires new expertise in polar operations and ship design.

- *Polar Code Implementation:* A mandatory IMO polar code could be fully developed by 2014; included will be sections on safety equipment, ice-navigator standards, polar ship-construction standards, and more. The Coast Guard should draft regulations and develop an implementation strategy for applying the polar code in U.S. Arctic waters.

- *Ice-Operations Capacity in the U.S. Arctic:* The Coast Guard has no ice-capable ships that can operate in the shallow, ice-covered coastal waters of Alaska (where deep-draft polar icebreakers cannot operate) or in deeper ice-covered waters when polar icebreakers are unavailable. An ongoing Arctic mission analysis should yield requirements to fill this gap in federal maritime capability in terms of enforcement and security. Ice-capable, multimission buoy tenders may be one answer, but more options need to be explored.

- *Antarctic Treaty Delegations:* The Coast Guard should be a regular member of the U.S. delegation to the annual Antarctic Treaty consultative meetings, and of working groups, especially when issues related to marine operations and marine tourism are discussed.

- *Arctic Oil-Spill Experts Group:* In the wake of BP's massive 2010 Gulf oil spill, the service should consider establishing a group of experts to review the issues and research needs for responding to an Arctic marine oil spill.

- *Future Polar Marine Operations:* The service should sponsor and engage fully in technical and operational forums to discuss the future of polar marine operations, including offshore development, fishing, marine tourism, commercial ship voyaging, and infrastructure needs.

These suggested tasks are not onerous or expensive. However, they are crucial to furthering U.S. interests in the polar regions. And being more engaged can surely be beneficial in arguing the nation's future polar icebreaker needs. The Coast Guard has the responsibility and the professional polar expertise to engage actively in these pursuits, and all of us expect no less.

Notes

1 Reprinted, with permission, from "The Fast-Changing Maritime Arctic," *Proceedings* 136, no. 5 (2010): 54–59. Copyright 2010, U.S. Naval Institute, www.usni.org.

2 "Arctic Sea Ice Extent Is Third Lowest on Record," NASA, October 6, 2009; http://www.nasa.gov/topics/earth/features/seaicemin09_prt.htm. In 2012, Arctic Ocean sea ice retreated even further to its lowest observed level. As NOAA's 2012 Arctic Report Card observed: "Based on estimates produced by the National Snow and Ice Data Center, on September 16, 2012 the sea ice cover reached its minimum extent for the year of 3.41 million km². This was the lowest in the satellite record; 18% lower than in 2007, when the previous record of 4.17 million km² was recorded. Overall, this year's minimum was 3.29 million km² (49%) below the 1979–2000 average minimum of 6.71 million km². The last six years, 2007–2012, have the six lowest minimum extents since satellite observations began in 1979." See: D. Perovich, W. Meier, M. Tschudi, S. Gerland, and J. Richter-Menge, "Sea Ice," Arctic Report Card: Update for 2012, National Oceanic and Atmospheric Administration (NOAA), December 3, 2012, www.arctic.noaa.gov/reportcard/sea-ice.html.

3 "A Shortcut through the Arctic Ocean," *Blue Line Magazine*, Beluga Shipping, Bremen, Germany, February 2010, 10–12.

4 R. Headland, "Transits of the Northwest Passage, 1903–2009," Scott Polar Research Institute, University of Cambridge, February 23, 2010.

5 Minister of Foreign Affairs of Canada, Chair's Summary of March 29, 2010, Arctic Ocean Foreign Ministers meeting.

6 U.S. Secretary of Commerce press release, August 20, 2009, "Approval of the Arctic Fishery Management Plan."

7 L. Jakobson, *China Prepares for an Ice-free Arctic*, Stockholm International Peace Research Institute, Insights on Peace and Security, No. 2010/2, Solna, Sweden.

8 T. Armstrong, "Icebreaker Voyage to the North Pole, 1977," *Polar Record* 19, no. 118 (1978): 67–68.

9 I. Frolov, "The 1987 Expedition of the Icebreaker Sibir to the North Pole," in L. Brigham, *The Soviet Maritime Arctic* (Annapolis, MD: Naval Institute Press, 1991), 33–44.

10 Discussions with G. Liljestrom (Stena) and N. Anders (Stena Drilling), Kalmar Maritime Academy, Sweden, March 2, 2010.

11 Sovcomflot press release, December 26, 2009, "Sovcomflot President and CEO Sergey Frank Meets with Prime Minister Vladimir Putin."

12 Lloyd's List, February 23, 2010, "SCF to test Northern Sea Route."

13 "The Coast Guard Must Enhance Its Polar Roles," is reproduced from the "Nobody Asked Me But …" column in *Proceedings* 136/8/1290 (August 2010): 290.

2. Can We Keep Up with Arctic Change?

Alun Anderson

The Arctic is changing rapidly and unpredictably. At the end of the summer in 2011, the total area of the ice left in the Arctic was 1.78 million square miles, down from the average of 2.72 million square miles seen in the last two decades of the twentieth century. An area of summer ice six times the size of California has vanished, leaving huge expanses of open water all around the Arctic shores.

No scientist expected to see change at such a startling rate. Just over five years ago, computer models predicted that the first ice-free summers in the Arctic would not arrive for almost a hundred years; now 2030 is seen as probable and 2015 as possible for the first year in which the ice will all melt away. As the ice goes, the unique animals of the Arctic, from the charismatic polar bear and the narwhal right down to the tiny, unseen creatures that live in fissures in the sea ice, will vanish too. Other animals from the south which flourish in warmer seas will arrive to replace them.

Humans are already arriving from the south: oil, gas, and mineral prospectors, tourists anxious to see the last polar bears, trawlers looking for new fishing grounds, cargo vessels taking Arctic oil and minerals away to resource-hungry nations, and the first few ships pioneering a fast route between Atlantic and Pacific. The people who have long lived in the Arctic now see their current way of life disappearing, sometimes along with their homes which are sinking into the thawing permafrost or being washed away by waves from newly open seas.

The five nations that ring the Arctic seas (United States, Canada, Russia, Norway, and Denmark, through Greenland) along with the other three nations which have territory within the Arctic Circle (Sweden, Finland, and Iceland) have all reacted by rewriting their policies for the High North. One broad theme runs through them: how to balance opportunities for the exploitation of resources with care for the environment and the rights of Arctic residents, while ensuring the region is free from conflict and that the Arctic nations, not outsiders, remain the key players in deciding what happens there.

A decade ago, concern over the Arctic might have stopped with these eight members of the Arctic Council, the region's only high-level forum, and the indigenous groups which have been given permanent participant status at the Council. But now environmental groups from far away and ever more distant nations demand a say in the region's future. China is busy building its second icebreaker, runs an Arctic research station and has begun investment in Arctic mines, oil, and gas. The European Union, Korea, and Japan are among many others who are scrabbling to boost their influence in the Arctic and, like China, want to gain permanent observer status at the Council.

The difficult questions of who should have what level of representation at which forums, where priorities lie between resource exploitation, environmental care, and people's rights, and which bodies should have responsibility for what, are far from resolved. Among the bigger issues that remain are how to drill safely for oil and gas, how oil spills can be effectively cleaned up, how ships can travel through the Arctic safely, how indigenous people should participate in development decisions, such as mining projects, which may bring them only a short-lived boom, which parts of the Arctic are vital to wildlife and should be totally protected, and whether some regions where ice will linger longest should be set aside as refuges for the Arctic's unique animals.

If the ice were not disappearing so fast, governments, policymakers, and Arctic residents might be able to keep up. But the pace is such that they must act faster or risk being left behind as the environment changes and new commercial interests rush in. The speed of change is perfectly symbolized by the voyage taken by eight Russians on a 60-foot yacht in 2010. They sailed the *Peter 1* right around the Arctic, first through the Northern Route from Murmansk across the top of Siberia to Alaska and then on, through the Northwest Passage to emerge in eastern Canada just ten weeks later, with ice hardly ever an obstacle. A century or so ago, when Baron Nordenskiold and Roald Amundsen sailed separately along these routes for the first time, an equivalent voyage would have taken six years. Perhaps the only phrase that truly captures the current speed of change in the Arctic, whether it's vanishing ice, thawing permafrost, rising temperatures, or the opening of Russian, Norwegian, and Greenlandic waters to oil exploration is "faster than anyone predicted." Action to look after the Arctic must accelerate too.

Russia Takes Off

Open a U.S. newspaper with a headline "Saving the Arctic" and you might think there is still time left. You'll likely be reading about the battles between big oil, indigenous people, and environmentalists in Alaska, which have held up oil exploration in the nearby seas. But Alaska is only a small slice of the Arctic. Elsewhere, there has already been a rapid move to exploit the Arctic seas, with Russia leading the pack, Norway coming up rapidly behind, and Greenland now taking off. Whatever environmentalists say, it is simply far too late now to "save the Arctic" with a pan-Arctic moratorium on its exploitation, as Greenpeace and others have called for. The issue now it to catch up and ensure that Arctic change is managed effectively.

Russia has been first to take advantage of the opening seas, escorting ever-larger vessels through the Northern Route across the top of Siberia with it powerful nuclear ice breakers. In 2010, for the first time, a 100,000-ton tanker, the *Baltica*, sailed from Murmansk to China. The transit took ten days. The same year, a special ice-breaking ore carrier went from the mines at Norilsk in Siberia to China and back without an accompanying ice-breaker.

The 11,320-mile round trip to Shanghai took only forty-one days, a huge saving over the usual 24,100-mile, 84-day journey through the Suez Canal. As Mikhail Belkin, Assistant Director of Rosatomflot, the Russian organization running its nine atomic icebreakers and one atomic container ship, put it in January 2011, "we proved that the Northern Sea route is navigable for huge commercial vessels.... the route is now economic and politically open for any vessel [of the right ice class] from any country."[1] Belkin considers that it is only a matter of time before the route can be kept open six to seven months a year with the right ships and icebreaker support. The 2011 season strengthened that view: it was the longest on record by a month with the first oil tanker

Fig. 1. Polar view. Look down on the Arctic and the immense span of coastline belonging to Russia stands out, with Canada, Norway, Greenland, and the United States having much smaller ocean frontages. Overlapping claims far out in the Arctic seas will need negotiation to settle. (Graphic: Nigel Hawtin.)

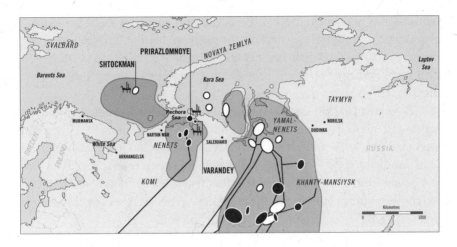

FIG. 2. ARCTIC OIL. THE RUSSIAN OIL AND GAS INDUSTRY HAS LONG BEEN ACTIVE IN THE ARCTIC AND IS NOW PUSHING INTO THE SEAS AT PRIRAZLOMNOYE AND SHTOKMAN AND INTO THE FAR NORTH ALONG THE YAMAL PENINSULA. HYDROCARBON BASINS ARE SHOWN IN GRAY, WITH EXPLOITABLE OIL RESERVES IN BLACK AND GAS RESERVES IN WHITE. BLACK LINES SHOW THE PIPELINES CONNECTING THE ARCTIC FIELDS TO THE SOUTH. (GRAPHIC: NIGEL HAWTIN.)

passing through at the end of June and the last in mid-November. Traffic is expected to boom, with Russia's Ministry of Transport predicting a thirty fold increase this decade, although most ships will be carrying raw materials out of Russia's North rather than taking a short-cut between Atlantic and Pacific. New and bigger nuclear icebreakers to escort traffic will be built, with the first planned for 2017, along with a chain of search and rescue centers.

Russian oil and gas companies are also moving north, both on land and into the sea. Foreign partners are currently welcome for their offshore drilling expertise and are cautiously forming partnerships with Russian ones, for while they are needed now, control of natural resources will always be Russia's top political priority.

In March 2011, the world's northernmost railway line running 350 miles across the permafrost and up into the middle of the Yamal peninsula was completed, opening up access to the huge Bovanenkovo field, which contains enough gas to supply the whole of Europe for a decade. The peninsula is best known for its nomadic reindeer herders, but they now must adapt to industrial development. A pipeline will take the gas west, back to Europe, beginning delivery in 2012, and a liquefied natural gas (LNG) terminal, to be built with help from France's Total, will provide access to the Northern Route for exports east.

In August 2011, Russia's first true offshore Arctic oil production facility was towed out to its home, forty miles offshore in the Pechora Sea. The giant steel platform, over 330 feet wide and weighing 100,000 tons, was weighted with another 400,000 tons of ballast to hold it firm on the sea bed, sixty-five feet below. Its first winter showed that the structure's enormous strength and weight were sufficient to defeat the crushing Arctic ice. A set of curving drill pipes will tap the reservoir beneath the sea bottom.

Much further out, almost four hundred miles from shore, work is continuing at Shtokman, the second-largest gas field in the world. This is the most ambitious engineering project in the entire Arctic. Here the water is much deeper (1,000 feet), so a production platform must float rather than sit on the sea bottom and deal with heavy fast-moving ice and occasional huge icebergs. A planned pipeline carrying the gas to shore will be longer than any built in this environment. Gazprom, Norway's Statoil and France's Total are working together on the project but when it will come into production – with 2018 an early forecast – depends on world gas prices and Russia's tax policies. The sudden rise of fracking techniques to exploit shale gas has upended predictions on future gas prices and raised doubts that Shtokman can be profitably exploited now, just as it has thrown doubts on plans to build pipelines to exploit stranded gas reserves on Alaska's North Slope and in Canada's Mackenzie River delta.

In another ambitious move into Russia's Arctic seas, Exxon is teaming up with Rosneft to explore a rich oil field to the east of Novaya Zemlya in the Kara Sea. Here the water is around three hundred feet deep, likely too deep to produce oil using a bottom-grounded structure like that at Prirazlomnoye. With ice cover for two-thirds of the year, the challenges are formidable. New technologies will have to be developed for floating production vessels that can cope with the ice, or for sea-bottom facilities that can work continuously beneath the ice. No one has ever produced oil in these conditions, yet alone tackled an oil spill. If the challenges of the Kara Sea can be safely overcome, the rest of the Arctic may look much easier to the oil industry,

Norway is now also rushing north, partly because of the surprise settlement in 2010 of its long-running sea border dispute with Russia and partly because its oil fields in the North Sea are running dry. In 2012, Norway and Russia followed up with an agreement to assess jointly the technology they would need for these previously disputed waters with production licenses expected as early as 2013–14. Encouraging news has already arrived from Norway's Arctic waters further to the west. In 2011, Statoil discovered a huge oil field at Skrugard, 125 miles out from land, and in early 2012, a second field close by.

Greenland too has embraced oil exploration in its coastal waters, despite heavy ice in winter and constant protests from Greenpeace boats. But Greenland has not been so lucky: exploration company Cairn Energy has spent over a billion dollars without yet hitting substantial oil reserves. Arctic oil exploration is a high-risk business.

Back in North America, the exploitation of the Arctic seas is proceeding much more cautiously. Shell began drilling exploration wells in Alaskan waters only in 2012 after over five years of delay, at immense expense, due to legal challenges. ConocoPhillips has announced plans to follow in 2014. The priorities are very different. Russia must move fast as its wealth and power come from energy. In 2007, the energy sector accounted for one-third of Russia's GDP, 60 per cent of its exports, and half of all government revenue. With existing oil and gas developments passing their peak, Russia must develop more; lawsuits do not stand in its way, and warnings of risks from environmental groups and the worries of reindeer herders are not slowing it up. Norway too needs oil; it is the world's eighth-largest oil exporter and the second largest gas exporter and relies totally on energy to support its exceptional standard of living. For Greenland, dreams of independence from Denmark for its 56,000 residents depend on exploiting petrochemicals in its sea and minerals on land.

Canada is the only Arctic nation where offshore oil exploration is on hold, although leases have been sold. Progress has been made on regulation. In late 2011, Canada's National Energy Board, reacting to the Gulf of Mexico disaster, stuck with rules that a company drilling in the Arctic would have to be capable of drilling a second relief well in the same season – which may be very short if winter ice is closing in – should there be a blowout.

Like Russia, North America has seen a boom in shipping too, but not because the Northwest Passage is opening for trade. Rather tourists and cruise

ships are flooding to the Arctic, sometimes sailing into dangerous, unchart-
ed waters. "Four years ago, we used to have 25 large tourist ships [around
Greenland]," says Aqqaluk Lynge, chairman of the Inuit Circumpolar Council
(ICC), "but last year [2010] we had more than 200."[2] It is just luck that so far
there have been only groundings and no major disasters.

Cooperation not Conflict?

Amid this rapid change, there has been a remarkable outbreak of political
cooperation, rather than conflict, among the Arctic nations. It didn't always
look that way. Back in August 2007, when a Russian miniature submarine
planted a titanium flag on the seabed beneath the North Pole, many western politicians panicked, thinking that Russia planned to seize territory the
old-fashioned way and a new era of territorial conflict was looming. That has
proved false.

At in a meeting in Ilulissat in Greenland hastily arranged by Denmark
soon after the Russian flag reached the seabed, the "Arctic Five" killed any
idea of an aggressive race to seize the North Pole and recognized that, "an extensive international legal framework applies to the Arctic Ocean." That legal
framework is the Law of the Sea (UNCLOS), which rules that an "extended
continental shelf" can only be claimed through geological data that proves
the sea bottom is a true, shallow extension of the land. After Ilulissat, all the
frontline states have been gathering data to extend their claims and have been
doing so cooperatively, often sharing research cruises.

Even better news came three years after the flag planting, when Russia un-
expectedly resolved its contentious forty-year-old Arctic border dispute with
Norway. The new border line was ratified unanimously by the Norwegian
parliament in February 2011, removing at one stroke the Arctic's most dangerous dispute for a NATO–Russia confrontation.

Other cooperative efforts are following. The eight Arctic nations that are
full members of the Arctic Council, signed an agreement to coordinate their
search-and-rescue operations across the Arctic in Nuuk, Greenland, in May
2011.

Such a flurry of cooperation is welcome. But the Law of the Sea can't
settle all potential territorial disputes among the Arctic Five. From the geological evidence that is now pouring in, it seems likely that Russia, Canada,

and Denmark-Greenland, will all have legitimate but overlapping claims to enormous areas of their nearby shallow shelf seas as well as along the shallow ridges that cross the Arctic. The question of who owns the Arctic will becomes one of how to settle boundaries when legitimate overlapping claims meet far out to sea. The Law of the Sea leaves it to the nations concerned to negotiate their boundary lines.

That is a job for the future and does not suggest a return to the bad old days of the Cold War when there were NATO bases in northern Norway, Greenland, and Iceland facing Soviet bases in the Kola Peninsula, with both sides ready for an invasion by the other. As Rear Admiral Trond Grytting, chief of the regional military crisis headquarters in Bodo on the north coast of Norway, put it in 2009: "the Cold War danger of inter-state or industrial war is today considered close to irrelevant in the north simply because it is impossible to see what can be gained. Military confrontation and tactical engagements in order to achieve political objectives can on the other hand not be ruled out."[3]

Certainly there may be "tactical engagements" intended to gain concessions in other disputes, including those far from the Arctic.[4] Europe is very dependent on Arctic gas already. Overall, the EU takes around one third of its gas supplies from Russia, one third from Norway and one third from elsewhere. As Russia and Norway explore the High North, Europe will become ever more dependent on the Arctic and on pipelines, including the new Nord Stream pipeline running though the Baltic all the way back to Yamal, for its energy. The fate of the EU and the Arctic are entwined. New trade routes opening through and around Russian waters will create new dependencies, involving China and the Far East too, with China and perhaps Japan set to take LNG from the Russian Arctic. Warming seas will also mean that valuable fish stocks will move in out of different fishing zones; some nations may gain but other loose badly and agreements may be disputed.

In response to the changing situation, Nordic countries, some of them NATO members (Iceland, Denmark, and Norway) and some not (Sweden and Finland), may move towards closer regional military cooperation. In 2009, an influential report from former Norwegian foreign minister Thorvald Stoltenberg pointed out the "increasing geopolitical and strategic importance following the Nordic waters' role as production and transit area for oil and gas to the European markets and the development of the Arctic" and called for joint air, maritime, and satellite surveillance and sharing of military resources.[5] "None of the Nordic countries will over the next 15–20 years be able to uphold the quality of their armed forces without engaging in a closer Nordic cooperation," Stoltenberg wrote. In January 2011, the British Prime Minister hosted the first Nordic–Baltic summit of prime ministers from Denmark, Finland, Iceland, Norway, Sweden, Estonia, Latvia, and Lithuania. That followed a meeting of defense ministers which the British defense minister explained had as one goal "that we create a NATO entity that Finland and Sweden feel a little more comfortable with, that we give further security to article 5 [mutual defense] in the Baltic states by being a nuclear power as part of that grouping, and that as a NATO grouping we are better able to deal with regional disputes with Russia."[6] The Russian media reacted unfavorably to what they saw as an attempt to create a new "mini-NATO" of the North. The following year, in March 2012, Britain signed a new agreement with Norway, its key supplier of gas, to enhance defense cooperation.

A Babble of Voices

The creation of new groupings and alliances highlights the bigger problem facing Arctic governance. A growing number of Arctic and non-arctic nations, as well as sub-national and cross-national groups, alongside numerous NGOs, now want to have a louder voice in Arctic affairs, and they do not want to leave decisions to the club of the "Arctic Five."

Finland, Sweden, and Iceland are Arctic nations that lack that prime location facing the Arctic seas, although they have territory within the Arctic. Although members of the Arctic Council, they were alarmed to be left out of the key meeting in Ilulissat organized by the coastal nations. Iceland is surrounded by sea but is just a little too far south to be a true Arctic seas nation. That is not how the Icelanders see it though. "We consider ourselves to be an Arctic coastal state," said Össur Skarphéðinsson, Iceland's Minister of Foreign Affairs, in January 2011, "we want to be included not excluded in deliberations on the Arctic region."[7]

Other nations and transnational groupings, including Japan, Korea, China, and the European Union, also want a seat at the Arctic table, now that its potential as a short-cut across the top of the globe and its enormous resources are apparent. China's rapid increase in the interest in the Arctic is particularly striking.

The largest embassy in Iceland belongs to China. Should a trade route up open between the Pacific and the Atlantic, Iceland is well placed to provide a hub port at its Atlantic end. Several high-level delegations from China, and one from Singapore, an established Asian hub port, have visited Iceland, although nothing concrete has been agreed. "I'm feeling like a girl at her first dance, being flattered by all the attention," Foreign Minister Skarphéðinsson joked.[8] Soon that attention may grow serious. Ships with Chinese crew and with cargoes bound for China have been among the first through the northern passage. The oil, gas, and mineral wealth of Russia and Scandinavia's Arctic region are of tremendous interest to China and the northern route may place them within easy reach. In November 2010, the China National Petroleum Corporation moved quickly to sign an agreement with the Sovcomflot Group to develop "the transportation potential of the Northern Sea Route, both for delivering transit shipments of hydrocarbons and for the transportation of oil and gas from Russia's developing Arctic offshore fields."[9]

Chinese mining companies have also shown strong interest in Greenland, which is rich in minerals and has large deposits of rare-earths, essential in many high-tech devices, and over which China has recently had a near monopoly. Greenland has a strong desire for autonomy, but it lacks the skills needed to build a mining industry; its future choice of partner may potentially bring in management, capital, and guest workers from far away and change the Arctic's political balance.

Then there are cross-national groups demanding greater control over the Arctic. Most powerful of them are the Inuit, with 100,000 of them living in Greenland and Canada and smaller numbers in Alaska, and just 1,600 remaining in eastern Russia. There are the Saami people, living across Norway, Sweden, Finland, and the Kola Peninsula of Russia who are moving towards greater unity; and many different indigenous groups spread across the top of Siberia.

The Inuit are of special importance as they have gone furthest towards gaining autonomy. Greenland, with 87 per cent of its 56,000 population Inuit, voted in 2008 to move towards economic independence from Denmark, which currently provides an annual subsidy equivalent to $10,000 per head, and on to political independence.

In the enormous Canadian Arctic territory of Nunavut, created in 1999, 85 per cent of the 30,000 population are Inuit and many powers have been devolved to its territorial government. It is no secret that Nunavut residents

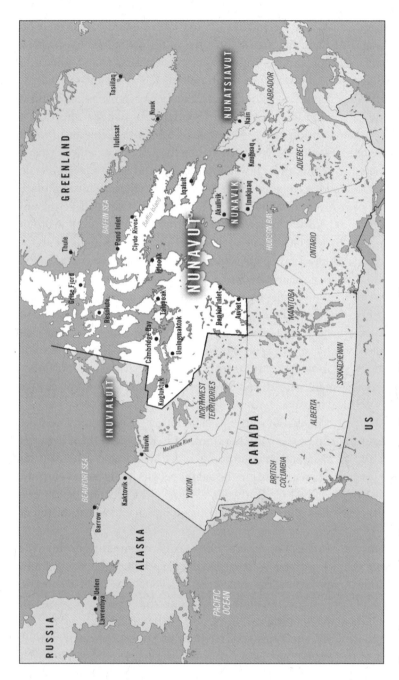

Fig. 3. Inuit homeland. Greenland and the Canadian Territory of Nunavut have a combined population of almost 90,000 people. Over 85 per cent of them are Inuit, and they are demanding greater autonomy and a louder voice in Arctic affairs. (Graphic: Nigel Hawtin.)

would like to see far greater devolution, with powers over their own affairs more akin to that of a Canadian province, rather than a territory. Canada has ten provinces and three territories, and a devolution agreement-in-principle between the Northwest Territories and the federal government, signed in 2011, has raised hopes that Nunavut too will gain control over the royalties that would flow from oil and mines.

Inuit across the Arctic are increasingly speaking with one voice through the ICC, especially as they have felt left out of discussions among the Arctic Five. In February 2011, Inuit leaders met in Ottawa to seek a common front on the kinds of Arctic mining and offshore drilling they should support. They did not agree on everything, in part because of Greenland's special enthusiasm to develop its resources. But leaders have always agreed that Inuit must be the first to benefit from minerals or oil found on their territories. "We cannot let industry from the outside simply walk in and take what we believe is not theirs," says ICC chairman Lyngge. "When Arctic resources are taken from our homeland, who will ultimately benefit? Is it those who have lived in the Arctic for thousands of years? Or is it those from the outside? Is the language of investing just a camouflage for taking?"[10]

The position of indigenous people has been strengthened by the UN Declaration on the Rights of Indigenous People, adopted in 2007. Among other things, it specifies the right to redress for any resources taken from their lands without their "free, prior and informed consent." Although it is a non-binding declaration, it has won support from the Obama administration and reluctant support from Canada.

With so many voices demanding to decide the future of the Arctic, the key issue is how they should all be represented and what legal regimes should apply. The Arctic Council is the region's most important high-level forum, with decisions reached by consensus among the eight Arctic states along with "permanent participation" from the ICC and five other indigenous groups. A range of non-governmental organizations have permanent observer status, as do representatives from France, Germany, Poland, Spain, the Netherlands, and the United Kingdom.

The council has no authority to make laws or set regulations, but it has been able to steer the priorities of the Arctic nations and issue authoritative reports (on Arctic climate change, for example), which have driven action by other bodies. Although the council lacks power, it has enormous influence. A strengthened Arctic Council is generally seen as the best hope of bringing all those with an interest in the Arctic together. A key issue is that the EU, China, Korea, Italy, and Japan have so far been denied permanent observer status at the Council, with the EU having significant disagreements with some members of the Council.

The EU contains Arctic states in Finland and Sweden (Denmark is an EU member but semi-autonomous Greenland quit in 1985 over fishery policy) and Iceland is seeking to join, but the union has met vigorous criticism from Inuit within Canada and Greenland. They are angry at bans on importing seal products into the EU, imposed by the European parliament to please animal rights activists. Many Inuit communities that exported sealskin in the past have been seriously hurt.

There are also differences between the EU and Norway over the status of the potentially oil-rich seas around the islands of Svalbard. Norway, which has sovereignty over Svalbard, sees them as part of its own continental shelf while the EU regards them as included within the unusual arrangements that give right to exploit Svalbard's wealth to all signatories of the 1920 Svalbard treaty (see "The Strange Case of Svalbard" in *After the Ice: Life, Death and Geopolitics in the New Arctic,* for a fuller explanation). A decision on permanent observer status for the EU, China, and others was expected at the Council's meeting in 2011 but has been delayed until 2013.

Beyond that, there is a consensus that the Council will have to meet more often, must have more resources to back it up with a permanent secretariat to be established in Tromsø, Norway, by 2013, and be more inclusive, but without imposing on the special rights and requirements of Arctic residents.[11]

New Rules from Old

Clearly much remains to be done. If there are no agreed rules to stop them, ships that aren't really suitable for the Arctic could travel there and risk oil spills. Among those ships there may be over-enthusiastic tourist liners, drug smugglers, and even terrorists seeking unpoliced routes. And there will certainly be pirate fishing boats, which will chase new stocks as they move into the newly warming Arctic. Ships are very mobile, and fish, whales, birds, and drifting oil spills don't recognize national boundaries, so it is not effective for each part of the Arctic to make up its own regulations. Nor can bodies that are responsible for just one sector (shipping or fishing, for example) build the best set of rules to protect the Arctic environment if each tackles its problems independently. Stresses from different causes (pollution plus overfishing, for example) add up, so the only effective way to look after the Arctic is by "ecosystem-based management," which looks at all the impacts from different causes as a whole. To move such an approach forward, far more data are needed about the "baseline" conditions in the Arctic: a recent fisheries study, for example, showed that the amount of fish being taken from the Arctic has been vastly underestimated[12] with the total catch 75 times higher than reported.

There is much in existing international rules and the Law of the Sea that can help. The Law of the Sea's Article 234 on "Ice-Covered Areas" allows states to apply rules on pollution that are stricter than international standards within their exclusive economic zones if they are ice-covered. Article 211(6) on "Pollution from Vessels" provides opportunities to protect defined areas that have special "oceanographical and ecological" conditions, after consultations through "the competent international organization." The International Maritime Organization (IMO) is one such organization. Annexes to its International Convention for the Prevention of Marine Pollution from Ships (MARPOL) allow "special areas" to be protected, which can include entire seas. The Mediterranean and Baltic seas have special protection against oil spills, for example.

Critical habitats can be identified as "Particularly Sensitive Sea Areas." Once an area is approved, as the seas around the Galapagos Islands and the Great Barrier Reef have been, maritime activities can be controlled and ships re-routed. Again, the lack of past long-term Arctic monitoring meaning there are not yet enough data to be clear how many regions deserve special protection. In 2011, the International Union for Conservation of Nature and the Natural Resources Defense Council made a first attempt, listing thirteen especially vulnerable areas. Action is needed immediately and so too is far more research.

The IMO also has a voluntary Polar Code (the IMO Guidelines for Ships Operating in Arctic Ice-Covered Waters), which it is now working to strengthen and make mandatory under its International Convention for the Safety of Life at Sea (SOLAS). It might seem strange, given the potential environmental damage from a ship wreck, that the Arctic lacks rules for ships that go there. Any rust bucket can set sail without an ice-strengthened hull, or a crew trained in ice navigation, into regions where there are no up-to-date charts and rescue many days away. Despite the obvious urgency, progress in re-writing the code is slow. Many nations are involved, and some have strong interests in the Arctic while others are more interested in shipbuilding and running shipping lines. Release of the draft code has already been delayed from its initial 2012 target and will not be ready before 2014 at the earliest, with further delays likely.

There are obvious gaps in Arctic governance. The Arctic Council has no mandate to deal with security or military issues. The Council has a weak interface with industry – including all those big international companies that are rushing to exploit the Arctic. Although international rules have been set up to deal with ships and fish, which move among different nations' waters, regulation of the oil and mining industry, and the way in which environmental risk are assessed, are dependent on each state's separate legislation, even though oil spills travel. That is why the ICC is now calling for an international fund to deal with compensation for Arctic oil spills. A hopeful sign is that Norway, which has some of the best ecosystem management and oil-drilling safety rules, may set high standards as it works with Russia in the Barents Sea.

Oil companies themselves have been running cooperative research project on oil spills and certainly don't want accidents; in 2012, they announced that they would expand past efforts in a new nine-company Joint Industry Program.[13] But history teaches that industry and regulators rarely have all the answers when they enter new territory and that disasters are the key drivers of change. The first international conventions on safety of life at sea were agreed upon after the *Titanic* sank; MARPOL was precipitated by the huge oil spill from the AMOCO Cadiz, and the *Exxon Valdez* disaster drove the switch to double-hulled tankers. The Deepwater Horizon Commission report summed up the problem when they wrote that the U.S. regulatory system is "fundamentally reactive and incapable of driving continuous improvement in policies."

Rapid change is taking us to an uncertain future. Arctic nations and all these other groups may cooperate, or quarrel, over long lists of things that each group feels are urgent. Perhaps a bigger set of rules and structures may be successfully put in place within the overall constitution provided by the Law of the Sea and looked after by the Arctic Council. Or maybe the five nations that front the Arctic will try to slam the door on everyone else, or each will go its own way. We may see cooperation, conflict, or a patchwork of partial solutions. The worst prospect is that the Arctic may simply outrun any attempt to govern it. The nightmare scenario would be a combination of environmental crisis and species extinctions, unregulated development and profiteering, disenfranchised indigenous peoples, and unresolved border disputes.

The Arctic ice could be approaching a tipping point at which it disappears ever faster, putting more stress on indigenous communities and opening up more parts of the Arctic, without time to make the best decisions. In the United States, it takes an estimated ten to fifteen years to win the budget for a new icebreaker and then design and build it. In a Korean yard, a new commercial icebreaking oil tanker can be ready in three months. If the ice vanishes in five or ten years, not thirty, the government of the Arctic and the protection of its environment and people could easily slip out of control while there is still just a babble of competing voices. And if that happens, as it may well do, the Arctic could take a wider revenge on the rest of the world. Already the Arctic's warmer seas are changing wind patterns and beginning to affect weather further south: as the ice vanishes, cold winds blast into Europe, bringing severe winters. Further ahead, when the huge dome of sparkling white ice which has covered the top of the globe for thousands of years disappears, we can expect huge releases of methane from thawing permafrost which may change the climate of the entire world.

Notes

1 Arctic Frontiers Conference, Tromsø, January 2011.

2 Ibid.

3 Arctic Frontiers Conference, Tromsø, January 2009.

4 Deutsche Welle, "Norway defends energy exploration in Arctic," *DW-World.de*, January 25, 2011; http://www.dw.de/norway-defends-energy-exploration-in-arctic/a-14785116.

5 Thorvald Stoltenberg, "Nordic Cooperation on Foreign and Security Policy: Proposals presented to the extraordinary meeting of Nordic foreign ministers in Oslo on February 9, 2009,"; http://www.mfa.is/media/Frettatilkynning/Nordic_report.pdf.

6 House of Commons Daily Hansard, November 8, 2010; http://www.publications.parliament.uk/pa/cm201011/cmhansrd/cm101108/debtext/101108-0001.htm.

7 Arctic Frontiers Conference, Tromsø, January 2011.

8 Ibid.

9 Sovcomflot Press Centre, "Sovcomflot Group and China National Petroleum Corporation Become Strategic Partners," November 22, 2010; http://www.sovcomflot.ru/npage.aspx?did=75963.

10 Arctic Frontiers Conference, Tromsø, January 2011.

11 The Arctic Governance Project; http://www.arcticgovernance.org/.

12 D. Zeller, S. Booth, E. Pakhomov, W. Swartz, and D. Pauly, "Arctic fisheries catches in Russia, USA and Canada: Baselines for neglected ecosystem," *Polar Biology* 34 (2011): 955.

13 Arctic Frontiers Conference, Tromsø, January 2012.

3. "Politicization" of the Environment: Environmental Politics and Security in the Circumpolar North

Lassi Kalevi Heininen

The environmental "awakening" started in the 1960s in many parts of the globe as a moral protest against belief in progress based on economic growth and modernization. One of the outcomes was that the term "the environment" was born; another that the environment became a target of political disagreements and conflicts, and thus "politicized."

This "politicization" is very much a process with cumulative effects which needs actors who are conscious and concerned and will act by themselves and convince others. Further, on the one hand, environmental politics became a field of activity for public authorities through, for example, environmental laws as well as a new field of foreign policy. On the other hand, the very meaning of security was extended beyond traditional concerns with "military" threats and national security to focus on environmental and human security problems, as indicated by the concept of "environmental security."

The Arctic is one of the purest regions of the world, rich in its biodiversity. But the region is also a sink of long-range air and water pollution, and thus both a victim and also a source of environmental degradation. In the early twenty-first century, climate change with its impacts is the most relevant and challenging factor for northern environmental politics, as well as a factor for changing northern security. Consequently, in the circumpolar North, there has been public concern on local, national, regional, international, and global levels about the state of the environment and increased demands for enhanced environmental protection. This environmental "awakening" started among northern indigenous peoples and environmental movements in response to concerns about long-range pollution and radioactivity.

This caused, indeed pushed, the Arctic states to become aware of, and concerned about, the degradation of the Arctic environment, particularly as a result of the Cold War's nuclear legacy. This soon led to joint international activity for environmental protection, particularly nuclear safety. Consequently, environmental politics came onto the political agenda of the Arctic states and became a part of their foreign policy. Current institutionalized northern cooperation, either inter-governmental or between non-state actors, is very much based upon the environment and on environmental protection. During the last decade in the High North, there has been a true "awakening" in terms of the recognition of challenge of climate change, particularly the issue of global warming, and this awakening is reminiscent of the great "environmental awakening" of the 1960s and 1970s.

This chapter is about the "politicization" of the environment, and it examines environmental politics and environmental security in the Arctic. First, it discusses the environmental "awakening," the "politicization" of the environment and environmental politics, and environmental security in general. Second, it describes and discusses environmental problems and politics, and environmental security in the Arctic. Third, it briefly describes the environmental "awakening" in the Arctic and how environmental protection as well as environmental security came onto the political agenda of the Arctic states and discusses interrelations between the environment and security in the Arctic context. Finally, this chapter ends with some brief conclusions.

From "Politicization" of the Environment to Environmental Politics

There have always been, and will be, changes in a nature. Change has happened and will happen in any case, and, moreover, change is the precondition for the very function of a nature. For example, Darwin did not only emphasize hard laws of competition in nature, but also said that there is broad cooperation based upon mutual interests, i.e., symbiosis either without harm to others or with benefit to both. Though a human being cannot destroy nature, he is able to change it, such as, for example, through mass-scale utilization, industrialization, and pollution, and with the assistance of technology, and thus destroy the very preconditions of human life.

Following from this, how to measure nature – is it subject or object? Is a man part of a nature, or apart from it? According to the Sprouts, "the earth and its inhabitants are tightly depending on each other … they are together one global comprehensive, ecological entity, the ecosystem" – this is called interdependence. Further, Passmore has said that physically a human being is able to live without a nature, if only it will not be totally destroyed. Nature has, however, very important immaterial values, such as "beauty."[1] What is relevant here is that a "nature" is different; what is the "environment?" The environment, as we now understand it, was born about forty to forty-five years ago – the process that we call the "environmental awakening." Since that time, it is possible to define the term "the environment" to mean the material basis for human existence, which is in a danger of being destroyed as a result of human activities.[2]

Correspondingly, the environmental "awakening" started in the 1960s, particularly at the turn of the 1960s/70s, in the West, but soon it became a more global movement. It was a moral protest against new kind of modernized socio-economic development, and the belief in progress based on economic growth and modernization.[3] A recent example of the same would be 'climatic awakening,' which finally became a global phenomenon at the early twenty-first century much due to (physical) impacts and possible risks of rapid climate change, particularly global warming.[4] It is likely to have an equal, if not greater, influence on societal norms and legislation, industrial economies, and human security.[5]

Environmental 'awakening' did not come alone, but together with thinking that there is a comprehensive, almost total, crisis between a society and the environment. And further, that there are limits for the humankind in the globe, and the globe is a closed system as one of the alternative discourses emphasized, as "The Limits of Growth" by the Club of Rome indicated in 1973. Ecological ideas came from the educated Western classes, thinkers, and intelligentsia, which emphasized ecological ethics, such as animal rights. For example, as Anna Bramwell put it: "Ecologism is a political box. It is a new box, into which many distinguished and important thinkers fit."[6] (Ecology, which actually means "the study of households," has a longer history; it is widely used in the normative sense, and "is now a political category" – and political categories have "a dual meaning" to be described as parties or policies, and as an ideology.[7]) Correspondingly, 'Environmental Science' became a field of research, and since then it has been "a science on everything!", which is, of course, impossible even as a thought.[8]

Actually, the environmental "awakening" of the 1960s is a paradox because almost all the information about environmental degradation was known before the Second World War, except radioactivity due to nuclear energy and tests, and distribution of man-made chemical compounds, which were made known and public by several pamphlets of the 1960s, such as *Silent Spring* by Rachel Carson in 1962. There are several examples of economic and political lessons learned of the dangers of environmental degradation by industry, such as a copper company at Copperhill which destroyed the landscape in Tennessee in the 1930s (the factory was not closed until 1988).[9] On the other hand, environmental "awakening" is understandable due to several environmental accidents in the 1960s and 1970s, such as the accident of the tanker *Torey Canyon* in 1967; "broken arrow," the crash of a nuclear-armed USAF SAC B-52 in Thule in 1968; dioxin leak in Seveso in 1976; nuclear accidents at Three Mile Island in 1979; methyl isocyanate release in Bhopal in 1984; and finally, the accident of the Chernobyl nuclear power plant in 1986. These accidents indicate, even emphasize, one of the well-known environmental discourses, the theory of a risk society by Ulrich Beck, saying that our modern and heavily industrialized societies are risk societies due to several environmental accidents and catastrophes with severe environmental and socio-economic impacts and damages.[10]

One of the outcomes was that the very meaning of security was extended (in discourses) beyond traditional concerns with "military" threats and national security to focus on environmental and human problems. Consequently, different discourses and concepts of security were started, and they had different premises and paradigms. This was also the case with northern security.

"Politicization" of the Environment

As a result of the birth of "the environment" and environmental "awakening," the environment and environmental issues became politicized. The main idea behind "politicization" of the environment is that the very different factors that include the human environment and determine its quality have become targets of political disagreements and conflicts. "Politicization" is a process: It can be started by a minor event, which is enough to catalyze people to do something that they have not done earlier. Correspondingly, this will cause others elsewhere to react in the same way, etc. Thus, it is like a chain reaction with cumulative effects, although it is not so common to agree on everything.[11]

Here "politics" means political activity, such as discussion, debate, implementation of political decisions, and political systems including environmental issues and conflicts, decisions concerning the environment, laws on the environment, and governance. Furthermore, "politics" is interpreted as relations and activities related to power, government, or authority among people and groups of people with distinct interests. Thus it means making decisions and implementing them, handling problems, and promoting and implementing interests using different forms of power. It also means making things political and making politics. Consequently, there is the precondition that "politicization" needs actors, i.e., individuals or communities who are conscious and concerned, and who will convince others to act. Behind is a constructivist research approach that emphasizes actors and their roles, and if there are several actors, there are also different and contradictory interests and conflicts of interest.[12]

Environmental conflicts or problems very much represent the "politicization" of the environment and are an important part of environmental politics. They are usually asymmetric, meaning that they are conflicts between different kinds of actors, mostly non-state actors. Environmental conflicts are often multifunctional and happen at many levels, and further, one of the main dimensions from the very beginning has dealt with the future of modern industrialized society.[13] Furthermore, environmental conflicts can be analyzed as discursive conflicts, where discourses consist of discussion plus social practices.

A relevant factor in international environmental politics, when trying to evaluate the state of, and relative importance of, environmental catastrophes and conflicts affecting people and societies, is a change in the perception of ecological problems as well as in threat or risk pictures in the public consciousness. This is especially so when dealing with global problems – such as climate change – and is a growing concern with regard to environmental protection from these problems.. Consequently, the importance of a single environmental problem or conflict is not possible to define based only on natural sciences, as it is always based on cultural and political points of view, which emphasize a problem-orientation.[14] Maybe the most important question for environmental politics is "problem definition," i.e., to define a problem which is *per se* a research problem.[15] For example, the basis of my research on interrelations between the military and the environment was to start to ask what kind of environmental degradation the military causes, and my research has continued to ask what kind of change in problem definition on security discourse(s), premise(s), and paradigm(s) might be needed, or possible, as a result.[16]

Another relevant point of view is to be cognizant of the interplay between politics and science. A good example, and maybe the most hegemonic environmental discourse, is the political strategy of "sustainable development." Although it is much discussed both theoretically and in the context of the Arctic region, it has not (yet) materialized, and we do not even agree what it really means, but we nonetheless discuss it.[17] Even more, the discourse is still very much based on the original definition by the report of the United Nations' World Commission on Environment and Development: "Development that meets present needs without compromising the ability of future generations to meet their own needs."[18]

This definition represents the thinking of the turn of the 1980s/90s that environmental problems can, and should, be "in control." This has raised criticism saying that the definition is based too much on faith in economic growth and technology and accepts industrialization as a global solution. There are also examples of other alternative discourses of environmental politics like the above-mentioned theory of a risk society; a discourse to emphasize the cultural point of view, i.e., that ecological modernization means competing interpretations, such as institutional learning, technological progress, and cultural politics as socially relevant;[19] and a discourse that environmental governance includes the danger that ecology has, or will, become a new discipline for "disciplining."[20]

From 'Politicization' to Environmental Politics and Environmental Security

All this has meant some sort of "environmental revolution" from 1973 to 1986 can be described as a process with several main steps, such as consciousness of the environment among citizens, establishment of new movements and organization, international agreements on the environment, and environmental governance and environmental laws. Consciousness of the environment, even "environmentalism," started to rise among the intelligentsia and other citizens. Consequently, new citizens' movements with one mission and spontaneous protests were born.

Also international organizations with strong and partly scientific expertise, such as the International Union for Conservation of Nature (IUCN), Greenpeace International, and the World Wildlife Fund for Nature, were established. Furthermore, official environmental agencies and governmental authorities on the environment, such as ministries of the environment, were established in the industrialized countries. Environmental protection also became a new field of legislation for environmental laws and more comprehensive collections of laws dealing with the environment.

As a part of this, traditional security was challenged by new discourses and premises of security-building linkages between peace, development, and the environment, such as common or comprehensive security, and environmental or ecological security, based on a few reports by the United Nations[21] and books by social scientists.[22] Consequently, the notion of security was exposed to new content, and the definition was widened toward a more human-oriented approach, which emphasized environmental and/or human aspects of security as alternative points of view to a narrow approach of military security. When defining environmental security, relevant hazardous environments and resource-based environmental conflicts are important,[23] and further, this new notion of security is based on salient interrelations between security and the environment.[24]

All this meant that the public sector took responsibility for the state of the environment, particularly environmental protection, and, consequently, "environmental politics" became a new area of socio-political activity and public politics of the state and society. Its goal and mission was "to take care of the relationship both a society and a human toward nature and their own living environment with a purpose to protect the biodiversity of a nature, to restore natural resources and to decrease and erase environmental damages and risks."[25] Further, environmental politics can be defined in a functional way, i.e., much influenced by activities of the public authority, or in an institutional way, i.e., activities implemented by the political and administrative regime, or through its goals, i.e., what are the goals and how they have been gained.

For example, although the 1st Community Law on the Environment of the European Communities is from 1959, the first Community Environmental Action Programme was adopted in 1973. Further, in 1987 environmental protection was recognized as a part of the legal competence of the EC through the signing of the Single European Act, and based on the 5th Environmental Action Program and its article 174 the major objectives of the European Union are defined, such as preserving, protecting, and improving the quality of the environment; the maintenance of continued access to natural resources; and increased environmental efficiency on energy.[26] According to John McCormick, environmental policy is one of the most rapidly expanding areas of the EU policy activity, and, consequently, the EU has a series of policies relating to specific environmental issues and key areas, such as water and air quality, fisheries conservation, radiation, chemicals, energy conservation, biodiversity, forestry, and organic agriculture.[27] Recently, the EU has subsequently begun to play a central role in international negotiations on climate change and has recognized the keen inter-relationship between climate change and (international) security.[28]

Correspondingly, "environmental politics" became a new field of foreign policy of the state, and international environmental politics a new field of international politics of the entire unified state system. This was implemented on the one hand by international conferences and other meetings on the environment: for example, the United Nations organized the Stockholm Conference on the Human Environment (UNCHE) in 1972, the first time representatives of a substantial number of national governments – 113 in total – met to discuss the environment, and consequently "the environment became a truly international issue."[29] As a result, the United Nations Environmental Program (UNEP) was established the next year, and later in the 1980s the Intergovernmental Panel on Climate Change (IPCC), which has played an important role in the High North.[30] Twenty years later, there was another UN conference on the environment, the Rio Summit in 1992, and then the 2009 climate summit in Copenhagen, the United Nations Framework Convention on Climate Change (UNFCCC), which was one of the most recent ones. On the other hand, this was implemented by international agreements and treaties dealing with the environment, particularly trans-boundary pollution. Among the first negotiated and signed agreements on the environment are the Convention for the Prevention of Marine Pollution by Dumping from Ships and Aircraft in 1972, the London Dumping Convention of 1972 to restrict dumping high-level radioactive material into the sea (this was mostly caused by the military), the 1973 MARPOL Convention for the prevention of marine pollution by dumping from ships, and the Convention on Long-Range Trans-boundary Air Pollution in 1979. If all these are universal and global, they must deal with the northernmost regions of the globe. The Agreement on the Conservation of Polar Bears in 1973 is particularly relevant in the High North as well as the Treaty for the Preservation and Protection of Fur Seals, which was already signed back in 1911. One of the best-known recent international agreements is the Kyoto Protocol on Climate Change as a part of the UNFCCC, which came into force, although the United States, China, and India did not ratify it.[31]

All in all, the environment became a common factor to describe problems of different relationships between humans and nature, such as air pollution influences on allergies in cities; oil leakages from oil tankers that kill birds; and forest clearcutting, which destroys reindeer herding. Also, the "politicization" of the environment happened, and that meant that there are many different environmental "voices" and that no one owns the environment. Further, the environmental "awakening" and the "politicization" of the environment turned into an "environmental revolution," and as a result there emerged international environmental politics and environmental security. Finally, environmental politics/policy has become a new public sector of society as well as a field of politics in addition to a new field of foreign policy of the state, and environmental, or comprehensive, security is now seriously taken into consideration.

Environmental Problems and Politics, and Environmental Security in the Arctic

There are several main reasons for environmental concerns and conflicts in the Arctic: one of them has to do with fisheries, meaning either competition for fish stocks or conflicts dealing with fisheries in northern waters, particularly in the Barents Sea, such as the "Cod War" between Iceland and the UK in the 1970s. These conflicts might probably be decreasing, simply because there are fewer fish, which could, however, be a reason for the opposite as well. Another typical "new" environmental problem with aspects of conflict is the nuclear problem, due to radioactive pollution and nuclear accidents, mostly in the seas – which I will discuss below. Correspondingly, a typical asymmetric environmental conflict, or a potential reason for conflict, is disagreement on how to use land. For example, the so-called Inari case in the northernmost part of Finland was this kind of multifunctional environmental conflict between forestry and reindeer herding.[32] It was also a classic conflict of interest between the *interests* of the actors, not necessarily between the actors themselves, which illustrates the complexity of asymmetric environmental conflicts in the post-Cold War North.[33]

The issue was, and is, not only local or regional but very much international, even global: long-range air and water pollution from southern latitudes to the northernmost latitudes, such as persistent organic pollutants from agriculture and air pollution from industry in Europe and North America, radioactivity from nuclear power plants and Arctic haze from big cities became known by the 1980s. A well-known example of these kinds of environmental problems is illustrated DDT, which was found in polar bears in the northernmost part of Greenland in the 1970s. Another is PCBs, as persistent organic pollutants were transported as long-range contaminants from the agricultural and industrialized areas in mid-latitudes of Europe and North America to the High Arctic by sea currents and air masses, and this was much hidden even to scientists until the 1970s.[34]

Perhaps the most challenging global environmental problem that people and societies face is rapid climate change. Its obvious and already existing physical impacts in the Arctic are all the more reason for increasing environmental concern. Already in 1997, the IPCC emphasized that in the Arctic, climate change is already occurring rapidly and clearly with several impacts. Further, according to the IPCC's Arctic Climate Impact Assessment Report, the Arctic has become an "indicator of climate change."[35] These kinds of phenomena are expected to continue, even to accelerate faster than earlier expected since the multi-year sea ice of the Arctic Ocean has become smaller – and, for example, the Northwest Passage was, for the first time, without sea ice in 2007.[36] Climate change always comes with physical impacts which are multifunctional and complex, such as evident rapid and global warming; thinning and melting of sea ice and glaciers; and thawing of permafrost. In addition, there is the "uncertainty" associated with climate change. For example, there is the collapse of man-made infrastructure and cities built on permafrost, with many societal consequences, and the rising sea levels in the world's oceans.[37]

Consequently, climate change creates major challenges and poses major risks to northern communities, forcing them either to adapt or for their residents to become environmental refugees.[38] For example, there is concern with food security since there is no longer "the continued and predictable availability and access to food, derived from northern environments through Indigenous cultural practices," resulting in a less traditional diet.[39] Furthermore, the scarcity of food, resulting in hunger and thirst among peoples of the North, might create new competition strategic resources, such as fresh water. These kinds of potential environmental conflicts are possible and might be accelerated by the fact that climate change opens new and improved possibilities for the utilization of natural resources and their transportation by the opening of new global sea routes for big oil tankers and container ships, and other activities – even smuggling of drugs and human trafficking.[40] All this indicates that climate change has a relevant security dimension and becomes a new factor for environmental and human security in addition to state sovereignty.[41]

Correspondingly, there are also several ways to list environmental problems and threats and causes of environmental conflicts in the High North. A basic and logical way is to categorize them functionally, according to the source of pollution, such as persistent organic pollutants, heavy metals, radioactivity, acidification and Arctic haze, petroleum hydrocarbons, and climate change.[42] Another basic and simple way is to divide them into global and regional environmental threats.[43] On the one hand, there are regional sources of pollution due to mass-scale utilization of natural resources, such as fishing, forestry, and oil and natural gas drilling; industrialization, such as smelters; and military activity, such as nuclear accidents. On the other hand, pollution also comes from outside the region, i.e., long-range and trans-boundary air and water pollution, and climate change is a global environmental challenge.[44]

Nuclear problems posed a special kind of international environmental and security problem. Radioactivity in the Arctic, particularly in the Barents Sea region, has also crossed national borders and either came from dumped nuclear waste and nuclear tests in the region or from Sellafield, the leaking UK nuclear power station on the coast of the Irish Sea. Consequently, nuclear safety – meaning problems and risks dealing with nuclear waste, spent fuel, and nuclear weapons and plants – became a concrete example of environmental "awakening" and environmental security, and consequently, came onto the political agenda of the Arctic states in the early 1990s. It also became a special issue for, even a symbol of, international cooperation on the environment between the Arctic states and other international actors in the region. Furthermore, it caused a change in problem definition in the northern security discourse.[45] Although the nuclear problem is no more acute, and indeed partly under control, it is still a relevant issue because it is so complex and multifunctional, and there is slowness in its progress.[46]

Another main reason for environmental concern is to find out what kind of plans and decisions are made, and by whom, or even before that, who is active in debate. Following from this, another way to list environmental problems and threats in the North is to have solution-orientation, and divide the reasons into three categories: "Ignorance," or insufficient scientific knowledge regarding physical and biological processes; "Technological poverty," i.e., knowledge, procedures, and equipment required to achieve certain goals; and "Political inability" to regulate the industrialization in the region.[47] This point of view is very much present in a hypothetical case study of the Siberian big rivers and socialism, which is so far hypothetical simply because it has not (yet) been implemented. However, *New Scientist* published an article in 2004 with the headline: "Russian scientists are reviving an old Russian plan to divert some of Siberia's mightiest rivers to the parched former Soviet republics of Central Asia."[48] This is the same old plan that was stopped as a concrete project by a decision of the Party Congress of the Communist party of the Soviet Union in the 1980s. As a research project, however, it managed to live on through the time of Glasnost and Perestroika, and the collapse of the Soviet Union itself, until the early twenty-first century. Even still the question remains: will the plan be implemented or not?

Environmental "Awakening" and Environmental Protection in the Arctic

The environmental "awakening" in northern regions very much started among indigenous peoples and by their organizations together with environmental movements. This was due to the fact that long-range air and water pollution, and radioactivity, as well as regional environmental wastes from industrial and military activities, have in the last decades been concentrated in northern regions. Thus, they became, and remain, a threat to indigenous peoples and their traditional livelihoods and cultures. This growing concern with the environment and increasing environmental "consciousness" has very much been targeting against modernized socio-economic development, such as uncontrolled industrialization and urbanization, and the consequent degradation of the environment, and the increased vulnerability to natural and technological hazards, unsustainable natural resource extraction, as well as related political instability and social unrest.

As a consequence, it is no wonder that that there was an environmental "awakening" among indigenous peoples like, for example, the Alta movement in 1980–81 against the harnessing of the Alta River in northern Norway. Although, the radical and trans-national Alta movement lost its fight over the dam, it spawned both an environmental and a national "awakening," particularly among young Saami and Saami artists.[49] Behind this was the fact that the indigenous peoples as well as other Northerners lived close to nature with their local or traditional ecological knowledge. Thus, to be concerned with the state of the environment is very natural, even a way of life to them, and a necessity for survival. During the last decade, there has been an "awakening" in terms of the recognition of problems of climate change, particularly the issue of global warming in the High North.

Furthermore, Indigenous peoples' organizations, such as the Inuit Circumpolar Council (earlier called the Inuit Circumpolar Conference) and the (Nordic) Saami Council, as well as environmental organizations such as Greenpeace International, became active in environmental protection and also in international environmental politics.[50] Indigenous peoples' organizations had their own agendas and were in close collaboration with other indigenous peoples and the scientific community, perhaps less with environmental movements. On the one hand, they have been acknowledged, for example, in the work of the Arctic Monitoring Assessment Programme (AMAP) for identifying the impacts of pollution in the Arctic,[51] which is partly due to the fact that six indigenous peoples' organizations are permanent participants of the Arctic Council.

On the other hand, they are an important actor and party in the epistemological cooperation of the Arctic.[52] For example, they actively pushed governments, and used the findings of this program to push governments into signing the global Stockholm Convention on Persistent Organic Pollutants (POPs), which can be seen as a success story of fruitful cooperation between northern indigenous peoples and the Arctic scientific community.[53] The Arctic Climate Impact Assessment[54] and the effects of climate change on northern traditional livelihoods are also examples of this collaboration. Indeed, there has been some influence, as the impacts of climate change have recently been taken seriously by governments and intergovernmental organizations, largely based on the concerns coming from the northern indigenous peoples and scientific information coming from the global scientific community.

All in all, indigenous peoples' organizations supported by both environmental organizations and movements, and groups of active researchers, have pushed governments to become active and to become involved in environmental protection, and they have been in close collaboration with the newly-born international northern institutions. This close relationship was not however clear, though obvious, at the very beginning of this new cooperation. Further, in general environmental advocacy by international environmental organizations (focusing on curbing nuclear dumping and marine mammal consumption) and protests and claims by indigenous peoples for their traditional livelihoods (against mining and forestry) have also created asymmetric environmental conflicts between indigenous peoples' organizations, national and regional authorities, local entrepreneurs, and industry.[55]

From Environmental Protection to International Northern Cooperation

Indeed, at the turn of 1980s/1990s, there was a boom in initiatives for international northern and Arctic cooperation in several fields by the Arctic states, such as the 1987 Murmansk Speech by former Soviet Premier Mikhail Gorbachev, and particularly for environmental protection, such as the Finnish initiative for Arctic environmental protection, based on the Murmansk Speech. This was followed first by the Arctic Environmental Protection Strategy (AEPS), signed by the eight Arctic states in 1991,[56] and second by new institutionalized intergovernmental forums, such as the Barents Euro-Arctic Region (BEAR) in 1993 and the Arctic Council (AC) and the Arctic Military Environmental Cooperation (AMEC), both in 1996. The common factor connecting all these initiatives and organizations is environmental protection, which became a part of the international agenda of northern cooperation between the Arctic states and other (international) northern actors. As a conclusion, environmental degradation was so seriously taken that it was put onto the foreign policy agenda of the Arctic states.

For example, the BEAR deals with functional cooperation across national borders in certain priority fields and sectors, such as environmental protection, particularly for nuclear safety, and social welfare, health, and well-being. Furthermore, the Arctic Council consists of environmental protection as its first pillar with several working groups, such as AMAP, and sustainable development as its second one, which is still rather weak. One critical question dealing with the Arctic Council is the balance between promoting environmental protection and sustainable development, including other interests surrounding the mass-scale utilization of natural resources, particularly offshore oil and natural gas drilling in the shelves of the Arctic Ocean. There were also new international agreements, such as the Stockholm Convention on POPs (in 2003). As new international forums, all these are examples of some sort of environmental regimes and assets for knowledge production.[57]

In this context, despite the contributions of the ICC and the Saami Council, and environmental organizations, the establishment of the AEPS as well that of the Arctic Council can be interpreted as a sophisticated mechanism whereby central governments could regain control over the fast-growing international cooperation by new international actors and reassert the primacy of their interests as sovereign states.[58] From the perspective of northern indigenous peoples, the Arctic Council can also be seen as an international mechanism through which to connect circumpolar environments, and thus better understand them.[59] Behind this is the fact that national interests often differ greatly from those of the indigenous peoples, which partly explains why northern indigenous peoples started to act and use their voice for environmental protection in the 1980s. For example, many of the northern indigenous peoples' homelands have strategic importance, both in military terms and in terms of energy security as a result of their natural resource endowments.

Environmental degradation *per se*, and the fact that it was taken onto the foreign policy agenda of the states, also made environmental protection in northern regions a sensitive issue.[60] This has led to disagreement, even conflicts, between indigenous peoples and state authorities when discussing the utilization of natural resources, particularly fisheries and the catching of marine mammals, and trying to define how to use land and waters. This might be continuing, when at the start of the twenty-first century, northern energy resources and their offshore utilization began to increasingly attract both the littoral states of the Arctic Ocean, as their ministerial meetings illustrate, and also actors with varying interests from outside the region.

Interrelations between the Environment and Security

This brings me to rethink whether, despite the current international cooperation on environmental protection, the environment is actually one of the fields of high politics, though it has traditionally been interpreted to be a field of low politics. An example of this is nuclear safety, which is said to represent "soft" security, though most radioactive wastes and nuclear accidents in the Arctic region are caused by the military.

Behind this is the fact that most of the special features of northern security and security policy[61] deal with the environment and environmental degradation, and interrelations between the environment and the military; for example, nuclear safety has already caused a change in problem definition in security discourses and premises.[62] Climate change has also been taken as a challenge to state sovereignty and the national security of the littoral states of the Arctic Ocean; for example, Canada has been asked to adopt "hard power" to defend its sovereignty over the Arctic Archipelago and the Northwest Passage. Consequently, climate change is not only an environmental issue and challenge but also has the potential for introducing new points of view into the theoretical discourse on and premises of security.

Following from this, environmental protection is one of the main fields of international cooperation in, and geopolitics of, the post-Cold War Arctic, and is influenced by three main themes: increased circumpolar cooperation by Indigenous peoples' organizations and sub-national governments; region-building with nations as major actors; and relationship between the circumpolar North and the outside world including global environmental problems. If this much deals with the first significant geopolitical change in the Arctic region, another significant and multifunctional geopolitical change has started in the early twenty-first century when the region has been taken into the globalized world system.[63] Furthermore, the entire Arctic region is playing a more critical role in environmental issues and is described as an environmental linchpin.[64] This is because the Arctic has traditionally been a "laboratory" for science and is now a "workshop" for multidisciplinary research on the environment as well as climate change and its impacts. Furthermore, current international Arctic cooperation started with environmental protection and has already achieved new technical innovations, for example, in nuclear safety and new attempts to build up the interplay between science and politics. Finally, the global relevance of this knowledge and the know-how in region-wide decision-making is sufficient to merit sustained efforts to communicate it to the outside world.

Conclusions

Traditional security policy and issues surrounding natural resource exploitation dominated the relationship between the circumpolar North and the outside world during the Cold War period. With its end, new and more global geopolitics entered into a new phase with implications for the North, such as the rise of new international non-state actors, and the importance of environmental protection in new northern cooperation based on the environmental awakening of northern non-state actors, such as indigenous peoples. Many kinds of global problems and flows of globalization, such as long-range air and water pollution, and radioactivity, influence the northern environment, and northern peoples and their communities. Therefore, the Arctic, one of the purest regions of the world, has turned into "a sink of pollutants." And recently, climate change very much illustrates the Arctic's vulnerability to global environmental problems.

The "politicization" of the environment in the High North has very much happened according to the global environmental "awakening," with many different environmental "voices." And environmental politics has become a new public sector and a new field of foreign policy of the Arctic states. Recently, the High North has become an environmental linchpin due to growing concerns with the state of the environment and the environmental "awakening." Nuclear safety became a special issue of environmental security and has caused a change in problem definition in the northern security discourse. Finally, climate change with its physical impacts and the related uncertainty has become the newest environmental challenge, even a threat, for many northern residents and communities. All this indicates that climate change has a relevant security dimension.

Notes

1 Robert Elliot and Arran E. Gare, *Environmental Philosophy: A Collection of Readings* (Melbourne: University of Queensland Press, 1983), 58–86.

2 Yrjö Haila, "Johdanto: Mikä ympäristö?" in Yrjö Haila and Pekka Jokinen, ed., *Ympäristöpolitiikka. Mikä ympäristö, kenen politiikka* (Jyväskylä: Osuuskunta Vastapaino, 2001), 9.

3 Ibid.

4 For example, see Sharon Begley, "The Truth about Denial," *Newsweek*, August 13, 2007, 36–43.

5 For example, see Lassi Heininen and Heather Nicol, "Climate change and Human Security – From a Northern Point of View," in Lassi Heininen and Heather Nicol, eds., *Climate Change and Human Security – From a Northern Viewpoint* (forthcoming).

6 Anna Bramwell, *Ecology in the 20th Century: A History* (New Haven, CT: Yale University Press, 1989), 13.

7 Ibid., 39–45.

8 Peter M. Haas, *Saving the Mediterranean: The Politics of International Environmental Cooperation* (New York: Columbia University Press, 1990), xviii. Haas has said that it is possible to claim that "Social Sciences have done relatively well at developing theories to explain periods of order and stability, but have done much less well at explaining the dynamics of periods of change … and have not been very good at analyzing complex, nonlinear systems such as international environmental issues seem to involve."

9 Eugene P. Odum, *Ecology and Our Endangered Life-Support Systems* (Sunderland, MA: Sinauer Associates), 63.

10 For example, see Ulrich Beck, "From Industrial Society to Risk Society: Questions of Survival, Social Structure and Ecological Enlightenment," in Mike Featherstone, ed., *Cultural Theory and Cultural Change* (London: Sage, 1992), 97–123.

11 Yrjö Haila, "Johdanto: Mikä ympäristö?" 11–14.

12 For example, see Lassi Heininen, "Euroopan pohjoinen 1990–luvulla. Moniulotteisten ja ristiriitaisten *intressien alue.*" *Acta Universitatis Lapponiensis* 21 – Arktisen keskuksen tiedotteita/ Arctic Centre Reports 30 (Lapin yliopisto, Rovaniemi), 1999.

13 For example, see: Ulrich Beck, "From Industrial Society to Risk Society: Questions of Survival, Social Structure and Ecological Enlightenment," in Mike Featherstone, ed. *Cultural Theory and Cultural Change* (London: Sage, 1992); and Yrjö Haila and R. Levins, *Ekologian ulottuvuudet* (Tampere: Vastapaino, 1992).

14 Further, in research on environmental conflicts, the reasons behind the conflicts are often specified and analyzed into differing facts, interests, and value. See: Markus Laine and Pekka Jokinen, "Politiikan ulottuvuudet," in *Ympäristöpolitiikka. Mikä ympäristö, kenen politiikka* (Jyväskylä: Osuuskunta Vastapaino, 2001), 47–65.

15 Yrjö Haila, "Johdanto: Mikä ympäristö?", 17–20.

16 For example, see: Lassi Heininen, *Sotilaallisen läsnäolon ympäristöriskit Arktiksessa – Kohti Arktiksen säätelyjärjestelmää (The Environmental Risks of Military Presence in the Arctic – Toward the Arctic Regime)* (Tampere: Tampere Peace Research Institute: Research Report No. 43, 1991); and Lassi Heininen, "Globalization and Security in the Circumpolar North," in Lassi Heininen and Chris Southcott, ed., *Globalization*

and the *Circumpolar North* (Fairbanks: University of Alaska Press, 2010), 221–63.

17 For example, see: Lassi Heininen, Jyrki Käkönen, and O-P Jalonen, *Expanding the Northern Dimension: The Final Report of the International Arctic Project of TAPRI* (Tampere: University of Tampere Peace Research Institute Research Report No. 61, 1995).

18 United Nations, *Our Common Future* (Oxford: World Commission on Environment and Development. Oxford University Press, 1987). 8.

19 M. A. Hajer, *The Politics of Environmental Discourse. Ecological Modernization and the Policy Process* (Guildford: Oxford University Press, 1995).

20 Yrjö Haila and Lassi Heininen, "Ecology: A New Discipline for Disciplining?" *Social Text* 42 (1995): 153–71.

21 For example, see Independent Commission on Disarmament and Security, *Common Security. A Blueprint for Survival*, UN/A/CN.10/38, January 1982.

22 For example, see Johan Galtung, *Environment, Development and Military Activity: Towards Alternative Security Doctrines* (Oslo-Bergen-Trondheim, 1982).

23 For example, see Jyrki Käkönen, *Konfliktit, turvallisuus ja ympäristö. Modernisaation kriisi* (Saarijärvi: Atena, 1995).

24 Johan Galtung, *Environment, Development and Military Activity: Towards Alternative Security Doctrines* (Oslo-Bergen-Trondheim, 1982); Arthur Westing, "The Environmental Component of Comprehensive Security," *Bulletin of Peace Proposals* 20, no. 2 (1989): 129–34; and Lassi Heininen, *Sotilaallisen läsnäolon ympäristöriskit Arktiksessa – Kohti Arktiksen säätelyjärjestelmää (The Environmental Risks of Military Presence in the Arctic – Toward the Arctic Regime)* (Tampere: Tampere Peace Research Institute. Research Report No. 43, 1991).

25 Translation by Lassi Heininen; Rauno Sairinen, Tytti Viinikainen, Vesa

Kanninen, and Arto Lindholm, *Suomen ympäristöpolitiikan tulevaisuudenkuvat* (Tampere: Gaudeamus Oy, 1999), 18.

26 See John McCormick, *Environmental Policy in the European Union* (New York: Palgrave, 2001).

27 Ibid., 17–40.

28 For example, see: European Commission, *Climate Change and International Security. Paper from the High Representative and the European Commission to the European Council*. S113/08, March 14, 2008. The Union has become a pioneer, or even a pathfinder, in international climate policy as the "20-20-20" decision by the European Council shows.

29 Annika E. Nilsson, *A Changing Arctic Climate: Science and Policy in the Arctic Climate Impact Assessment* (Linköping: Linköping University, Department of Water and Environmental Studies, Linköping Studies in Arts and Science No. 386, 2007), 14.

30 Ibid., 70–80.

31 These countries were parties to the Asia-Pacific Partnership of Clean Development and Climate in 2005, together with Australia, Japan, and South Korea, to decrease greenhouse gases, which Australian prime minister John Howard claimed would be more effective and fair.

32 See: Mari Riipinen, "Local community as a stage for land use discourse – before and after a global actor." A Presentation in the Calotte Academy, Inari, Finland, May 26–28, 2005 (mimeo). The key actors were the Saami on one side, and newcomers, including the Finns, on the other side, and the focus was how to use northern forests, for cutting, as most the Finns would like, or for reindeer herding, as most of the Saami would like, and both dealt with livelihoods and thus economy, but reindeer herding is also a part of the Saami culture.

33 See Lassi Heininen, "Euroopan pohjoinen 1990-luvulla."

34 *Arctic Pollution 2002.* Arctic Monitoring and Assessment Program, Oslo, Norway, 2002.

35 *Arctic Climate Impact Assessment. Policy Document.* Issued by the Fourth Arctic Council Ministerial Meeting, Reykjavik, November 24, 2004.

36 Lawson W. Brigham, "Marine Access and Transportation." Presented at the Conference on Emerging from the Frost, Security in the 21st Century Arctic, Tromsö, Norway, 2007.

37 *Arctic Climate Impact Assessment. Policy Document.* Issued by the Fourth Arctic Council Ministerial Meeting, Reykjavik, November 24, 2004.

38 For example, see: "Report and Recommendations," *Report and Recommendations from a workshop "The Arctic and Canada's Foreign Policy,"* sponsored by The Walter and Duncan Gordon Foundation, October 4–5, 2006, 12–13; and M. Nuttall, "Epistemological Conflicts and Cooperation in the Circumpolar North," in Lassi Heininen and C. Southcott, ed., *Globalization and the Circumpolar North* (Fairbanks: University of Alaska Press, 2010), 149–78.

39 C. D. James Paci, Cindy Dickson, Scott Nikels, Laurie Chan, and Christopher Furgal, *Food Security of Northern Indigenous Peoples in a Time of Uncertainty: Position Paper for the 3rd NRF Open Meeting,* Yellowknife, NWT, September 15–18, 2004.

40 For example, see: Rob Huebert, "Climate Change and Canadian Sovereignty in the Northwest Passage," *Isuma* 2, no. 4 (Winter 2001), 86–94.

41 Lassi Heininen, "Globalization and Security in the Circumpolar North,"; also Lassi Heininen and Heather Nicol, "Climate Change and Human Security – From a Northern Point of View," in Lassi Heininen and Heather Nicol, eds., *Climate Change and Human Security – From a Northern Viewpoint* (forthcoming).

42 For example, see *Arctic Pollution Issues* (Oslo: Arctic Monitoring and Assessment Program, 1997).

43 For example, see Lassi Heininen, "An Introduction," in Lassi Heininen, ed., *Arctic Environmental Problems.* TAPRI. Occasional Papers No. 41 (Tampere: Tampereen Pikakopio Oy, 1990), 7–20.

44 Other categories of global problems, many of them playing relevant role in the Arctic, are the proliferation of nuclear weapons and other security problems, economics and problems with development, scarcity of natural resources, refugees and other human rights problems, diseases and pan-epidemics. H. Hakovirta, *Globaaliongelmat ja globaalipolitiikka: koeporauksia* (Turku: Turun yliopisto, Valtio-opin laitos, 1996).

45 Lassi Heininen, "Globalization and Security in the Circumpolar North."

46 Lassi Heininen and Boris Segerståhl, "International Negotiations Aiming at a Reduction of Nuclear Risks in the Barents Sea Region," in Rudolph Avenhaus, Victor Kremenyuk, and Gunnar Sjöstedt, eds., *Containing the Atom: International Negotiations on Nuclear Security and Safety* (New York: Lexington Books; International Institute for Applied Systems Analysis, 2002), 243–70.

47 O. S. Stokke, "Environmental Threats in the Arctic," in Lassi Heininen, ed., *Arctic Environmental Problems.* TAPRI. Occasional Papers No. 41 (Tampere: Tampereen Pikakopio Oy, 1990), 22–41.

48 *New Scientist,* "Russia Revives Epic River Plan," February 7, 2004.

49 For example, see: Declaration of Murmansk, 16th Annual Sami Conference in Murmansk, Russia, October 15–18, 1996; and Lassi Heininen, "Circumpolar International Relations and Cooperation," in Lassi Heininen and C. Southcott, eds., *Globalization and the Circumpolar North* (Fairbanks: University of Alaska Press, 2010), 265–304.

50 For example, see: Greenpeace, *Nuclear Free Seas: The Greenpeace Campaign for Nuclear Free Seas*, 1987 (pamphlet).

51 C. D. James Paci, "Connecting Circumpolar Environments: Arctic Athabaskan Council and Arctic Council Programmes," in *Circumpolar Connections: Supplementary Proceedings of the 8th Circumpolar Cooperation Conference* (Whitehorse: Circumpolar Universities Association and Yukon College, 2003), 18–26.

52 For example, see: M. Nuttall, "Epistemological Conflicts."

53 AMAP, *Arctic Pollution 2002*. Arctic Monitoring and Assessment Program, Oslo, 2002, 36; S. Meakin and T. Fenge, "Indigenous Peoples and the Stockholm Convention on Persistent Organic Pollutants," in *Arctic Human Development Report* (Reykjavik: Stefansson Arctic Institute, 2004).

54 *Arctic Climate Impact Assessment. Policy Document*. Issued by the Fourth Arctic Council Ministerial Meeting, Reykjavik, November 24, 2004.

55 For example, see: Lassi Heininen, "Euroopan pohjoinen 1990-luvulla": 242–55.

56 Rovaniemi Declaration, Signed by the Eight Arctic Nations, June 14, 1991, Rovaniemi, Finland.

57 Annika E. Nilsson, *A Changing Arctic Climate*.

58 "Jyrki Käkönen, Kestävä kehitys ja demokratia Arktiksessa," in Jyrki Käkönen, ed., *Kestävä kehitys arktisilla alueilla*. Rauhan- ja konfliktintutkimuslaitos, Tutkimustiedotteita No. 49, 1992, 16–34.

59 C. D. James Paci, "Connecting Circumpolar Environments: Arctic Athabaskan Council and Arctic Council Programmes," in *Circumpolar Connections: Supplementary Proceedings of the 8th Circumpolar Cooperation Conference* (Whitehorse: Circumpolar Universities Association and Yukon College, 2003), 18–26.

60 For example, see Jens Brösted and Mads Fægteborg, "Expulsion of the Great People When U.S. Air Force Came to Thule: An Analysis of Colonial Myth and Actual Incidents," in *Native Power: The Quest for Autonomy and Nationhood of Indigenous People* (Bergen: Universitetsforlaget, 1985), 213–38; Frances D. Abele, and Thierry Rodon, "Inuit Diplomacy in the Global Era: The Strengths of Multilateral Internationalism," *Canadian Foreign Policy* 13, no. 3 (2007): 56.

61 These include, first, implementation of the technology models of geopolitics; second, nuclear safety; third, relations between the environment and the military; fourth, relations between indigenous peoples and traditional security; and finally, climate change as global problem.

62 Lassi Heininen, "Globalization and Security in the Circumpolar North," in Lassi Heininen and C. Southcott, eds., *Globalization and the Circumpolar North* (Fairbanks: University of Alaska Press, 2010), 221–63.

63 Lassi Heininen, "Post-Cold War Arctic Geopolitics: Where are the Peoples and the Environment?" in M. Bravo and N. Triscott, eds., *Arctic Geopolitics and Autonomy*. Arctic Perspective Cahier No. 2 (2010), 89–103.

64 For example, see: Arctic Human Development Report, Akureyri: Stefansson Arctic Institute, Iceland, 2004, 24–25; M. Nuttall, "Epistemological Conflicts."

4. Conceptualizing Climate Security for a Warming World: Complexity and the Environment-Conflict Linkage[1]

Daniel Clausen and LTJG Michael Clausen, USCG

Introduction

Currently, a new concern is circulating among policy-makers, think tanks, and scholars: securing the planet's climate. This interest has accelerated as analyses of the security implications of climate change have made their way into think tank reports, popular books, and, most importantly, official national-al security documents like the *National Security Strategy* and *Quadrennial Defense Report*.[2] In addition to acknowledging the challenge of decreasing GHG emissions, these reports also examine the various regional effects of climate change and how the military might be tasked with responding to regional contingencies involving disasters or violence influenced by environmental factors. These reports tend to converge on a common representation of climate change as a "threat multiplier."[3] As these reports predict, as climate change impacts ecosystems, it will cause critical food and water shortages, spur mass migration, and strain government capacities and credibility, thus leading to more conflict and the collapse of order. According to these reports, the first victims will likely be states that lack reserve capacities in capital, scientists, engineers, or flexible political institutions able to adjust to the effects of climate change. In addition, the reports state that these ecologically induced crises could destabilize entire regions, feeding terrorist movements and sparking interstate conflicts and civil wars.[4]

While the common image these reports depict is both plausible and analytically useful, it also suffers from multiple uncertainties, not the least of which is that stemming from the environment-conflict linkage. Currently, the exact interaction between environmental factors, political institutions, and outcomes are anything but certain. Scholars who are actively engaged in studying what has been termed "environmental security" often disagree in stark terms on the precise relationship between environmental variables and the onset of conflict, both civil war and interstate.

This chapter will begin by recounting how climate change has evolved as an object of national security thinking and discourse, beginning from the 1980s and stretching to the recent "Climategate" issue. It will then examine the research climate change scientists and national security-oriented think tanks have done in terms of formulating plausible scenarios with a special focus on the way climate change has been defined as a "threat multiplier." It will then examine how different scholarly traditions have studied and depicted the environment-conflict linkage. As this chapter will show, one of the particular complications of studying the environment-conflict linkage is that the relationship between environmental factors and conflict is rarely straightforward, and, thus, is left open to interpretation by scholars from different backgrounds and theoretical orientations.

Sometimes acrimony between different schools can take place on either definitional grounds or even on differences on what is worthy of study. Environmental factors can encompass anything from environmental degradation, to renewable resource scarcity, to non-renewable resource scarcity, to resource abundance (having a commodity that is highly valued on the world market).[5] Scholars have disagreed on which if any of these variables is important in conflict onset and intensity. In addition, there is disagreement about how to study environmental factors, whether the environment or resources can or should be theorized outside of the political institutions that are established to manage it, or even outside of larger world patterns of consumption that condition environmental processes.[6] The paradox of the environmental security literature is that the environment is often acknowledged as an increasingly important factor in understanding the unfolding dimensions of world politics even as it is identified as a potential source misunderstanding and obfuscation.

For this reason, future policy-makers and scholars need to think critically about how exactly the environmental factors can "cause" conflict. Because of the importance of the environment-conflict linkage for understanding world politics, the essay will finish with some suggestions for how scholars can further explore the relationship and integrate the insights into scenarios for climate change.

The Rise of Climate Change as an Object of National Security

Since the 1980s, the issue of climate change has been on and off the political agenda – to say nothing of its framing as a national security issue. After James Hansen (then director of NASA's Goddard Institute of Space Studies) famously asserted in 1988 that climate change was near certain,[7] speculation and research began on the linkages between national security, climate change, and environmental degradation. That same year, the IPCC was created under the guidance of the UN Environmental Programme (UNEP) and World Meteorological Organization (WMO) to represent the consensus of scientists on the issue of climate change. It wasn't until the 1990s, however, that the Strategic Environmental Research and Development Program (SERDP) was created within the DoD to address issues of environmental concern. This corresponded with a gradual rise in policy statements placing the environment and environmental degradation within the sphere of national security.

The 1991 *National Security Strategy* features a brief section on the environment that mentions issues of food security, ozone depletion, water supply, deforestation, biodiversity, and treatment of wastes, in addition to the problem of climate change.[8] In addition, a Global Environmental Affairs Directorate at the National Security Council and an Office of Environmental Security led by a Deputy Undersecretary of Defense were established to address the rising interest in the connections between the environment and security. Around this same time, the idea that environmental scarcity could fuel a future anarchy of ungovernable spaces was first elaborated in the scholarship of Thomas

Homer-Dixon and then popularized by Robert Kaplan in his famous 1994 article for the *Atlantic Monthly*,[9] an article that was widely circulated among policy-makers. This popular speculation would lead to the creation of the new subfield of environmental security and a flurry of new initiatives for securing the environment within the Clinton administration. Thus, the 1997 *National Security Strategy* reflected Kaplan's concerns of resource scarcity fueling an increasing number of post-modern conflicts.[10]

Despite a growing awareness of climate change, the issue remained largely neglected. The Kyoto Protocol of 1997, though signed by the United States, was never sent to the Senate for ratification. Bipartisan resistance to the protocol centered on its failure to address pollution from rising industrial powers like China and India. While the Pentagon did commission one report in 2003 that garnered some media attention, the issue remained largely undervalued as a national security priority.[11] Even though interest was growing in some circles of the defense community about the linkages between environmental degradation and conflict, without national leadership, these projects remained largely on the back burner. As the national security community dealt first with the immediate threat of Al Qaeda and addressing gaps in homeland security, then wars in Afghanistan and Iraq, and then rising nuclear threats from Iran and North Korea, the issue of climate change was neglected, both as a political issue and as a security concern.

Since 2007, however, there has been a dramatic rise in the attention paid to climate change, both as an international political issue and as a mounting security threat. That year both Al Gore and the IPCC won the Nobel Peace Prize for their work in raising awareness of the issue. The IPCC's 2007 synthesis report judged that the evidence for climate change is "unequivocal"[12] and that the evidence that human-generated greenhouse gases are the cause of increased temperatures is "very likely" (over 90 per cent).[13] That year also saw the issuance of an influential report by the Center for Naval Analysis (CNA) backed by retired generals framing climate change as a "threat multiplier."[14] In addition, the Triangle Institute for Security Studies hosted a conference that addressed the impacts of climate change on national security.[15] Following these influential reports, several other studies and volumes were published, along with a National Intelligence Assessment issued by the Office of the Director of National Intelligence.[16]

Most importantly, the notion of climate change as a security issue has now captured the attention of political and military senior leadership.

Whereas the 2006 *Quadrennial Defense Review* made no mention of climate change or environmental security, the DoD 2008 *National Defense Strategy* acknowledged both that "climate pressures may generate new security challenges" and that there was a need to "tackle climate change."[17] Riding this new wave of engagement with the issue of climate change, the 2010 DoD *QDR* and *NSS* devote entire sections to the subject. The *QDR* addressed the full range of effects that climate change is likely to have on the security environment, and what needs to be done to tailor future force structure, mitigate the DoD's carbon footprint, and help spur new technological developments in clean energy;[18] the *NSS* meanwhile emphasizes the risk climate change poses to national security and the need for a broad shift toward an energy efficient economy. As the 2010 stated: "The danger from climate change is real, urgent, and severe."[19]

Estimates, Scenarios, and the Special Role of the Scientific Epistemic Community

It is not an insignificant point that many of the recent reports and scholarship that connect climate change to national security point to climate change's already perceptible influences – from the increased likelihood of hurricanes, to the spread of desertification in parts of Africa, to increased tension over scarce water resources in the Darfur region of the Sudan. As Buzan, Waever, and de Wilde write about past attempts to frame environmental issues as security threats: "Environmental issues often point to an unspecified, relatively remote future and therefore involve no panic politics."[20] The vagueness of environmental predictions often conflicts with a national security culture that privileges threats that are certain, proximate, and grounded in an understanding of the international system as a competition among states.

While most reports on climate change note the ambiguity involved in modeling environmental systems, the consensus among scientists is that, not only is climate change verifiable, but predictions up until this point have been too conservative. Because of the ambiguities involved in modeling environmental systems, one group of scholars (a combination of former government officials and Brookings Institute, Center for Strategic and International Studies, Center for Naval Analyses, and Center for New American Security scholars) has purposely used the word *scenarios* rather than prediction to describe their approach.[21] These authors argue that because climate change involves a complex relationship of interlinked variables that are difficult to predict – demography, energy policy, technological change, and their interactions with complex ecological systems – one should not dwell on the most likely scenario, but rather, examine a range of plausible ones. This logic applies not only to rate of climate change but also to its effects. As many scholars have pointed out, the linkages among environmental stress, environmental shocks, and trends such as political violence, migration, and the spread of disease are difficult to theorize with precision.[22]

Currently, the average obtained from IPCC climate change scenarios projects that over the next twenty to thirty years the earth's average temperature will rise by 1.3 degrees Celsius. This scenario assumes that there are no trigger effects or feedback loops and thus extrapolates largely from trends known to date.[23] While the geographical impact of climate change will vary, in the next twenty to thirty years vulnerable regions will face prospective food shortages, droughts, and flooding. Among the possible implications of these environmental changes will be pandemics, political instabilities, and potential energy and food shocks. These ecologically induced crises could destabilize entire regions, feeding terrorist movements and sparking interstate and civil conflicts. What is significant about this scenario is that it has been described as inevitable.[24] Though climate change may bring some benefits to the United States in the form of near-term increases in agricultural yields,[25] these benefits will be offset by irregular weather patterns and political and economic losses from the failure of poorer countries to cope with climate change.

Another plausible scenario, explored by Leon Fuerth,[26] assumes that various tipping points and feedback loops are activated and thus that the earth's temperatures increase more rapidly. In this scenario, methane released from melted ice sheets, the decline in carbon-absorbing forests, and the rate of rapid industrialization lead to double the climate change increase predicted in the first scenario – temperatures increase over the next twenty years by 2.6 degrees Celsius instead of the expected 1.3 degrees. Water scarcities increase, crop yields decline rapidly, coastal regions are subject to drastic flooding, and global fisheries decline as a result of coral bleaching and ocean acidification.[27] These multiple ecological breakdowns strain political institutions (especially in the less-developed world), leading to mass migration, intra- and interstate conflict, and possibly the resurgence of virulent fascist ideologies.[28] As many scholars have stressed, however, because of the many complex systems involved in predicting these events – both ecological and political – speculation on the consequences of abrupt climate change are at best useful stories for understanding what is at stake.[29]

Seeing Climate Change through its Effects: Climate Change as a "Threat Multiplier"

Currently, much of the national security literature designates climate change as a "threat multiplier."[30] The idea is that climate change's impact on ecosystems will cause critical food and water shortages, spur mass migration, and strain governments' capacities and credibility, thus leading to more conflict and anarchy – especially in those countries that lack the resources to deal with these effects. According to this research, the first victims will likely be states that lack reserve capacities in capital, scientists, engineers, or flexible political institutions able to adjust to the effects of climate change.[31] This is not to reinforce stereotypes of the poor in the Global South as the inevitable seed of world anarchy – to suggest as much would in any case ignore the source of much carbon pollution.[32] Though there is currently a wealth of research challenging these neo-Malthusian assumptions of easy connections between environmental scarcities and violent conflict,[33] the saliency of the environment-conflict linkage will likely increase as the severity of environmental shocks increases. As current environmental security thinking suggests, because of this threat of expanded ungovernable spaces, the United States will need to continue to secure U.S. energy supplies, most likely through increased stability operations in unstable areas of the world where energy is abundant, and expand capabilities for guarding sea lanes in newly opened up areas of the Arctic Ocean.[34]

Analysts who examine the threat of climate change to U.S. security often point out that potential ecological catastrophes threaten the "resilience of the international community,"[35] creating dangerous imbalances between nations that have the capacity to deal with climate change and those that do not. While some might quibble that some of this language conflates global justice with the Unites States's vital security interests, the connection is analytically useful for a number of reasons. As weak states become afflicted by environmental stresses, the United States will have to face the possibility of a rapid surge in migration, the spread of pandemics, and the breakdown of political stability in energy-rich countries and countries that are becoming increasingly embedded in the global economy, thus affecting the economic security of U.S. citizens.

There is a growing consensus that the impact of climate change will continue to strain the United States's credibility as a global security provider, peace broker, and disaster relief provider. As the United States and other countries try to attenuate the impact of climate change on their own soil, security scholars are worried that the United States and the world will lose established levels of international cooperation – the current state of the international community as such. This loss of cooperation could affect U.S. efforts to uproot terrorism, stop nuclear proliferation, and confront rogue regimes.

Though accurate and analytically useful, the term "threat multiplier" could also lead to some dangerous gaps in understanding how to respond to climate change. The idea of climate change as a threat multiplier leads the defense community to focus more on responding to the outcome of climate change (an intensified environment of threats defined in the usual terms of disaster relief, increased terrorism, rogue and collapsed states) than attenuating its causes – greenhouse gas emissions.[36] As the current *QDR* illustrates, however, the DoD has taken proactive steps toward lowering its carbon footprint and establishing programs that spur important technological developments in energy efficiency and alternative fuels.

However, out of all the claims made about the negative impacts of climate change, the prediction that conflict – both interstate and intrastate – will be more frequent and intense is the most contentious. As the following review of the academic literature will demonstrate, conceptualizing the linkage between environment change and conflict is anything but a straightforward intellectual task. Different Perspectives in the Study of Environment and Conflict

The three major traditions that deal with the environment-conflict linkage – neo-Malthusianism, neoclassical economics, and political ecology – disagree in often stark terms about, not only how the environment can be said to "cause" conflict, but also, what types of variables should be studied, how they should be studied, and what type of language should be used to portray conclusions. Despite these differences, each has something different to offer security planners seeking to understand the environmental causes of conflict. This is perhaps best demonstrated by Colin Kahl's Demographic and

Environmental Stress Model, which integrates many of the insights from the three approaches. Taken together, each of the traditions should give future students of the environment-conflict linkage pause before making simplistic and automatic assumptions about the way scarcity and degradation cause conflict.

Reading through the literature, one is often struck by the sheer number of issues that are explored under the environmental security label. The literature on environmental security discusses instances when states or substate groups come into conflict directly over resources, when subnational groups use a valuable resource to finance rebellion, when degradation or scarcity produces grievance-based violence, or when environmental problems overwhelm government legitimacy and thus provide permissive conditions for rebellion.[37] Within this hodgepodge of concerns, the "environment" can come to stand for land scarcity, soil erosion, depletion of freshwater, timber, or fish stocks, demographic pressure that can lead to these effects, or even strategically valuable resource wealth like petroleum and mineral reserves. In addition, "security" can mean anything from threats to regime security, threats to regional or international order, or threats to people's health and livelihood. Given that many of the issues within what is called the "environmental security" literature often deal with grievances, distributional justice, and/or structural violence (rather than threats to "national security" narrowly defined) some authors have argued that it is more accurate to describe the enterprise as the study of environmental *insecurity*.[38]

Generally speaking, there are three different traditions of examining the linkage between environmental causes, politics, and conflict: 1) neo-Malthusianism, 2) neoclassical economics, and 3) political ecology.[39] Each of these three approaches represents a different theoretical tradition, angle of vision, and political objective. The neo-Malthusian approach emphasizes the way trends in demography and the environment create acute scarcities that contribute to violent conflict. Alternatively, the neoclassical economics tradition stresses the adaptability of human systems (especially free market and democratic systems) in dealing with problems of the environment. Political ecology approaches, while more varied and difficult to lump together, generally share a concern for the liberation of impoverished and oppressed groups and try to deconstruct the way specialized forms of knowledge and discourse have been used to oppress marginalized groups. In addition to these three approaches, I also examine the claims of environmental skeptics as a fourth "school" for discussion. Typically, skeptics have come from both the neoclassical econom-ics and the political ecology groups (though often for different reasons).

As my short sketches will demonstrate, though each approach has very important – and in some case irreconcilable – differences, they also have im-portant linkages and create forms of knowledge that complement the other.

1. THE NEO-MALTHUSIAN APPROACH

Neo-Malthusians generally point to accelerating pressures on natural re-sources and planetary life-support systems as a major cause of conflict in the future. Though the notion that population growth itself puts strains on the planet has long been refuted, this groups often links population growth with environmental degradation and the failure of political institutions to manage environmental uses.[40] These failures can lead to increased migration, threats to state stability, increased state oppression to pre-empt threats to the state, and conflict between the state and aggrieved ethnic or political groups. Homer-Dixon's work in the nineties in particular has been very influential. Homer-Dixon's chief argument is that, as opposed to earlier times when human adaptive capacities were activated, mutually reinforcing patterns of degradation make the current crises – in particular the environmental effects of climate change – more difficult to overcome.[41] The later contributions of the scholars in what is called the Toronto School (including Homer-Dixon's work) explore the complexity involved in the environment-conflict linkage using primarily case study analysis. Many of these studies found that, while environmental factors were rarely necessary or sufficient conditions, they nevertheless lead to structural opportunities for violence.

Critics have pointed to neo-Malthusianism's pension for environmental determinism. Neo-Malthusians have been accused of ignoring both interac-tions with political institutions that make conflict more likely and the way political institutions and ideas help produce scarcity to begin with. Though scholars such as Barnett[42] laud the sophistication of case study work done by Homer-Dixon and others as part of the Toronto School's Project on Environment, Population, and Security, critics still suggest that the "positiv-ist vernacular"[43] used by neo-Malthusians often denotes a linear relationship between environmental stress and conflict that has yet to be proven.

Because neo-Malthusians focus on the environment as an independent variable, they also ignore important dynamics involved in civil war onset. As the literature on civil strife points out,[44] revolts are often difficult to start because of problems of coordination and the free-rider dilemma. The free-rider problem in civil wars amounts to this: how does a revolt start when the risk taken on by the initial organizers is so much greater than the risk taken on by those who decide to bandwagon later on? Thus, critics of the neo-Malthusian approach point out that an emphasis on resource scarcity over-predicts the occurrence of civil strife.

2. NEOCLASSICAL ECONOMICS

In the neoclassical economic approach, much more of an emphasis is put on the human capacity to cope with environmental change and, in a rebuttal to neo-Malthusians, resource abundance (not scarcity) is linked with conflict.[45] For scholars in this group, the market mechanism plays an important role. Market incentives triggered by scarcity lead to new innovations in technology and management to create coping mechanisms. In a similar way, representative governments respond to political demands to obviate critical scarcities that affect their constituencies. In addition, those who focus on the "resource curse" could be placed into this group. The abundance of a highly valued commodity severely stunts the development of sophisticated, variegated market economies by giving incentives for parties to find and hold valuable resources rather than innovate. The availability of resources also stunts the development of governments responsive to citizen needs, giving incentives for the government to be just strong enough to hold valuable territory and live off rents from its resources. In what is termed the "honey pot" hypothesis, resource abundance creates incentives for groups to capture resources. Where there is a weak state, substate groups can compete with the government for control of these resources. This literature tends to emphasize "greed" (defined as opportunities for banditry or state capture in order to generate income) over "grievance" (defined as human rights abuses and political oppression) as motivation for intrastate conflict.

Critics of the neoclassical economics approach have pointed out that on a local scale the mechanisms for mediating resource scarcity, in the form of a market mechanism or a responsive government, are often imperfect or absent in much of the less-developed world. On a global scale, critics point out that – in contrast to past claims of impending demographic doom – current negative trends of population growth, consumption, and environmental limits are much more embedded and reinforcing than was ever the case before. As

Homer-Dixon argues, these patterns lend themselves to reinforcement and trigger effects that stress the environment in irreversible ways.[46]

In addition, a great deal (though not all) of the "honey pot" theories tend to focus more on non-renewable resources than on renewable resources that have been overstressed. Forestry, fisheries, and agriculture – resources that are renewable when used in moderation – tend to contribute to the employment of large populations. When these resources are depleted, much larger portions of the population suffer, leading to grievance-based violence.

Moreover, the neoclassical economics approach ignores the way "resource curse" explanations can be linked with the neo-Malthusian literature:[47] the availability of resource rents from non-renewable resources like oil might prevent the government from undertaking policies to manage renewable resources like fisheries or agricultural land in ways that benefit the larger population. Over time, this neglect could lead to clashes among substate groups over increasingly scarce resources. These critical scarcities might also create better incentives for people to join rebel groups (the "greed" explanation) to capture valuable nonrenewable resources.

3. Political Ecology

Though very difficult to encapsulate in a thumbnail sketch, political ecology can be described as a mix of post-structural and critical theory, non-equilibrium ecology, and rich ethnographic case study analysis. While this captures some of the essence of the approach, another way to think of this tradition is in terms of its normative objectives. Political ecology tends to focus less on accumulating and testing generalizable theories and more on interrogating the complexity of social and ecological relationships. In particular, the literature is interested in exposing how systems of environmental management often disenfranchise the poor.[48] Thus, as the title of Peet and Watt's book *Liberation Ecologies* suggests, a key theme in political ecology is creating a scholarship that can foster the liberation of marginalized people.

Much of the literature is also hostile to the neo-Malthusian approach and the way its scholarship has informed U.S. strategic thinking since the mid-90s. A common accusation of political ecologists is that neo-Malthusians posit simplistic linkages between environmental degradation, scarcity, and conflict. In addition, they criticize neo-Malthusians for ignoring the way scarcities are conditioned by larger systems – domestic and local systems, but in some cases world systems – of production and consumption.[49]

For Kahl, political ecology's focus on regimes of production and distribution misses just how much material factors matter. Kahl criticizes political ecologists for downplaying the role of environmental stress in conflict; instead, he highlights the way the material fact of demographic stress conspires with systems of inequality to cause conflict.[50] Even though political ecology's case study approach to environmental factors has provided a solid contribution to the field, political ecologists have nonetheless been dismissive of the contributions and nuance of Toronto school (neo-Malthusian) case studies.[51] Perhaps the strongest criticism of political ecology has to do with its lack of policy relevance. Because political ecology studies often seek to upset simplistic ways of viewing the world, their work often suffers from a high degree of indeterminacy.[52] Thus, unlike for example the work of think tank policy papers, their conclusions are rarely reducible to easy-to-read executive summaries or bullet points. This is at once a major strength of political ecology studies, but also a major limitation on their ability to reach mainstream audiences.

4. ENVIRONMENTAL SECURITY SKEPTICISM

Finally, it should be noted that there is also a strain of literature that questions the salience of the environment-conflict linkage. In a sense, this is a continuation of the skepticism found in the neoclassical and political ecology approaches. This literature, however, is important enough to include in its own section because it questions the very merit of the explosion of interest in "environmental security." Raleigh and Urdal, for example, note that statistical literature studies that include a large number of cases (a large N) is at best mixed on the association between resource scarcity and violence.[53] While the State Failure Task Force Report of the late 1990s[54] found that soil degradation, deforestation, and freshwater scarcity were not directly linked to conflict, Hauge and Ellington (1998) found that the same factors, with high population density, were highly associated with civil war – but also, that these factors were secondary to political factors.[55] Theisen, however, is unable to replicate the results of Hauge and Ellington in his statistical study. He concludes that, because the Hauge and Ellington study is so frequently the sole statistical study cited in the environmental security literature, and because these results are not subject to replication, the relationship between scarcity, degradation, and conflict has very little support in the large statistical study research.[56]

In addition, criticisms of the environmental security literature have also come from the political ecology camp. Environmental security models that rely on understandings of the environment as an "independent variable" often simplify complex processes that reflect the issue of resource *distribution* and discourses that drive these distribution patterns. As Benjaminsen argues, reading the neo-Malthusian literature one "often gets the impression that degradation is something measurable" when the idea of degradation is always subject to "conflicting views regarding how the land should be used and what the landscape ought to look like."[57] In addition, the environmental security literature tends to treat "conflicts as internal to 'groups' or 'societies' with little or no analysis of interactions with the international political economy."[58] This approach, then, leaves larger issues of global environmental justice unexplored.

Colin Kahl's DES Model

Thus far, Kahl's Demographic and Environmental Stress Model (DES) has done the most to integrate environmental and political variables into one comprehensive account. The independent variable in the model – demographic and environmental stress (DES) is a composite variable that encompasses (1) rapid population growth, (2) the degradation of renewable resources, and (3) the maldistribution of renewable resources. It should be noted that the third variable assumes that political, social, and economic processes have an important impact on the way scarcity is produced in populations (a concession to political ecology). A resource may be in ready supply, yet nevertheless experienced as scarce by local populations because the resource is so poorly distributed or managed.

The author contends that there are two main pathways through which DES can cause violence – *state failure* and *state exploitation*. The state failure pathway creates incentives for "social groups to engage in violence via the logic of the security dilemma."[59] In other words, as crucial resources become scarce, rival states or substate groups will be more likely to compete for these resources. When this happens within the state, fierce competition can reduce the government to merely one competitor amongst other comparatively powerful groups. The state exploitation pathway, however, assumes a different dynamic. In this pathway, better organized and powerful state elites are able to pre-empt competition from competitor groups or capture scarce resources through violence in order to protect their own narrow self-interests.[60] Kahl argues that *groupness* (the degree to which people align with an ethnic, religious, or class group over the state) and institutional *inclusivity* (the degree to which important government institutions allow diverse groups to influence policy through legitimate processes) are important for understanding whether DES leads to conflict.[61] In the case of groupness, strong cleavages in group affiliations within the state and the absence of cross-cutting loyalties and identifications help to overcome the collective action problem early in revolts (the free-rider problem identified in the civil strife literature noted above). By contrast, an ethnically homogenous state, a unified national identity, or cross-cutting identifications can help neutralize conflict.[62] Similarly, an inclusive government with legitimate processes for protesting policies can also help neutralize violent conflict. In contrast, government processes that exclude large populations with high levels of groupness will fuel the logic of the security dilemma.

The strength of the state to deter violence plays a significant role in determining the pathways of violence. When elites are unified against a weaker minority, higher levels of DES will be needed to push minority groups toward violent revolt. In this case, state exploitation is the most likely pathway. In cases where the minority is especially weak and state capacities for oppression extremely advanced, violence may not even register because it is deeply submerged in state structures of human rights abuses. In the case of state weakness, substate actors will find it easier to garner support among their in-group and challenge the state for ever scarcer resources, thus leading to greater challenges to state authority.[63]

By taking into account the importance of demographic and environmental stresses as an independent variable, Kahl's work addresses the neo-Malthusian "independent variable"; however, by acknowledging the way distribution systems *create* scarcity, he also acknowledges some of the concerns of political ecology. Finally, by demonstrating how dysfunctional coping methods are the pathways toward conflict, Kahl demonstrates how the insights of the neoclassical economics approach can inform studies of the environment-conflict linkage.

The Limitations of the DES Model

Though Kahl's model is a significant achievement, there are nevertheless several important gaps that need to be explored.

First, along the lines of political ecology, the model fails to take into account the complex ways that DES is a product of the deep structural processes of power within the world system. Though DES assumes maldistribution as a key process which produces scarcity in disadvantaged populations, the model leaves the global systems of production and consumption that help to create scarcities un- (or under-) theorized.[64] For example, Kahl's model fails to take into account how much the measured "stress" in the independent variable is due to the combination of oil shocks, rising interest rates, falling/rising commodity prices, and the structural adjustment programs during the period of conflict. Though a discussion of these factors does appear in Kahl's discussion section, they are largely exogenous to his model. Maldistribution, in other words, may be the condition of a larger story that includes more than just relations between civil society and local government. This larger story may also be more important theoretically if our concern is the welfare of vulnerable populations in the Global South.[65]

Second, along the lines of neoclassical economics, the model fails to take into account the processes of productive institutions and mechanisms that can reflect back on DES to alleviate these problems to begin with. In other words, Kahl never closes the circle. As the neoclassical economic position notes, market mechanisms and democratic institutions can not only relax mechanisms of civil strife but also help alleviate the problem of DES through adaptive processes. These adaptive processes should not be limited to so-called rational management approaches to the environment either. There is a wealth of scholarship, for example, that points to effective indigenous methods for land management. This problem remains unresolved because Kahl's concern is civil strife, not processes of environmental management. Yet, as many authors have argued, understanding what process are available for managing environmental stress is just as important as understanding why conflict occurs.[66]

My third critique regards the positioning of DES as an important independent variable. As my review of the "skeptics" above notes, the statistical literature currently finds only a weak association between environmental degradation and conflict. While demographic stress and the grievance of populations makes this independent variable more significant, lumping the three together into a composite variable misses just how different each of these variables are in their relationship to the onset of violence. Thus, one could imagine the model drawn much differently. Theisen's conclusion that political dysfunction and poverty have much more explanatory power than resource scarcity,[67] for example, suggests that political issues and poverty should be positioned as the independent variable, with the environmental factors positioned as intervening variables.

A fourth critique can be directed at Kahl's methodological approach. Because Kahl relies heavily on two case studies to elucidate his claims (the Philippines and Kenya), his study is limited to a thick description of DES and the intervening variables of groupness and institutional inclusivity to demonstrate the utility of his model. As he states, one of the reasons he decides to take this route is because much of the data he needs is not easily quantifiable. In addition, Kahl claims that statistical approaches are not very effective at answering "how" questions.[68] Though Kahl is largely correct, his approach nevertheless does little to counter environmental security skepticism. Future scholars will need to think creatively of ways to test Kahl's model through large *N* statistical studies.

My criticisms of Kahl's model are purposely unfair: they ask the model to provide answers to questions and to perform tasks it was never intended to do. Yet these criticisms point to important avenues of further research, facilitated by future conjunctions between research agendas. While future research should not try to include everything, it should attempt to make important connections between currently disparate approaches – for example, that between qualitative case study research and large quantitative statistical studies, or that between the neo-Malthusian/neoclassical economics approaches and political ecology. Though Kahl's approach is a good starting point, there is still much to be done.

Conclusion: New Paths of Exploration and Synthesis

As this essay has shown, greater efforts to link the concerns of different traditions in environmental security can help to construct a more nuanced understanding of the role the environment plays in the onset and intensity of conflict. By incorporating *both* the environment and regimes of resource distribution, Kahl's model avoids the either/or tradeoff between the two that is assumed in other approaches. As my criticisms have shown, however, Kahl's approach is far from perfect. Still, there are good reasons why researchers should continue to look across traditions for insights on how environmental factors can contribute to conflict. Even as defense planners begin to think about how climate change can lead to civil war onset and interstate conflict, they will do well to remember the points made by environmental security skeptics and especially the weak linkages that are found between environmental factors and conflict in the statistical literature. As these studies have found, variables such as soil degradation, deforestation, and water scarcity are at best secondary to issues of poverty, low economic growth, and high dependence on primary commodities for export.[69] These studies serve to remind us that environmental factors are one part (sometimes even a relatively small part) of a larger picture.

Despite the work done by Kahl and other scholars, there are still quite a few avenues for improving the state of knowledge on the role of environmental causes on conflict. Scholars and security planners should continue to:

- Create greater synergies between statistical studies that look for relationships among a large number of cases and more nuanced case studies that take into account how environmental factors work in different political and social contexts. This will allow scholars and security planners to understand the limit of generalizations about the environment and conflict.

- Direct more attention to smaller political units like provinces in order to complement larger studies that use the state as their unit of analysis.[70]

- As a way of addressing environmental security skeptics, investigate the degree to which instances where conflict does not register are actually instances where populations are suffering from acute forms of political oppression and structural violence (in other words, environmentally facilitated insecurity).[71]

- Examine the feedback loops that allow political institutions, ideas, and activism to react back on environmental "independent variables" – both positively and negatively. This may mean thoughtful engagement with the environmental management literature. The implication is that understanding which state capacities are best at obviating environmental stress is just as important as understanding how environmental stress causes conflict.

- And finally, researchers should seek to avoid the mysticism that often accompanies positioning the environment scarcities or valuable resources as "strong" independent variables. Scholars can do so by looking at the role of political entrepreneurs in either promoting or helping to prevent violent conflict in contexts of high environmental stress.[72] By doing so, scholars and security planners will also help to create more policy-relevant studies for those looking to intervene in future crises.

As security planners continue to develop regional scenarios for climate change, it is important to remember that there is nothing automatic about linkages between environmental causes and violence. The evolution of politics in different regions will depend quite a bit on complex political and ecological variables that are rarely clear-cut. By comparing and contrasting the insights of statistical studies and in-depth case studies, security scholars can begin to understand that limitations of generalizations about environmental variables as well as begin to identify new hypothesis for testing. An attention to building nuance and sophistication in our understanding of the environment-conflict linkage will ultimately benefit decision-makers and policy planners as they seek to understand the environmental factors in the future of world politics.

Though the environmental security literature will continue to inform our understanding of conflict onset and intensity in the twenty-first century, one should also be aware of the limitations of this research. Much of the current and future literature, whether case studies or large statistical analyses, will be based on what has happened in the past. An understanding of past cases may be of limited utility in comparison with a very unique future. This future may include more acute forms of environmental stress than could ever be found in studies of the recent past. Thus, even as scholars continue to probe for relationships between different environmental causes and conflict, it is important for security planners and analysts to be bolder than their academic counterparts. Whereas the scholarly community is more apt to proclaim that the future is not evidence,[73] security planners will need to actively think about the limits of current studies and account for the worst of all possible cases.

Notes

1 The first part of this chapter was originally published in *Strategic Insights* 9, no. 2 (2010): 13–25; http://calhoun.nps.edu/public/bitstream/handle/10945/11519/SI_V9_I2_2010_Clausen_13.pdf.

2 See, for example: Center for Naval Analysis (CNA), *National Security and the Threat of Climate Change* (2007), http://www.cna.org/reports/climate; Thomas Finger, *National Intelligence Assessment on the National Security Implications of Global Climate Change to 2030* (Office of the Director of National Intelligence, 2008), http://www.dni.gov/testimonies/20080625_testimony.pdf; Peter Schwartz and Doug Randall, *An Abrupt Climate Change Scenario and its Implications for United States National Security* (Pasadena: Jet Propulsion Laboratory Pasadena, October 2003), http://www.edf.org/documents/3566_AbruptClimateChange.pdf; Kurt M. Campbell and Christine Parthemore, "National Security and Climate Change in Perspective," in *Climatic Cataclysm: The Foreign Policy and National Security Implications of Climate Change*, ed. Kurt M. Campbell (Washington, D.C.: Brookings Institute Press, 2008); Kurt Campbell, Jay Gulledge, J. R. McNeill, John Podesta, Peter Ogden, Leon Fuerth, R. James Woolsey, Alexander T. J. Lennon, Julianne Smith, Richard Weitz, and Derek Mix, *The Age of Consequences: The Foreign Policy and National Security Implications of Global Climate Change* (Center for Strategic and International Studies/ Center for American Security; November, 2007); Joshua W. Busby, "Who Cares about the Weather?: Climate Change and U.S. National Security" *Security Studies* 17, no. 3: 468–502; White House, *National Security Strategy* (2010); White House, *National Security Strategy* (2010).

3 The term "threat multiplier" is specifically used in by the Center for Naval Analysis (CNA), *National Security and Climate Change* (2007), 3 and 6.

4 The scenario described above is generally consistent with the reports cited in the first note. See especially: Cambell and Parthemore (2008), 14; for an exploration of linkages between climate change and terrorism, see Paul J. Smith, "Climate Change, Weak States and the 'War on Terrorism' in South and Southeast Asia." *Contemporary Southeast Asia* 29, no. 2 (2008): 264–85.

5 In many of the studies surveyed, important variables are under-represented: the effect of extreme weather events, coastline erosion, and the impact of environmental refugees on state legitimacy. These are important research issues.

6 A particularly important problem is that of endogeneity. It is difficult to clearly delineate whether environmental degradation and scarcity cause bad political institutions and thus lead to conflict, or whether conflict and dysfunctional political institutions are the cause of environmental degradation and scarcity.

7 Kurt M. Campbell and Christine Parthemore, "National Security and Climate Change in Perspective," in *Climatic Cataclysm: The Foreign Policy and National Security Implications of Climate Change*, ed. Kurt M. Campbell (Washington, D.C.: Brookings Institute Press, 2008), 4.

8 White House. *National Security Strategy* (1991).

9 Thomas Homer-Dixon, "On the Threshold: Environmental Changes as Causes of Acute Conflict," *International Security* 16, no. 2 (1991): 76–116; Robert Kaplan, "The Coming Anarchy," *Atlantic Monthly*

(February 1994): 44–76; http://www. theatlantic.com/doc/199402/anarchy.

10 White House. *National Security Strategy* (1997); http://www.fas.org/man/docs/ strategy97.htm.

11 Peter Schwartz and Doug Randall, *An Abrupt Climate Change Scenario and its Implications for United States National Security* (Pasadena: Jet Propulsion Laboratory Pasadena, October 2003); http://www.gbn.com/articles/pdfs/ Abrupt%20Climate%20Change%20 February%202004.pdf.

12 Intergovernmental Panel on Climate Change, *Climate Change: Fourth Assessment Report* (AR4) (WMO/ UNEP, 2007), 30; http://www.ipcc.ch/ publications_and_data/publications_ipcc_ fourth_assessment_report_synthesis_ report.htm.

13 Ibid., 39.

14 Center for Naval Analysis (CNA), *National Security and the Threat of Climate Change* (2007); http://www.cna.org/reports/climate.

15 For video recordings of the presentations at this conference, see: http://tiss.sanford. duke.edu/ClimateChangeVideo-Recording. php.

16 Thomas Finger, *National Intelligence Assessment on the National Security Implications of Global Climate Change to 2030* (Office of the Director of National Intelligence, 2008), http://www.dni.gov/ testimonies/20080625_testimony.pdf.

17 Department of Defense (DoD), *Quadrennial Defense Review* (2010): 5.

18 Ibid., 84–88.

19 White House, *National Security Strategy* (2010): 47.

20 Barry Buzan, Ole Weaver, and Jaap De Wilde, *Security: A New Framework for Analysis* (Boulder, CO: Lynne Rienner, 1998), 83.

21 Jay Gulledge, "Three Plausible Scenarios of Future Climate Change," in *Climatic Cataclysm: The Foreign Policy and National*

Security Implications of Climate Change, ed. Kurt Campbell (Washington, D.C.: Brookings Institute Press, 2008), 50–51.

22 See Homer-Dixon, "On the Threshold"; Colin Kahl, *States, Scarcity, and Civil Strife in the Developing World* (Princeton, NJ: Princeton University Press, 2006); CNA (2007); Carolyn Pumphrey, "Introduction," in *Global Climate Change: National Security Implications,* ed. Carolyn Pumphrey (Strategic Studies Institute/ Triangle Institute for Security Studies, 2008), 1–22, http://www. strategicstudiesinstitute.army.mil/pubs/ display.cfm?PubID=862.

23 John Podesta and Peter Ogden. "Scenario 1: Expected Climate Change over the Next Thirty Years," *Climatic Cataclysm: The Foreign Policy and National Security Implications of Climate Change,* ed. Kurt Campbell (Washington, D.C.: Brookings Institute Press, 2008): 97–132; Finger (2008); Kurt Campbell, Jay Gulledge, J. R. McNeill, John Podesta, Peter Ogden, Leon Fuerth, R. James Woolsey, Alexander T. J. Lennon, Julianne Smith, Richard Weitz, and Derek Mix, *The Age of Consequences: The Foreign Policy and National Security Implications of Global Climate Change* (Center for Strategic and International Studies / Center for American Security. November, 2007).

24 Podesta and Ogden, "Scenario 1," 97; Campbell et al., *Age of Consequences,* 42.

25 Finger, *National Intelligence Assessment.*

26 Leon Fuerth, "Scenario 2: Severe Climate Change over the Next Thirty Years," *Climatic Cataclysm: The Foreign Policy and National Security Implications of Climate Change,* ed. Kurt Campbell (Washington, D.C.: Brookings Institute Press, 2008): 133–54.

27 Fuerth, "Scenario 2," 133–35; Campbell et al., *Age of Consequences,* 42–43.

28 Fuerth, "Scenario 2," 143; Ken Booth, *A Theory of World Security* (Cambridge: Cambridge University Press, 2007).

29 For more on the difficulty of predictive analysis and climate change, see Joshua Busby, "Who Cares about the Weather?: Climate Change and U.S. National Security," *Security Studies* 17, no. 3 (2008): 468–504.

30 CNA (2007); DoD (2010), 85, refers to climate change as an "accelerant of instability or conflict."

31 Campbell and Parthemore, "National Security and Climate Change in Perspective," 14; Homer-Dixon, "On the Threshold".

32 This is a point that cannot be stressed enough. As Peluso and Watts argue, much of the literature on environmental security often recreates the world's poor as the threat to civilization; while I would suggest this is at best a thematic shadow that haunts the literature, environmental security scholars should be clear whenever possible to acknowledge the sources of economic insecurity for the poor. For a fuller discussion, see Nancy Peluso and Michael Watts, "Violent Environments," in *Violent Environments*, ed. Nancy Peluso and Michael Watts (Ithaca, NY: Cornell University Press, 2001), 3–38.

33 The criticisms of neo-Malthusian assumptions of the easy linkage between scarcity and conflict vary by different concerns. Edited volumes such Peluso and Watts, *Violent Environments*, examine some of the ways environmental security narratives reinforce stereotypes of the poor (especially in the Global South) as the basis for anarchy and disorder. Another author examines the way the environment-conflict linkages can possibly justify endless interventions by the Global North into the sovereign political domains of the Global South: see Jon Barnett, "Destabilizing the Environment-Conflict Thesis" *Review of International Studies* 26 (2000): 271–88; other scholars find little empirical evidence in statistical studies to support the strong linkage between renewable resource scarcity and conflict: see Clionadh Raleigh and Henrik Urdal, "Climate Change, Environmental Degradation, and Armed Conflict," *Political Geography* 26 (2007): 674–94; Ole Magnus Theisen, "Blood and Soil? Resource Scarcity and Internal Armed Conflict Revisited," *Journal of Peace Research* 45, no. 6 (2008): 801–18; and Henrik Urdal, "People vs. Malthus: population pressure, environmental degradation, armed conflict revisited," *Journal of Peace Research* 42, no. 4 (2005): 417–34. This is just a small sample of the literature from what we term the "environmental security skeptics."

34 Pew Center on Global Climate Change, *National Security Implications of Climate Global Change* (August 2009); http://www.pewclimate.org; DoD (2010), 84.

35 Campbell and Parthemore, "National Security and Climate Change in Perspective," 17.

36 One author, for example, Anthony Patt, criticizes a recent volume that evaluates climate change as a national security problem for not focusing enough on the issue of mitigation. See Anthony Patt, "Book Review: *Climatic Cataclysm: The Foreign Policy and National Security Implications of Climate Change*," *Global Environmental Politics* 9, no. 2 (2009): 129–31.

37 Elizabeth Chalecki, "Environment and Security," in *The International Studies Encyclopedia*, ed. Robert A. Denemark (Blackwell, 2010); Simon Dalby, "Environmental Security and Climate Change," in *The International Studies Encyclopedia*, ed. Robert A. Denemark (Oxford: Blackwell, 2010).

38 Jon Barnett, "Destabilizing the Environment-Conflict Thesis," *Review of International Studies* 26 (2000): 271–88; see also Peluso and Watts (2001), 3–38; B. Hartmann, "Will the Circle Be Unbroken? A Critique of the Project on Environment, Population, and Security," in *Violent Environments*, ed. N. Peluso and M. Watts (Ithaca, NY: Cornell University Press, 2001): 39–63.

39 Colin Kahl, *States, Scarcity, and Civil Strife in the Developing World* (Princeton, NJ: Princeton University Press, 2006), 4–25; see also Chalecki, "Environment and Security" and Dalby, "Environmental Security and Climate Change."

40 For examples of the neo-Malthusian literature, see: Norman Myers, "Population, Environment, and Conflict," *Environmental Conservation* 7 (1987): 15–22; Thomas Homer-Dixon, *Environment, Scarcity, Violence* (Princeton, NJ: Princeton University Press, 1999); Thomas Homer-Dixon and Jessica Blitt (eds.), *Ecoviolence: Links among Environment, Population and Security* (Lanham, MD: Rowman and Littlefield, 1998).

41 Homer-Dixon, "On the Threshold."

42 Jon Barnett, "Destabilizing the Environment-Conflict Thesis."

43 Ibid., 283.

44 See, for example, Jack Goldstone, *Revolutions of the Late Twentieth Century* (Boulder, CO: Westview, 1991).

45 For examples of this literature, see Richard M. Auty, "Natural Resources and Civil Strife: A Two-Stage Process," *Geopolitics* 9, no. 1 (2004): 29–49; Indra de Soysa, "The Resource Curse: Are Civil Wars Driven by Rapacity or Paucity?", in *Greed and Grievance: Economic Agendas in Civil War*, ed. M, Berdal and D. Malone (Boulder, CO: Lynne Rienner, 2000): 113–35; Indra de Soysa, "Ecoviolence: Shrinking Pie or Honey Pot?", *Global Environmental Politics* 2, no. 4 (2002): 1–34.

46 Homer-Dixon "On the Threshold"; Kahl, *States, Scarcity, and Civil Strife*, 17.

47 Kahl, "On the Threshold," 20.

48 For a concise introduction and exploration of political ecology research, see Roderick Neumann, *Making Political Ecology* (New York: Hodder Arnold, 2005). For other representative writings, see: Tania Murray Li, *The Will to Improve* (Durham, NC: Duke University Press, 2007); Richard Peet and Michael Watts, "Liberating Political Ecology," in *Liberation Ecologies: Environment, Development, Social Movements*, ed. R. Peet and M. Watts (New York: Routledge, 2004), 3–47; Michael Watts, " Violent Environments: Petroleum Conflict and the Political Ecology of Rule in the Niger Delta, Nigeria," in *Liberation Ecologies: Environment, Development, Social Movements*, ed. R. Peet and M. Watts (London: Routledge, 2004), 273–98.

49 Peet and Watts, "Liberating Political Ecology," 12; for one particularly acrimonious exchange between Homer-Dixon and Peet and Watts, see *ECSP Report-Issue 9* (2003): 89–96.

50 Kahl, "On the Threshold," 115.

51 See Homer-Dixon for a critique, *ECSP Report-Issue 9*.

52 Kahl, "On the Threshold," 25.

53 Raleigh and Urdal, "Climate Change": 674–94. See also, Henrik Urdal, "People vs. Malthus: population pressure, environmental degradation, armed conflict revisited," *Journal of Peace Research* 42, no. 4 (2005): 417–34.

54 Daniel C. Esty, Jack. A. Goldstone, Ted Robert Gurr, Barbara Harff, Marc Levy, Geoffrey D. Dabelko, Pamela Surko, and Alan N. Unger, *State Failure Task Force Report: Phase II Findings* (McLean, VA: Science Applications International, for State Failure Task Force, 1998).

55 Wenche Hauge and Tanja Ellingsen, "Beyond Environmental Scarcity: Causal Pathways to Conflict," *Journal of Peace Research* 35, no. 3 (1998): 299–317; see also, Raleigh and Urdal, "Climate Change,, 680.

56 Ole Magnus Theisen, "Blood and Soil? Resource Scarcity and Internal Armed Conflict Revisited," *Journal of Peace Research* 45, no. 6 (2008): 801–18.

57 Tor Arve Benjaminsen, "Does Supply-Induced Scarcity Drive Violent Conflicts in the African Sahel? The Case of the Tuareg Rebellion in Northern Mali," *Journal of Peace Research* 45, no. 6 (2008): 821.

58 Neumann, *Making Political Ecology*, 160; also see Simon Dalby, *Environmental*

Security (Minneapolis: University of Minnesota Press, 2002), 89–90.

59 Kahl, "On the Threshold," 26.

60 Ibid., 26.

61 Ibid., 27.

62 For a visual illustration, see ibid., 52.

63 For a complete visual of this theoretical design, see ibid., 59.

64 For an alternative diagram model taking into account these processes, see Watts and Peet, *Liberating Political Ecology*, 30.

65 In this regard, Paul Collier's suggestions regarding what countries in the Global North can do to be ethical consumers of valuable resources is essential reading. See, especially, Paul Collier, *The Bottom Billion* (Oxford: Oxford University Press, 2007).

66 Barnett, "Destabilizing the Environment-Conflict Thesis"; Dalby, "Environmental Security and Climate Change."

67 Theisen, *Blood and Soil*, 801.

68 Kahl, "On the Threshold," 60.

69 See Thiesen, *Blood and Soil*; see also, Esty et al., "State Failure," and Raleigh and Urdal, "Climate Change"; for more on the robust connection between civil war and poverty,

low economic growth, and primary commodity dependence see Paul Collier and Anke Hoeffler, "Greed and Grievance in Civil War." *Oxford Economic Papers* 56, no. 4 (2004): 563–95.

70 Raleigh and Urdal's (2007) study is a good first attempt at examining the environment/conflict relationship at smaller scales. They use 100 km square units to examine the relationship between land degradation, freshwater availability, and population density and the risk of violence. However, in the future, a focus on more salient *political* units smaller than the state (for example at the province level) might be more instructive.

71 See: Philippe Le Billon, "Diamond Wars: Conflict Diamonds and Geographies or Resource Wars," *Annals of the Association of American Geographers* 98, no. 2 (2008): 347.

72 See, for example, Daniel Moran's comments regarding how easy it is to lose sight of human agency when strong "independent variables" are considered. Daniel Moran, "Climate Change and Climate Politics" *Strategic Insights* 9, no. 2 (2010): 8.

73 Raleigh and Urdal, "Climate Change,", 674, 676; see also, Nils Petter Gleditsch, "Armed conflict and the environment," *Journal of Peace Research* 35, no. 3 (1998): 393.

COOPERATION AND CONFLICT: PATHS FORWARD

5. Cooperation or Conflict in a Changing Arctic? Opportunities for Maritime Cooperation in Arctic National Strategies[1]

Ian G. Brosnan, Thomas M. Leschine, and Edward L. Miles

Introduction

"Arctic neighbors draw up battle lines." – *BBC News*, August 11, 2007[2]

This vivid hook used by the BBC is representative of countless headlines and a fair number of academic papers published since 2007 regarding relations in the Arctic Ocean.[3] Concerns that the Arctic will be the scene of international conflict are the result of several converging circumstances, including the dramatic retreat of summer sea-ice that has historically been a major barrier to accessing shorter shipping routes and Arctic natural resources, long-standing unresolved Arctic maritime boundaries, and approaching deadlines for several of the Arctic states to submit information respecting the outer limit of their continental shelf beyond 200 nautical miles to the United Nations.

Although many of the arguments for Arctic conflict found in the popular press are built on oversimplifications of complex multidimensional issues, conflict in the region seems possible. However, the possibility of conflict is also a possibility for cooperation and examination of the opportunities for cooperation in the Arctic is needed. The United States, Canada, Russia, Norway, and Denmark have recently published new or updated Arctic strategies and policies (henceforth referred to collectively as strategy statements). Here, we examine these strategies and identify common issues that can serve as avenues for cooperation between the Arctic states. A more complete exploration of the opportunities and potential character of cooperation between the Arctic powers can be found in Brosnan, Leschine, and Miles, "Cooperation or Conflict in the Arctic?" *Ocean Development and International Law* 42 (2011): 173–210.

Our focus on the so-called "Arctic Five," the United States, Canada, Denmark, Norway, and Russia, merits some explanation. Our article is the result of a report prepared for the National Assembly of Korea and the Korea Maritime Institute. A combination of littoral geography and geopolitical and economic circumstances, as well as our interpretation of our funder's interests and the short time-line to produce our report, led us to focus on the "Arctic Five." As the list of signatories to the recent Arctic Search and Rescue Agreement, the Arctic Council's first legally binding instrument, attests, there are more concerned Arctic parties than just the United States, Canada, Denmark, Norway and Russia. Sweden, Finland, and Iceland are also signatories to the agreement and Arctic Council members. They participate, to varying degrees, in other international Arctic fora such as the International Maritime Organization bodies concerned with Arctic shipping. A growing number of countries and international bodies, including, *inter alia*, Britain, the EU, China, and India, are requesting to join the Arctic Council as observers. Many of the themes identified below are as applicable to the Arctic Council members, observers, and permanent participants as they are to the "Arctic Five." Our focus on the "Arctic Five" should not detract from the fundamental message that there are numerous avenues for cooperation in the Arctic; conflict is not inevitable.

Five Arctic Strategies

The United States updated its Arctic Region Policy (U.S. ARP) on January 9, 2009, apparently in response to geopolitical and environmental changes.[4] It was released during the final days of President George W. Bush's administration, which raised questions about its merit as a guide to future U.S. policy. However, the contents seem to have been carefully crafted to serve as a flexible, long-term policy for U.S. activities in a changing region rather than a partisan move to influence long-term U.S. Arctic conduct. There was no indication during President Obama's first term that the policy would be updated,[5] nor has it been a focus of the 2012 presidential election campaign. Barring significant new developments in the region, we anticipate that the current policy will remain in place for some time. The U.S. ARP identifies U.S. interests in seven topical areas and lays out implementing steps. U.S. interests include: 1) Arctic national and homeland security; 2) international governance; 3) extended continental shelf and boundary issues; 4) international scientific cooperation; 5) maritime transportation; 6) economic and energy issues; and 7) environmental protection and conservation of living marine resources.

Canada's "Northern Strategy: Our North, Our Heritage, Our Future" was released on July 26, 2008, as a document and a website.[6] The strategy is built on four pillars: 1) exercising Arctic sovereignty, which includes establishing and maintaining a physical presence in the Arctic and mapping of the continental margin to substantiate claims to an extended continental shelf; 2) protecting environmental heritage, including conducting scientific research and environmental protection; 3) promoting social and economic development through resource exploration, development and infrastructure improvements; and 4) improving and devolving northern governance, which involves streamlining regulatory processes in the three northern territories and transferring authorities over land and resources to territorial and indigenous governments. There is also a foreign policy component of Canada's "Northern Strategy" that identifies Canada's bilateral projects with its Arctic partners and describes the Arctic Council and other international fora in which Canada participates.

Norway's "High North Strategy" was signed on December 1, 2006.[7] It clearly identifies Norway's interest in the sustainable development of Arctic energy and fisheries resources but is also notable for balancing development with environmental management concerns and a strong focus on regional and international cooperation. It is also the oldest of the Arctic state strategy documents. However, despite its vintage, it remains relevant. The government that authored the Report remained in power through the 2009 elections and the new government has not replaced or updated the Strategy. In a 2010 address to the Norwegian Parliament, the Norwegian Foreign Minister affirmed many of its policies.[8] Norway's "High North Strategy" is divided into nine subject areas: 1) foreign policy, including focus on energy and the environment, regional forums, and presence of Norwegian armed forces in the Arctic; 2) knowledge generation and competence building in marine, climate, and polar research, petroleum research and development, and environmental monitoring and emergency response; 3) indigenous peoples' issues; 4) people-to-people cooperation in the North through cultural exchange; 5) environmental issues related to climate change, long-range transboundary air pollution, and integrated management of northern seas; 6) management and utilization of marine resources; 7) petroleum activities; 8) marine transportation; and 9) business development.

The Russian Federation's "Arctic Strategy" was approved on September 18, 2008.[9] It is built on five central objectives: 1) social and economic development, particularly natural resource development and expanded use of the Northern Sea Route; 2) military security and protection of the state borders; 3) environmental protection, including protection and preservation of the Arctic and management of anthropogenic development impacts; 4) scientific and technological research and development in areas of climate change, resource exploitation, and social issues; and 5) foreign affairs, including establishing or maintaining positive bilateral relationships and determining limits of the Russian continental shelf beyond 200 nautical miles. The strategy also describes the measures and mechanisms for achieving these objectives and three stages of implementation that are to be completed by 2020. The Statement makes it clear that Russia's priority is to secure its Arctic territory for use as a strategic resource pool.

Denmark's Arctic strategy is now contained in two documents. The first, "Arctic in a time of change"[10] was released in May 2008 has two foci, fostering Greenlandic independence through economic development and Denmark's role as an Arctic nation.[11] The former receives greater emphasis throughout the Statement. "Arctic in a time of change" discusses eleven key issue areas: 1) Home Rule; 2) asserting sovereignty, including physical presence and continental shelf mapping; 3) Arctic and Nordic cooperation; 4) indigenous peoples; 5) energy and minerals development; 6) protection and sustainable use of living natural resources; 7) the environment, including addressing climate change and pollution; 8) research, particularly into climate change and pollutant impacts; 9) shipping and aviation infrastructure development; 10) encouraging commerce and industry; and 11) cultural cooperation.

Details of a new Danish Arctic strategy, "Strategy for the Arctic 2011–2020," were leaked shortly before its official publication in August 2011.[12] This new strategy document explicitly notes that the May 2008 strategy, "Arctic in a time of change," continues to serve as a foundation for Danish activities in the Arctic whilst the new strategy focuses on the Kingdom of Denmark's strategic priorities for the development of the Arctic through 2020.[13] The new strategy is more focused but does not represent a significant departure from the 2008 strategy. Its publication in English indicates that it is a guide for external actors as well as domestic audiences. "Strategy for the Arctic 2011–2020" contains four principal sections. 1) "A Peaceful, Secure and Safe Arctic" covers sovereignty, surveillance, and maritime safety. 2) "Self-sustaining Growth and Development" discusses the use of energy, mineral, and natural resources, integration with global trade, social development, and efforts to improve Arctic health. 3) "Development with Respect for the Arctic's Vulnerable Climate, Environment, and Nature" describes Denmark's efforts to better understand the effects of climate change and implement protections for the environment and biodiversity. Finally, 4) "Close Cooperation with our International Partners" covers regional and global cooperation and the representation of Danish interests in the international arena.

Common Themes

Six themes are common to the Arctic strategy statements: sovereignty; scientific research; resource development; shipping; environmental concerns; and governance. Each theme can be divided into several component issues (see Table 1).

1. Sovereignty

Under the theme of sovereignty, the coastal Arctic states contend with two issues, the determination of the extent of their extended continental shelves and the projection of sovereign presence in the Arctic. With the exception of Norway, all the states emphasize the need to map and delimit the extent of their continental shelves.[14]

All five states address sovereign Arctic presence. Sovereign presence traditionally covers a range of activities such as establishing a fixed human presence, military exercises, or police activity.[15] The latter, police activity to deter, detect, and interdict illegal activity receives emphasis in the various state strategy statements and is the more intuitive place to look for cooperation on issues of sovereign presence. The states vary in their specification of what illegal activity they are concerned with: all address illegal fishing; some smuggling and illegal migration; and only the United States and Russia address terrorism. However, the methodologies of deterrence and interdiction are sufficiently similar that they can be collapsed under the rubric of sovereign activity to deter, detect, and interdict illegal activities.

2. Scientific Research

Arctic scientific research can be synthesized into just two issues in all five strategies. The first is research to better inform national activities and priorities. There is individual variation across the nations as to which areas of research are highlighted, but generally they include socioeconomics, human health, impacts of anthropogenic activities on the environment, and resource assessments. The second common research issue is improved understanding and forecasting of Arctic climate change and its physical and biological impacts. This issue is a subset of the first but is highlighted because of the emphasis it receives across all the strategy statements.

3. Resource Development

Resource development is at the heart of the strategies of all five states, and issues of energy resources and fisheries are common to all. However, the United Nations Convention on the Law of the Sea (UNCLOS) already provides the states with sovereign jurisdiction over the vast majority of Arctic resources through the 200 nautical mile exclusive economic zone (EEZ) and rights to the resources of the continental shelf beyond 200 nautical miles.[16] Where the states have sovereign control over resources, they can pursue their interests through independent decision-making. Consequently, the theme of resource development is applicable to cooperation where it applies to the resources over which the coastal states may not enjoy complete sovereignty, specifically energy resources in areas of overlapping, unresolved territorial claims and transboundary fish stocks.[17]

4. Shipping

Arctic shipping appears in all five strategy statements through two overarching issues, governance and infrastructure/services. Both issues are clearly important to all states, although states vary in the level of detail they accord to the issues. For example, the United States identifies specific governance mechanisms and infrastructure needs, and Norway describes infrastructure needs, whereas Canada is relatively nondescript in its treatment of both. This is likely a function of the five states' different interests in Arctic shipping. Russia hopes to develop the Northern Sea Route as a shorter alternative to current global shipping routes. Canada sees ongoing environmental and political challenges to development of the Northwest Passage.[18] The United States, Norway, and Denmark's concerns seem to stem from their position at the terminuses of both routes and possibility of increased shipping in their waters as a result of expanded use of both routes. The United States is also clearly concerned with the right of transit passage in the Northwest Passage and portions of the Northern Sea Route.

5. Environmental Concerns

Environmental issues described in the Arctic strategy statements can be divided into two categories. The first category includes "legacy" issues such as the long-range transport and impacts of pollutants, remediation of contaminated Cold-War military and industrial sites, and radioactive contamination from dumped nuclear material. As the categorization of these issues as "legacy" suggests, they have largely been addressed, although not necessarily solved, by international cooperation.[19] There are opportunities for Arctic cooperation that center on the second category: addressing the environmental impacts of new or expanded anthropogenic activity and preservation of Arctic biodiversity.

Table 1. Common themes in the strategies of the five coastal Arctic states.

	United States	Canada
Environmental Concerns	Environmental protection and conservation of living marine resources	Arctic stewardship
		Environmental protection of northern lands and waters
Resource Development	Economic issues, including energy resource development	Social and economic development via resource exploration and development, and addressing critical infrastructure needs
Sovereignty	National and Homeland Security interests	Physical presence in the Arctic
	Map and define the continental margin	Map and submit extended continental shelf claim
Governance	Create or update appropriate international governance regimes	Engage international partners, and a strong Arctic Council
Scientific Research	Encourage international scientific cooperation, climate change monitoring and forecasting.	Conduct research and advance knowledge
		Ensure leadership in Arctic science
Shipping	Address Arctic marine transportation needs	Address critical infrastructure needs

Sources: Compiled from the strategy statements of the five coastal Arctic states. See notes 3, 5, 6, 8, 9, and 11.

Norway	Russia	Denmark / Greenland
Climate change, long-range transboundary pollution, integrated marine management, environmental monitoring and response	Protection/preservation of the Arctic environment, management of human development impacts	Protection and sustainable use of natural resources
Management and utilization of marine resources	Development of resources as a base for social and economic development; improved resource exploitation technology and infrastructure	Exploration, development of energy and minerals, industry investment in exploration
Petroleum development activities		Encouraging industrial growth
Resolve maritime boundaries, ensure presence of Norwegian armed forces in the Arctic	Military security and border protection improvements	Assertion of sovereignty through surveillance, military presence
	Delimitation of the continental shelf	Map/submit extended continental shelf claim
Create/sustain energy and environmental policies and regional forums	Establish and maintain good bilateral and regional relationships	Develop, maintain Arctic and Nordic cooperation, strengthen environmental governance
Conduct marine, climate, and polar, social, petroleum research	Develop Arctic technologies, understand and predict climate change, conduct indigenous research	Characterize climate change, social impacts strengthen climate research cooperation
		Conduct research to inform national activities (shipping, etc.)
Marine transportation, integrated management	Develop the Northern Sea Route	Develop infrastructure (ports, monitoring)

6. Governance

Governance, generally the formal and informal policies and processes that steer human activities in the Arctic, appears as a theme throughout all five strategy statements. It is woven into resource development, shipping, environmental issues, and scientific research. All five states also address the application of the law of the sea principles as the international legal regime for the Arctic. The U.S. ARP recognizes the value of accession to UNCLOS and seeks the advice and consent of the U.S. Senate, while the other states affirm their commitment to resolving Arctic legal issues through UNCLOS. In 2008 all five states affirmed their commitment to adhere to the law of the sea through the Illulissat Declaration.[20] The issue of the international legal regime governing the Arctic appears to have been settled; future cooperation on governance issues is likely to be tightly coupled to sectoral issues and can be examined in that context.

Avenues for Cooperation

Brosnan et al. (2011) provide an in-depth examination of specific avenues for cooperation between the Arctic states and the shape that such cooperation could assume. We briefly review the major findings here and highlight areas where cooperation is already occurring. (See Table 2.)

Mapping Margins and Projecting Sovereign Presence

Mapping continental margins is a technically challenging and expensive task. It typically requires the use of multiple techniques to map seafloor topography and sediment characteristics and can involve the employment of two ships, one to perform mapping activities and the other to provide icebreaking services.[21] Similarly, efforts to deter, detect, and interdict illegal activities such as smuggling, terrorism, and illegal fishing, require combinations of enforcement vessels (aircraft and ships), trained personnel, and monitoring and surveillance capabilities.

Collaborative efforts can conceivably result in better outcomes. Nations that are engaged in mapping may find access to more ship-time through collaboration, comparative advantages in mapping equipment and ship capabilities may be realized, and duplication of effort may be avoided. Ultimately, mapping, submission, and approval may proceed more quickly, leading to cost savings and political stability that companies investing in resource exploitation value.[22] For enforcement, bilateral and multilateral efforts to deter, detect, and interdict illegal activities can serve as force multipliers, maximizing the use of limited resources. For example, when the police force of one party participates in a "ride-along" of another state's maritime patrol, the authority and jurisdiction of two states can be projected at once from one vessel rather than two.[23] Comparative advantages in equipment and capability can also be realized if nations have invested in unique platforms for enforcement or surveillance, including satellite deployments. Such advantages need not be identified post-hoc; the Arctic states are reviewing their surveillance and operational capabilities and there are already cooperative mapping efforts underway.[24]

Scientific Research

Answering scientific questions begins with observations and data collection. Resulting data sets can be analyzed, synthesized, and used in scientific modeling. Many important research questions in the Arctic cannot be addressed solely with data collected within nationally controlled or high seas areas. Arctic ocean circulation, which affects sea ice extent and ecosystem function, is a prime example. There are strong incentives for all of the states to forgo unilateral research efforts related to understanding the Arctic and predicting changes in the regions and to cooperate. An Arctic monitoring network, which the United States specifically addresses, would provide more complete observations and data sets to researchers. These data sets can be used to establish baseline conditions, feed operational models, and detect subsequent changes.[25] Climate, weather, ocean circulation, and other operational models may generate more useful results from data sets that provide more complete understanding of the biological, physical, and chemical characteristics of the Arctic Ocean and atmosphere. Incomplete access to physical data from Russian Arctic waters, for example, has historically hindered Western scientists' understanding of Arctic Ocean circulation.[26] Understanding emerging potential threats to the environment such as methane seeping from melting permafrost or released from warming marine gas hydrates requires that

research be conducted throughout the Arctic; no country can fully characterize such threats using only local research results.[27] Scientific understanding of
the biology, health, and sustainable harvest levels of migratory species, such
as marine mammals and transboundary/straddling fish stocks, would benefit
from international cooperative research for the same reason.

There are other practical considerations beyond improving the science
where cooperation may provide more optimal outcomes. The Arctic states'
ice-capable research fleets are aging and ship-time is at a premium; cooperation may result in researchers having greater opportunities to conduct
at-sea research or leveraging opportunities for multidisciplinary crises.[28] A
similar principle applies to Arctic research satellites. Joint operation of future
research satellites or deployment of complementary rather than duplicative
equipment could result in significant cost savings and greater benefits to scientific understanding of the Arctic.

Oil, Gas, and Fish

Under the UNCLOS framework, resource development outcomes that may
require cooperation in order to be realized include transboundary fish stocks
and energy resources in areas of overlapping claims. These appear to be bilateral issues in the Arctic, so it is useful to consider the potential dilemmas of
the Arctic states in the context of four regions: a Norwegian/Russian region
(the Barents Sea area); a Canadian/Danish region that includes the Lincoln
Sea and two small areas of overlapping claims; a Canadian/U.S. region in the
Beaufort Sea that also includes an overlapping territorial claim; and a U.S./
Russian region north of the Bering Strait.

In the first case, Russia and Norway have had a long, at times troubled, history of fisheries regimes to manage Barents Sea fish stocks. These agreements,
such as the 1978 Grey Zone Agreement, governed the harvest limits, catch
allocations, fishing gear, and division of enforcement authority in the Grey
Zone.[29] On energy issues, Norwegian state-owned StatoilHydro and Russia's
Gazprom have agreed in the past to work jointly to develop the Shtokman
natural gas field.[30] In 2010, Russia and Norway settled their differences and
signed a treaty on maritime delimitation and cooperation in the Barents Sea
and the Arctic Ocean, effectively eliminating political uncertainty that has
been one barrier to development of Barents Sea resources.[31]

In the remaining three regions, and in contrast to the Barents Sea region, the economic potential of oil, gas, and fisheries is promising, but still speculative, and the area of overlapping claims is small.[32] However, as interest in Arctic resources grows, the positive aspects of the Norwegian/Russian history in the Barents Sea may serve as a model for cooperation in the development of resources where maritime boundaries have not been settled or resources are transboundary.

Ships and Shipping

There are ten general topics related to shipping that appear in the Arctic strategies; aids to navigation (ATON), Vessel Traffic Services (VTS), ports, weather and navigation services, iceberg and sea-ice reports, shipping monitoring, standards for Arctic ships, environmental response, and search and rescue. Port development, ATON placement, and weather/navigation services have traditionally been national activities, but there are incentives for cooperation on the remaining topics. There are successful models for joint vessel traffic and monitoring services and sea-ice and iceberg services, such as VTS Puget Sound and the International Ice Patrol, that provide unique benefits to cooperating nations and could be adapted to the Arctic as shipping develops.[33] On May 12, 2011, an Agreement on Cooperation on Aeronautical and Maritime Search and Rescue (SAR) in the Arctic was signed by Canada, Denmark, Finland, Iceland, Norway, the Russian Federation, and Sweden.[34] A similar environmental response agreement could be useful as oil, gas, and shipping resources are developed.

Arctic Environment and Biodiversity

While there are already nascent coordination efforts and some long-standing global regimes applicable to the Arctic, e.g., the IMO Guidelines for ships intended for Polar service, the Arctic Council's guidelines for Arctic offshore oil and gas development, the 1995 UN Fish Stocks Agreement, and the Association of Arctic Expedition Cruise Operator's (AECO) voluntary environmental guidelines for Arctic tourism, there is opportunity for the Arctic states to strengthen coordination to address environmental concerns, either by adapting existing institutions or implementing Arctic specific

Table 2. Avenues for Arctic cooperation contained within the strategies of the United States, Canada, Russia, Norway, and Denmark.

Theme	Issues	Opportunities
Sovereignty	• Continental Shelf Mapping • Policing Illegal Activity	• Engage in collaborative mapping efforts. • Leverage joint operations and comparative equipment advantages.
Scientific Research	• Informing Activities and Priorities • Climate Change	• Conduct Arctic-scale data collection and analysis, collaborative ship-use, and complementary equipment deployments.
Resource Development	• Energy • Fisheries	• Explore new bilateral development and management agreements where transboundary resources or unresolved claims exist.
Shipping	• Shipping Standards • Infrastructure and Services	• Implement Vessel Traffic Services, sea-ice and navigation services, environmental and search & rescue agreements modeled on successful examples.
Environmental Concerns	• Anthropogenic Impacts • Biodiversity	• Strengthen existing guidelines (energy, shipping, tourism) through binding agreements. Implement Arctic Climate Impact Assessment biodiversity recommendations.

agreements.[35] For example, the Arctic Council's guidelines for oil and gas development could be codified and made binding, as could the guidelines for ships operating in polar waters. Existing IMO conventions permit states to introduce ballast water standards that are stronger than existing international standards and define special areas where stronger pollution control methods may be mandated.[36] Standards for developing new Arctic fisheries, which could include temporary moratoriums as a standard to ensure that the fisheries and ecosystem studies precede commercial fishing, would strengthen existing measures. The geographic scope of the AECO Guidelines, currently limited to Greenland, Svalbard, and Jan Mayen, could be expanded to cover the remainder of the Arctic either through inclusion of the guidelines in regulation or government pressure for industry-voluntary adoption.

With regards to Arctic biodiversity, the Convention on Biological Diversity has been ratified by the United States, Canada, Denmark, Norway, and Russia; monitoring and recording of Arctic biodiversity is underway.[37] However, the Arctic Council's Conservation of Arctic Flora and Fauna (CAFF) Working Group is presently implementing only the first three of the 2004 Arctic Climate Impact Assessment's suite of biodiversity recommendations: documenting existing biodiversity; identifying changes; and recording changes.[38] The fourth, managing biodiversity requires attention and could be suitable for a unique multilateral Arctic agreement.

Conclusions

Common themes in the Arctic Strategies of the United States, Canada, Denmark, Norway, and Russia provide a high-level view of potential avenues for cooperation in the Arctic region and a useful counterpoint to claims of pending conflict; indeed, cooperation is already occurring on several of the themes identified in the strategies. It is also notable that incentives to cooperate in some thematic areas have not yet materialized because the issues are not yet salient. A lack of cooperation regarding Arctic resource development and related environmental issues has been a source of public concern because the alternatives are believed to be conflict. But if incentives to cooperate are largely linked to developments that remain emergent, then a lack of cooperation should not be alarming. After all, cooperation is occurring on some important issues, including resource development in the Barents Sea and creation of an Arctic-observing network. Additional cooperation is possible as issues become increasingly salient. For example, the IMO Guidelines for ships operating in polar waters may be codified and made legally binding in the coming years.

Arctic Ocean conflict is not inevitable. Numerous avenues for cooperation exist and new options, alternative conceptualizations, and different perspectives can influence policy decisions.[39] Thus, in a dynamic, sometimes uncertain environment such as the Arctic, it is perhaps more useful to explore and illuminate the avenues for cooperation than to attempt to predict conflict.

Notes

1 Based on *Ocean Development and International Law* 42, no. 1–2 (2011): 173–210. Copyright 2011. Reproduced by permission of Taylor & Francis Group, LLC., http://www.taylorandfrancis.com. The authors gratefully acknowledge the Korea Maritime Institute's support for this work. Their generous funding for research and publication at the School of Marine and Environmental Affairs made this chapter, and a larger work appearing in *Ocean Development and International Law* 42, no. 1 (2011): 173–210, possible.

2 Lee Carter, "Arctic Neighbors Draw Up Battle Lines," Toronto: BBC News, August 11, 2007.

3 See Oran R. Young, "Whither the Arctic? Conflict or Cooperation in the Circumpolar North," *Polar Record* 232 (2009): 73–82.

4 United States, *Arctic Region Policy*, 2009, 48 I.L.M. 374.

5 U.S. Arctic Policy Expert, *Interview*, 2009. Interviews were conducted in 2009.

6 Canada, *Canada's Northern Strategy: Our North, Our Heritage, Our Future*, 2009; http://publications.gc.ca/site/eng/330644/publication.html.

7 Norwegian Ministry of Foreign Affairs, *The Norwegian Government's High North Strategy*, 2006; http://www.regjeringen.no/upload/UD/Vedlegg/strategien.pdf.

8 See Norway, Minister of Foreign Affairs, J. G. Store, *Debate on High North/Arctic Strategies*, Oslo, 2010; http://www.regjeringen.no/en/dep/ud/Whats-new/Speeches-and-articles/speeches_foreign/2010/highnorth_debate.html?id=592606.

9 Russian Federation, *The Fundamentals of State Policy of the Russian Federation in the Arctic in the Period up to 2020 and Beyond (Osnovy Gosudarstvennoi Politiki Rossiiskoi Federatsii v Arktike Na Period do 2020 Goda i Dalneishuiu Perspektivu)*, 2008; http://www.scrf.gov.ru/documents/98.html, translated by Google Translator.

10 Denmark, *Arctic in a Time of Change. Proposed Strategy for Activities in the Arctic Area (Arktis i En Brydningstid. Forslag Til Strategi for Aktiviteter i Det Arktiske Område)*, 2008; http://www.um.dk/NR/rdonlyres/962AFDC2-30CE-412D-B7C7-070241C7D9D8/0/ARKTISK_STRATEGI.pdf, translated by Google Translator.

11 Denmark's Arctic strategy is heavily focused on Greenland, which has historically had a colonial relationship with Denmark and is now seeking greater independence. Various authorities for activities in Greenland, and thus the Arctic, have been devolved to Greenland. In a referendum that

went into effect on June 21, 2009, Greenland adopted Self-Government, a progression from Greenlandic Home Rule (adopted in 1979), wherein Greenland became an autonomous entity in the Kingdom of Denmark. The adoption of Self-Government by Greenland means new changes to the Denmark–Greenland relationship, including requiring the Danish government to consult with the Greenlandic government on all bills affecting the island, separating the economies and reducing subsidies provided by Denmark as natural resource revenues in Greenland expand, and permitting the Greenlandic government to enter into agreements and bilateral/multilateral relationships with other states. The *Act on Greenland Self-Government Act*, no. 473 (June 12, 2009), http://uk.nanoq.gl/Emner//media/6CF403B6DD954B77B-C2C33E9F02E3947.ashx, provides for the transfer of authority for security at sea, ship registration and maritime matters, charting, navigation aids, lighthouses, and pilotage areas, the marine environment, mineral resources, aviation, and radio-based maritime emergency and security services to the Greenland government. Greenland's government is responsible for fishing, shipping, national and regional planning activities, infrastructure, transportation, hunting, and conservation and protection of the environment and nature out to three nautical miles from shore. The Danish government has jurisdiction for the area extending from three nautical miles out to the extent of the exclusive economic zone. See generally, Greenland-Danish Self-Government Commission, *Report on Self-Government in Greenland*, 2008; http://uk.nanoq.gl/sitecore/content/Websites/uk,-d-,nanoq/Emner/Government//media/4618 5A4413C54A3D89D3D16F1D38F0D3.ashx.

12 Denmark, *Strategy for the Arctic 2011–2020*, 2011; http://uk.nanoq.gl//media/29cf0c2543b344ed901646a228c5bee8.ashx; Christoffersen, J. "Denmark wants to claim the North Pole," 2011; http://www.information.dk/268404, translated by Google Translator.

13 Denmark, *Strategy for the Arctic 2011–2020*, 11.

14 Norway submitted its information on the outer limits of the continental shelf to the Commission on the Limits of the Continental Shelf (a body created by UNCLOS, supra note 12, Annex II) on November 27, 2006, before it published the "High North Strategy." The Commission has made its recommendations respecting Norway's submission on March 27, 2009. *Summary of the Recommendations of the Commission on the Limits of the Continental Shelf in Regard to the Submission Made by Norway in Respect of Areas in the Arctic Ocean, the Barents Sea, and the Norwegian Sea on 27 November 2006*, 2009; http://www.un.org/Depts/los/clcs_new/submissions_files/nor06/nor_rec_summ.pdf. Russia also submitted its information to the Commission before publishing its latest Arctic strategy document but received a request from the Commission for more data. See United Nations, *Oceans and the Law of the Sea: Report of the Secretary General. A/57/57/Add.1*. 2002; http://www.un.org/Depts/los/general_assembly/general_assembly_reports.htm.

15 Historical occupation has been used to defend territorial claims of ownership. Canadian domestic land claims acts are based on an extensive study of historical Inuit land use in the Canadian Arctic, and observers have suggested that Canadian claims to sovereignty over waters in the Arctic could also be so based. Barry Scott Zellen, *On Thin Ice: The Inuit, the State, and the Challenge of Arctic Sovereignty* (Lanham, MD: Lexington, 2009); T. Fenge, "Inuit and the Nunavut Land Claims Agreement: Supporting Canada's Arctic Sovereignty," *Policy Options* 29, no. 1 (2008): 84–88.

16 United Nations Convention on the Law of the Sea, 1833 *U.N.T.S.* 397, Articles 55, 56, 76 and 77.

17 Specifically, those stocks that are, or may become, commercially valuable.

18 Zellen, *On Thin Ice*, 2.

19 Examples include: the Stockholm Convention on Persistent Organic Pollutants, 2256 *U.N.T.S.* 119, and the Declaration among the Department of Defense of the United States of America, the Royal Ministry of Defence of the Kingdom of Norway, and the Ministry of Defence of the Russian Federation on Arctic Military Environmental Cooperation, 1996; http://www.denix.osd.mil/international/upload/Declaration.pdf.

20 The Ilulissat Declaration, Ilulissat, Greenland, 2008, 48 I. L.M 362.

21 See United States Department of State, "Extended Continental Shelf Project," September 11, 2009; continentalshelf.gov/ and Elizabeth Riddell-Dixon, "Not for the Faint-Hearted: Mapping Canada's Arctic Continental Shelf," *Policy Options* 30, no. 4 (2009): 60–64.

22 See United States "Extended Continental Shelf Project" ; Riddell-Dixon, "Not for the Faint-Hearted," 62; and Ron Mcnab, "Complications in Delimiting the Outer Continental Shelf" (PPT Slides), present at Changes in the Arctic and the Law of the Sea, Seward May 20–23, 2009; http://www.virginia.edu/colp/pdf/Macnab-outer-c.s.pdf.

23 For a more extensive description of the benefits of joint efforts to deter, detect, and interdict illegal fishing activity, see Kevin W. Riddle, "Illegal, Unreported, and Unregulated Fishing: Is International Cooperation Contagious?" *Ocean Development & International Law* 37 (2006): 265–97.

24 United States, "Extended Continental Shelf Project."

25 There are efforts underway to establish an Arctic Observing Network. See Sustained Arctic Observing Network (SAON), "The SAON Process" [cited 2010]; http://www.arcticobserving.org/index.php?option=com_content&view=article&id=42&Itemid=52.

26 This represents what nations may perceive to be a cost to cooperation on scientific matters. Environmental data such coastal geophysical or oceanographic particulars also represent tactical intelligence for military operations.

27 K. M. Walter, S. A. Zimov, J. P. Chanton, D. Verbyla, and F. S. Chapin, 3rd. "Methane Bubbling from Siberian Thaw Lakes as a Positive Feedback to Climate Warming." *Nature* 443, no. 7107 (2006): 71–75; Bilal U. Haq, "Natural Gas Deposits: Methane in the Deep Blue Sea." *Science* 285, no. 5427 (1999): 543–44.

28 See U.S. Arctic Science Expert, *Interview*, 2009; U.S. National Research Council, Committee on the Assessment of U.S. Coast Guard Polar Icebreaker Roles and Future Needs, *Polar Icebreakers in a Changing World: An Assessment of U.S. Needs* (Washington, D.C.: National Academies Press, 2007); Norway, Minister of Foreign Affairs, J. G. Store, *Perspectives on International Research Collaboration in the North: Minister of Foreign Affairs J. G. Store's Speech at the Research Council of Norway's High North Conference* (Kirkenes, 2008); http://www.regjeringen.no/en/dep/ud/Whats-new/Speeches-and-articles/speeches_foreign/2008/research_collaboration.html?id=537458; and "New Arctic Research Vessel for Norway," *Barents Observer*, May 5, 2010; http://barentsobserver.com/en/sections/society/new-arctic-research-vessel-norway.

29 See Robin R. Churchill and Geir Ulfstein, *Marine Management in Disputed Areas: The Case of the Barents Sea* (London: Routledge, 1992), 95 and 111.

30 Energy Information Agency, *Country Analysis Briefs – Norway*. Energy Information Agency, August 1, 2009; http://www.eia.gov/countries/country-data.cfm?fips=NO.

31 Jonas Gahr Store and Sergey Lavrov, "Joint Statement on Maritime Delimitation and Cooperation in the Barents Sea and the Arctic Ocean," Oslo: April 27, 2010; http://www.regjeringen.no/upload/UD/Vedlegg/

Folkerett/100427-FellesuutalelseEngelsk. pdf. See also "Treaty between the Kingdom of Norway and the Russian Federation concerning Maritime Delimitation and Cooperation in the Barents Sea and the Arctic Ocean," September 15, 2010; http://www.regjeringen.no/en/dep/smk/press-center/Press-releases/2010/treaty.html?id=614254.

32 U.S. North Pacific Fishery Management Council (NPFMC), "Fishery Management Plan for Fish Resources of the Arctic Management Area," 2009; http://alaskafisheries.noaa.gov/npfmc/fmp/arctic/ArcticFMP.pdf. D. L. Gautier, K. J. Bird, T. E. Moore, Z. C. Valin, R. R. Charpentier, T. R. Klett, J. K. Pitman, C. J. Schenk, M. E. Tennyson, C. J. Wandrey, A. Grantz, D. W. Houseknecht, J. H. Schuenemeyer, and K. Sorensen, "Assessment of Undiscovered Oil and Gas in the Arctic" *Science* 324, no. 5931 (2009): 1175–79. International Boundaries Research Unit, *Maritime Jurisdiction and Boundaries in the Arctic Region* (Durham: IBRU, September 2010); http://www.dur.ac.uk/resources/ibru/arctic.pdf. David H. Gray, "Canada's Unresolved Maritime Boundaries," *IBRU Boundary and Security Bulletin* 5, no. 3 (1997): 61–73.

33 U.S. Coast Guard, Report of the International Ice Patrol in the North Atlantic, 2011 Season, Bulletin No. 97 (CG-188-6): 58; http://www.navcen.uscg.gov/pdf/iip/2011_IIP_Annual_Report.pdf.

34 United States Department of State, "Fact Sheet: Arctic Search-and-Rescue Agreement," May 12, 2011; http://iipdigital.usembassy.gov/st/english/texttrans/2011/05/20110512190727su0.5350698.html#ixzz1NINbMQkh.

35 International Maritime Organization, *Guidelines for Ships Operating in Arctic Ice Covered Waters* (London: International

Maritime Organization, 2002); http://docs.imo.org. Arctic Council, Protection of the Arctic Marine Environment Working Group, *Arctic Offshore Oil and Gas Guidelines,* 2009; http://arctic-council.org/article/2009/6/updated_oil_and_gas_guidelines. Agreement for the Implementation of the Provisions of the United Nations Convention on the Law of the Sea of 10 December 1982 Relating to the Conservation and Management of Straddling Fish Stocks and Highly Migratory Fish Stocks, 2167 *U.N.T.S.* 3. Association of Arctic Expedition Tour Operators (AECO), "Guidelines," 2010; http://www.aeco.no/guidelines.htm.

36 International Maritime Organization, *International Convention for the Prevention of Marine Pollution from Ships, 1973, as modified by the Protocol of 1978 relating thereto (MARPOL 73/78),*1340 U.N.T.S. 69, and International Maritime Organization, *International Convention for the Control and Management of Ships Ballast Water and Sediments*; http://www.imo.org/publications/Pages/Home.aspx.

37 Framework Convention on Biological Diversity, 1760 *U.N.T.S.* 79. Arctic Council, Conservation of Arctic Flora and Fauna (CAFF), "CAFF"; http://arctic-council.org/working_group/caff. Louise McRae, Christoph Zockler, Michael Gill, Jonathan Loh, Julia Latham, Nicola Harrison, Jenny Martin, and Ben Collen, *Arctic Species Trend Index 2010: Tracking Trends in Arctic Wildlife* (Akureyri, Iceland: CAFF International Secretariat, 2010); http://www.asti.is/.

38 Arctic Council, *Arctic Climate Impact Assessment* (Cambridge: Cambridge University Press, 2005),540, and "CAFF."

39 Arthur A. Stein, *Why Nations Cooperate: Circumstance and Choice in International Relations* (Ithaca, NY: Cornell University Press, 1990), 208.

6. Energy and the Arctic Dispute: Pathway to Conflict or Cooperation?[1]

Nong Hong

The melting of the Arctic ice pack in combination with developments elsewhere concerning future energy security are creating scenarios that range from low-level friction to potential conflict between the Arctic littoral states.[1] Much attention has been devoted to maritime boundary disputes involving the Arctic littoral states: Canada, Denmark, Norway, Russia, and the United States. In addition to this, the emerging interest of non-Arctic states in shipping, polar research, and non-living resource exploitation also adds uncertain elements to the Arctic's geopolitical development. Many Arctic states' populations are skeptical about non-Arctic states' intentions in the Arctic, thus raising such questions as, "Is China going to take away our oil and gas from the Arctic to meet its energy needs?" and "Why are Japan and South Korea interested in observer status in the Arctic Council?" Associated with these concerns is the essential question, "Is the energy factor a curse to Arctic cooperation or an opportunity to a peaceful settlement of Arctic maritime disputes?"

Arctic Geopolitics

During the Cold War, the Arctic was a security flashpoint with U.S. and Soviet nuclear submarines patrolling under the North Pole and bombers airborne over the region. Today, the Arctic is largely disassociated from great power politics. New concerns, challenges, and opportunities, however, are arising as the Arctic is perceived to be increasingly more accessible.

Countries with military/security interests and naval capacity in the Arctic include Russia, Canada, Norway, Denmark, and the United States. Russia has been the headline grabber with the Chilingarov expedition planting a Russian flag on the sea bed under the North Pole and the resumption of bomber overflights in August 2007.[2] Russian military interests center on the Kola Peninsula, home to the Russian nuclear submarine fleet, and on re-building the northern fleet. The United States also released its revised U.S. Arctic Regional Policy in January 2009, which reiterated the importance of the Arctic for U.S. national security and defense.[3] Denmark and Norway, which control Greenland and the Svalbard Islands, respectively, are also anxious to establish their claims. For Greenland, which has just approved a new self-government relationship with Denmark, the focus is on developing a cooperative infrastructure in the Arctic, i.e., through the Arctic Council and the International Maritime Organization (IMO). Greenland's desire to have direct participation in the deliberations of Arctic states is complicated by Danish policies, which are focused on Europe and can be at odds with the interests of Greenlanders.[4] Canada is also defending its political interests, for example, by making vessel notifications in the Northwest Passage mandatory and making clear it will not cede anything in the North. Canadian Prime Minister Stephen Harper, in July 2007, announced funding for new Arctic naval patrol vessels,[5] a new deep-water port, and a cold-weather training center along the Northwest Passage.

There are also international governmental organizations and major powers from outside the region which take an interest in the North. For example, the new Northern Dimension is interpreted to mean a common policy of the European Union (EU), the Russian Federation, Iceland, and Norway in Northern Europe. In addition, northern issues are finally being given a higher priority on the EU's agenda, and matters relating to the North have been an important concern of the United Nations (UN) for years. For example, the UN has special duties in the region through the UN International Law of the Sea.

Major powers from outside the region, such as the UK, France, Germany, China, Japan, and South Korea are taking a growing interest in many aspects of the North, such as in scientific research. Finally, there is a growing worldwide, even global, economic and political interest toward the north-ernmost regions of the globe, particularly due to estimated fossil fuels in the shelves of the northern seas and visions of new trans-Arctic sea routes. Consequently, transnational corporations (TNCs) have strong commercial interests in becoming present to utilize energy resources.[6]

Arctic Energy Resources in Perspective

The melting ice coverage has led some analysts to believe that previously inaccessible oil and gas deposits may now be accessible permanently or pe-riodically.[7] Successful development of these reserves would help to alleviate the pressure on the global oil and gas markets and potentially enhance energy security as a result.[8]

While there are deposits of uranium and coal scattered throughout the area north of the Arctic Circle, the main energy resources of interest for com-mercial operators are oil and gas. The precise quantities of these resources remain unknown. However, a study conducted in 2008 by the U.S. Geological Survey suggests the Arctic may contain approximately 13 per cent of the glob-al mean estimate of undiscovered oil, which is approximately 618 billion bar-rels of oil.[9] While the Eurasian side of the Arctic is more natural-gas-prone, the North American side is more oil-prone. The North American side of the Arctic is estimated to have about 65 per cent of the undiscovered Arctic oil, but only 26 per cent of the undiscovered Arctic natural gas.[10]

The Arctic Alaska region, the Amerasia Basin, and the East Greenland Rift are expected to hold about 48.6 billion barrels of undiscovered oil, which is about 54 per cent of the total undiscovered Arctic oil. Approximately 2.5 billion barrels of oil have already been discovered in large fields in both the Amerasia Basin and the Northwest Canadian Interior Basins that are not yet being produced.[11]

The estimated amount of undiscovered gas is more significant – approx-imately three times as much as the estimated oil on an energy-equivalent basis. The median estimated amount represents some 30 per cent of global estimated undiscovered gas.[12] Of course, the existence of these resources does not mean that they will all be exploited. Ultimately, this will most likely be decided by the price of the resource weighed against the extraction, process-ing, and transportation costs of getting it to market.

Current estimates of hydrocarbon resources in the Arctic vary between 3 and 25 per cent of the world total. Most are likely within established Russian territory, but the extent of deposits in disputed or international spaces is unclear, and the viability of extraction depends on a host of shifting economic and technological variables.[13]

Much attention has been devoted to maritime boundary disputes involving the Arctic littoral states: Canada, Denmark, Norway, Russia, and the United States. Some analysts believe that the Arctic might witness conflicts between the littoral states caused by the quest for energy resources.[14] The melting of the Arctic ice pack in combination with developments elsewhere concerning future energy security are creating scenarios that range from low-level friction to potential conflict between the eight nations surrounding the Arctic region, which leads to the question under the legal framework: who owns the energy resources in the Arctic?

Legal Aspects: Who Owns the Arctic's Energy Resources?

With energy resource playing a significant role in the Arctic's geopolitics, it is important to clarify the ownership of these rich resources. To do that, an unfolding of the disputes among the Arctic states will help clear off the uncertainty.

A framework to resolve boundary disputes in the Arctic exists in the form of the United Nations Convention on the Law of the Sea (UNCLOS). UNCLOS contains provisions regarding the delineation of the outer limits of continental shelves and maritime boundaries. It obliges states to submit their boundary claims to the UN Commission on the Limits of the Continental Shelf (CLCS) within ten years of ratifying UNCLOS.[15] Russia, the United States, Canada, and Norway have all claimed a twelve-nautical-mile (nm) territorial sea and a 200-nm Exclusive Economic Zone (EEZ) in the Arctic Ocean. Like the EEZ, the continental shelf automatically extends out to 200 nm, save for the need for a boundary with a neighboring state. The international law on how to define a continental shelf beyond 200 nm is found in Article 76 of UNCLOS. Within the extended continental shelf, a state has sovereign rights on and under the seabed, including hydrocarbons (e.g., oil, gas, and gas hydrates), minerals, etc.

Each of the five coastal Arctic states has an Extended Continental Shelf (ECS) in the Arctic Ocean. Russia was the first to make a submission to the Commission in December 2001. The Commission issued recommendations at its June 2002 meeting that included a recommendation that Russia make a revised submission that includes additional data for the central Arctic Ocean. Russia is collecting and analyzing these data now. Norway has proceeded the farthest of any Arctic state to define its ECS. It made a submission in 2006 that covers three areas – the Banana Hole, the Loop Hole, and a small area north of Svalbard. The CLCS issued recommendations in March 2009. Norway has publicly accepted those recommendations.

Canada has ECS in the central and western portions of the Arctic Ocean as well as off its East Coast. Canada has two separate cooperative data collection efforts, one with Denmark (since 2005) on the Lomonosov Ridge and another with the United States (since 2008) on the Canada Basin and the Chukchi Borderland. Canada's submission is due in July 2013. Denmark has ECS in five areas: two areas off the Faroe Islands and three areas off Greenland. Denmark's submission is due in November 2014. The United States has been gathering and analyzing data to determine the outer limits of its extended continental shelf since 2002 but has been collecting data in the Arctic Ocean since 2003.

Five Arctic states issued the Ilulissat Declaration on May 28, 2008, affirming that each state would remain committed to the legal framework of the law of the sea to resolve any overlapping claims.[16] The agreement by the Arctic states to resolve their disputes through the UNCLOS framework suggests that the overlapping boundary issues will be settled amicably, although it is likely that they will take some time to be finalized.

Article 136 of UNCLOS provides that the "Area" beyond national jurisdiction and its resources are the common heritage of mankind. No state shall claim or exercise sovereignty or sovereign rights over any part of the Area or its resources. All rights in the resources of the Area are vested in mankind as a whole, on whose behalf the International Seabed Authority, an autonomous international organization that administers mineral resources in the Area, shall act. The non-Arctic states and international organization can seek interests in the exploration and exploitation of the natural resources only in the seabed beyond the jurisdiction of any Arctic states in this region. However, the general conduct of states in relation to the Area shall be in accordance with the provisions of UNCLOS, the principles embodied in the Charter of the United Nations and other rules of international law in the interests of maintaining peace and security and promoting international cooperation and mutual understanding. It is clear that none of the non-Arctic states challenge the territorial claims in the Arctic and the related claims for jurisdiction rights. It does appear that UNCLOS must be interpreted in the broader perspective of humankind.

Challenge and Cooperation in Energy Development

Political challenges for oil companies that show interest in energy extraction may stem from unresolved boundary disputes. Besides, the opening up of Arctic sea routes once only navigable by icebreakers threatens to complicate delicate relations between countries with competing claims to Arctic territory – particularly as once inaccessible areas become ripe for exploration for oil and natural gas. The United States, Russia, and Canada are among the countries attempting to claim jurisdiction over Arctic territory alongside Nordic nations.

Analysts say Japan, South Korea, and China are also likely to join a rush to capture oil and gas trapped under the region's ice.[17] The Arctic states are very concerned about these non-Arctic states' position on Arctic status. It is clear that China has an agenda and is looking to use existing regimes to advance its interests at the multilateral and bilateral level. China has recently entered into bilateral discussions with both Norway and Canada. Due to China's fast economic growth and military capacity-building, suspicions about China's intentions in the Arctic also arise, driven by what Western analysts call the "China Threat Theory," though China defends with the "Peaceful Development Theory." Although Hu Zhengyue, Chinese Deputy Minister of Foreign Affairs, has said "China does not have an Arctic strategy," China does appear to have a clear agenda regarding the Arctic.[18] In his speech at Svalbard, Hu acknowledged that the Arctic is mainly a regional issue but said that it is also an inter-regional issue due to climate change and international shipping. Unsurprisingly, China would like to see the Arctic states recognize the interests of non-Arctic states.[19]

Economic challenges also exist. Finding large Arctic oil and natural gas deposits is difficult and expensive; developing them as commercially viable ventures is even more challenging. Arctic oil and natural gas resource exploration and development are expensive because of the challenges from harsh winter weather that requires that the equipment be specially designed to withstand frigid temperatures, limited transportation access, and long supply lines that reduce transportation options and increase transportation costs, physical environment that requires additional site preparation to prevent equipment and structures from sinking, and operating costs that are increased by ice-pack conditions that extend over much of the Arctic Ocean.[20] In addition, while the Arctic has the potential to become a more important source of global oil and natural gas production sometime in the future, the timing of a significant expansion in Arctic production is difficult to predict. Statoil, a global energy company, announced in April that it had made the most significant discovery off Norway in the past decade at its Skrugard prospect in the western Barents, breathing new life into Norway's hitherto declining oil prospects. But producing oil and gas in Norway's remote "High North" might entail higher costs and possibly greater risk of spills.[21]

In addition to political and economic challenges, technological concerns should not be neglected, as the feasibility and thus the cost of extracting oil and gas in the Arctic will depend heavily on the state of the available technology as well as climatic developments which may produce a more or less hospitable environment in which to operate. Extraction technology has been grappling with extreme-climate marine drilling for decades, but the pace of new advancements will dictate the feasibility of exploitation in coming years.[22]

It is more challenging to forecast the level of offshore hydrocarbon extraction in the future. As noted, operating in the Arctic environment is made more challenging by the presence of ice and the generally severe weather conditions. In order to manage the risk that flows from these conditions, hydrocarbon extraction operations must design safety and protection into their infrastructure and procedures. Moreover, given the more fragile nature of the Arctic environment in comparison to other hydrocarbon-producing areas of the world, companies will be expected to operate with increased environmental safeguards in the Arctic. Together, these higher standards will result in increased operating costs for the oil and gas companies. These costs may convince some companies that the potential gains are not worth the risks of investing in the region.[23]

Opportunity for Cooperation

The high cost of doing business in the Arctic suggests that only the world's largest oil companies, most likely as partners in joint venture projects, have the financial, technical, and managerial strength to accomplish the costly, long-lead-time projects dictated by Arctic conditions. Incentives to settle outstanding disputes would rise with the increasing potential economic returns posed by exploitation and the resulting polarization within the international system.[24]

While there are disagreements between the Arctic states on maritime boundaries, there are still reasons to believe that these disagreements can be resolved amicably. The prospect for conflicts relating to unresolved boundary disputes seems remote. The existing vehicles for dispute resolution and cooperation in the region, UNCLOS and the Arctic Council, will also help to reduce tensions.

Joint management of resource fields is another option that might come into play as countries involved in a dispute might see more advantage in approaching the disagreement this way rather than losing a claim in an international tribunal. Cooperation between Norway and Iceland regarding the development of the Dreki field could serve as a model for similar arrangements in the future. Another example is the continental shelf dispute concerning an area rich in natural gas between Russia and Norway in the Barents Sea. Both countries dispute the other's interpretation of where their borders extend into the offshore EEZ.[25] While it is possible that there could be a conflict between the two countries over this area, it seems highly unlikely, given the potential costs versus the potential benefits. Both countries have substantial reserves within the undisputed areas of their continental shelves so to risk conflict over what would be an incremental increase in total reserves would be nonsensical. Indeed, on June 5, 2009, Russia and Norway signed a Memorandum of Understanding to explore ways to jointly develop the contested areas.[26] There is already cooperation between the gas companies of the two.[27]

Geopolitical issues are not exclusively conflicts over interests, although such concerns tend to dominate. They can also reflect cooperative, multilateral initiatives by which a state pursues its interests vis-à-vis others. Such cooperative ventures are often considered desirable and even unavoidable when a state is seeking a result that cannot be achieved unilaterally. At the same time, cooperation frequently establishes a level of governance – in some cases formally, in others less formally – by which mutual understanding can clarify intentions and help to build trust.

Recognizing and respecting each other's rights constitutes the legal basis for cooperation between Arctic and non-Arctic states. In accordance with UNCLOS and other relevant international laws, Arctic states have sovereign rights and jurisdiction in their respective areas in the region, while non-Arctic states also enjoy rights of scientific research and navigation. To develop a partnership of cooperation, Arctic and non-Arctic states should, first and foremost, recognize and respect each other's rights under the international law. Examples between Arctic and non-Arctic states are there. On November 22, 2010, the Sovcomflot Group (SCF) and China National Petroleum Corporation (CNPC) signed a strategic long-term cooperation agreement. The parties agreed to develop a long-term partnership in the sphere of seaborne energy solutions, with the SCF fleet serving the continually growing Chinese imports of hydrocarbons. Taking into account the significant experience gained by Sovcomflot in developing the transportation of hydrocarbons in the Arctic seas, SCF and CNPC agreed upon the format for coordination in utilizing the transportation potential of the Northern Sea Route along Russia's Arctic coast, both for delivering transit shipments of hydrocarbons and for the transportation of oil and gas from Russia's developing Arctic offshore fields to China. A new fleet of tankers designed to operate in ice as well as additional heavy-duty icebreakers will be built to that end. South Korea's Samsung Industries is looking into filling the technological gap to make it possible to deliver Arctic natural gas across the Pacific Ocean to East Asia. Russia is building massive duel-bowed oil tankers, which, while traveling forward, move as they normally would through open water. While traveling forward, the ships move as they normally would through open water. But when the vessels move backward, they can act as ice-breakers.

Conclusion

The Arctic has recently witnessed a manifold growth in its geostrategic importance due to the huge deposit of oil and natural gas and the potential contribution of northern sea routes for global shipping. As a result of this, northern regions and seas have become a target area for the growing economic, political, and military interests of the Arctic states as well as of major powers outside the region and transnational companies.

While it is important to look at the Arctic issue from a law of the sea perspective, with the Arctic states resorting to the Commission of Limits of Continental Shelf (CLCS) for advice on the outer limit of their continental shelves, and major powers and transnational corporations are seeking opportunities to develop the region within the framework of a "common heritage of mankind" beyond national jurisdictions; political, economic, and technological concerns also challenge oil companies in further investment in energy development in the Arctic. By the same token, however, joint management of resources is another option that might come into play as countries involved in a dispute might see more advantage in approaching the disagreement this way rather than losing a claim in a zero-sum game. The energy factor, rather than a curse for the Arctic, could serve as an opportunity for regional cooperation in the region.

Notes

1 This paper draws mainly from my article, "Arctic Energy: Pathway to Conflict or Cooperation in the High North?", *Journal of Energy Security* (May 2011); http://www.ensec.org/index.php?option=com_content&view=article&id=310:arctic-energy-pathway-to-conflict-or-cooperation-in-the-high-north&catid=116:content0411&Itemid=375. Reprinted with permission of the *Journal of Energy Security*.

2 Scott G. Borgerson, "Arctic Meltdown: The Economic and Security Implications of Global Warming," *Foreign Affairs* 87, no. 2: 63–77.

3 Thomas Omestad, "Bush Signs Off on New U.S. Arctic Policy," *USNews.com*, January 12, 2009.

4 Borgerson, "Arctic Meltdown."

5 "Ottawa buying up to 8 Arctic patrol ships," *CBC News*, July 9, 2007.

6 J. Robinson, "The Power of Petroleum," *Newsweek*, November 4, 2007, 21.

7 Scott G. Borgerson, "The Great Game Moves North," *Foreign Affairs*, March 25, 2009; George Kolisnek, "Canadian Arctic Energy Security," *Journal of Energy Security* (December 2008); http://www.ensec.org/index.php?option=com_content&view=article&id=172:canadian-arctic-energy-security&catid=90:energysecuritydecember08&Itemid=334.

8 Peter F. Johnston, "Arctic Energy Resources and Global Energy Security," *Journal of Military and Strategic Studies* 12, no. 2 (2010): 1–22.

9 Gautier Donald, Kenneth J. Bird, Ronald R. Charpentier, Arthur Grantz, David W. Houseknecht, Timothy R. Klett, Thomas E. Moore, Janet K. Pitman, Christopher J. Schenk, John H. Schuenemeyer, Kai Sørensen, Marilyn E. Tennyson, Zenon C. Valin, and Craig J. Wandrey, "Assessment

of Undiscovered Oil and Gas in the Arctic," *Science* 324, no. 5931 (May 29, 2009): 1177–78.

10 "Arctic Oil and Natural Gas Potential," U.S. EIA website; http://www.eia.doe.gov/oiaf/analysispaper/arctic/footnote.html.

11 Ibid.

12 Gautier et al., "Assessment of Undiscovered Oil and Gas," 1178.

13 "Arctic Oil and Natural Gas Potential."

14 Barry S. Zellen, "Viewpoint: Cold Front Rising – As Climate Change Thins Polar Ice, A New Race for Arctic Resources Begins," *Strategic Insights* 7 (February 2008): 1–10; http://calhoun.nps.edu/public/handle/10945/11478.

15 Vsevolod Gunitskiy, "On Thin Ice: Water Rights and Resource Disputes in the Arctic Ocean," *Journal of International Affairs* 61, no. 2 (2008): 261–62.

16 "The Ilulissat Declaration," Arctic Ocean Conference. Ilulissat, Greenland, May 27–29, 2008.

17 James Joyner, "Arctic Thaw Brings NATO Security Risks"; http://www.acus.org/new_atlanticist/arctic-thaw-brings-nato-security-risks.

18 X. Ning, '地球未来的缩影—外交部部长助理谈"北极研究之旅"' [A microcosm of the world's future – Assistant Minister of Foreign Affairs talks about 'High North Study Tour'], *Shijie Bolan* 349, no. 19 (2009): 58.

19 Ning, 2009.

20 Joyner, "Arctic Thaw Brings NATO Security Risks."

21 Wojciech Moskwa and Melissa Akin, "Analysis: Huge Barents Oil Find Shifts Focus Back to Arctic," *Reuters*, April 5, 2011; http://www.reuters.com/article/2011/04/05/us-arctic-oil-idUSTRE7343B620110405.

22 Joyner, "Arctic Thaw Brings NATO Security Risks."

23 Ibid.

24 Phillip Cornell and Jochen Kleinschmidt, "Energy and High North Governance: Charting Uncertainty," *Journal of Energy Security* (June 2009); http://www.ensec.org/index.php?option=com_content&view=article&id=202:energy-and-high-north-governance-charting-uncertainty&catid=96:content&Itemid=345.

25 Zellen, "Viewpoint: Cold Front Rising," 5.

26 Energy Information Agency, "Norway," Country Analysis Briefs.

27 *Xinhua/Devapriyo Das*; http://english.peopledaily.com.cn/90001/90777/90853/7363531.html. Putin's first visit to Denmark in late April 2011 and comments about energy security and Arctic cooperation shed further light on prospects of cooperation between Russia and Denmark. As reported by *Xinhua* during Putin's visit, "Both Denmark and Russia are members of the 5-country Arctic Council, currently chaired by Denmark, and see considerable economic opportunities, not least the opening-up of trade routes, in the region. 'We believe, and our experts believe that in the years to come, there might be a 10-fold increase of the amount of ships going through the Northern Sea Route because it's less expensive than the Suez canal, reduces transport costs and costs of goods,' Putin said," and "added that any maritime boundary disputes and claims on the Arctic, 'should be settled by the Arctic countries on the basis of existing international norms and the UN Convention on the Law of the Sea.'" See Yang Jingzhong and Devapriyo Das, "Putin talks energy security, Arctic cooperation on first official visit to Denmark," *Xinhua*, April 27, 2011; http://news.xinhuanet.com/english2010/world/2011-04/27/c_13847262.htm.

7. Maritime Boundary Disputes in East Asia: Lessons for the Arctic[1]

James Manicom

Arctic strategy is being made in a rapidly changing environmental, political, and economic context. While the rate of environmental change is subject to some debate, it is certain that the Arctic environment is getting warmer, with associated costs and consequences for the circumpolar ecosystem as well as for northern peoples.[2] The international political consequences of this catastrophe are as yet unknown. The Arctic region is home to many unsettled boundaries over potentially resource-rich areas; of all Arctic boundaries, only the Denmark–Norway and Russia–Norway maritime boundaries are undisputed.[3] Article 76 of the UN Convention on the Law of the Sea (UNCLOS) grants states the right to claim an extended continental shelf as far as 350 nm from its baselines, or 100 nm from the 2,500 m isobath, no later than ten years after ratification of UNCLOS. Making these claims is a technically complex and costly endeavor, and thus all submissions are evaluated by the Commission on the Limits on the Continental Shelf (CLCS). Created by UNCLOS, the CLCS is a non-political body composed of experts tasked with assessing, and by extension legitimizing, states' claims to extended continental shelves. It is not a judiciary body and responsibility for dispute resolution rests with the parties involved. The stakes of this endeavor are high. Recognition of a state's claim brings jurisdiction over the seabed and subsoil of the extended continental shelf. In addition to disputes over the potentially resource-rich seabed, some analysts fear added political tension in the event that state intentions for disputed areas, such as over conservation or environmental standards, are incompatible.[4]

In this context, it is vital that policy-makers consider the international political implications of the pending maritime boundary dispute over the extended continental shelf in the Arctic. While there has been growing attention on this issue internationally, Ottawa has been criticized for lacking a coherent Arctic strategy.[5] In the final days of the Bush presidency, the White House published its Arctic policy document, which in addition to reiterating American policy on the Northwest Passage noted that "energy development in the Arctic region will play an important role in meeting growing global energy demand as the area is thought to contain a substantial portion of the world's undiscovered energy resources."[6] Russia released an Arctic strategy document in September 2008, which, while less belligerent than previous iterations, nevertheless emphasized that the development of the Arctic region is "vital to Russia's relevance in world affairs."[7] By contrast, the Harper government's "Canada's Northern Strategy" focused primarily on the domestic aspects of Canada's North and simply noted that Canada's continental shelf mapping efforts would be complete by 2013 and that the process "is not adversarial."[8]

While all three documents emphasize the multilateral and cooperative intentions of the states involved, it remains to be seen whether these ideals will prevail. In light of the possibility that extended continental shelf claims in the Arctic may overlap[9] and combined with the optimistic assessment of regional resource wealth, the ingredients are present for an explosive maritime boundary dispute.[10] Canada, Denmark, and Russia have all undertaken surveys of the seabed in an effort to map the limits of their extended continental shelves beyond 200 nm. In light of a resurgent Russian foreign policy and the primacy of resource development in Russian political economy, the potential exists for overlapping claims to the extended continental shelf to increase political tensions in the circumpolar North.[11] Broadly, the track record on maritime disputes indicates that they are prone to frequent and protracted political crisis and in some cases violent conflict.[12] Given that any dispute will not crystallize until Canada and Denmark formalize their extended continental shelf claims in 2013 and 2014 respectively, the time is right to explore what Arctic states can expect from a maritime boundary dispute of this nature.[13]

With a view to contributing to this important policy debate, this chapter draws comparative insights from East Asian coastal states with overlapping maritime claims in an effort to outline how Arctic states can best respond to this emerging dispute.[14] The geography of East Asia is characterized by a series of semi-enclosed seas, which combined with the widespread adoption of UNCLOS have given rise to a number of overlapping maritime boundary claims. It is thus an ideal place to look for policy-relevant lessons for Arctic policy-makers, as East Asian leaders confront these issues on a daily basis. The international legal regime that governs state claims to extended continental shelves is still emerging; the CLCS has thus far only ruled on eleven of the fifty-three submissions.[15] Therefore, the time is right to explore the trajectory of the pending Arctic dispute over the extended continental shelf by comparing it with maritime boundary disputes in other regions. The first section of the paper elaborates on the basis for the comparison by surveying current debates on Arctic politics and drawing parallels with East Asia. These debates appear to be divided between a perspective that foresees conflict over increasingly accessible Arctic resources and an optimistic perspective that emphasizes the order of the international legal process and Arctic states' capacity for cooperation. The next section elaborates on the East Asian experience with the international political challenges of disputed maritime boundary issues. The final section explores the direction of the Arctic dispute and identifies issues that Arctic policy-makers may wish to consider as they move forward.

East Asia and the Arctic: The Basis for Comparison

This study should be regarded as a plausibility probe into the relationship between disputed maritime space and inter-state conflict in the Arctic. Disputed maritime boundaries are not new to Arctic states, although they have arguably never been perceived with such urgency due to the deadlines for CLCS submission and due to the anticipated impact of climate change on the accessibility of the region's resources. As illustrated below, the literature on the extended continental shelf dispute posits three variables that determine the level of tension between Arctic states. These variables overlap with explanations of the ebb and flow of tension over East Asian maritime boundaries. Nevertheless, there are clear limits to the comparison that need to be recognized.

The current debate in the literature can be divided into two camps, a pessimistic "resource race" view and a more benign assessment. According to the former, the potential for overlapping claims and the resource needs of the claimant states is a recipe for violent conflict.[16] This appears to be an extension of the "resource wars" literature that assumes a linear relationship between territorial disputes, resource wealth, and war.[17] The U.S. Geological Survey (USGS) has noted that "the extensive Arctic continental shelves may constitute the geographically largest unexplored prospective area for petroleum remaining on Earth" with an estimated ninety billion barrels of oil.[18] Combined with high demand for hydrocarbons, it follows that states will seek to exploit the resource-rich Arctic region. According to this perspective, jurisdiction over extended continental shelves is the final frontier in the last unexplored resource-rich region in the world. For many analysts, the primacy of hydrocarbon resource development in the Russian economy necessarily implies an assertive Russian posture to undefined boundaries.[19] Likewise, Canadian leaders have been candid about their interest in the resource potential of Canada's North.[20]

The benign view offers a compelling corrective to this pessimistic perspective and rests on three arguments. First, the resource wealth of the Arctic is unknown. There have not been detailed seismic surveys of any part of the Arctic region. The USGS methodology merely suggests that the Arctic Circle has the geological conditions consistent with the formation of hydrocarbons. Moreover, the development of these resources will remain costly compared to onshore alternatives for decades to come. Combined with the inaccessibility of the Far North, spending money on demonstrations of 'sovereignty' is a fool's errand.[21] Second, a track record of cooperation exists between the Arctic states. These states have created institutions to militate against conflict, which in turn has helped the cooperative development of the North.[22] Examples include the Arctic Council and the University of the Arctic, among others.[23] The former increases multilateral contact and transparency between the Arctic states, while the latter serves as a confidence-building measure. Finally, the benign view argues that the process for making claims to extended continental shelves is an orderly one and one that has thus far been characterized by cooperation between the claimant states. The technical and scientific requirements to map the sea floor are expensive, and the operations are made particularly more costly by the harsh environment.[24] Thus, the officials involved have a long track record of comparing notes and pooling resources.[25]

For example, in 2007 Canada and Denmark enlisted the aid of a Russian nuclear-powered ice-breaker for their mapping missions.[26] Furthermore, there has been talk of a trilateral submission to the CLCS by Russia, Canada, and Denmark.[27]

While both views are compelling, both overlook an important dimension of territorial and maritime boundary disputes; the role of national identity. Disputes over land and maritime space can become linked with a state's perception of itself and its perception of rival claimants as 'others.' This can create a set of domestic political circumstances that militates against cooperation.[28] This is evident in both regions. While the resource wealth of the Arctic is a clear motivator of Russian policy, there is also evidence that Russian leaders view the Arctic dispute as part of a nation-building project. According to Pavel Baev, in addition to political legitimacy, Russia's economic fortunes and by extension internal cohesion has always been tied to its strength as a resource state.[29] Indeed, following a meeting of the Russian Security Council in October 2008, Russian President Dmitry Medvedev stated, "the solution of the country's long-range objectives and its competitive capability in the global market is connected to the [Arctic] region's development."[30] Thus, the driving force behind Russia's posture is not only a material one, but an ideational force designed to adhere to myths contained within Russian great power identity. Appeals to national identity can also be detected in Canada's response to perceived threats of Arctic 'sovereignty.' According to one former Conservative party staff member, Stephen Harper was able to undermine the Liberal charge of pro-American bias by inflating the threat of American submarines passing under a thawing Northwest Passage.[31] This set the stage for much of Canada's subsequent activism on the Arctic.[32]

Similar perspectives surround East Asian maritime boundary disputes. Contrary to Buzan's (1978) expectations, it appears that maritime boundary disputes have indeed attracted popular emotional attachment and have acquired domestic political salience.[33] In East Asia, the region's divergent national identities and unsettled historical record has given rise to a host of nationalist groups that have pressured political leaders to adopt confrontational policies toward territorial and maritime boundary issues.[34] Combined with the widespread adoption of UNCLOS in the mid-1990s, East Asian coastal states found that disputes that were formerly over disputed islands now included overlapping maritime jurisdictional claims to potentially resource-rich sea areas. While the widespread adoption of UNCLOS created these disputes, many find grounds for optimism based on this consensus on the relevant international legal principles as well as recurrent pledges by pol-icy-makers to peacefully resolve their disputes based on these principles.[35] Nevertheless, many analysts warned that the nexus of contested resource-rich territory, high energy demand, and competing national identities would cre-ate a 'perfect storm' for conflict in light of rising military spending across East Asia.[36] This conclusion was predicated on the view that in the absence of the common strategic priorities dictated by the Cold War, East Asian states would find formerly dormant territorial disputes to be of renewed importance.[37]

The latter two explanations of East Asian maritime boundary issues have not surfaced in recent debates about the Arctic. First, the end of the Cold War appears to have been less salient as a structural change with regard to Arctic boundary disputes. The end of the Cold War has actually precipitated an era of cooperation between Arctic states, whereas East Asian states have remained at odds over their disputed maritime claims.[38] Secondly, regional military spending trends have been uneven across the Arctic claimants, while East Asian states have invested heavily in the naval capabilities required to press their claims.[39] Canadian military acquisitions are focused on maintain-ing an operational presence in the North but lack the power projection capa-bilities necessary to threaten rival states. Likewise, the Russian Northern fleet has become more active, but it has not acquired any significant hardware, and concerns persist about the feasibility of military modernization plans.[40] There are thus three common explanations of the trajectory of maritime boundary disputes that underwrite the basis for comparison.

1. High expectations of resource wealth, particularly hydrocarbons, fuel political tension.

2. National sovereignty, even the limited jurisdiction granted over the extended continental shelf, is a domestically salient political issue.

3. These motivations for conflict are purportedly balanced by internationally recognized legal principles and dispute-resolution mechanisms that facilitate cooperation between claimant states.

There are clearly differences between the challenges raised by Arctic sovereignty disputes and those raised by East Asia's maritime disputes, not least due to the differences between the two regions themselves. The density of population in East Asia has led to a vibrant economic interdependence, which according to some stabilizes the region's maritime boundary disputes.[41] Conversely, the sparsely populated circumpolar region has created a different economic dynamic, wherein local indigenous populations battle with far-off southern capitals for basic development assistance.[42] However, these apparent differences are less compelling than they may appear. According to Oran Young, the Arctic region is distinct from state-centered regions such as Southeast Asia and the Middle East. Regions such as the Arctic have no political actors that exclusively occupy the region; rather, outside actors use it as an arena to pursue their interests.[43] Nevertheless, a sense of "Northernness" exists amongst the eight Arctic states.[44] This northern identity excludes states, such as Germany or China, that view themselves as having Arctic interests but which are not recognized as such by Arctic states. The region is ultimately composed of states – or parts of states – that accept the inherent legitimacy of the pursuit of national interests. It is thus not as distinct from other regions of the world as Young suggests.

Finally, many of East Asia's maritime boundary disputes stem from contested sovereignty over offshore islands and related overlapping Exclusive Economic Zones (EEZ) and continental shelf boundaries. While there are similar delimitation disputes in the Beaufort, Lincoln, and Barents seas, the emerging issue of overlapping continental shelf jurisdiction differs somewhat in its legal entitlement. Unlike the EEZ and continental shelf, jurisdiction over the extended continental shelf is limited to the seabed and the subsoil.[45] Nevertheless, these raise similar political challenges because state entitlements to the seabed are identical under the EEZ and the extended continental shelf. From an international legal perspective, there is nothing unique about Arctic boundary disputes.[46]

Questions and Lessons from East Asia

The East Asian response to overlapping jurisdictional claims may identify what questions Arctic states and peoples need to ask themselves if they are to advance a coherent and peaceful Arctic strategy. The discussion proceeds along the three parallels noted above; the purported. salience of resource wealth, the role of identity politics, and the commitment to cooperation based on UNCLOS principles.

The relationship between resource wealth and political tension over maritime boundaries is well documented in East Asia. All East Asian economies rely on fossil fuels for their economic growth, and the region's relative resource poverty suggests that areas rich in hydrocarbon resources necessarily attract attention. In East Asia the bulk of these resource deposits are offshore in areas of contested jurisdiction. For instance, the Senkaku/Diaoyu islands dispute erupted following reports of high resource wealth in the seas that surround them.[47] While this occurred against the backdrop of high energy prices due to the Oil Shocks, neither Japan nor China was as insecure about energy then as they are now. Following China's shift to net oil importer status in 1993, energy was increasingly viewed as a motivator in the South and East China Sea disputes.[48] In this view, a rising great power such as China – with growing energy demand needed to power the engine of economic growth – would assert its claims to disputed maritime space with greater intensity, thereby increasing the potential for war. China's economic growth is linked to the domestic political legitimacy of the Chinese Communist Party (CCP); energy security is thus viewed as integral to the perpetuation of the regime. From a geopolitical perspective, the fact that these disputes are against Japan, a regional rival, or against a collection of smaller Southeast Asian powers bodes poorly for continued stability. In the former case, domestic leaders derive legitimacy from confrontation,[49] whereas in the latter there is little other than the countervailing power of the United States keeping the peace.[50]

Nevertheless, these "resource wars" never materialized. Some argue that China's relative military weakness vis-à-vis its neighbors accounts for this, but this does not explain China's recent efforts to cooperate with its neighbors when its relative military strength is at its highest. There is clearly an underlying set of processes that enable resource concerns to shift towards ambitions for joint development. As Schofield and Storey observe, the track record in East Asia reveals that resource wealth is consistent with both cooperation and confrontation.[51] On the one hand, this is unremarkable; resources are a material object that can be divided between claimants. On the other hand, the desire to control resource-rich territory is often a motivator for confrontation. Ralf Emmers[52] has argued that resource concerns must be separated from geopolitical calculations and domestic identity politics in order to be a litmus issue targeted for cooperation. In this view, following a relaxation of geopolitical tensions, East Asian states have been able to pursue cooperation over disputed resource-rich territories. China and Japan signed a consensus on the joint development of parts of the East China Sea in June 2008 and China, the Philippines, and Vietnam signed an agreement on seabed resource exploration in a section of the South China Sea in March 2005. In short, the presence of hydrocarbon resources in a disputed area is not necessarily a recipe for conflict.

Turning to the second parallel, there is a strong relationship between territorial identity and political legitimacy in the East Asian region.[53] In many cases, political elites in East Asian states use this nationalist sentiment to legitimize their own rule.[54] According to Buhk, both conservative and progressive factions of the Japanese government used the Russian occupation of the Northern Territories to articulate their construction of Japanese postwar identity.[55] Combined with the unsettled historical record between Asian states, this legitimization process has given rise to domestic nationalist groups within several states that pressure their leaders when perceived challenges to territorial sovereignty arise. For instance, Beijing seeks to legitimize its rule by fostering a nationalist narrative that highlights both the achievements of the CCP, as well as injustices suffered at the hands of external power, in particular Japan and the United States.[56] In Japan, a vocal conservative minority has grown tired of Japan's deference to China and insists that Japan adopt a more assertive posture towards China. These minorities have pressured their central governments to adopt controversial policies on issues that are vital to each party's contested national identity, such as the treatment of historical issues, military spending and particularly vis-à-vis the contested sovereignty over the Senkaku/Diaoyu islands dispute.[57]

While the relationship between national identity and territorial sovereignty is clear, the relationship between national identity and the jurisdictional claims over maritime space are less obvious. Nevertheless, as popular sentiment between China and Japan has become more antagonistic, these grievances have been aired, not only with regard to the disputed islands, but also against the exercise of EEZ jurisdictional entitlements, most recently China's resource development of the Chunxiao gas field in the East China Sea in April 2005.[58] Likewise, nationalist groups in Vietnam protested outside Chinese consular offices in response to more heavy-handed Chinese assertions of jurisdiction in the South China Sea.[59] As a consequence, state elites are constrained by these domestic political costs if they attempt to pursue cooperative approaches to these disputes.[60] The danger is that maritime boundary delimitation disputes may become as intractable as territorial disputes. Nevertheless, as noted above, East Asian states have been able under certain circumstances to overcome these nationalist pressures and cooperate in a limited fashion on maritime jurisdictional issues.[61] While dispute settlement remains elusive, the nexus of hydrocarbon wealth and disputed identities is not necessarily a portent for conflict.

Finally, like their Arctic counterparts, East Asian states have repeatedly issued assurances that they will abide by UNCLOS principles in their search for a solution to their maritime boundary disputes. All East Asian states, with the exception of Cambodia and North Korea, have ratified UNCLOS and in some cases this development facilitated the management of the region's fisheries resources. However, this normative development has done little to smooth political tensions on overlapping maritime boundaries. Assertions by states of the consistency of their policies with UNCLOS are partly undermined by the nature of UNCLOS itself, which does not specify a preferred method of boundary delimitation. According to Clive Schofield, this gap can be viewed "as offering either great flexibility to coastal states, or ... considerable scope for conflicting interpretations."[62] The East Asian experience has been the latter. For instance, China and Japan differ fundamentally on the basis for their maritime claims: the EEZ regime versus the continental shelf regime. Both find evidence for their view in international legal jurisprudence. Although there is no mention of the Japanese median line concept in UNCLOS, International Court of Justice delimitation decisions increasingly favor an equidistance line based on 'relevant factors.' China points to the 1969 North Sea case, which argued that length of coastline and continental shelf are the most important factors in delimitation. Thus, in the Chinese view, in light of UNCLOS's emphasis on 'equity,' delimitation should consider factors such as the length of the Chinese coastline and the natural prolongation of the continental shelf.[63] China regards Japan's median line as inconsistent with UNCLOS because it was declared "unilaterally" and divides the East China Sea in half.[64] Japan meanwhile points to the more recent (1985) Libya/Malta case, which held that equidistance lines are in keeping with the wording of UNCLOS that delimitation must achieve an equitable solution and which discounted the relevance of geomorphologic factors.[65]

These differences are more than simply abstract debates about international law; they have direct bearing on inter-state cooperation. The median line presented the most significant barrier to concluding the Consensus on Resource Development reached in June 2008 between China and Japan. The parties could not agree on where to locate the joint development zone (JDZ). From the Chinese perspective, it needed to be located beyond the median line, in the area of overlap. From the Japanese perspective, the JDZ should bisect the median line since it represents the equidistance point between the two coastlines. In the end, China agreed to a JDZ that includes space on the Chinese side of the median line. While there is no doubt this was integral to concluding the agreement,[66] this concession reportedly attracted criticism from hardliners within China and arguably explains the delay in implementing the agreement. As of July 2012, there is little evidence that exploration will proceed in the JDZ in light of recurrent tensions over the exercise of maritime jurisdiction in contested sea areas.

Furthermore, the existence of disputed maritime boundaries has politicized the international processes surrounding UNCLOS. For example, ahead of its submission to the CLCS, the Philippines had still not yet defined the baselines of its maritime zones: the territorial sea, the contiguous zone, and the EEZ. Because the constitution contains the geographic definition of the Philippine state, outlining baselines required a constitutional amendment.[67] Attempts to amend the 1987 Constitution raised the question of whether or not to include disputed Kalayaan area of the Spratly islands as part of the territorial definition of the Philippines.[68] During this process, it was revealed that President Arroyo was considering not including the Kalayaan claim in the declaration for fear of offending China, a rival claimant, which precipitated a protest from the opposition.[69] Consistent with its own claims to the Spratlys, Beijing expressed its opposition to the constitutional amendments. Manila consequently moved to alter the wording in its UN submission from a restatement of sovereignty, to a claim to a 'regime' of islands whose sovereignty is contested. According to the Philippines' delegate to UNCLOS, Estelito Mendoza, to claim Kalayaan would be "absurd," because the Philippines has never treated it as its own territory and because it does not have the military might to defend its claim.[70] This fuelled speculation from opposition politicians that Arroyo was prepared to bargain away Philippine territory in exchange for Chinese aid dollars and investment. The Philippines Baselines Law was signed in early 2009, just ahead of the Philippines' CLCS submission and elicited condemnations and military posturing from Vietnam and China.[71] This occurred despite the fact that the law did not outline baselines in the Spratlys, but declared a "regime of islands" in the disputed areas that the Philippines claims. It is small wonder, therefore, that some scholars have argued that UNCLOS has created more problems than it has solved.[72]

Implications for Policy-makers in Arctic States

This brief comparison has highlighted many challenges and opportunities for Arctic states. First, the optimistic assessment that boundary delimitation is occurring in a fashion consistent with international process does not necessarily preclude conflict. The East Asian experience reveals that states can be parties to UNCLOS, maintain a verbal commitment to peaceful resolution, yet have deep disagreements over the methods used to settle disputes. Like East Asia, the abstract and technical issue of Arctic boundary delimitation risks being caught up in domestic identity politics. The well-publicized planting of a Russian flag on the Arctic seabed is one indication of this trend, as is the raucous Canadian reaction. Similarly, following the CLCS's request that Russia submit further data in 2001, a Russian Defense Ministry newspaper accused the UN body of bias.[73] Nevertheless, the politicization of boundary delimitation has made cooperation by East Asian states difficult, but not impossible.

Secondly the "resources race" narrative is not a self-fulfilling prophecy. Hydrocarbons can be divided and shared among willing participants. While the resource value of the Arctic remains unknown, and the most profitable areas are currently within undisputed areas close to shore, the East Asian experience reveals that proven commercial resources are not necessary for heightened tensions. In a political context, the burden of proof for commercial resource exploitation in disputed areas is low. Simultaneously, the East Asian experience reveals that the existence of commercial resources is consistent with cooperation as well as conflict. While recent evidence suggests that states have been able enter into joint development talks and agreements, this occurred after a period of posturing. Policy-makers appear to view resource wealth as an acceptable motivation for brinksmanship, possibly to strengthen their bargaining posture. With reference to the Arctic, both Canada and Russia are on record as being deeply interested in seabed resource exploitation. In August 2008, Prime Minister Harper announced a new geo-mapping mission to exploit the "precious resources buried under the sea ice and tundra."[74] Likewise Nikolay Patrushev, the secretary of the Russian Security Council, argued that the Arctic must become Russia's primary resource base for the future.[75] The East Asian experience indicates that this rhetoric is most dangerous when coupled with the existence of domestic political prerogatives articulated in identity terms. Both the aforementioned joint development agreements between China and Japan and between China, Vietnam, and the Philippines have collapsed due to opposition from within claimant states. While Arctic states do not appear to be beholden to the kind of assertive nationalism that is present in East Asia, there is no shortage of insecure national identities among them.

The analysis above indicates an important lesson that can be drawn from the East Asian approach to disputed maritime boundaries. It is imperative to marginalize and isolate domestic opposition to cooperation. This can be accomplished through confidence-building measures that are well publicized as such to domestic audiences. Prior to reaching the joint development agreement in the East China Sea, China and Japan went through eleven rounds of working level discussions and concluded agreements that increased transparency between coast guards en route to the agreement.[76] In this vein, joint mapping missions between Canada, Russia, and Denmark are an important first step.[77] Joint Coast Guard search and rescue simulations, such as those between Canada and Denmark, are also effective confidence-building measures.[78] These have the added benefit of institutionalizing cooperative tendencies. Problematically, these efforts are rarely publicized on Arctic government websites or by political leaders. Instead domestic talk of protecting "sovereignty" risks undermining bilateral cooperation as well as multilateral confidence-building efforts through the Arctic Council. While Canada and Denmark are unlikely to view this sort of rhetoric as hostile, their partnership, combined with the role of identity politics in Russia, may exacerbate Russian threat perceptions. In this context, it is unfortunate that Russia did not participate in Canada's annual military exercises in the North, which in 2010 featured for the first time U.S. and Danish forces. The omission of even a Russia observer does little to alleviate Russian suspicion of a united NATO front that rejects Russia's continental shelf claims. Furthermore, there is evidence that some Russian media sources view the opposition to Russia's continental shelf claims as part of a conspiracy by Western Arctic states.[79] As the East Asian experience has demonstrated, agreement to follow the "orderly and legally-established process outlined within UNCLOS" does not necessarily prevent conflict.[80]

While this paper has focused on three parallels between Arctic and East Asian maritime boundary disputes, there may be others. Specifically, there is a trend in East Asia that is consistent with Bernard Oxman's[81] concerns over "creeping jurisdiction"; the thickening of state sovereignty over ocean areas where state jurisdiction is incomplete. State sovereignty is the most diluted over the extended continental shelf, as states have only exclusive rights to the seabed and subsoil. They have no entitlement to living resources in the water column or to police the maritime activities of foreign vessels in those waters. Nevertheless, there is a perception among some in Canada that asserting "territorial control" over the extended continental shelf is Canada's "most pressing sovereignty issue."[82] This suggests a wider interpretation of state jurisdiction than is consistent with that outlined in article 76 of UNCLOS. This interpretation is broadly consistent with Chinese and Indian efforts to maximize their jurisdiction over claimed waters, such as their move to ban all forms of marine research and military activities in the EEZ on national security grounds. It remains to be seen whether this phenomenon will emerge in the Arctic's thawing waters. According to one legal interpretation, Arctic states could make an argument that they are entitled to govern marine research if it relates to the seabed of the extended continental shelf.[83] This could create the kind of exchanges that have recently been witnessed in the East and South China Seas between Chinese vessels and their Japanese and American counterparts. This is an area for future research.

The East Asian experience in managing its many maritime boundary disputes appears to yield helpful insights for Arctic policy-makers. Leaders may wish to ask themselves whether casting the Arctic issue in terms of national identity risks reducing the political space for cooperative policy options. For example, the private members bill tabled by Conservative MP David Kramp, which would add the word "Canadian" to the Northwest Passage, has echoes in East Asia. South Korea has been attempting, with moderate success, to change the name of the Sea of Japan to the East Sea. Unsurprisingly, South Korea and Japan have a contested maritime boundary, as well as a disputed island in the waters concerned. Casting the dispute in these terms can reduce the political appetite for cooperative resource development. Likewise, Arctic policy-makers might think more carefully about how their domestic messages are received by other Arctic states. The most important lesson, however, is that the apolitical process of making submissions to the CLCS is not as benign as some argue. While the process of gathering data and making submissions should not be of concern,[84] the fact remains that the results of these efforts can be exploited for domestic political purposes, which in turn could exacerbate tensions. Certainly this has been case when similar matters arose in East Asia.

Notes

1 This article previously appeared as "Maritime Boundary Disputes in East Asia: Lessons for the Arctic," *International Studies Perspectives* 12, no. 3 (2011): 327–40. This research was funded by a Social Sciences and Humanities Research Council of Canada postdoctoral fellowship.

2 Barry S. Zellen, "Toward a Post-Arctic World," *Strategic Insights* 8, no. 1 (2009); http://calhoun.nps.edu/public/bitstream/handle/10945/11477/Toward%20a%20Post-Arctic%20World.pdf?sequence=1; accessed December 20, 2012.

3 Scott G. Borgerson, Statement to U.S. House of Representatives Committee on Foreign Affairs. March 25, 2009.

4 Michael Byers, *Intent for a Nation: What Is Canada For?* (Vancouver: Douglas & McIntyre, 2007), 167.

5 Terry Fenge and Tony Penikett, "The Arctic Vacuum in Canada's Foreign Policy," *Policy Options* 30, no. 4 (2009): 65–70.

6 White House, *National Security Presidential Directive /NSPD 66 Arctic Region Policy* (Washington, D.C.: Office of the Press Secretary, 2009), 7.

7 Katarzyna Zysk, "Russia's Arctic Strategy: Ambitions and Constraints," *Joint Forces Quarterly* 57, no. 2 (2010): 105.

8 Government of Canada, *Canada's Northern Strategy: Our North, Our Heritage, Our Future* (Ottawa: Minister of Public Works

and Government Services Canada, 2009), 12.

9 International Boundaries Research Unit, *Maritime Jurisdiction and Boundaries in the Arctic Region* (University of Durham, 2009); Alex G. Oude Elferink, "The Outer Continental Shelf in the Arctic: The Application of Article 76 of the LOS Convention in a Regional Context," in *The Law of the Sea and Polar Maritime Delimitation and Jurisdiction*, edited by Alex G. Oude Elferink and Donald R. Rothwell (Dordrecht: Martinus Nijhoff, 2001): 139–56.

10 Scott G. Borgerson, "Arctic Meltdown: The Economic and Security Implications of Climate Change," *Foreign Affairs* 87, no. 2 (2008): 63–77.

11 Ariel Cohen, Lajos F. Szaszdi, and Jim Dolbow, "The New Cold War: Reviving the U.S. Presence in the Arctic," Backgrounder 2202, Heritage Foundation, 2008, http://www.heritage.org/research/reports/2008/10/the-new-cold-war-reviving-the-us-presence-in-the-arctic; accessed December 20, 2012.

12 Robert W. Smith and Bradford Thomas, "Island Disputes and the Law of the Sea: An Examination of Sovereignty and Delimitation Disputes," in *Security Flashpoints: Oil, Islands, Sea Access and Military Confrontation*, edited by Myron H. Nordquist and John Norton Moore

(The Hague: Martinus Nijhoff, 1998), 55–104; Geoffrey Till, "Martime Disputes in the Western Pacific," *Geopolitics and International Boundaries* 1, no. 3 (1996): 327–45.

13 Donald R. Rothwell, "Issues and Strategies for Outer Continental Shelf Claims," *International Journal of Marine and Coastal Law* 23, no. 1 (2008): 191.

14 This paper was presented at the 2009 ISSS/ISAC conference in Monterey, California, the New Scholars conference at Carleton University, and as part of the seminar series at the Asian Institute, University of Toronto. The author wishes to thank Franklyn Griffiths, Elizabeth Riddell-Dixon, Scott Simon and three anonymous reviewers for comments. This research was funded by a Social Sciences and Humanities Research Council of Canada postdoctoral fellowship. This paper has previously been published as James Manicom, "Maritime Boundary Disputes in East Asia: Lessons for the Arctic," *International Studies Perspectives* 12, no. 3 (2011): 327–40.

15 United Nations, Submissions, through the Secretary-General of the United Nations, to the Commission on the Limits of the Continental Shelf, 2010 (updated May 14, 2010).

16 Scott Borgerson, "Arctic Meltdown" 63–77; Barry Scott Zellen, "Cold Front Rising: As Climate Change Thins Polar Ice, a New Race for Arctic Resources Begins," *Strategic Insights* 7, no. 1 (2008); https://calhoun.nps.edu/public/bitstream/handle/10945/11478/zellenFeb08.pdf; accessed December 20, 2012.

17 Michael T. Klare, *Resource Wars* (New York: Henry Holt, 2002).

18 U.S. Geological Survey, *USGS Arctic Oil and Gas Report: Estimates of Undiscovered Oil and Gas North of the Arctic Circle*, July 2008; http://www.eurasiareview.com/21122011-estimates-of-undiscovered-oil-and-gas-north-of-the-arctic-circle-analysis/; accessed December 20, 2012.

19 Ariel Cohen, "Russia's Race for the Arctic," Heritage Foundation Web Memo 1542, 2007, http://www.heritage.org/Research/RussiaandEurasia/wm1582.cfm; accessed April 30, 2009; Vladimir Folov, "The Coming Conflict in the Arctic: Russia and U.S. to Square Off over Arctic Energy Resources," July 17, 2008, http://www.globalresearch.ca; accessed April 30, 2009.

20 Stephen Harper, "Securing Canadian Sovereignty in the Arctic," Iqaluit, Nunavut, 2006.

21 Paul Wells, "The Cold Truth," *Maclean's*, September 7, 2009.

22 Oran R. Young, "Governing the Arctic: From Cold War Theatre to Mosaic of Cooperation," *Global Goverance* 11 (2005): 9–15.

23 See the cases collected in *Polar Politics: Creating International Environmental Regimes*, edited by Oran R. Young and Gail Osherenko (Ithaca, NY: Cornell University Press, 1993).

24 Elizabeth Riddell-Dixon, "Canada and Arctic Politics: The Continental Shelf Extension," *Ocean Development and International Law* 39, no. 4 (2008): 348–51.

25 Ron Macnab, Paul Neto, and Rob van de Poll, "Cooperative Preparations for Determining the Outer Limit of the Juridical Continental Shelf in the Arctic Ocean," *IBRU Boundary and Security Bulletin* (2001): 86–96; Jacob Verhoef and Dick MacDougall, "Delineating Canada's Continental Shelf According to the United Nations Convention on the Law of the Sea," *Journal of Ocean Technology* 3, no. 1 (2008): 1–6.

26 Elizabeth Riddell-Dixon, "Canada and Arctic Politics: The Continental Shelf Extension," *Ocean Development and International Law* 39, no. 4 (2008): 350.

27 Michael Byers, *Who Owns the Arctic? Understanding Sovereignty Disputes in the North* (Toronto: Douglas & McIntyre, 2009), 97.

28 Todd L. Allee and Paul K. Huth, "When Are Governments Able to Reach Negotiated Settlement Agreements? An Analysis of Dispute Resolution in Territorial Disputes, 1919–1985," in *Approaches, Levels and Methods of Analysis in International Politics: Crossing Boundaries*, edited by Harvey Starr (New York: Palgrave Macmillan, 2006).

29 Pavel Baev, "Russia's Race for the Arctic and the New Geopolitics of the North Pole," *Jamestown Occasional Paper* (Washington, D.C. Jamestown Foundation, 2009).

30 Vitaliy Denisov, "The Arctic Is the Future," *Krasnaya Zvezda*, October 6, 2008.

31 Tom Flanagan, *Harper's Team: Behind the Scenes in the Conservative Rise to Power*, 2nd ed. (Montreal: McGill-Queen's University Press, 2009), 246.

32 For the academic debate, see Franklyn Griffiths, "The Shipping News: Canada's Arctic Sovereignty Not on Thinning Ice," *International Journal* 58, no. 2 (2003): 257–82; and Rob Huebert, "The Shipping News Part II: How Canada's Sovereignty Is on Thinning Ice," *International Journal* 58, no. 3 (2003): 295–308.

33 Barry Buzan, "A Sea of Troubles? Sources of Dispute in the New Ocean Regime," Adelphi Paper 143 (Oxford: International Institute for Strategic Studies, Oxford University Press, 1978).

34 Andrew Mack, "Island Disputes in Northeast Asia," Working Paper 1997/2 (Canberra: Department of International Relations, Australian National University, 1997); Mark J. Valencia, "Domestic Politics Fuels Northeast Asian Maritime Disputes," *Asia Pacific Issues* 43 (2000): 1–8.

35 John Donaldson and Alison Williams, "Understanding Maritime Jurisdictional Disputes: The East China Sea and Beyond," *Journal of International Affairs* 59, no. 1 (2005): 135–56.

36 Richard K. Betts, "Wealth, Power, and Instability: East Asia and the United States after the Cold War," *International Security*

18, no. 3 (1993/1994): 34–77; Kent E. Calder, *Asia's Deadly Triangle: How Arms, Energy and Growth Threaten to Destablize Asia Pacific* (London: Nicholas Brealey, 1996).

37 Aaron L. Friedberg, "Ripe for Rivalry: Prospects for Peace in a Multipolar Asia," *International Security* 18, no. 3 (1993/1994): 5–33; Gerald Segal, "The Coming Confrontation between China and Japan?" *World Policy Journal* 10, no. 2 (1993): 27–32.

38 Oran R. Young, "Governing the Arctic: From Cold War Theatre to Mosaic of Cooperation," *Global Goverance* 11 (2005): 9–15.

39 Richard Bitzinger, "A New Arms Race? The Political Economy of Maritime Military Modernization in the Asia-Pacific," *Economics of Peace and Security Journal* 4, no. 2 (2009): 32–37.

40 Katarzyna Zysk, "Russia's Arctic Strategy: Ambitions and Constraints," *Joint Forces Quarterly* 57, no. 2 (2010): 103–10.

41 Min Gyo Koo, *Island Disputes and Maritime Regime Building in East Asia* (New York: Springer, 2009).

42 Barry S. Zellen, *Breaking the Ice: From Land Claims to Tribal Sovereignty in the Arctic* (Lanham, MD: Lexington, 2008).

43 Oran R. Young and Arkady I. Cherkasov, "International Co-Operation the Arctic: Opportunities and Constraints," in *Arctic Alternatives: Civility of Militarism Is the Circumpolar North*, edited by Franklyn Griffiths (Toronto: Science for Peace/ Samuel Stevens, 1992), 9.

44 E.C.H. Keskitalo, *Negotiating the Arctic: The Construction of an International Region* (New York: Routledge, 2004), 45–47.

45 East Asian states have also made claims to extended continental shelves and in many cases these extend or reinforce existing maritime boundary disputes. See Clive Schofield and Ian Storey, "Energy Security and Southeast Asia," *Harvard Asia Quarterly* 9, no. 4 (2005): 36–46; and Clive Schofield and I Made Andi Arsana, "Beyond the Limits?: Outer Continental

Shelf Opportunities and Challenges in East and Southeast Asia," *Contemporary Southeast Asia* 31, no. 1 (2008): 28–63.

46 Robin Churchill, "Claims to Maritime Zones in the Arctic: Law of the Sea Normality or Polar Peculiarity?", in *The Law of the Sea and Polar Maritime Delimitation and Jurisdiction*, edited by Alex G. Oude Elferink and Donald R. Rothwell (Dordrecht: Martinus Nijhoff, 2001), 105–24.

47 Selig S. Harrison Harrison, *China, Oil and Asia: Conflict Ahead?* (New York: Columbia University Press, 1977); and Victor H. Li, "China and Offshore Oil: The Tiao-Yu Tai Dispute," in *China's Changing Role in the World Economy*, edited by Bryant G. Garth (New York: Praeger, 1975), 143–62.

48 Mamdouh G. Salameh, "China, Oil and the Risk of Regional Conflict," *Survival* 37, no. 4 (1995–96), 133–46; Mark J. Valencia, "Energy and Insecurity in Asia," *Survival* 39, no. 3 (1997): 85–106; Michael T. Klare, *Resource Wars* (New York: Henry Holt, 2002).

49 James C. Hsiung, "Sea Power, Law of the Sea, and a Sino-Japanese East China Sea 'Resource War'," in *China and Japan at Odds: Deciphering the Perpetual Conflict*, edited by James C. Hsiung (New York: Palgrave Macmillan, 2007), 133–53.

50 Bob Catley and Makmur Keliat, *Spratlys: The Dispute in the South China Sea* (Aldershot: Ashgate, 1997).

51 Clive Schofield and Ian Storey, "Energy Security and Southeast Asia," *Harvard Asia Quarterly* 9, no. 4 (2005): 36–46.

52 Ralf Emmers, *Geopolitics and Maritime Territorial Disputes in East Asia* (London: Routledge, 2010).

53 Jean-Marc F. Blanchard, "Maritime Issues in Asia: The Problem of Adolescence," in *Asian Security Order: Instrumental and Normative Features*, edited by Muthiah Alagappa (Stanford: Stanford University Press, 2003), 424–57.

54 Youngshik Daniel Bong, *Flashpoints at Sea? Legitimization Strategy and East Asian Island Disputes*, PhD thesis, University of Pennsylvania, 2002.

55 Alexander Bukh, "Identity, Foreign Policy and the 'Other': Japan's Russia," *European Journal of International Relations* 15, no. 2 (2009): 319–45.

56 Peter Hays Gries, *China's New Nationalism: Pride, Politics and Diplomacy* (Berkeley: University of California Press, 2004).

57 Phil Deans, Deans, "Contending Nationalisms in the Diaoyutai/Senkaku Dispute," *Security Dialogue* 31, no. 1 (2000): 119–31; Chien-peng Chung, *Domestic Politics, International Bargaining and China's Territorial Disputes* (London: RoutledgeCurzon, 2004), 26–60.

58 James Manicom, "The Interaction of Material and Ideational Factors in the East China Sea Dispute: Impact on Future Dispute Management," *Global Change, Peace and Security* 20, no. 3 (2008): 375–91.

59 Roger Mitton, "Vietnam, China Clash Again over Spratlys: Chinese Navy Fires at Vietnamese Fishing Boats in Oil-Rich Region," *The Straits Times*, July 19, 2007; Ian Storey, "Trouble and Strife in the South China Sea: Vietnam and China," *China Brief* 8, no. 8 (2008): 11–14.

60 Chien-peng Chung, "Resolving China's Island Disputes: A Two-Level Game Analysis," *Journal of Chinese Political Science* 12, no. 1 (2007): 49–70.

61 Erica S. Downs and Philip Saunders, "Legitimacy and the Limits of Nationalism: China and the Diaoyu Islands," *International Security* 23, no. 3 (1998/1999): 114–46.

62 Clive Schofield, "The Trouble with Islands: The Definition and Role of Islands and Rocks in Maritime Boundary Delimitation," in *Maritime Boundary Disputes, Settlement Processes and the Law of the Sea*, edited by Seoung-Yong Hong and John M. Van Dyke (Leiden: Martinus Nijhoff, 2009), 32.

63 "Ambassador Wang Yi on China's Japan Policy," *People's Daily*, October 19, 2004.

64 Sun Pyo Kim, *Maritime Delimitation and Interim Arrangements in North East Asia* (The Hague: Martinus Nijhoff, 2004), 27. It should be noted that Japan refuses to publish the exact points used to draw the median line.

65 Alexander M. Peterson, "Exploration of the East China Sea: The Law of the Sea in Practice," *bepress Legal Series* (1730). (2006): 23.

66 James Manicom, "Sino-Japanese Cooperation in the East China Sea: Limitations and Prospects," *Contemporary Southeast Asia* 30, no. 3 (2008): 455–78.

67 Abigail Kwok, "RP Delegate to UNCLOS: 'Don't Include Kalayaan Group of Islands in Baselines Bill,'" *Inquirer.net*, August 7, 2008.

68 "Proposed Federal Constitution Includes Kalayaan in RP," *Manila Times*, July 19, 2008.

69 Efren L Danao, "Nene Scores Miriam on Disputed Islands," August 12, 2008.

70 Abigail Kwok, "RP Delegate to UNCLOS.".

71 Heda Bayron, "New Philippine Border Law Re-Ignites Territorial Disputes in South China Sea," *VOA News*, March 17, 2009; http://chinhdangvu.blogspot.com/2009/03/new-philippine-border-law-re-ignites.html; accessed December 20, 2012.

72 Sam Bateman, "UNCLOS and Its Limitations as the Foundation for a Regional Maritime Security Regime," *Korean Journal of Defense Analysis* 19, no. 3 (2007): 27–56.

73 Vladimir Kuzar, "A Pole of Pretension – the Arctic," *Krasnaya Zvezda*, October 20, 2008.

74 Stephen Harper, "Prime Minister Harper Announces the Geo-Mapping for Northern Energy and Minerals Program," August

26, 2008; http://www.pm.gc.ca/eng/media.asp?id=2256; accessed May 11, 2009.

75 "Arctic Must Become Primary Strategic Resource Base," *DNI.ru Daily News*, October 22, 2008.

76 James Manicom, "Sino-Japanese Cooperation in the East China Sea: Limitations and Prospects," *Contemporary Southeast Asia* 30, no. 3 (2008): 455–78.

77 Jacob Verhoef and Dick MacDougall, "Delineating Canada's Continental Shelf According to the United Nations Convention on the Law of the Sea," *Journal of Ocean Technology* 3, no. 1 (2008): 5.

78 "Update: Denmark's Arctic Assets and Canada's Response – Northern Deployment 2009: Danish Navy & CCG in the High Arctic," *Canadian-American Strategic Review* (2009); http://www.casr.ca/id-arcticviking-northern-deployment-09.htm; accessed December 20, 2012.

79 "Battle for the Arctic Continues," *Krestyanskaya Rus*, October 9, 2008. Western in this context refers to the "West," rather than geographical orientation.

80 Foreign Affairs and International Trade Canada Foreign Affairs and International Trade Canada, Joint Statement on Canada–Russia Economic Cooperation, November 28–29, 2007.

81 Bernard H. Oxman, "The Territorial Temptation: A Siren Song at Sea," *American Journal of International Law* 100, no. 4 (2006): 830–51.

82 Ken S. Coates et al., *Arctic Front: Defending Canada in the Far North* (Toronto: Thomas Allen, 2008), 198.

83 Ron Macnab, Olav Loken, and Arvind Anand, "The Law of the Sea and Marine Scientific Research in the Arctic Ocean," *Meridian* (fall–winter 2007): 1–6.

84 Michael Byers, *Who Owns the Arctic? Understanding Sovereignty Disputes in the North* (Toronto: Douglas & McIntyre, 2009), 92.

8. Babysteps: Developing Multilateral Institutions in the Arctic

Maj. Henrik Jedig Jørgensen

Preface

As climate-change skeptics are increasingly won over from "the dark side" to accept the fact that climate change is a fact, the Arctic coastal states are struggling to find ways to adapt their national strategies to the changing geo-political situation that is a result of the warming of the Arctic. At the same time, scholars from all over the world are struggling to understand the future possibilities and challenges of the Arctic in the light of this changing scenario – and their projections vary across a continuum stretching from a scenario of peaceful development with a multiple of beneficiaries on one end to one of a new "Cold War" or even military confrontation on the other.[1] At the centre of this forecasting, we find two variables: First, all projections expect the quest for power (or in some cases this is reduced to the constituents of power, e.g., resources or territory) to be central to the future of the Arctic. Second, although some projections tend to hold cooperation as a constant – either assuming that conflict is inevitable or that cooperation is a natural condition – the degree of cooperation is a central variable that is common to most studies.

This chapter assumes that the ongoing quest for power in the Arctic can be regulated and that the Arctic coastal states have a common interest in establishing fora, rules, and regulations to deal with actual and potential future challenges – both within the security domain and in other, softer domains. The existing fora that could be used for dialogue and cooperation in the Arctic are all established on Cold War premises and on the premise that Arctic change is taking place at a slow and incremental pace. Consequently, they are insufficiently institutionalized and lacking in power – and therefore incapable of assuming an overarching responsibility for historical reasons. This chapter discusses the need for, possibilities of, and challenges to empowering the weak existing fora with the aim of increasing the degree of practical and binding Arctic cooperation, and reducing the level of militarization and risk of conflict against the option of establishing new and more potent fora. It will also discuss the future need for institution-building with the short-term aim of being able to keep up with the pace of Arctic change and the long-term aim of establishing Arctic institutions with the potential to carry out UN mandates under Article VIII of the UN Charter.

Why the Need for Arctic Cooperation and Institutions Is Pressing

The need for future development of cooperation in the Arctic is determined by the change in human activities in the region. Basically it can be said that the present limited Arctic cooperation is a function of the scarce amount of human activity in the past. But there is no longer any doubt that the patterns of human behavior in the Arctic is changing: In the 2007 Norshipping Report *Arctic Shipping 2030* that examined scenarios for the future of Arctic shipping,[2] part of the conclusion reads: "ice class technology and surveillance technology will be important in all the scenarios." The report goes on to conclude that as a consequence of climate change and globalization, Arctic shipping will increase. But as a consequence of climate change, extreme weather conditions will continue to be a – or may even become a more extreme – factor to consider for the duration of the analysis (i.e., at least until 2030). Therefore reliable meteorological predictions, including predictions of distribution and movement of the sea ice will become one important factor, while ice-class technology will remain another important factor to international commercial freight.

The flip-side of this conclusion also needs to be considered: If ships will require ice-class technology to guarantee their safe passage through Arctic waters and surveillance technology to predict the extent and thickness of sea ice, this means that by implication the report assumes that Arctic shipping will be running calculated risks to cross Arctic waters. The conclusions in the Norshipping report are consistent with most other reports and assessments. For example, the Arctic Council in 2009 published the *Arctic Marine Shipping Assessment* report: The report points to the conclusion that: "It is highly plausible there will be greater marine access and longer seasons of navigation, except perhaps during winter, but not necessarily less difficult ice conditions for marine operations."[3]

While there is no longer any doubt that human activities in the Arctic are increasing, there are a few determining factors to consider. Predominantly the speed of global climate change, the existence or non-existence of natural resources, the development of extraction and transportation technologies and the "temperature" of the world market are three variables that will have an impact on the level of activity. Together with my colleague Jon Rahbek-Clemmesen, I discussed these parameters in a 2009 report from Danish Institute for Military Studies, under the title: *Keep it Cool*. The discussion of the central factors concluded that the combination of demand, technology and availability/accessibility could basically be boiled down to one single question: If it pays to do something in the Arctic – be it exploitation of natural resources, Arctic maritime transportation, or cruise-ship tourism – it will be done.[4]

In our 2009 report – for lack of substantive meteorological predictions – we assumed that the global climate change was a slowly progressing phenomenon that would influence both the possibility to search for resources and the accessibility of the resources that might be found. The assumption that climate change was a slowly progressing phenomenon had some impact on the conclusions of the report: if the time perspective for Arctic development is long, there is also considerable time to establish cooperation, rules, and regulations. But since we published the report, however, most predictions seem to indicate that Arctic change is occurring much faster than we assumed – and this leaves less time for the establishment of new Arctic fora and the development of existing ones to take care of matters that are suddenly seen to surface.

The combination of increased traffic in the Arctic poses a risk in itself: where no ships are sailing, no collisions or shipwrecks will occur, so the sheer increase in traffic should be considered a risk driver. But while long-term meteorological predictions forecast a reduced ice-coverage in the Arctic, they also envision an increase in extreme weather phenomenon with "greater ice movement and wave action, which will increase the risks of sailing and operations in the Arctic."[5] Altogether, "This new Arctic Ocean of increasing marine access, potentially longer seasons of navigation and increasing ship traffic requires greater attention and stewardship by the Arctic states and all marine users."[6] But what does stewardship mean in this context: who has the legitimate right or legal obligation to steward the Arctic? And what elements of stewardship are required?

Why Cooperation Is Lacking

On a practical level – like search and rescue (SAR) or environmental protection – a number of initiatives are already in place – be it national, bilateral, or multinational – but until recently, a truly broad and all-encompassing Arctic cooperation was generally lacking. I suggest that such practical and binding cooperation in the Arctic was traditionally lacking for three reasons: First, cooperation has been hampered by historical mistrust between Russia and the four Arctic NATO members. This historical factor prevented the Arctic states from entering into a concrete security cooperation – and by extension it had a negative effect on the development of a concrete Arctic cooperation outside of the high-politics domain. Second, the Arctic states have only recently begun to realize that climate change and changing traffic patterns will be altering their national priorities – they are all on the outside of the so-called OODA loop and they are only just entering the "Decide" phase.[7] Third, cooperation was hampered by weak institutional frameworks, competing interests, and the risk of influence-dilution in the existing fora.

1. Historical Mistrust

States generally prefer to cooperate with other states that resemble themselves and where relations are both friendly and based on repeated successful examples of cooperation. This explains, for example, why Norway has been a keen supporter of establishing an Arctic dimension in NATO. But it also explains why Russia is not going to be so happy with such a development. The role of NATO will be discussed in greater detail later in the paper, but for now I will conclude that Russia and NATO historically have been antagonistic – and this will continue to effectively prevent any practical cooperation in the *high-politics* domain.

But historical security concerns can also influence cooperation in the low-politics domain; logic would have it that where states with a complicated security relationship seek to build closer relations, they should begin by approaching each other in areas that are not perceived as vital by any of them. Such low-politics cooperation could have a mitigating effect on a sore relationship. The Agreement on Cooperation on Aeronautical and Maritime Search and Rescue (SAR) in the Arctic, or as it is more commonly known, the Arctic SAR Agreement – the first binding international treaty concluded among the member states of the Arctic Council that was signed on May 12, 2011 – could be seen as an example of such an issue. The Arctic states all have a responsibility to be able to coordinate SAR at sea within their territories. And while the ongoing increase in Arctic traffic pushes the general need for SAR capacities, the unpredictability of the distribution of territories following a distant UNCLOS decision makes the distribution of future national responsibilities unclear. So the question needing to be addressed was: should each Arctic state develop individual capabilities to cover the areas where it makes a claim, or should the Arctic states establish cooperation to pool their mutual capabilities to support the common task? The answer may seem to be a clear "yes," but there is also a risk that diplomatic efforts at building cooperation within the low-politics domain can be perceived within the high-politics security domain. If this logic applied to Arctic cooperation, the development of concrete and binding agreements would then be hampered because states would fear such initiatives could be perceived by the others as a means of de-securitization. In this case, the Arctic states would simply be afraid to discuss concrete cooperation for fear of drawing attention to the risk of a confrontation.

2. Slow Realization of the Influence of Climate Change

Slow realization of the influence of climate change and changing traffic patterns is another reason why cooperation was for so long insufficiently institutionalized because the Arctic states have only recently begun to realize the impact of climate change. The understanding that climate change was pushing the need for cooperation has been promoted – among other factors – by the fact that the Arctic states have been struggling to document their claims to UNCLOS for their territorial rights in the Polar basin. The value of international cooperation has been clearly demonstrated by the fact that it has been a precondition for most states to be able to support their territorial claims. For example, the Danish ability to document any claims would be severely challenged if Russian or Swedish icebreakers could not be chartered.

3. Weak Institutional Frameworks, Competing Interests, and the Risk of Influence-Dilution in the Existing Fora

The third reason why practical cooperation was slow to materialize in the Arctic has to do with the composition and construction of the fora that could be used to develop such cooperation. First, where the Arctic Council is concerned, it has the disadvantage of including states that are not Arctic coastal states. Should these states be allowed a deciding role in the establishment of Arctic capabilities? If so, how should burden-sharing be arranged? Second, the Arctic Council has been struggling to sort out how to deal with a growing number of observer states. Third, the Arctic Council to some extent gains its legitimacy from the special representation of indigenous peoples: but if the Council is transformed into an organization with permanent representation, these groups will have good reason to fear marginalization. Fourth, the Arctic Council is prevented from covering military issues by the Ottawa declaration: it may deal with *high-politics* on the diplomatic level, but many of the concrete tasks that need coordination will have a military dimension. And finally: if the Arctic states shift their attention to "Arctic 5" (A5), cooperation will carry the same problems concerning indigenous peoples as mentioned above – and at the same time, the Nordic countries will have to kiss the "Nordic dimension" goodbye.

What Should Cooperation Include?

International cooperation could be initiated for various reasons. On a practical level, it should be designed to optimize the effect of national funding against effect: when operating individually, the Arctic coastal states – no matter how powerful they may be – are up against a tremendous challenge in case of a future worst-case scenario. If a Gulf of Mexico-like scenario were to take place in Arctic waters, the combined efforts of the Arctic states would be better served by a coordinated and pre-arranged multinational effort than the sole effort by any individual state. And any practical cooperation would have to consider a range of scenarios to be covered – which would force the Arctic states to discuss their own ambitions against those of the other – and thus facilitate dialogue. Of course, this dialogue would also expose differing agendas – but the alternative to the Arctic states discussing agendas and scenarios theoretically and in advance is discussing them when they confront each other on practical terms.

But Arctic cooperation should also serve to reduce security tensions among the Arctic states. Of course there are already elements of dialogue and transparency – both relatives of security – in already-existing Arctic cooperation, but these relatives are much more distant than their cousins: coordination and cooperation. Broad military coordination or cooperation would tie individuals on all sides of the Arctic rim closer together and form the basis of formalized channels of dialogue much stronger than those of today. It would offer Russia a better communications platform than risking her aging bombers by taking them across the Arctic Basin, and it would offer politicians a set of closed channels to voice their frustrations.

And finally Arctic cooperation should be able to handle future external threats and challenges like illegal fishing, piracy, illegal immigration, smuggling, and other criminal activities as well as potential security threats from external state actors. Fear – or claims of fear – of such activities could be used by individual Arctic states as excuses to unilaterally bolster their defences in the Arctic – and therefore they are likely sources of future insecurity if not handled in time. The Arctic states need all these effects – and they need to start the dialogue soon. If one state or another decides to act on its own against a perceived potential threat that could be manifest in a decade, it will probably have to start building capabilities today in order to be able to employ them tomorrow.

Cooperation where all the Arctic states are included is illustrated in the matrix in Figure 1. As shown in the matrix, broad Arctic cooperation is isolated to the diplomatic dimension. Initiatives concerning cultural issues and environmental protection have traditionally been handled by the Arctic Council, but binding agreements and concrete cooperation has been scarce. Even the budding cooperation within the SAR area was long isolated to the diplomatic level and only recently came to fruition in the form of the May 2011 binding Arctic SAR Agreement.

Ideas for further concrete cooperation could include issues such as meteorological forecasting, including monitoring of ice-movements, fisheries inspections, environmental protection, or pollution fighting. On a much longer horizon, the vision for cooperation should not exclude the potential for the Arctic coastal states to engage in a military cooperation that would enable them to act commonly in the Arctic on behalf of the UN, for example under Article VIII of the UN charter.

Closer cooperation between the Arctic coastal states would also enable them to better influence global organizations and the establishment of common international standards. For example, the Arctic coastal states have a special interest in influencing the United Nations International Maritime Organization when it is working to formalize its Polar directives.

Building Blocks for Future Cooperation: Arctic Institutions

Arctic cooperation is already taking place on many levels. On the most basic level, individuals have always had to cooperate in order to survive the harsh climate. Where profit is involved, companies cooperate to be able to extract resources. Where cross-boundary interests are at stake, interest groups cooperate to promote their agendas and learn from each other. And state cooperation takes place for a multitude of reasons in order to balance the wish to fulfil national interests uncompromisingly against the cost of doing so alone.

But in the areas where cooperation between the Arctic coastal states has been all-inclusive (i.e., including Russia), it has taken place within the framework of the Arctic Council, and cooperation has been limited only to the soft politics domain. In the domain of hard security, broad cooperation has been hampered by traditional security concerns and mistrust: The only hard security institution operating in the Arctic is NATO, and the prospect of including Russia in that organization remains distant, bordering on non-existent.

The Arctic Council is the only internationally recognized Arctic institution, and the possible development of the Arctic Council or alternatively the Arctic 5 will be the focus of this chapter. But as the only multinational security actor in the Arctic, NATO also has an important role to play – or perhaps at best, NATO has an important role *not* to play. No matter what new dimensions the Arctic Council does develop, NATO will always be the famous "invisible elephant" in the room, and whether the Arctic Council can be developed to assume a larger role will to a great extent be dependent on what role NATO plays or does not play in the Arctic.

NATO

The interest in the Arctic of both NATO and the Soviet Union during the Cold War was mostly motivated by the fear of nuclear attacks either from submarines operating in the Arctic sea or from missiles or bombers that could bring their deadly cargo across it. Early-warning stations in the Arctic were supposed to alert NATO militaries in case Soviet missiles were launched – and Soviet bases in Northern Siberia and on the Kola Peninsula were tasked with air defense against NATO attacks. Bomber and missile units were allocated offensive tasks on both sides of the Arctic.

Another reason to keep an eye on the Arctic had to do with the relatively landlocked position of the Soviet Union and its consequent need to use the Arctic Sea for maritime purposes: with access to only a few warm-water ports, most of them easily containable by NATO, the Soviet Union had to rely on its formidable Northern Fleet, situated in Murmansk, to disrupt the transfer of troops and equipment from the United States across the Atlantic to a European war theater in case of a war. For both NATO and the Soviet Union maritime operations in the Atlantic were vital – and control of the passage from the Arctic to the Atlantic was thus of the utmost importance.

After the Cold War and the dissolution of the Soviet Union, the security agenda of both the NATO states and Russia has dramatically changed. The Arctic, however, has not entirely lost its perceived importance to military security: Russia still has a (decaying) Northern Fleet in Murmansk with ice-capable nuclear-powered submarines, and it maintains its bomber regiments and nuclear missiles and is very much aware that it is still facing NATO – and, in the Arctic, this poses a special challenge, since the other four Arctic Coastal states are all NATO members. As I put it in an earlier study: "with four of the Arctic states belonging to the same alliance – and with Russia being the only non-NATO Arctic state, there is a particular risk that actions undertaken by individual states will be perceived as part of a coordinated alliance gesture directed against Russian interests. This will be especially problematic if the stakes regarding the distribution of potential gains in the Arctic are seen to be altered. In this situation it is likely that Russia will perceive any change of military posture as an alliance move aimed at intimidating or even compelling Russia from asserting its perceived rights."[8] In other words, while each of the four Arctic coastal states that are NATO members may perceive their individual military actions as part of national strategies, there is a risk that Russia will interpret these same actions as part of a coherent NATO strategy rather than as part of a set of respective national strategies.

But there is also a risk that Canada, Denmark, Norway, and the United States will tend to see Russian military actions through the Cold War lens: in a matter of years rather than decades, the decaying Russian Northern Fleet will need renovation – and units within that fleet will need to be replaced. At the same time, it should be remembered that the decay of the Russian Northern Fleet is taking place alongside the development of Russian economic interests in the Arctic and as the natural protection of Russian territories is literally melting away; the significance of Russian dependence on oil and gas extracted from the Arctic as well as the insecurity connected with the disappearance of the traditional protection offered by an inhospitable ice-desert both speak in favor of maintaining a strong defensive military force in the Arctic region.[9] Adding to this insecurity and need for protection of vital interests, Russia also has to consider the emerging power of China. I will not deal with this issue in detail but simply conclude that the Russian military posture in the Arctic will also have to be considered against the need to protect its interests elsewhere and from other players than the Arctic coastal states.

In light of the above-mentioned considerations, the Arctic coastal NATO member states will have to consider the impact of their individual military actions. If any of them are uncomfortable with Russian military actions or with the development of Russian military capabilities, this could trigger a bilateral confrontation or even initiate an arms race between Russia and the

Arctic coastal states. But before that, NATO members could be tempted to invite NATO north to bolster their national position, demonstrate alliance solidarity, or even compel Russia. On the "ladder of escalation," a NATO response to a bilateral confrontation could prove hazardous to the development of peaceful Arctic relations.

NATO and Russia have come a long way towards a mutual understanding since the end of the Cold War. Indeed, there are even examples of cooperation – like when NATO was allowed to use Soviet airspace in the war in Afghanistan. And the NATO-Russia Council has been a forum for consultation since 2002, but this is also a fragile forum, as it was demonstrated after cooperation was suspended from August 2008 to March 2009 following the 2008 war between Russia and Georgia and the Russian occupation of South Ossetia.

The Arctic Council

The broadest and most encompassing Arctic institution is the Arctic Council. Founded on the basis of the Arctic Environmental Protection Strategy, the Arctic Council was established in 1996, absorbing the environmental dimension and broadening its mandate to cover all other issues in the Arctic except military ones.[10] Based on a core of Arctic and Subarctic states (Canada, Denmark, Finland, Iceland, Norway, Russia, Sweden, and the United States), the Arctic Council gains an increased legitimacy from including the indigenous Arctic population, represented by transnational Aboriginal organizations. Furthermore, the Arctic Council is open to observers – the only requirement for observer status being the demand to comply with the founding principles of the Council.

Much hard work has been put into adapting the Arctic Council to the changing situation in the Arctic. In some cases, the Arctic Council has established working groups to supplement the original four working groups from AEPS.[11] This goes for the Sustainable Development Working Group (SDWG). In other cases, the Arctic Council has proven instrumental in establishing and promoting new knowledge – for example, when the U.S.-funded Arctic Climate Impact Assessment (ACIA) was conducted under the auspices of Arctic Council.

But while the Arctic Council has proven successful in serving as a forum for dialogue on soft-policy issues and a body for coordinating research and knowledge-sharing – and even raising Arctic climate change to the international agenda – its statute sets some limitations to the wider use of the Council: First of all the absence of military issues from the agenda means that issues that could be meaningfully covered in the only truly pan-Arctic forum will have to be coordinated elsewhere – for example in the NATO-Russia Dialogue. The NATO-Russia Dialogue construction has the disadvantage of historical bias – and, as noted above, it has been disbanded on several occasions over issues that had nothing to do with the Arctic, such as the Russia-Georgia war in 2007, or the Kosovo conflict in 1999.

Another obstacle to developing the Arctic Council towards something more functional is the meeting rhythm of the council. In an environment of accelerated change, biennial meetings are simply not enough: The Council needs a permanent representation to be able to coordinate ongoing activities and monitor the rapid changes that can be observed in the Arctic. Steps are already taken to increase the pace of cooperation: at the 2009 Tromsø meeting, the Council: "Decide[d] to further strengthen the political role of the Arctic Council by having a meeting at deputy Minister level, with representatives of Permanent Participants, to discuss emerging issues between Ministerial meetings."[12] But although annual meetings could increase the pace of institutional development, there would still be a strong need for a permanent body to address the challenges that are rapidly emerging as the level of activity is increasing.

The first stepping stone toward AN Arctic Council permanent representation was made in 2007, when Norway agreed to host a secretariat at Tromsø through the period 2006–12.[13] Although the activities of such a secretariat does not hold any decision-making authority and is probably largely unable to coordinate ongoing activities, it could provide a platform for a more robust future representation with actual agencies and a larger organization. The secretariat may technically seem to be a temporary institution – but the fact that the 2009 Tromsø Declaration concludes that the Arctic Council: "appreciate[s] the Secretariat's contribution to the increased efficiency of the work of Arctic Council,"[14] can only point to a more permanent future structure for Arctic Council. Although new funding mechanisms may be required, and although its activities will probably be restricted to the coordination of

8. BABYSTEPS

meetings and agendas, it may provide the opportunity to lift ongoing coordination out of national frameworks and into a multinational agenda.

But changing the position of the Arctic Council will be difficult, if the participants maintain that the Council shall remain little more than a biennial forum for the exchange of ideas and coordination of environmental and cultural issues. In order to bring the Arctic Council to prominence, it will need to be empowered to be able to act on short notice against arising challenges, and it should have a concrete set of tasks to coordinate or even direct. The establishment of a permanent secretariat is a step on the way, but that secretariat must be developed to be able to lasso ideas and tie them to reality. This will require a competent permanent staff, new procedures and competencies within the secretariat (possibly a secretary general), and a number of functional agencies to provide limbs for the Arctic Council body. The following section will discuss the possibilities for empowering the Arctic Council through institutional approaches. In doing so, it will lend inspiration from the Subarctic areas where such cooperation has been ongoing for years.

Empowering the Arctic Council

If the Arctic Council is to be developed into a more potent institution, it will need a permanent representation. The pace of Arctic change is going faster than the meeting rhythm of Arctic Council, and consequently the Council will be unable to react in time to emerging challenges as Arctic traffic is quickly increasing. A permanent representation should include a secretariat – but also a command structure led by a secretary general or a similar construction. It would also need a permanent staff and a headquarters. Once established, the Council (which would start to look more like an organization) could start to assume responsibility for coordinating the tasks that emerge as Arctic traffic increases. The decision as to what staff functions should be included in the organization could be determined by "supply and demand" mechanisms: all coastal states are struggling with the same considerations – and it should not be hard to identify a couple of "starters" like ice-forecasting, or coordinating SAR activities as agreed to by the Arctic Council members in May 2011.

But the Arctic council will need to change its statute in order to gain the necessary potency. This is a major challenge since development of binding structures will push state administrations closer to the centre of decisions at the expense of indigenous peoples. This is primarily because funding and state responsibilities will become a core mechanism in all discussions of an empowered Arctic Council. As long as Arctic Council does not engage in high-politics or at least focuses its efforts on soft issues like culture and environment, the organizations representing indigenous peoples are likely to maintain their special position somewhere between member states and mere observers. But if the scope and focus of Arctic Council is changed to address high politics and security, this special position could be at stake, possibly causing the indigenous peoples to lose influence.

Arctic states may continue to be reluctant to discuss expanding the mandate and statute of the Arctic Council or establishing innocent bilateral fora for cooperation simply because this could be interpreted as maneuvers to create alternative channels to handle security issues in case of a crisis, and thus draw unwanted attention to the potential conflicts of the Arctic. In other words, fear of drawing attention to the security dimension of the Arctic may prevent the establishment of highly relevant fora for cooperation that could in fact serve the purpose of alternative channels for dialogue in case the traditional channels close because of a crisis. But at some point, the members of Arctic Council will have to consider where to coordinate Arctic military issues. And at that point states will be the dominant actors with NGOs playing only marginal roles.

The Arctic 5 (A5)

The Arctic 5 or A5 is a fairly new invention. The forum includes the Arctic coastal states in what could be termed an "Arctic Land Owners Association."[15] The first formal A5 initiative was the Ilulissat meeting in May 2008 that produced the Ilulissat Declaration. The A5 gains its legitimacy from the public safety dimension, which can be roughly explained by the fact that any occurrence that will need handling in the polar basin will have to be handled by one or more of the Arctic coastal states, but may have influence on all of them.[16]

The Ilulissat Declaration was a unigue achievement in three ways: first, it demonstrated that by reducing the Arctic Council to a forum with concrete security concerns, it was able to deal with matters of security in a binding way.

Second, to achieve a binding agreement, it established that the Arctic coastal states had special common interests and responsibilities and thus succeeded in carving Iceland, Sweden, and Finland out of the Arctic equation. Indeed, it even demonstrated to states with no Arctic presence whatsoever – like China – that the Arctic coastal states considered themselves the core actors of the polar basin.[17] Third, it succeeded in committing the United States to decisions reached under the aegis of UNCLOS, although the United States is still not a signatory to that convention.

Although the outcome of the Ilulissat meeting – the Declaration – was widely praised in the five Arctic coastal states, the forum has been criticized for virtually excluding indigenous people from influence and thus rein-forcing the primacy of states over peoples.[18] At the same time, the Ilulissat Declaration has been observed with scepticism and even anger in the Nordic countries that do not have Arctic coast lines, and there seems to be a fault line in Denmark between politicians who endorse the Arctic Council over the A5 and vice-versa.

In this respect Denmark may have to choose between promoting the A5, which excludes Finland, Sweden, and Iceland from the cooperation, and a Nordic dimension in Arctic cooperation that rests on the Stoltenberg report and especially the common ambition to use the consecutive Nordic (Norwegian, Danish, and Swedish) chairmanship of the Arctic Council to promote the recommendations from the Stoltenberg report.[19] The two fora may not necessarily be mutually exclusive, but in this early phase of develop-ment, Danish domestic political considerations may dictate a choice between the two.

The United States does not seem too enthusiastic about A5 either. After the March 2010 meeting, U.S. Secretary of State Hilary Rodham Clinton stated that: "Significant international discussions on Arctic issues should include those who have legitimate interests in the region.… I hope the Arctic will always showcase our ability to work together, not create new divisions."[20] This led Professor Rob Huebert of the University of Calgary's Centre for Strategic and Military Studies to conclude, "I think that's effectively dead.… I can't see any other country running forward to make it work." Professor Michael Byers from the University of British Columbia commented: "This has thrown that particular dimension of [the Canadian government's] policy into an impossible position … from now on, they have to include the other

Arctic Council members and they also have to make sure there is indigenous representation."[21]

Although these statements could still prove to be prophetic, it is too early to remove the A5 from the equation: It may well prove to have the potential to deal with future challenges that will appear as the ice melts and the quest for resources becomes manifest. If the Arctic Council proves unable to transform itself and adapt to the changing circumstances in the Arctic – like establishing a permanent formal organization to serve as an anchor-point for concrete initiatives – let alone handle concrete security issues like military cooperation, the principal actors (the coastal states) will need to take matters elsewhere. Although the Arctic Council has a special legitimacy because of the representation of indigenous peoples, it will be naïve to rely on a forum with no permanent representation and with a biannual (or even annual if we include the latest initiatives) meeting rhythm to coordinate the events in an environment that changes faster than the meeting rhythm.

Empowering the A5

Although enthusiasm for A5 may be limited to some of the Arctic coastal states, it is still worth considering what role this forum would be able to play in case the Arctic Council fails to develop the institutional capacity needed to suit an Arctic environment with a lot more activity than what can be observed today. In that case, there will be an Arctic institutional vacuum that will leave it up to the individual states whether to act alone or seek coordination and cooperation. This could emphasize bilateral arrangements – or introduce other institutions whether old ones or new.

In that case, the A5 could prove to be a better alternative than bilateral arrangements or the obvious fall-back option for those Arctic coastal states that are NATO members. For the moment, this scenario might seem distant – but as Arctic maritime traffic increases, the decision date for establishing capacities is also pushed closer. This means that the Arctic states will have to develop capacities before they can fully predict the costs and benefits of capacity-building. They may seek to share the burden with other actors – and the prize will be a dilution of influence as contributors will make demands before committing resources.

So the A5 may have some disadvantages when it comes to legitimacy – and it may arouse some controversy among the Arctic Council members who will lose influence if binding decisions and formal cooperation is transferred to A5. But on the other hand, non-state actors and non-coastal Arctic states are unlikely to commit resources on any significant scale in exchange for influence on capacity-building and institutional development of the Arctic Council. In any case, the location of the headquarters of any future multinational Arctic organization is likely to be in one of the Arctic-rim states, and any capacity constructed for an Arctic future will be based in the rim states as well. Disregarding these facts is naïve and will lead to postponement of important cooperation initiatives.

The concrete cooperation initiatives that could empower the A5 are similar to those mentioned in the discussion of Arctic Council. But as a basis for the cooperation, an "Arctic 5 declaration," should be designed. Once in place, the declaration should institutionalize the cooperation and establish the basis for a an organization with a permanent headquarter staffed with a secretary general and a secretariat, and with appropriate staff functions to initiate cooperation in the domains that could commonly be identified as relevant.

Conclusion

In this chapter, I have described the consequences of the changing conditions to navigation in the Arctic. I have made the point, that practical cooperation by the Arctic coastal states within a number of areas like search and rescue, surveillance, environmental protection, and pollution containment will continue to be required, and that the changing security dynamics that come from Arctic change also need a forum of attention.

In a matter of just a few decades, the Arctic could become a region of such importance that the world economy and well-being of millions could be at stake in case of a regional crisis – be it in the security domain or elsewhere. This speaks in favor of establishing a regional framework of cooperation that could be empowered by a UN resolution coordinating on behalf of the United Nations whatever effort might be required – or even acting under Article VIII of the UN charter.

If this vision is to come true, the right forum will have to be established – either based on existing structures or entirely new ones. The only institution to include all the central Arctic actors is the Arctic Council, but the Arctic Council is currently not geared to support such a vision of cooperation in an environment of rapid change. If the Arctic Council is to be able to coordinate any ongoing effort, it will have to establish itself as a permanent structure, headed by a secretary general, situated in a headquarters, surrounded by a staff and fitted with a secretariat. But this will require fundamental changes to the statutes of the Arctic Council. And even more drastic changes will be needed if the Council is to be able to coordinate any efforts in the security domain. But the only other multinational security actor in the Arctic, NATO, is no realistic alternative because of the historical bias that surrounds it.

Small steps have been taken to increase the responsiveness and efficiency of the Arctic Council, but there is still a long way to go: expanding the secretariat is an important step, but establishing a permanent staff with a dedicated leadership would make better sense if the Council had its own operations or development programs to coordinate.

The groundbreaking work of the Arctic Council Taskforce on Search and Rescue, culminating in the binding May 2011 Arctic SAR Agreement, could provide an opportunity for creating a permanent body to be attached to the secretariat. But if the Arctic Council proves unable to deliver the premises for broad and functioning international operational cooperation in the Arctic, other options must be considered. A cooperation vacuum will be too dangerous and too expensive – and therefore, the A5 should be carefully considered as a less legitimate but probably more effective alternative.

Letting go of the idea of A5 means easing the pressure on the development of the Arctic council – or put another way, the idea that A5 could take the role of Arctic operational cooperation will put pressure on those actors within the Arctic Council that resist much-needed development of the Council. Finally, perhaps the question of empowering the Arctic Council versus the Arctic 5 is not one of "either-or" but could be one of "both-and," with the Arctic Council serving as a forum for dialogue while the A5 serves the purposes of formal agreements and cooperation on the operational level.

Notes

1 See the work of Scott Borgerson, Rob Huebert, Karina E. Clemmensen, and Sven G. Holtsmark, among others.

2 Norshipping, *Arctic Shipping 2030*, ECON Report 2007-70, 24.

3 Arctic Council, Key finding 7, *Arctic Marine Shipping Assessment* (AMSA) (2009), 35.

4 This is largely consistent with the findings in Arctic Marine Shipment Assessment 2009, 124.

5 AMSA, 9.

6 AMSA, 25.

7 In its simplest form, the OODA loop consists of four phases of an actor's decision cycle: Observe—Orient—Decide—Act. Each phase contains a number of sub-processes and the loop represents a recurring cycle where the actor's own action spurs the need for new observation, orientation, decision, and action.

8 Henrik Jedig Jørgensen, "No Hands – No Cookies," Paper presented at the ISA Conference, February 2010, 13.

9 Rob Huebert, "The Newly Emerging Arctic Security Environment," *Canadian Defence and Foreign Affairs Institute* (2010): 3–5; http://www.cdfai.org/PDF/The%20Newly%20Emerging%20Arctic%20Security%20Environment.pdf; accessed on December 20, 2012.

10 As specified in the Ottawa Declaration of 2004.

11 The original working groups were: Arctic Monitoring and Assessment Programme (AMAP), Conservation of Arctic Flora and Fauna (CAFF), Protection of the Arctic Maritime Environment (PAME), and Emergency Prevention, Preparedness and Response (EPPR).

12 Tromsø Declaration, April 29, 2009, 8; http://library.arcticportal.org/1253/1/Tromsoe_Declaration%2D1..pdf.

13 See: http://arctic-council.org/article/2007/11/common_priorities.

14 Tromsø Declaration, April 29, 2009, 8; http://library.arcticportal.org/1253/1/Tromsoe_Declaration%2D1..pdf.

15 *Berlingske Tidende*, March 31, 2010, an article by former Danish Minister of Foreign Affairs, Uffe Ellemann Jensen; http://uffeellemann.blogs.berlingske.dk/2010/03/31/%E2%80%9Darctic-5%E2%80%9D-%E2%80%93-et-dansk-initiativ-som-ikke-ma-tabes-pa-gulvet/; accessed on December 20, 2012.

16 Barry Scott Zellen, *Arctic Doom, Arctic Boom: The Geopolitics of Climate Change in the Arctic* (Santa Barbara, CA: Praeger, 2009), 103–9.

17 Ibid.

18 Ibid.

19 Norwegian, Danish, and Swedish Common Objectives for their Arctic Council Chairmanships 2006–12, Arctic Council website: http://arctic-council.org/article/2007/11/common_priorities; accessed on August 15, 2010.

20 "Arctic Summit Freezes Out Arctic Peoples and Three Nations," *SIKU News*, March 30, 2010; http://www.sikunews.com/News/International/Arctic-Summit-freezes-out-Arctic-peoples-and-three-nations-7352; accessed on August 28, 2010.

21 "Clinton's Arctic Comments Cheer Inuit," *CBC News*, March 31, 2010; http://www.cbc.ca/canada/story/2010/03/31/clinton-arctic.html; accessed on August 28, 2010.

REGIONAL PERSPECTIVES

Europe and the High North Atlantic

9. Structural, Environmental, and Political Conditions for Security Policy in the High North Atlantic: The Faroe Islands, Greenland, and Iceland[1]

Rasmus Gjedssø Bertelsen

1. Introduction

Security policy in the Faroe Islands, Greenland, and Iceland has historically taken place in a nexus of structural, environmental, and political conditions which pose particular challenges for such policy – a situation that continues and which will continue to take place. This chapter examines these conditions for broad security policy-making and implementation in the region in a historical, current, and future perspective.[2] It shows how these three societies have historically addressed and currently address security policy, where the experience of Iceland as the only fully independent state is enlightening. On this basis, the chapter discusses how these societies can address future developments with regard to climate change and increased self-government in the case of the Faroe Islands and Greenland, which is a central, but often overlooked, political development in the region. Security policy here is conceived broadly as covering the exercise of sovereignty, participation in international security orders such as NATO, well-grounded and researched debate and policy-making, law enforcement, intelligence, civil defense, marine resource management, environmental protection, provision of search and rescue, air and sea surveillance, among other issues.

This chapter identifies structural, environmental, and political conditions as well as public administration and finance challenges for security policy in section 2: *Conditions and Challenges for Security Policy in the Faroe Islands, Greenland, and Iceland.* The conditions are: microstates with very limited absolute capabilities, but responsibilities over vast strategically important air and sea spaces; Arctic and Subarctic climatic and geographic conditions, including climate change, which affects political and economic conditions and in turn increases strategic interest and pressure on the region; the geopolitical role of the region, including short-term political changes such as the U.S. withdrawal from the Keflavik base and long-term political changes, such as increasing Faroese and Greenlandic self-government and possible eventual independence from the Kingdom of Denmark.

There is, presently, one independent microstate, or very small state, Iceland, and two microsocieties, the Faroe Islands and Greenland, that are overseas autonomies of a small state, the Kingdom of Denmark. Despite their current absence of sovereignty, the Faroe Islands and Greenland are called microstates in this chapter in light of their historical movement toward greater self-government and possible full independence from the Kingdom of Denmark. The author defines microstates as less than 1 million inhabitants.[3] Such a capabilities-centered definition is valid for the purposes of this chapter. The term 'Kingdom of Denmark' is used for what in Danish is called "Rigsfællesskabet," the unity of Denmark, the Faroe Islands and Greenland under the crown. "Denmark" refers to the Continental European part of the kingdom.

Based on the above-mentioned conditions, public finance and administration as well as security policy challenges are identified (section 2, continued): these microstates have very narrow tax and personnel bases for supplying the means of security policy. Therefore, how can these microstates exercise effective sovereignty over vast, strategically important air and sea spaces; contribute to international security order; conduct well-grounded and researched debate and policy-making; protect society against terrorism, organized crime, and illegal trafficking; supply environmental protection and civil defense; provide search and rescue services, etc?

Iceland responds to these challenges through its security policy, and with expanding self-government and possible independence, the Faroe Islands and Greenland will have to design policies to do likewise (section 3: *Overview of Historic, Current, and Future Icelandic, Faroese, and Greenlandic Security Policies*). These case studies show how Iceland successfully has overcome the challenges to security policy-making through a combination of domestic capabilities and external partnerships, which is part of its successful independence. The Icelandic experience indicates ways for the Faroe Islands and Greenland to handle their security policy under changing conditions of both climate change and increasing self-government.

2. Conditions and Challenges for Security Policy in the Faroe Islands, Greenland, and Iceland

This chapter identifies a number of central structural, environmental, and political conditions for formulating and exercising security policy in the region of Greenland, Iceland, and the Faroe Islands. Based on these conditions, this chapter highlights intertwined public finance and administration as well as security policy challenges for the Faroe Islands, Greenland and Iceland.

Structural Conditions: Highly Developed, Strategically Located Microstates in the High North

The *structural conditions* are the combination of the small population sizes and the policy demands made on these highly developed microstates in the High North with vast, strategically important air and sea spaces with Arctic and Subarctic climatic and geographic conditions.

Iceland has a population of around 313,000, the Faroe Islands 48,000, and Greenland 56,000. All these societies are highly developed, thus, with large capabilities *relative* to their populations, but very limited capabilities in *absolute* terms. Highly developed states face largely similar policy tasks, which the less populated states have to face with less-absolute resources and smaller organizations and, thus, possibilities for specialization. A fascinating aspect of Icelandic government and society is how tasks are solved at very high levels of proficiency by very small public, private, and civil society organizations with limited internal possibilities for specialization. The level of proficiency is evident from Iceland's very high level of human development, ranking third globally in 2009.[4]

The term *microstate* is an important analytical category and should be used here, although it is sometimes substituted in political discourse by *small state*: the Faroe Islands, Greenland, and Iceland face different conditions than, for instance, Sweden with its population of around 9,045,000, which is a small state with a large territory including Arctic and Subarctic regions.

Environmental Conditions: Constant and Changing Climate with Social Consequences

The *environmental conditions* for North Atlantic security policy are both permanent and changing. Permanent environmental conditions include difficult Arctic and Subarctic climatic conditions as well as great distances over sea and ice (especially in the case of Greenland), which make all kinds of communication, transportation, projection of capabilities much more difficult and thus expensive. These conditions and the sheer distance of the region from areas of conflict kept the region out of European conflicts for centuries. Technological advances, especially in long-range flying during World War II and to even a greater extent during the Cold War, as well as in nuclear submarines, canceled those distances and integrated the region into global politics and conflict. This development led to an unprecedented militarization, which has, however, been replaced by greater cooperation after the Cold War.[5]

Other environmental conditions include abundant resources. Marine resources have caused conflict in the 1950s–1970s – most notably between Iceland and Britain, resolved through the international law of the sea. The region's rich renewable geothermal and hydroelectric energy resources and possibly hydrocarbons are drawing increasing attention and investment. Although difficult to export, the renewable energy resources are sought after as a response to greenhouse gases. This fact is clear from technology export and recent and proposed investments in power generation and energy-intensive aluminum and other industries in Iceland and Greenland. High, although volatile, oil prices also focus attention on possible hydrocarbon resources in the region, where, for instance, the United States Geological Survey predicts with varying probability around 51.8 billion barrels of oil and oil-equivalent natural gas around Greenland.[6]

The environmental conditions are also changing due to climate change, which is particularly pronounced in the High North. Global warming is affecting, for instance, the sea ice in the Arctic Ocean and is "very likely" to improve access to energy exploration and shipping.[7] Improved marine access may place these societies much more centrally in global energy and transportation systems than hitherto possible through oil and gas exploration in their economic exclusion zones or on their continental shelves, as well as through new trans-Arctic shipping lanes linking the North Atlantic and the North Pacific.[8]

Such changes will have profound social, political, and economic impacts. New economic opportunities fostered by climate change may contribute to increased Faroese and Greenlandic self-government and possible independence through reducing fiscal dependence on Denmark. Energy exploration and important shipping lanes for the global economy will also further increased outside strategic interest and pressure on the region.

Political Conditions: Superpower Interests, and Constitutional Ties to Denmark

As mentioned, technological developments have firmly integrated the North Atlantic and the Arctic in European, trans-Atlantic, and trans-Arctic geopolitics. Because of the location, the area cannot keep out of any conflict in Europe involving trans-Atlantic connections (as evident in WWII and the Cold War) or between North America and Eurasia (as the Cold War or future strategic competition between the United States and China, where the Arctic is the shortest route).

The areas concerned in this chapter are either overseas autonomies (the Faroe Islands and Greenland) of a small state (Kingdom of Denmark) or an independent microstate (Iceland). They all depend on the military protection of larger powers and alliances. This fact is reflected in the NATO membership of both the Kingdom of Denmark and Iceland and the U.S. bases in Greenland and, until 2006, Iceland.

The European Union plays a growing role in broader societal security questions and will take a greater interest in North Atlantic and Arctic affairs following increased energy exploration and shipping in the region. The relationship between Iceland, the Faroe Islands, and Greenland and the EU is, however, complicated. Iceland has stayed out of the union (while joining the Internal Market through the European Economic Area). The Faroe Islands did not follow Denmark into the European Community in 1973 and Greenland left the EC in 1985. The prospect of Icelandic EU membership is discussed below.

Short-term *political changes* have, for instance, included the U.S. withdrawal from the Keflavik base in Iceland in September 2006. This action removed the capabilities of a superpower from the region, leaving it in the hands of microstates (Faroe Islands, Greenland and Iceland) and a small state (Kingdom of Denmark). Iceland was forced to rethink its security policy in light of this loss of, for instance, search and rescue as well as air policing capabilities in the region, which led to innovative policy-making covering the entire spectrum of security policy that is further discussed below.

An overlooked, but an equally very important long-term *political change* in the region is increasing Faroese and Greenlandic self-government and possible independence from the Kingdom of Denmark. This development gradually transfers responsibility to these microstates and would ultimately remove the small state, the Kingdom of Denmark, with its naval and other capabilities from the region. Part of the success of independent Iceland has been to formulate and execute a successful security policy, and the Faroe Islands and Greenland must do the same in taking on greater and perhaps eventually full responsibility.

Public Finance and Administration Challenges: Few Taxpayers and Small Organizations

First of all, the complexity of the structural, climatic, and geographic conditions of microstates in the North Atlantic with vast strategically important air and sea spaces lead to the following public finance and administration dilemma: There is a narrow tax basis for large capital investments and expenditures to implement security policy, for example, ocean-going patrol vessels, surveillance aircraft, search and rescue helicopters, etc., not to mention any kind of combat forces.

Likewise, organizations are very small with limitations to their internal specialization, for instance, military assessments, law enforcement, and intelligence work. As an example, the reader can note that the Defense Department in the Icelandic Ministry of Foreign Affairs has a staff of now five, previously three, and in the aftermath of the U.S. withdrawal from Keflavik the U.S. negotiation team counted twenty-six, while the inter-ministerial Icelandic team counted nine.[9] The Foreign Ministry of the Faroe Islands has a staff of twenty-six also covering trade and tourism promotion.[10] The Directorate of Foreign Affairs of the Greenland Home Rule has a staff of 9 covering Arctic cooperation, EU, indigenous cooperation, the bilateral relations with the United States, foreign trade and promotion, and foreign and security policy.[11]

Because of the small absolute size of organizations, there are few opportunities to reap returns to scale. There are high average costs in operating patrol vessels, search and rescue helicopters, surveillance aircraft, which in larger organizations can be spread over more units (a problem which becomes more serious from the narrow tax basis). These microstates must therefore design policies to counter these public finance and administration challenges.

At the ideational level, values and preferences also condition the security policy-making of the societies in this chapter. All three societies have, on one hand, neutralist traditions and, on the other hand, no military traditions, which together works against the establishment of domestic military forces (for instance, in the Icelandic case after the U.S. exit from Keflavik in 2006 in the view of Alyson Bailes).

Security Policy Challenge: Limited Absolute Resources and Large Responsibilities

These public finance and administration challenges are the basis of a pivotal security policy challenge: how microstates with very limited absolute capabilities, but responsibility over vast, strategically important air and sea spaces, can pursue an effective security policy and thereby exercise effective sovereignty over this space; contribute to the international security order, such as NATO; conduct well-grounded and researched debate and policy-making; provide efficient law enforcement and intelligence against terrorism, organized crime, and trafficking; and provide environmental protection, search and rescue services?

A practical example of how the means of exercising effective sovereignty can be beyond the capabilities of a country is that Iceland does not field interceptor fighter jets to police its air space (and at the small state level, for instance, the Royal Danish Navy has abandoned submarines). Historically,

Iceland has relied on the United States to supply air policing through the bilateral U.S.–Icelandic Defense Agreement of 1951 and fighters stationed at the Keflavik base. Since the U.S. abandonment of the Keflavik base, Iceland has relied on NATO allies rotating fighter jets through Keflavik to provide such policing. This NATO policy is also pursued in the case of other member states with very limited absolute capabilities as Estonia, Latvia, Lithuania, Luxembourg, and Slovenia. These Icelandic and other historical and present arrangements are examples of how microstates must create policies around these challenges.

The microstates in this chapter have no military traditions, and because of their resource-base their military options are extremely limited. Therefore, they have to design policies to have civilian authorities carry out some military tasks and collaborate with foreign, military counterparts. Iceland has had to design specialized policies for its civilian authorities to work with allied military and intelligence authorities, which would otherwise be handled by a similar military or intelligence body.[12]

This security policy challenge of limited absolute resources and large responsibilities will be even greater for increasingly self-governing and perhaps eventually independent Faroe Islands and Greenland with their population bases of around 50,000 to 60,000 individuals or about one-sixth that of Iceland. This difference is sizeable, and the similarities between, on the one hand, the Faroe Islands and Greenland and, on the other hand, Iceland should not be overestimated either. Faroese and Greenlandic society today rely on the ships and helicopters of the 1st Squadron of the Royal Danish Navy, together with the overall security capabilities of the small state of the Kingdom of Denmark. Faroese and Greenlandic self-rule governments are becoming increasingly involved in security and defense policy. Increasingly self-governing and possibly fully independent Faroe Islands and Greenland will have to devise policies to replace those Danish assets and reach out to allies and partners in Europe, North America, and the North Atlantic.

3. Overview of Historic, Current, and Future Icelandic, Faroese, and Greenlandic Security Policies

The Faroe Islands, Greenland, and Iceland have all, throughout their history, had to address the security policy challenges outlined above and design policies around them. These historical, present, and possible future policy responses are outlined here. The Icelandic case is substantially longer than the Faroese or Greenlandic, since Iceland is the only one to have run the full course to independence. Therefore, Iceland is the only community to have had to design and implement the full range of security policy.

Iceland: Setting the Direction for North Atlantic Microstate Security Policy

The history of the independence politics of Iceland and how its foreign and security affairs have been managed at various stages of self-rule is of value for discussing current and future Faroese and Greenlandic self-rule and possible independence. The independence trajectory of Iceland has inspired Faroese independence politics in particular and is therefore important for understanding self-rule developments in the Faroe Islands and Greenland.

The Viking settlers of Iceland in the 800s and 900s (AD) formed an independent commonwealth, which in 1262 was absorbed by the Kingdom of Norway. In 1380 the Kingdom of Denmark and the Kingdom of Norway merged under a common king, which brought Iceland, Greenland, the Faroe Islands, Shetland, and Orkney into this union. In 1814, Norway was forced into a union with Sweden at the Kiel peace after the Napoleonic wars but left the Faroe Islands, Greenland, and Iceland under the Danish crown. In 1845, the Viking age assembly, the Althingi, was reconstituted as a consultative assembly to the absolutist king of Denmark, and in 1874 it gained legislative, budgetary, and taxation powers over domestic affairs, leaving the executive under Danish administration. In 1904, Iceland gained home rule with an Icelandic executive under an Icelandic minister responsible to the Althingi.[13]

The Kingdom of Iceland emerged as a sovereign independent state in 1918 tied to the Kingdom of Denmark in a personal union of a common king. Denmark willingly agreed to this step to press rights of self-determination for Danes in North Schleswig under German rule in view of the World War I settlement. This acquiescence is an example how Denmark will give up sovereignty in the North Atlantic for interests closer to home. The Kingdom of Denmark executed the foreign affairs of the Kingdom of Iceland and represented it diplomatically, but the foreign policy was set by parliament in Reykjavik, which, for instance, chose not to enter the League of Nations for neutrality reasons. This personal union was mutually dissolvable after twenty-five years, and in 1944 Iceland dissolved the union and declared the republic. The Kingdom of Denmark played no role in the foreign or security affairs of Iceland after the German occupation of Denmark on April 9, 1940.[14] The Danish-Norwegian navy had operated sporadically in the North Atlantic since the late 1500s, exercising Danish-Norwegian sovereignty. With home rule in 1904, Denmark decided to build the first purpose-built inspection vessel, Islands Falk, completed in 1906. In 1913, the Althingi adopted the law on the Coast Guard Fund laying the financial ground for Icelandic coastguard activity. With the union treaty of 1918, coastguard duties were carried out by the Kingdom of Denmark until the Kingdom of Iceland would take them over, which was expected. The Royal Danish Navy continued some inspection duties around Iceland until 1940. In 1919, Althingi adopted legislation authorizing the leasing or buying of coastguard vessels. The Fisheries Association of the Westman Islands south of Iceland bought a used trawler in 1924 as a rescue and support vessel, Þór, which quickly became sponsored by the Icelandic state as a coastguard ship and armed in 1924. In 1924, the first purpose-built Icelandic coastguard vessel, Óðinn, was commissioned in Denmark and entered service in 1926. The Icelandic coastguard was particularly successful in enforcing Icelandic jurisdiction over territorial waters and the economic exclusion zone in the cod wars with the UK in 1958, 1972, and 1975.[15]

Michael Corgan in his overview of Icelandic security policy[16] since the settlement of the island in the late 800s shows the core security policy to have been the sheer distance from European conflicts. Internal Icelandic conflict, however, opened the door to Norwegian domination in 1262. This security through distance was fundamentally broken during World War II by technological advances in long-range flying, making Iceland a strategically vital location for control over North Atlantic air and sea space and the connection between North America and Europe. This development led to first British and shortly thereafter American occupation of Iceland during World War II.

Iceland's strategic importance increased further with the onset of the Cold War. Icelandic political leaders addressed this strategic pressure through continued partnership with the United States regarding the airfield at Keflavik, its founding membership in NATO, and the bilateral U.S.–Icelandic defense agreement from 1951, basing troops and aircraft at Keflavik. This policy firmly placed Iceland under the protection of the United States against covert or overt Soviet pressure. In addition, the base earned valuable foreign currency for Iceland, and the search and rescue helicopter assets were valuable additions to Icelandic emergency services.

The base was also an extremely contentious element in Icelandic politics and society and was seen by many as a threat to cultural and linguistic uniqueness. Corgan explains well to readers unfamiliar with Icelandic society and history the concern of this society to preserve its language and culture. This concern is a *de facto* security policy concern for Icelanders as well as other nations and groups with small populations. The development and preservation of the language and culture of a very small society is a particular challenge. The Icelandic nation has been particularly successful in this endeavor through a consistent linguistic policy of creating logical Icelandic words for new terms. This policy has the democratic advantage that a new word through its components ought to be understandable to any speaker of the language without the educational background to know the meaning of the ancient Greek or Latin words behind many words in other Western languages.

For Iceland, being a microstate with very small institutions (though very competent, proven by the nation's very high level of human development) and with no military heritage, hampers domestic debate and policy-making. Corgan shows the value of the development of indigenous security policy and research institutions for Icelandic debate and policy-making as well as for creating a native vocabulary in the field: the parliamentary Icelandic Commission on Security and International Affairs and the Department of Defense Affairs in the Ministry of Foreign Affairs since 1979. Creating a native security policy and strategic studies vocabulary was a particular challenge because of the lack of military tradition, small, less-specialized organizations and the linguistic "defense" policy. Corgan shows the importance of such a native vocabulary and how, especially, the above-mentioned parliamentary commission contributed to the development of this vocabulary and broader knowledge of these questions. Since the end of the Cold War and the U.S. withdrawal from Keflavik, the demand for renewed debate and analysis has reappeared. A security studies institute was agreed to by the Conservative–Social Democratic government (2007–2009), which, however, did not materialize. The threat assessment commission established by the then foreign minister has been inactive and has not delivered any report.

These lessons are extremely relevant for the Faroe Islands and Greenland, facing identical structural and historical conditions as microstates with little, if any, military heritage. They must develop such vocabularies in Faroese and Greenlandic together with domestic expertise. The Faroese can, because of close linguistic ties, benefit much from the Icelandic efforts. The Greenlandic efforts can hopefully contribute to Inuit empowerment around the North Pole.

The 2006 U.S. withdrawal from Keflavik was a shock to Icelandic security policy and forced Icelandic authorities to undertake a wide-ranging review of security policy, organization, and capabilities, which is the topic of Gunnar Þór Bjarnason's study.[17] When the U.S. government informed the Icelandic government on March 15, 2006, that it would withdraw its four fighters with search and rescue helicopter support from Keflavik before the end of September of that year, it was a major defeat for Icelandic policy. The conservative Independence Party-led governments since the end of the Cold War had averted U.S. disengagement from Keflavik and maintained the twin aim of avoiding unilateral U.S. decisions and maintaining U.S. air defense capabilities at Keflavik. The U.S. decision was a negation of both aims.

This new situation forced the Icelandic government and authorities to review organization, legislation, and capabilities with substantial development and innovation of Iceland's broad security policy, authorities, and capabilities. Initially, Minister of Justice and Ecclesiastical Affairs Björn Bjarnason seized the initiative in the policy response to the U.S. exit. Bjarnason was a central and internationally well-connected, security policy-maker for many years and a leading personality on these questions in the pro-U.S. and pro-NATO Independence Party. In the 2007–2009 Independence Party–Social Democratic coalition, the foreign minister was Ingibjörg Sólrún Gísladóttir from the pro-EU Socialdemocratic Alliance. These two individuals and their ministries were the main actors and competitors responding to the U.S. withdrawal and the response was divided between their organizations.[18]

Under the Ministry of Foreign Affairs, the Icelandic Defense Agency was established with the first defense policy act from April 2008. The agency's main task is operating the Icelandic Air Defense System with the NATO radar installations in the country. In addition, the agency maintains the security area at Keflavik reserved for visiting NATO forces, collaboration with NATO, and other defense and security-related tasks. This situation is an example of a civilian authority conducting the affairs of a military or a ministry of defense. In the absence of an Icelandic military, practical security and defense policy is divided between the Ministry of Foreign Affairs and the Ministry of Justice and Human Rights.

The domestic security functions under the then Ministry of Justice and Ecclesiastical Affairs, now the Ministry of Justice and Human Rights, were particularly developed. The police services and Icelandic Coast Guard fall under this ministry. A driving force here was that the search and rescue capabilities of U.S. forces at Keflavik would no longer support the Icelandic Coast Guard and other emergency services.[19] Revised civil defense legislation established a Security and Civil Defense Council responsible for policy, composed by the prime minister (chair), the minister of Justice and Ecclesiastical Affairs, minister of Transportation, minister of Environment, minister of Health, minister of Foreign Affairs, and minister of Industry, together with relevant senior civil servants and heads of agencies. The legislation also established a new coordination and control center for all civil defense and search and rescue work, bringing together relevant authorities and emergency services supported by a new Tetra communications system.

The Coast Guard leased new helicopters, acquired a new DASH 8 Q300 surveillance aircraft, and commissioned a new ship. The national police has established an intelligence analysis unit. A North Atlantic Coast Guard Forum has been established inspired by its namesake in the North Pacific collaborating on security issues as illegal migration and drug trafficking, fisheries, environment, and search and rescue. Icelandic Minister of Justice and Ecclesiastical Affairs, Björn Bjarnason, suggested developing this Forum into a standing multilateral coast guard force in the area. The domestic security functions have close cooperation and joint contingency plans and have established cooperation with their sister organizations in neighboring states, in particular Norway, Denmark, Britain, and the United States.[20]

Climate change presents Iceland with both challenges and opportunities. As a highly developed country, Iceland is seeking to reduce its greenhouse gas emissions. Climate change in the Arctic may affect Iceland profoundly, socially and environmentally, for instance, through the reduction of sea ice cover giving access to increased energy exploration throughout the Arctic or to trans-Arctic shipping. Increased energy production in Siberia has resulted in greatly increased oil- and gas-tanker traffic through Icelandic waters to markets in North America. This traffic carries potentially great environmental hazards in case of accidents and oil-spills.[21]

The long-term opportunities for trans-Arctic shipping between the North Pacific and the North Atlantic have raised significant attention from the Icelandic government evidenced in the detailed 2005 report *Fyrir stafni haf: Tækifæri tengd siglingum á Norðurslóðum* (*Open Sea Ahead: Possibilities regarding Navigation in the Arctic*) and the 2007 international stakeholder conference *Ísinn brotinn: Þróun norðurskautssvæðisins og sjóflutningar* (*Breaking the Ice: Arctic Developments and Maritime Transportation*). The Icelandic authorities see a number of environmental and socio-economic drivers pushing for trans-Arctic international shipping in the future: The fundamental environmental driver for the socio-economic drivers is climate change, where the extent of sea ice cover in the Arctic Ocean over the summer is significantly reduced and predicted to be reduced much further and thickness of ice throughout the year as well.[22] The socio-economic drivers are the growth in world trade, which is mainly shipborne, and energy and mineral exploration in the Arctic. The world economy is dominated by the North Atlantic and North Pacific areas, where the Northern Sea Route along the Siberian coast and the Northwest Passage north of Canada are the shortest connecting routes. The present gateways through the Panama and the Suez canals are used close to capacity and limit the future use of very large vessels, while there are no limitations in the Arctic Ocean. Significant advances in ship building technology allow for ships to break through single-year ice without icebreaker support.[23]

These environmental and socio-economic drivers have converged in Iceland to the formulation of a vision to make Iceland the North Atlantic trans-shipment facility at one end of the trans-Arctic route. The vision is a shuttle service by Arctic purpose-built ships between Iceland and, for instance, the Aleutian Islands, which would be serviced by normal ships serving respectively the North Atlantic and the North Pacific.[24]

The EU is playing a greater role in societal security. Iceland has, in the wake of the financial crisis and the challenges of operating a very small independent currency, submitted a membership application to the EU, and the formal negotiation process has begun. However, only one party in the parliament, Althingi, the ruling Socialdemocratic Alliance, is wholeheartedly behind the application. The public has turned increasingly and decisively against EU membership since autumn 2008.[25] The main argument for EU membership was joining the Euro, but the sharp depreciation of the Icelandic Króna helped much in turning around the Icelandic trade deficit and improving competitiveness under the financial crisis and has greatly helped Iceland recover from the crisis.. There are two classic explanations for Iceland remaining outside the EU which still apply: the material unacceptability of the Common Fisheries Policy for a country basing its economy on fisheries, and the rhetorical unacceptability of ceding sovereignty to a supranational body for a country which has gained independence after centuries of foreign rule.[26] A recent and influential reason for voter rejection of the EU is the Icesave conflict over deposit insurance of British and Dutch depositors in Landsbankinn, where the United Kingdom and the Netherlands backed by the EU coerced Iceland into politically taking on the Icesave obligations.[27]

The European Commission published a communication to the European Parliament and Council on November 20, 2008, on *The European Union and the Arctic Region* in response to the European Parliament Resolution of October 9, 2008, on Arctic governance.[28] This communication addressed three areas of engagement in the Arctic for the EU: 1) protecting and preserving the Arctic in unison with its population; 2) promoting sustainable use of resources; and 3) contributing to enhanced multilateral Arctic governance. The utility of this EU strategy for Iceland was subsequently set out in a Ministry of Foreign Affairs note. Iceland noted the interest of the European Commission in trans-Arctic shipping, where Iceland sees great prospects for providing trans-shipment. The Icelandic Ministry of Foreign Affairs concluded that Iceland as an EU member would be the gateway of the EU toward the Arctic Ocean and expected increased European investments in Iceland in. Arctic research, energy exploration, and transportation in connection with resource exploitation in the Arctic and new navigation routes. There is no trace in the EU Commission communication of the EU taking on traditional security responsibilities, which NATO currently covers. Concerning immigration and law-enforcement, Iceland has been a member of the Schengen area since 2001 with access to common databases, etc.

Faroe Islands: Broad-Spectrum Security Concept and Partnership with Denmark

The Faroe Islands were also settled by Viking settlers and eventually absorbed by the Kingdom of Norway around 1035, and thus eventually coming under the Danish-Norwegian crown. Independence-minded Faroese have always looked to Iceland and there were family ties between independence political families in the two societies around 1900 when Iceland gained home rule. The Faroe Islands were fully integrated as a county in Denmark, and the ancient assembly and court of law, the Løgting, was reconstituted in 1852 as a consultative and later county assembly.[29]

The Faroe Islands were equally drawn into European conflict during World War II and occupied by Britain because of their strategic location in the North Atlantic. After the war, the Faroe Islands remained in the Kingdom of Denmark, gaining home rule in many domestic issues in 1948, forty-four years after Iceland, with the Løgting as legislative assembly. The Faroese home rule act excludes the constitution of the Kingdom of Denmark, citizenship, monetary affairs, and foreign, defense, and security policy. The act divides between *A* and *B* areas of legislation, where the Løgting could take over the *A* items at its own or Danish request, and which especially cover social policy, health care, business, education, and infrastructure. The *B* items, covering, of relevance here, police, radio, air traffic, and natural resources, could be taken over by mutual agreement. This constitutional status left security policy, including law enforcement and intelligence matters, in the hands of government authorities in Copenhagen, and integrated the Faroe Islands together with the Kingdom of Denmark into NATO during the Cold War.[30]

In 2005, an expansion of the existing 1948 home rule legislation was adopted in equal partnership between the Kingdom of Denmark and the Faroe Islands, whereby the Faroe Islands can take over all issue areas except the constitution, citizenship, the Supreme Court, and foreign, security, and defense policy as well as currency and monetary policy. The only areas of relevance here that the Faroe Islands have not taken over are police and air traffic. At the same time, legislation was passed, which authorizes the Faroe Islands to enter into international agreements on issues it has taken over and opens the possibility for Faroese membership of international organizations in areas covered by self-rule.[31]

During World War II, Britain established a LORAN radio navigation station in the islands, which Britain, the United States, and others were keen to maintain after the war. Copenhagen was keen to keep foreign forces out of the Faroe Islands, so the Royal Danish Navy took over the station despite great technical difficulty and established a previously unseen level of presence in the islands. As with Greenland and Iceland, the Faroe Islands were important for NATO to close the Greenland-Iceland-United Kingdom (GIUK) gap to keep the Soviet navy out of the North Atlantic and protect trans-Atlantic lines of communication. The Royal Danish Air Force operated a NATO radar facility at Sornfelli from 1963 to 2007. Today, the Royal Danish Navy usually has an inspection vessel of the Thetis class (112 m long) with helicopter in the area. The Faroese home rule government through Faroese Islands Fisheries Inspections operate the two patrol and rescue vessels *Brimil* (60 m long) and *Tjaldrið* (42 m long), and the national carrier, Atlantic Airways, has a Bell 412 helicopter on 24/7 standby for search and rescue work.[32]

The Faroese parliament, Løgtingið, has on several occasions since 1940 expressed a stand emphasizing keeping the Faroe Islands out of international conflict and keeping military forces out of the islands. Danish and NATO military activities were only partially disclosed to Faroese authorities according to Jákup Thorsteinsson's 1999 report on the Faroe Islands during the Cold War. The Faroese self-rule government does not refer to security policy on its website, unlike the Greenlandic, which points to the lack of a common strategic culture among Iceland, the Faroe Islands, and Greenland. This lack is an important hurdle to overcome in the development of broad security policy in the region. The Løgting today adapts a broad security concept and is concerned with topics such as organized crime and trafficking. In the modernization of the Faroese home rule in 2005, it was emphasized in the Danish-Faroese legislation that foreign, defense, and security policy does not fall under the home rule. On the other hand, the Kingdom of Denmark and the Faroe Islands agreed to involve the Faroe Islands as an equal partner in foreign and security policy deliberations concerning the islands.[33]

Faroese society bears resemblance to Iceland culturally and historically. Both are descendants of Viking settlers in the 800s with mutually intelligible languages. Socially, both are highly developed microstates and knowledge-based societies with roots in fisheries and sheep farming. They share political and historical roots as North Atlantic autonomies of the Kingdom of Denmark, and possible Faroese independence is likely to follow a path similar to that which led to Icelandic independence, with sovereignty in a union as Iceland between 1918 and 1940/1944. The Danish-Icelandic union was clearly the inspiration for the Faroese proposal in 1998 for Faroese sovereignty in a personal union with Denmark. This proposal fell on unresolved Faroese fiscal dependency on Denmark, which seems the stumbling block for further or full independence for now. In the Løgting, independence-minded parties, Tjóðveldi (8), Fólkaflokkurin (7) and Miðflokkurin (3), have a slight majority out of thirty-three members.

Security policy-making and implementation in the Faroe Islands will continue to face the public finance and administration dilemmas identified above. These dilemmas exist for current policy carried out under self-rule, such as fisheries inspection, and will be accentuated by taking over important areas as law enforcement and air traffic, as is predicted in current self-rule legislation. These dilemmas will also be accentuated by increased energy exploration and shipping, which, however, also gives economic opportunities for further self-government. As in the Icelandic case, these dilemmas must be faced through a combination of developing domestic capabilities, organizations, policies, and vocabulary to the possible extent and building outside alliances for addressing tasks beyond domestic capabilities. Increased regional collaboration and integration through, for instance, joint deployment of assets, procurement, maintenance, and training may ameliorate these dilemmas by expanding the basis of organizations and the organizations themselves allowing for greater efficiency, returns to scale, and specialization.

The Faroe Islands can replicate Iceland with domestic civilian security, law enforcement, and coast guard organizations. For replacing the assets of the Kingdom of Denmark, the Faroe Islands can also replicate Iceland with NATO membership with security guarantees and air policing directly from Britain or Norway. The importance of the GIUK gap depends on the state of the international system. Today, the gap is of little importance as reflected in the closure of the Royal Danish Air Force Sornfelli NATO radar station. If the gap regains importance and the Faroe Islands have gained independence, the Faroe Islands could replicate the Icelandic Defense Agency establishing civilian air surveillance integrated into NATO.

Greenland: North American Security and U.S.–Danish–Greenlandic Relations

Greenland straddles circumpolar Inuit and Nordic culture and history. Inuit have migrated from North America to Greenland since prehistoric times. Norse settlers arrived in the Viking age from Iceland and were absorbed in the Kingdom of Norway, but disappeared in the Middle Ages. Danish-Norwegian missionary Hans Egede arrived in Greenland in 1721 to rediscover the Norse and reassert the Danish-Norwegian claim to Greenland. Greenland remained a colony of the Kingdom of Denmark until it was integrated on an equal standing in the kingdom as a county in 1953, the old status of both Iceland and the Faroe Islands. In 1979, Greenland gained home rule similar to Faroese home rule, seventy-five years after Iceland and thirty-one years after the Faroe Islands.[34]

Greenland's steady movement to greater self-government and a more independent role in the world is clear, as with the Faroe Islands. In 2005, the Kingdom of Denmark and Greenland agreed – as in the Faroese case – to grant Greenland the right to enter into agreements with foreign countries and international organizations on issues Greenland had taken over. Greenland also received the right to join international organizations in these domains, usually as associate member. In 2009, the Kingdom of Denmark and Greenland agreed on self-rule for Greenland, which recognizes the Greenlanders as a people under international law, awards the rights to natural resources to Greenland, and gives the self-rule government the right to take over all issue areas except the constitution, citizenship, currency and monetary policy, and foreign, defense, and security policy. The areas Greenland can and desires to take over in due course involve important broad security policy areas such as police, justice, immigration, transportation, and other areas. The self-rule agreement explicitly grants Greenland the right to pursue full independence and thus shows Danish acceptance of this goal. The self-rule agreement received 75.5 per cent support in a referendum in Greenland on November 25, 2008, showing the strong popular support for increased self-government.[35]

Greenland has played a key role in North Atlantic and North American security since its occupation by U.S. forces during World War II, the U.S.–Danish agreement on the defense of Greenland from 1941, and the defense agreement from 1951. The United States kept forces and facilities in a number of bases in Greenland. Today, the only facility is the Thule radar, which is part of the National Missile Defense project, showing the continued central strategic role of Greenland. The Royal Danish Navy operates inspection vessels of the Thetis class with helicopters and the patrol vessel class Knud Rasmussen, and the national carrier, Air Greenland, has a fleet of fifteen helicopters.[36]

The Greenland home rule government has been keen to take a greater and equal role in the foreign, defense, and security policy deliberations concerning the island. Whereas the Faroe Islands seem concerned with a broad spectrum of security challenges, Greenland is focused on the U.S.–Danish–Greenlandic relationship and the presence of U.S. forces in Greenland. In addition, Greenland is focused on developing its relations with the United

States in other areas, such as economic development, science, and education, etc., which are seen as important to socio-economic development, the pre-condition for independence.

An important achievement for Greenland was the U.S.–Danish–Greenlandic foreign ministers' meeting at Igaliku in Southern Greenland on August 6, 2004. Here, Colin Powell, Per Stig Møller, and Josef Motzfeld agreed on involving the Greenland home rule government and authorities in the hitherto bilateral U.S.–Danish relationship regarding the defense agreement and the U.S. forces in Greenland. This agreement was a Greenlandic condition for allowing the upgrade of the Thule radar for the National Missile Defense project. In addition, the parties made joint declarations on the environmental aspects of the U.S. presence in Greenland and economic and technical cooperation between the United States and Greenland with a tripartite joint committee to support this collaboration.[37]

Greenland is keenly pursuing increased energy and mineral exploration, where offshore hydrocarbon resources are seen as a way to replace financial support from the Kingdom of Denmark and thus pave the way for greater and eventually, full independence.[38] Large incomes from hydrocarbon exploitation may supply the financial basis for increased and perhaps full Greenlandic independence but does not solve the public administration dilemma pointed out in this chapter of very small organizations with very limited possibilities for specialization. Greenland is also much more dependent on trained civil servants, etc., from Denmark than the Faroe Islands. Greenland needs to achieve a higher level of education through both domestic efforts and studies abroad, where Iceland is a successful example of transferring much knowledge and technology through education abroad.

As pointed out by Corgan, domestic security policy expertise and vocabulary is vital for informed debate and policy-making. The Faroe Islands and Greenland must (to the extent they have not done so already) follow in the footsteps of Iceland and develop the domestic vocabularies and expertise to assess military, strategic, and other security issues. An important challenge and aim will be to develop a common regional strategic culture of security and surveillance for a common space increasingly exploited for energy and marine resources and traversed by international shipping rather than Cold War standoffs. Existing organizations can help in forming the relationships to create such a common strategic culture, such as the West Nordic Council, the Nordic Council, and the Arctic Council. The West Nordic Council chose safety at sea and international cooperation for its thematic conference in 2008 and made recommendations to the Nordic Council.

Increased Greenlandic self-government and possible independence will be highly dependent on the ability to create and staff highly qualified indigenous organizations and services such as bureaucracies, coast guard, and law-enforcement. As in the case of the Faroe Islands, Greenland will, with growing self-government and perhaps full independence, have to combine solving some security policy tasks domestically and others in collaboration with outside parties, as is the case currently with the Kingdom of Denmark. Greenland could and is expected to remain a member of NATO with a bilateral defense agreement with the United States and to host the U.S. Air Force base at Thule. Such an arrangement would supply the guarantees of Greenland's defense and could supply other assets. Only the U.S. commitment to the security of the region can assure convincing escalation domination against Russia, and, in the future, China. Futhermore, large-scale civilian emergencies will be outside the capabilities of the present and future actors in the region and will demand outside assistance. Greenland is also expected to work closely with Canada concerning the Northwest Passage.

Regarding Denmark's interest in North Atlantic security, it must, first of all, be emphasized that the only reason for Denmark's involvement in the Arctic and North Atlantic is naturally the Faroe Islands and Greenland being part of the Kingdom of Denmark. The day these societies might gain full independence from the kingdom, Denmark will, in all likelihood, be as completely removed from their security policy as it is from that of Iceland (apart from cooperation because of the Faroe Islands and Greenland or NATO collaboration). Denmark will remain involved during a time of union, as with Iceland between 1918 and 1940.

It is clear from current Danish foreign and security policy that its primary defense interest is in combat-like operations in areas such as the Middle East, Central Asia, and the Horn of Africa, etc. These are the missions of the future for the Danish military and the Royal Danish Navy, rather than its rich North Atlantic history, which in all likelihood will end with the possible independence of the Faroe Islands and Greenland. There is no reason to believe there will be political will or interest in Denmark to maintain – and certainly not renew – the present significant Danish Arctic naval capabilities in the event of Faroese and Greenlandic independence.

Conclusion: Smart Microstate Solutions of Small Domestic Organizations and Outside Collaboration

Security policy-making and implementation in the North Atlantic region of Greenland, Iceland, and the Faroe Islands take place under demanding structural, environmental, and political conditions, which cause significant public finance and administration and security policy challenges. This chapter identifies these conditions and challenges, describes how these three microstates historically and currently address these conditions and challenges, and points toward future environmental and socio-political developments.

The structural conditions are that the Faroe Islands, Greenland, and Iceland all are highly developed microstates, thus with large relative but limited absolute capabilities. These conditions are intensified by the difficult Arctic and Subarctic environmental, such as climatic and geographic, conditions, which make communication, transportation, and projection of capabilities difficult and expensive. Environmental conditions are changing with climate change, where, for instance, melting sea ice is very likely to improve access to oil and gas exploration and trans-Arctic shipping. These processes may further Faroese and Greenlandic self-government and possible independence through economic opportunities but will also increase outside strategic interest and pressure on the region. Political conditions are changing with, in the short term, the U.S. abandonment of the Keflavik base, which removed the capabilities of a superpower leaving behind three microstates and a small state. In the longer term, a crucial political change in the region will be increased Faroese and Greenlandic self-government and perhaps eventual independence from the Kingdom of Denmark.

Based on these conditions, the three microstates face the public finance challenge of a very narrow tax basis for the capital investments and expenditures of security policy as ocean-going patrol vessels, search and rescue helicopters, and surveillance aircraft. Equally, they face the public administration challenge of very small organizations with limited possibilities for specialization, for instance, in strategy, law enforcement, and intelligence. This complex of conditions and challenges pose the security policy challenge of how these three microstates with large, strategically important air and sea space can pursue security policies to effectively exercise sovereignty; contribute to international security; conduct well-grounded and researched debate and policy-making; protect society from organized crime, illegal trafficking, or terrorism; and provide search and rescue as well as environmental protection.

Iceland has successfully faced these challenges, which is part of its successful independence. The Faroe Islands and Greenland must equally formulate and implement successful security policies as part of increasing self-government and possible eventual independence. Sheer distance and difficult environmental conditions isolated the region from international conflict until World War II and the Cold War. NATO membership and the U.S. presence at Keflavik, together with domestic capabilities addressed Iceland's security needs during the Cold War and fifteen years after. The U.S. withdrawal from Keflavik forced Iceland to review its security policy, legislation, and capabilities. The Faroe Islands and Greenland benefit from Danish capabilities, which they will have to design policies to replace under greater self-government and responsibilities and possible full independence.

The public finance and administration and ultimately, security policy challenges addressed in this chapter are not unique to the North Atlantic. The Caribbean, the Pacific, and the Indian oceans all have island states with very limited absolute capabilities while they have very large air and sea space with serious security issues in areas such as illegal trafficking. If the very small societies in the North Atlantic can present innovative and smart solutions to address and overcome these challenges, these societies can make a unique and important contribution to security policy-making and implementation of countries with very limited absolute resources, especially island nations, around the world.

Notes

1 This paper previously appeared in *Strategic Insights* 9, no. 2 (2010): 26–52; https://calhoun.nps.edu/public/bitstream/handle/10945/11518/SI_V9_I2_2010_Bertelsen_26.pdf?sequence=1.

2 I thank the following for their valuable comments: the participants at the 5th Open Assembly of the Northern Research Forum, Anchorage, September 24–27, 2008; the Arctic Science Summit Week, Bergen, March 23–28, 2009; the postdoctoral conference 'Many Faces of Security in a World of Complex Threats,' Stiftung Wissenschaft und Politik, Berlin, September 16–17, 2009; the United Nations University Institute of Advanced Studies research dialogue, April 7, 2010; and the International Polar Year Oslo Science Conference, Oslo, June

6–12, 2010; The Icelandic Minister of Justice and Ecclesiastical Affairs Björn Bjarnason, Head of Department Þórunn Hafsteinn, Icelandic Ministry of Justice and Ecclesiastical Affairs, Director Inuuteq Holm Olsen, Greenland Self Rule government, Herálvur Joensen, Representative of the Faroe Islands in Copenhagen, Associate Professor Michael Corgan, Boston University, and Visiting Professor Alyson Bailes, University of Iceland.

3 Dag Anckar, "Regime Choices in Microstates: The Cultural Constraint," *Commonwealth and Comparative Politics* 42, no. 2 (2004): 206–23.

4 "Human Development Report 2009 – HDI Rankings," in United Nations Development Programme [database online]. [cited 2010]. Available from http://hdr.undp.org/en/statistics/.

5 Michael T. Corgan, *Iceland and Its Alliances: Security for a Small State* (Lewiston, NY: Edwin Mellen Press, 2002), 270; Jóannes Eidesgaard, *Uppskot til samtyktar um trygdarpolitikk Føroya* (*Statement on Faroese Security Policy*), April 13, 2004; Lassi Heininen, *Geopolitics of a Changing North*, position paper for the 5th NRF Open Assembly, September 24–27, 2008 (Anchorage, AK: 2008); Oran R. Young, "Whither the Arctic? Conflict or Cooperation in the Circumpolar North," *Polar Record* 44 (2008): 1–10; Willy Østreng, *Extended Security and Climate Change in the Regional and Global Context: A Historical Account*, position paper for the seminar "The Politics of the Eurasian Arctic: National Interests and International Challenges," Ocean Futures and the Northern Research Forum, Oslo, June 24, 2008 (Oslo, 2008).

6 United States Geological Survey, *Circum-Arctic Resource Appraisal: Estimates of Undiscovered Oil and Gas North of the Arctic Circle* (Menlo Park, CA: United States Geological Survey, 2008).

7 Arctic Climate Impact Assessment, *Impacts of a Warming Arctic: Arctic Climate Impact Assessment*, 1st ed. (Cambridge: Cambridge University Press, 2004).

8 Trausti Valsson, *How the World Will Change with Global Warming* (Reykjavik: University of Iceland Press, 2006), 156; Barry Zellen, *Arctic Doom, Arctic Boom: The Geopolitics of Climate Change in the Arctic* (Santa Barbara, CA: Praeger, 2009), 232.

9 Gunnar Þór Bjarnason, *Óvænt áfall eða fyrirsjáanleg tímamót? Brottför Bandaríkjahers frá Íslandi: aðdragandi og viðbrögð* (*Unexpected Shock or Predictable Turning Point? the Departure of the U.S. Military from Iceland: Antecedents and Responses*) (Reykjavík: Háskólaútgáfan, 2008), 168.

10 "Starvsfólk í heimatænastuni (Personnel in the home service)," in Uttanríkisráðið [database online]. Tórshavn [cited 2010].

11 "Ansatte i Udenrigsdirektoratet (Personnel in the Directorate of Foreign Affairs)," in Grønlands Selvstyre [database online]. Nuuk, August 5, 2010, [cited 2010]. Available from http://dk.nanoq.gl/Emner/Landsstyre/Departementer/Landsstyreformandens%20Departement/Udenrigsdirektoratet/Ansatte.aspx.

12 "Okkar ábyrgð – öryggi og varnir Íslendingar: Erindi á fundi Samtaka um vestræna samvinnu og Varðberg, 29. mars, 2007(Our Responsibility – Security and Defense of the Icelandic Nation: Speech at Icelandic Atlantic Association Varðberg)," in Björn Bjarnason [database online]. 2007 [cited 2008]. Available from http://www.bjorn.is/greinar/2007/03/29/nr/3960; "Viðtækar öryggisráðstafanir: Kynning fyrir starfshóp utanríkisráðherra um hættumat 13. desember 2007 (Extensive security precautions: Presentation for the minister of foreign affairs' working group on risk assessment December 13, 2007)," in Björn Bjarnason [database online]. [cited 2008]. Available from http://www.bjorn.is/greinar/2007/12/13/nr/4284.

13 Jóhannes Nordal and Valdimar Kristinsson, eds., *Iceland, the Republic:*

Handbook (Reykjavik: Central Bank of Iceland, 1996).

14 Ibid.

15 "Saga LHG (History of the Icelandic Coast Guard)," in Landhelgisgæsla Íslands [database online]. Reykjavik [cited 2010]. Available from http://www.lhg.is/sagan/.

16 Corgan, *Iceland and Its Alliances*, 270.

17 Bjarnason, *Óvænt áfall eða fyrirsjáanleg tímamót? Brottför Bandaríkjahers frá Íslandi: aðdragandi og viðbrögð (Unexpected Shock or Predictable Turning Point? The Departure of the U.S. Military from Iceland: Antecedents and Responses)*, 168.

18 Alyson J.K. Bailes, and Th. F. Gylfason, "'Societal Security' and Iceland," *Stjórnmál og Stjórnsysla* 2008/1, University of Iceland; http://www.stjornmalogstjornsysla. is/?p=369.

19 Bjarnason, *Óvænt áfall eða fyrirsjáanleg tímamót? Brottför Bandaríkjahers frá Íslandi: aðdragandi og viðbrögð (Unexpected Shock or Predictable Turning Point? The Departure of the U.S. Military from Iceland: Antecedents and Responses)*, 168.

20 "The Civilian Role in Safety in the North Atlantic: 2008 Conference of Arctic Parliamentarians, Fairbanks, Alaska, 11 to 14 August," in Björn Bjarnason [database online]. August 12, 2008 [cited 2009]. Available from http://www. bjorn.is/greinar/nr/4579; Bjarnason, *Víðtækar öryggisráðstafanir: Kynning fyrir starfshóp utanríkisráðherra um hættumat 13. desember 2007 (Extensive Security Precautions: Presentation for the Minister of Foreign Affairs' Working Group on Risk Assessment 13 December 2007)*; ibid; "Iceland and the Civil Dimension of Maritime Security: NATO Parliamentary Assembly 53rd Annual Session Reykjavik, Iceland, 6 October 2007, Committee on the Civil Dimension of Security," in Björn Bjarnason [database online]. October 6, 2007, [cited 2009]. Available from http://www.bjorn.is/greinar/2007/10/06/nr/4189.

21 Utanríkisráðuneytið, *Ísinn Brotinn: Þróun norðurskautssvæðisins og sjóflutningar (Breaking the Ice: Arctic Developments and Maritime Transportation)* (Reykjavik: Utanríkisráðuneytið, 2007); Utanríkisráðuneytið, *Fyrir stafni haf: Tækifæri tengd siglingum á norðurslóðum (Open Sea Ahead: Possibilities regarding Navigation in the Arctic)* (Reykjavik: Utanríkisráðuneytið, 2005), 1–63.

22 Arctic Climate Impact Assessment, *Impacts of a Warming Arctic*.

23 Utanríkisráðuneytið, *Fyrir stafni haf: Tækifæri tengd siglingum á norðurslóðum (Open sea ahead: Possibilities regarding navigation in the Arctic)*, 1–63; Utanríkisráðuneytið, *Ísinn Brotinn: Þróun norðurskautssvæðisins og sjóflutningar (Breaking the Ice: Arctic developments and maritime transportation)*.

24 Utanríkisráðuneytið, *Fyrir stafni haf (Open sea ahead)*; Utanríkisráðuneytið, *Ísinn Brotinn (Breaking the Ice)*.

25 Samtök iðnaðarins, *Viðhorf almennings til ESB: Mars 2010 (Public Opinion on the EU: March 2010)* (Reykjavik: Samtök iðnaðarins, 2010), 1–8.

26 Christine Ingebritsen, *The Nordic States and European Unity* (Ithaca, NY: Cornell University Press, 1998), 219; Eiríkur Bergmann, "'Hið huglæga sjálfstæði þjóðarinnar': Áhrif þjóðernishugmynda á Evrópustefnu íslenskra stjórnvalda" (Sense of Sovereignty: How National Sentiments Have Influenced Iceland's European Policy) (PhD diss., University of Iceland, 2009), 1–370.

27 Guðni Th Jóhannesson, *Hrunið: Ísland á barmi gjaldþrots og upplausnar (The Fall: Iceland on the Verge of Bankruptcy and Chaos)* (Reykjavik: JPV Útgáfa, 2009), 1–427.

28 Commission of the European Communities, *The European Union and the Arctic Region* (2008), 1–12.

29 Kirsten Harder, *De dansk færøske forhold 1945–48* (Odense: Odense Universitetsforlag, 1979), 1–199; Zakarias

Wang, *Stjórnmálafrøði (Political Science)*, 2nd ed. (Hoyvik: Forlagið Stiðin, 1989), 1–262; Vagn Wåhlin et al., *Mellem færøsk og dansk politik: Den Parlamentariske Kommission, Fúlabók'en og Adressesagen i perspektiv 1917–1920 (Between Faroese and Danish Politics: The Parliamentary Commission, the Fúlabók and the Address Case in Perspective 1917–1920)* (Tórshavn; Århus: SNAI – North Atlantic Publications, 1994), 1–256; "The Faroese Parliament," in Løgtingið [database online]. Tórshavn [cited 2010]. Available from http://www.logting.fo/files/File/2008/faldari_EN_web.pdf.

30 "The Faroese Parliament," in Løgtingið [database online]. Tórshavn [cited 2010]. Available from http://www.logting.fo/files/File/2008/faldari_EN_web.pdf; Jákup Thorsteinsson, *Føroya í kalda krígnu: Hernaðarmál og politikkur. Avegisfrágreiðing um støðu Føroya í kalda krígnum (The Faroe Islands in the Cold War: Military Affairs and Policy. Report on the Status of the Faroe Islands in the Cold War)* (Tórshavn: Løgmansskrivstovan (Prime Minister's Office), 1999), 1–135.

31 Løgtingið, *The Faroese Parliament*, 1–16; "Den færøske selvstyreordning" (The Faroese Self-Rule Arrangement), in Statsministeriet [database online]. Copenhagen [cited 2010]. Available from http://www.stm.dk/_a_2565.html.

32 Thorsteinsson, *Føroya í kalda krígnu: Hernaðarmál og politikkur. Avegisfrágreiðing um støðu Føroya í kalda krígnum (The Faroe Islands in the Cold War: Military Affairs and Policy. Report on the Status of the Faroe Islands in the Cold War)*, 1–135; "Search and Rescue," in Atlantic Airways [database online]. [cited 2010]. Available from http://www.atlantic.fo/Default.aspx?pageid=5080; "Færøernes Kommando (Faroe Islands Command)," in Forsvaret [database online]. [cited 2010]. Available from http://forsvaret.dk/FRK/Pages/default.aspx.

33 Thorsteinsson, *Føroya í kalda krígnu: Hernaðarmál og politikkur.*

Avegisfrágreiðing um støðu Føroya í kalda krígnum (The Faroe Islands in the Cold War: Military Affairs and Policy. Report on the Status of the Faroe Islands in the Cold War), 1–135; 2005. Per Stig Møller and Jóannes Eidesgaard, *Fælles principperklæring mellem Danmarks Regering og Færøernes Landsstyre om Færøernes medvirken og inddragelse i udenrigs- og sikkerhedspolitikken (Fámjin erklæringen) (Common Declaration of Principles between the Government of Denmark and the Self Rule Government of the Faroe Islands on the Participation and Involvement of the Faroe Islands in the Foreign and Security Policy (the Fámjin Declaration))*, 2005; Jóannes Eidesgaard, *Uppskot til samtyktar um trygdarpolitikk Føroya (Statement on Faroese Security Policy)*, 2004; Jóannes Eidesgaard, *Fráboðan til danska uttanríkisráðharran juni 04 um tingsamtykt (Letter to Danish Foreign Minister on Parliamentary Decision)* 2004.

34 Finn Gad, *Grønland (Greenland)* (Copenhagen: Politiken, 1984), 336.

35 "Den grønlandske selvstyreordning (The Greenlandic Self Rule Arrangement)," in Statsministeriet [database online]. Copenhagen [cited 2010]. Available from http://www.stm.dk/_a_2566.html.

36 "Our Aircraft and Helicopters," in Air Greenland [database online]. [cited 2010]. Available from http://airgreenland.com/om_air_greenland/fly_og_helikoptere/; "Grønlands Kommando (Greenland Command)," in Grønlands Kommando [database online]. [cited 2010]. Available from http://forsvaret.dk/GLK/Pages/default.aspx; "Peterson Air Force Base," in United States Air Force [database online]. [cited 2010]. Available from http://www.peterson.af.mil/units/821stairbase/index.asp.

37 Colin Powell, Per Stig Møller, and Josef Motzfeldt, *Joint Declaration by the Government of the United States of America and the Government of the Kingdom of Denmark, including the Home Rule Government of Greenland, on Economic and*

Technical Cooperation, 2004; Colin Powell, Per Stig Møller, and Josef Motzfeldt, *Joint Declaration by the Goverment of the United States of America and the Government of the Kingdom of Denmark, including the Home Rule Government of Greenland, on Cooperation on the Environment in Greenland*, 2004; Colin Powell, Per Stig Møller, and Josef Motzfeldt, *Agreement between the Government of the United States of America and the Government of the Kingdom of Denmark, including the Home Rule Government of Greenland, to amend and supplement the Agreement of 27 April 1951 pursuant to the North Atlantic Treaty between the Government of the United States of America and the Government of the Kingdom of Denmark concerning the Defense of Greenland (Defense Agreement) including relevant subsequent Agreements related thereto,* 2004.

38 Andrew Ward and Sylvia Pfeifer, "Greenland sees oil as key to independence," *Financial Times*, August 27, 2010, 3–3.

North America

10. U.S. Arctic Policy: The Reluctant Arctic Power[1]

Rob Huebert

Introduction

By virtue of both its standing as a superpower and its purchase of Alaska in 1867, the United States is an Arctic nation. But throughout much of its history, it seldom recognized this fact. At an individual level, it has produced outstanding polar explorers such as Robert Peary and Richard Byrd, as well as modern-day Arctic scientists such as Robert Corell and Waldo Lyon. Furthermore, the Arctic was central to the United States' nuclear deterrent posture during the Cold War. But the Arctic has seldom figured prominently in U.S. policy discussions. Thus the United States may be characterized as the "reluctant" Arctic power.

Indeed, U.S. Arctic policy could be traditionally characterized as reactive, piecemeal, and rigid. While the Arctic is important to the United States, that fact seldom reached the attention of U.S. policy-makers and the U.S. public. But this has started to change. The Arctic is changing fundamentally due to climate change, resource development (in particular, energy), globalization, and geopolitical factors. Given the developing situation in the Arctic, even if the United States wanted to continue avoiding Arctic issues, it cannot. Furthermore, the selection of Alaskan governor Sarah Palin as the

Republican vice-presidential nominee in 2008 reminded Americans of their most northern state – if only for the duration of that election.

This chapter begins with a review of the existing U.S. Arctic policy. To the surprise of many observers, in its last days in power, the George W. Bush administration released a new U.S. Arctic policy on January 9, 2009.[2] The U.S. government had previously set out an Arctic policy in 1994.[3] Senior U.S. officials began the process to develop a new policy in 2007, and observers expected it would be released before the 2008 election. When this did not occur, many simply assumed that the crafting of the new policy would be left to the new Obama administration. Thus, its unveiling in 2009 caught most observers off guard. An Arctic only Region Policy is a departure from previous U.S. Traditionally, U.S. policy has dwelt with the Arctic and Antarctic simultaneously. This time, the decision was made to develop an Arctic-only policy. The policy is both frank and direct, and it has significant ramifications for all Arctic nations – Canada included. The Obama administration has accepted the policy and taken a more proactive position on some Arctic issues. Thus the 2009 policy offers a clear picture of what the United States considers to be its core Arctic policy objectives and provides a guide on how to achieve them. The task of developing this policy has been challenged by the reality of a changing Arctic. The United States has to deal, not only with the low priority traditionally given the Arctic, but also with the fact that the Arctic is changing in ways that are not yet understood. An additional problem facing the Americans is the larger political issues surrounding the political deadlock that has developed between President Obama and Congress. The unwillingness to seek compromise has limited the American ability to respond to the economic crisis that developed in 2008. Issue areas such as the Arctic which lack substantial political support, have tended to be ignored in this very toxic political environment.

Thus understanding American Arctic policy is very confounding. This chapter will provide an introduction of the existing policy framework and then examine and assess the core Arctic issues facing the United States. It will focus on the issues of energy development and international relations in the region.

1. U.S. Arctic Policy

Although the U.S. government's Arctic Region Policy provides guidance for American action in the Arctic, its major utility seems to be in the process of its creation. Officials close to the system have suggested that the process of policy formation "reminds" the various core departments that the United States has Arctic interests and that it needs to think seriously about the Arctic. The document thus provides important insights into what U.S. policy-makers think is important – when they think about the Arctic at all.

The policy's preamble states:

> The United States is an Arctic nation, with varied and compelling interests in the region.
> This directive takes into account several developments, including, among others:

1. Altered national policies on homeland security and defense;
2. The effects of climate change and increasing human activity in the Arctic region;
3. The establishment and ongoing work of the Arctic Council; and
4. A growing awareness that the Arctic region is both fragile and rich in resources.[4]

This focus changes the 1994 policy in two important ways. First, the earlier policy stated that the "United States has been an Arctic nation,"[5] while the 2009 document states that the "United States *is* an Arctic nation" (emphasis added). Second, the new document focuses on Alaska as at the core of U.S. Arctic interests: as the rest of the document makes clear, Alaska is a central reason the United States has Arctic interests, but these interests are national in character, not simply related to the concerns of one state.

These seemingly innocuous changes signify that the United States now understands that the Arctic is changing in ways that concern its vital national interests. To that end, Arctic Region Policy lists six objectives, as follows:

It is the policy of the United States to:

1. Meet national security and homeland security needs relevant to the Arctic region;

2. Protect the Arctic environment and conserve its biological resources;

3. Ensure that natural resource management and economic development in the region are environmentally sustainable;

4. Strengthen institutions for cooperation among the eight Arctic nations (the United States, Canada, Denmark, Finland, Iceland, Norway, the Russian Federation, and Sweden);

5. Involve the Arctic's indigenous communities in decisions that affect them; and

6. Enhance scientific monitoring and research into local, regional, and global environmental issues.[6]

These are the same basic objectives as in the 1994 document, but the order has been altered, with the need to meet national security moved from last to first. Moreover, homeland security has now been added to national security – clearly a reflection of the changes after 9/11. Thus, in 1994, U.S. officials were already becoming aware of the changes in the Arctic and drafted a policy to respond to them. That policy identified three main themes: a focus on natural resources and the need to develop them in a sustainable manner; recognition of the fragile nature of the Arctic environment and the need to better understand it; and recognition of the international nature of the Arctic. However, although both the 1994 and 2009 policies contain broad general objectives, nowhere in these documents is there guidance on what the Americans are supposed to do or how they are to achieve these objectives. The questions thus arise: what has U.S. policy been on resource development in the North and on the Arctic's international dimension, and what have been the actions taken by the Obama administration? And what will be the ramifications of these U.S. policy objectives for Canada, the United States' most important Arctic neighbor?

2. U.S. Resource Issues in the Arctic

The heart of U.S. Arctic resource policy and actions is Alaska. The U.S. view of its most northern state tends to focus on its abundant resources. From its extensive oil and gas reserves, both on land and offshore, to its fisheries and natural beauty, Alaska is seen as a wilderness to be used. But how this is to be done is a question Americans have grappled with for a long time. Alaska's attraction to outsiders has always been in terms of its natural resources. Prior to the U.S. purchase of Alaska, the Russians had come to its northern shores in search of fish and whales. The subsequent discovery of gold in Canada's neighboring Klondike region created a gold rush that still resonates in both the Yukon and Alaska. Other resources also drew outsiders to the state. The main point is that certain themes developed then that still exist today. The discovery of substantial amounts of natural resources brought to Alaska a large number of outsiders who had to deal with the challenge of a formidable climate, a challenge exacerbated by the considerable distance between Alaska and the continental United States. The United States then had to pay attention to its relations with Russia, Canada, and the United Kingdom, which still controlled Canadian foreign and defense policy at the time. When considered in this light, it should be apparent that the "new" Arctic reflects the old Arctic, despite the changes that are occurring.

The six objectives of the 1994 policy were:

1. Protecting the Arctic environment and conserving its biological resources;

2. Assuring that natural resource management and economic development in the region are environmentally sustainable;

3. Strengthening institutions for cooperation among the eight Arctic nations;

4. Involving the Arctic's indigenous people in decisions that affect them;

5. Enhancing scientific monitoring and research on local, regional, and global environmental issues; and

6. Meeting post-Cold War national security and defense needs.[7]

The largest economic issues facing Alaska pertain to the development of oil and gas reserves and the means to transport these resources to southern markets.[8] While both the 1994 and 2009 U.S. Arctic policy documents state that any such development should take place in a sustainable fashion, neither says anything about the tempo of development. This is perhaps because of the ongoing political debate in Alaska, and in the United States in general, about how those resources should be exploited. Debate rages over development of the Arctic National Wildlife Refuge (ANWR) and the offshore regions of the Chukchi Sea and the Beaufort Sea and typically focuses not on how to proceed in a sustainable fashion but on whether or not drilling should occur at all.[9] ANWR was made a Federal Protected Area in 1960 and given further protection under the 1980 Alaska National Interests Land Conservation Act, which stipulated that drilling could occur on these lands only with the approval of the U.S. Congress. While incentives to drill in the region diminished with the fall in oil prices in the 1980s, the issue took on an international dimension in 1987 when the United States and Canada signed an agreement regarding the conservation of the Porcupine caribou herd – whose calving grounds are located in the ANWR – that requires each party to notify the other if it plans to engage in economic activity that could affect the herd. In fact, much of the opposition to drilling in the area – especially on the part of Canada – is based on fears of the negative impact it could have on the herd.

In the offshore areas, Aboriginal, local, and environmental groups challenged a planned drilling program by Shell Oil despite the company's assurances to mitigate environmental damage.[10] Even though Shell had received approval from the necessary federal agencies to begin drilling, a November 2008 court decision temporarily halted the company's plans, ruling that the U.S. government should have undertaken a more thorough environmental study of the ramifications of the proposed drilling. This has now been done..[11]

A further complicating factor was the Deepwater Horizon Disaster in the Gulf of Mexico. On April 20 2010, there was an explosion and subsequent fire that resulted in the deaths of 11 workers and the largest oil spill in American waters.[12] As a direct result, President Obama through the Department off the Interior issued a 6 month moratorium on all deepwater drilling in May 2010.[13] At the same time, the department also did not approve any applications in shallow waters. As a result, the moratorium did not technically affect any planned drilling in Alaskan waters, since all of the proposed sites were occurring in waters of no more than 150 feet in depth.[14] However, the net effect was that all proposed drilling was placed on hold. The state of Alaska then sued the Federal government on the grounds that it had not been properly consulted.[15] Ultimately, the moratorium was lifted in October 2010, but the Department of Interior began to require that companies wishing to drill demonstrate more concrete plans and abilities to deal with accidents and spills. Shell began exploratory drilling in 2012. However a series of minor setbacks resulted in a reduced number of wells being drilled. Shell had hoped to drill two wells in the Beaufort Sea and three in Chukchi Sea.[16] Delays with their equipment and ice conditions resulted in a substantially reduced number of wells dug. The company suspended its drilling program in mid September 2012, but expects to be back in 2013.[17]

The 2012 presidential election has highlighted the political divide between the Obama administration and Alaska, which is very supportive of the Republicans. The governor of Alaska has been openly critical of what he has characterized as an overtly anti-development Obama administration. However, the Obama administration has pointed out that it has allowed Shell Oil to proceed with offshore exploratory drilling. But at the same time his Secretary of the Interior has recommended that half of the ANWAR region be placed off limits for development.[18]

Ultimately the ongoing debate is driven by concerns about the sustainable development of oil and gas in the Arctic. The issue has developed into an argument between two fundamentally opposed groups. One side takes the position that opening Arctic lands and waters for oil and gas exploitation is a means to ensure domestic U.S. energy security – which the development of the resources in the ANWR will reduce U.S. American dependence on Middle Eastern supplies.[19] The other side is dominated by those who argue that the contribution of oil and gas in these regions to satisfying U.S. demand is insufficient to justify the risk to the local environment.[20]

Going beyond the concerns of strong vested interests, however, the cornerstone of the debate is the amount of oil and gas that actually exists in Alaska and its offshore regions. Extensive exploration of these areas in the 1960s and 1970s led to the discovery of the North Slope fields that now currently fuel the entire Alaskan production, but no other finds of that magnitude were made. Then, in the 1980s, the price of oil fell and almost all Arctic exploration ceased. Interest in exploration renewed at the beginning of 2000, driven by three factors.

First, the continuing conflict in the Middle East, combined with the hostility of states such as Iran, meant that U.S. dependency on Middle Eastern oil remained part of the core of U.S. foreign policy debates; the prospect of northern sources of oil offered at least a partial solution to this dependency. Very recently there have been two complicating factors on this issue. In the fall of 2012 there have been a series of crisis in the region that have raised the possibility of open conflict. Relations between the United States and Iran have become very tense as a result of the continued efforts of the Iranian regime to develop nuclear weapons. The ongoing conflict in Syria has also raised the possibility of escalation into its neighbors. Most recently in November 2012, the conflict between Israel and Palestine has also escalated. Any one of these conflicts has the potential of expanding. Such an expansion would have an impact on oil supplies from the region. But in the long term there has been some evidence that the United States is now moving to increased domestic production on the basis of new technologies that are allowing for a significant expansion of the development of oil resources within the United States. Some analysis has suggested that the United States could become self sufficient in the near future because of these developments.[21]

Second, the rising price of oil meant that Alaskan oil and gas was becoming more economically viable; some analysts suggest, off the record, that Alaskan oil deposits are viable above about $80 per barrel for offshore deposits and about $55 per barrel for land-based sources.[22] These prices have been reached; throughout most of 2012, the price of oil has hovered around $80–$100 per barrel.[23] At the same time, there is concern that if new sources are not soon found, the Alaska Pipeline may need to be shutdown. It requires a set minimum amount of oil in order to function. Overall production from the north slope has been decreasing since 1988. If trends continue without new sources of oil the pipeline may face closure by 2025.[24]

Third, there is growing evidence that the Arctic region might contain very large unexploited supplies of both oil and gas. The U.S. Geological Survey, the best-known source of current speculation, suggests that more than 30 per cent of the world's undiscovered gas and 13 per cent of undiscovered oil reserves may be in the Arctic, with by far the largest estimated deposit (some 30 billion barrels) to be found in the waters immediately off the north coast of Alaska.[25] Of course, only drilling will determine the accuracy of these estimates. Moreover, it is easy to be confused about what such figures mean. Governor Sarah Palin was severely criticized for allegedly not understanding

Alaska's energy production when she was quoted as saying that the state accounts for 20 per cent of U.S. domestic energy production – in fact, Alaska's share is only about 3.5 per cent, but even if she had actually meant to say oil, rather than energy, Alaska's total production in 2007 was only 14 per cent of the U.S. total.

In addition to the ANWR, the other areas of great interest for resources are the offshore regions in the Chukchi Sea and Beaufort Sea. At one time, the Department of the Interior's periodic lease sales on blocks of ocean space for exploration and development in these regions attracted little interest from industry, but this began to change in the early 2000s.[26] The lease sale of February 8, 2008, saw a record-breaking $2.6 billion in winning bids on leases for development in the Chukchi Sea.[27] Shell Gulf of Mexico Inc. has had the greatest interest in these areas, but ConocoPhillips has also been active. Another issue directly related to the development of oil and gas is how they should be delivered to southern markets. When oil was first discovered on the North Slope in the late 1960s, the United States considered two options regarding delivery. One was to build a pipeline across Alaska from the north to the southern port of Valdez and then to use supertankers to carry the oil to the west coast. The other option was to use ice-strengthened supertankers to carry the oil directly from the North Slope to the east and west coasts of the United States. Going east, however, would have required a transit of the Northwest Passage. When the United States tested the viability of this route in 1969 and 1970, it sparked a political row with Canada, which claims the Northwest Passage as its internal waters and requires all foreign vessels to request Canadian permission to enter. The United States regards these waters as an international strait, however, and takes the position that, as long as vessels comply with international standards and rules, no permission is required from Canada. The voyage of the test vessel, SS *Manhattan*, created considerable tension between the two countries, and in any case the ship experienced considerable difficulty transiting the passage during the most favorable time of the year. Canada dispatched an icebreaker to demonstrate its control of the passage and to assist the *Manhattan* – indeed, without such help, the U.S. vessel might not have completed its voyage at all.

The difficult passage of the *Manhattan* convinced the oil companies involved that it would be better to build a pipeline to Valdez and ship oil from there instead. By 1977, the Trans Alaska Pipeline System (TAPS) – more than 800 miles of 48-inch-diameter pipe – was completed, at a total cost of

$8 billion.[28] The pipeline is owned by a consortium of oil companies – principally BP, with 47 per cent of the shares, ConocoPhillips, and ExxonMobil – under the name Alyeska. Four companies – Alaska Tanker Company, Polar Tankers Inc., SeaRiver Maritime Inc., and SeaBulk Tankers Inc. – deploy fifteen supertankers to move the oil from Valdez to southern U.S. markets.[29] This route, however, is not without its hazards. On March 24, 1989, the single-hulled *Exxon Valdez* ran aground and spilled more than 11 million gallons of oil into Prince William Sound.[30] As a result of that environmental disaster, in 1990 the U.S. Congress passed the Oil Pollution Act (OPA) and mandated the use of double-hulled tankers by all companies engaged in the TAPS trade. Under OPA, all new tankers built in the United States must now be double-hulled, and all existing single-hull tankers must be phased out by 2015. The International Maritime Organization is now attempting to upgrade international standards to match those under U.S. law.

The United States was able to act unilaterally with respect to shipbuilding standards as a result of its protectionist Jones Act,[31] which requires that all goods transported between U.S. states must be carried by a U.S.-built vessel manned by a U.S. crew, so that only U.S.-owned and -built tankers can carry oil from Alaska to ports in the continental United States. U.S. protectionism was further fostered by legislation banning the sale of Alaskan oil to foreign producers from 1974 to 1995, and 2000 legislation banning direct foreign sales of Alaskan oil.[32] Thus, the effect of such legislation is U.S. control of the shipping of all Alaskan oil through international waters.

The United States will soon face a key issue regarding how new oil and gas finds – if they are discovered - will be moved to U.S. markets, and a particularly challenging one if and when offshore deposits are found in the Chukchi Sea or Beaufort Sea. Will these be carried by underwater pipeline or by tanker, or perhaps some combination of the two? The Russians are currently addressing this issue in their development of the Stokman Gas field in the Barents Sea. Whatever the United States decides, important economic, environmental, and international issues will have to be considered.

What should be obvious to most observers is the tremendous activity that is now occurring in Alaska surrounding the development of oil and gas. Key decisions, however, are not being made on the basis of a coordinated policy, but in terms of critical political battles. The key battleground for oil and gas prospects on land is the U.S. Congress, and whether it will decide to allow drilling to take place in the ANWR as well as the new regulatory regime that has been put in place following the Deepwater Horizon disaster. This long-term battle has hinged on possible environmental damage versus the partial relief these resources provide for U.S. dependency on foreign sources of energy. The challenge is that there is no definitive understanding of how much damage could occur (particularly to the Porcupine caribou herd) or of how much oil and gas exists in these reserves. Furthermore, there is the new possibility that the United States may be able to meet its domestic demands through the development of oil fields in the lower 48. These would be much easier to get to market. In many ways, the debate is based on elements of faith and has more to do with the various political ideologies and beliefs among U.S. business and environmental groups. In such an atmosphere, it is not surprising that a policy framework agreeable to all has been impossible to fashion.

Impact on Canada

The U.S. focus on resource development in the Arctic has several ramifications for Canada. From a positive perspective, the potential supply of Canadian Arctic energy supplies to the North American market is bound to be viewed by the Americans as a positive development. U.S. Geological Survey studies and the exploration efforts of Exxon and BP make it clear that substantial amounts of oil and gas can be expected to be found in the Canadian North. Since the North American Free Trade Agreement (NAFTA) basically treats all oil and gas as a part of a common market in energy, any new Canadian supplies would help to address U.S. demand and reduce U.S. dependency on "foreign" supplies.

On the other hand, U.S. efforts to develop its Arctic supplies risk placing strains on Canada. There are two main areas of concern: the development of oil and gas on lands in the ANWR, and the development of oil and gas resources in the disputed zone of the Beaufort Sea. As mentioned earlier, Canada is on record as stating that it opposes the development of oil and gas in the ANWR because of the risk that such action poses to the Porcupine caribou herd. Should the U.S. government ultimately decide to go ahead with the drilling, Canada will find itself obligated to publicly oppose the U.S. action. While it is doubtful that Canadian opposition would have a significant impact on the U.S. decision, it will be seen as an irritant in the relationship.

A more recent development in Canadian American energy relations has emerged over the issue of pipeline construction and the identification by some American interest groups that the production of oil from the Albertan oil sands represents an environmental threat.[33] As a result there has been resistance in the United States over the construction of pipelines to carry the oil sands product from Canada into the United States. This has alerted Canadians to the reality that they cannot simply assume that the United States will automatically be willing to consume Canadian production.

Further complicating American Canadian arctic relations are the Beaufort Sea boundary issue and the status of the Northwest Passage. The United States' 2009 Arctic Region Policy has sharply narrowed the focus on both issues. As for the Beaufort Sea, the new U.S. policy, after explaining the U.S. position on this ongoing dispute, goes on to state the need to "[p]rotect United States interests with respect to hydrocarbons reservoirs that may overlap boundaries to mitigate adverse environmental and economic consequences related to their development."[34] This is something that was not mentioned in previous policy statements. What this should tell Canadian officials is that the United States has paid renewed attention to this issue.

A solution could be found, however, if the two states' political leaders were willing to help create a joint venture in the disputed zone in the Beaufort Sea. Since any oil and gas developed in the region would be transported to the North American market under the terms of NAFTA, it is not an issue of either side wanting the resources for itself. It is also important to note that the multinational corporations developing these resources are already working on both sides of the border. If Canada and the United States agreed to disagree about the formal border of the region, but also agreed to the establishment of a joint venture to develop oil and gas in the disputed zone, a potential political crisis could be averted. Both states have already stated that any development must be conducted with the strongest environmental protection, so this should not be an issue. What would remain would be a plan that equitably shares the economic returns of any development. A joint management plan would give the companies the political stability they need and would allay any concerns Canada might have about "losing" either its sovereignty in the Arctic or its energy security. All sides would emerge winners.

3. U.S. Circumpolar Relations

The most significant international issues facing the United States in the Arctic, as identified in both the 1994 and 2009 Arctic policies, are strengthening institutions for cooperation among the eight Arctic nations and meeting post-Cold War national security and defense needs. What is most striking is that, while U.S. policy states a desire to improve relations with its circumpolar neighbors, the United States is more likely to take steps that hinder, rather than foster, Arctic cooperation. Since the end of the Cold War, the Americans have participated in Arctic multilateral action only with great reluctance. Had they not been continually pressured by Canada, it is unlikely that they would have joined any of the new multilateral initiatives that developed at the end of the Cold War. As it stands, the U.S. position is that of a reluctant participant even when it is clearly in its interest to join. There are three main sources of multilateral activity in the Arctic: the Arctic Environmental Protection Strategy (AEPS), the Arctic Council, and the United Nations Convention on the Law of the Sea (UNCLOS). All three involve a hesitant and reluctant United States.

The Arctic Environmental Protection Strategy and the Arctic Council

In 1987, toward the end of the Cold War, then-Soviet leader Mikhail Gorbachev made several proposals during a speech in Murmansk in 1987 calling for the end of hostilities in the Arctic.[35] Western leaders, including those in the United States, initially ignored this initiative. When it became apparent that Gorbachev's reforms were going to revolutionize the USSR, leaders from the other Arctic nations began to develop plans to create new multilateral Arctic institutions. The two most important were the Arctic Environmental Protection Strategy, led by Finland and supported by Canada, and the Arctic Council, which was a Canadian initiative. The U.S. response to both was very tepid. The Reagan administration was opposed to the creation of any new multilateral organization and was specifically worried that an Arctic organization could negatively affect its security interests in the North. It preferred to approach the North on either a unilateral or a bilateral basis.

Canadian prime minister Brian Mulroney had proposed the creation of an "Arctic Council" as early as 1989. Canadian officials pushed for a multilateral body to be created by a new Arctic treaty that would bind its members to action on a wide range of issues. However, the Americans' negative reaction convinced Canadian officials that the time was not right. At this point, Finnish officials began to push for the creation of a more limited body – a multilateral body that would tie the Soviets to more cooperative behavior in the Arctic. They did not particularly care what the body was to do, only that it needed to exist and then expand. After consultations with the other Arctic nations, they decided that the body should focus on international environmental issues. The Finnish officials argued that addressing a shared problem such as environmental degradation could act as the means of establishing a dialog. The Finns sought the assistance of Canadian officials in developing this dialog because of Canada's known ability to operate in a multilateral forum. Drawing almost directly on a Canadian domestic policy titled the Arctic Environmental Strategy, the Finns and Canadians developed a draft strategy called the Arctic Environmental Protection Strategy (AEPS).

Then, in October 1988, the Finns and Canadians launched a series of negotiations with the six other Arctic states – the Soviet Union, Iceland, Sweden, Norway, Denmark (for Greenland), and a very reluctant United States. In June 1991, in Rovaniemi, Finland, the eight Arctic states signed a declaration on the protection of the Arctic environment and accepted the accompanying AEPS. The strategy identified six main tides of pollutants – persistent inorganic pollutants (POPs), oil pollution, heavy metals, noise, radioactivity, and acidification – and called for existing mechanisms and agreements to be dedicated to protecting the Arctic environment and for new initiatives to be considered. Finally, the strategy called for action to be taken to counter the pollutants. Four working groups addressing different Arctic environmental issues were created to support these actions. A ministerial meeting of the AEPS was to take place every two years. The second occurred in September 1993, in Nuuk, Greenland, at which it was decided to create a fifth working group – the Task Force on Sustainable Development (TFSD) – and that northern indigenous peoples needed greater institutional support to allow them to participate in a more meaningful manner.

To that end, the main northern indigenous peoples' organizations should be invited to become permanent participants in the AEPS. The United States resisted this suggestion at first, viewing it as a Canadian strategy to gain additional support for its national position, which it assumed the indigenous peoples' groups would closely support on a wide range of issues. The

Americans further argued that since state representatives on the new body already represented the various aboriginal organizations, giving these groups official standing was to give these people two votes. They later reluctantly agreed that the northern peoples be granted status as permanent participants but insisted that there could never be more permanent participants than state parties in the organization. This meant that, as long as there were eight state parties to the AEPS, there could never be more than seven permanent participant organizations. The Americans also insisted that only the state parties be allowed to vote on any budgetary issues. The first three organizations to accept the ultimately proffered invitation to join the AEPS were the Inuit Circumpolar Conference (ICC) – whose board would also have representation from U.S. Inuit[36] – the Nordic Saami Council, and the Russian Association of Indigenous Peoples of the North (RAIPON).

The AEPS proved a successful forum in which the eight Arctic nations could bring together their best experts on issues of international pollutants in the Arctic. The process was an important learning process for the eight nations and resulted in several reports highlighting common environmental challenges. It soon became apparent to many of those involved in the process, however, that an expanded system was necessary, which, in the early 1990s, led Canadian officials in the Mulroney government to resume efforts to create an Arctic Council that would have a mandate beyond environmental issues.

Even into the Clinton administration, however, the United States remained aloof to the Canadian initiative. The Americans attended two international meetings, in May 1992 and May 1993, but only as observers. The May 1993 meeting led to the decision to create an Arctic Council that would follow many of the practices of the AEPS. Its core membership would be the eight Arctic states, and permanent participant membership would be given to major northern indigenous peoples' organizations. In Canada, in 1994, the new government of Jean Chrétien continued to support the Mulroney government's initiative and to prod a reluctant United States to join. In early 1995, following a series of bilateral discussions with Canada, the U.S. government dropped its resistance to participate and agreed to support the initiative.

U.S. participation, however, now meant the need to accommodate U.S. concerns.[37] The Canadian government originally had hoped that, as an international organization with treaty-mandated powers, the Arctic Council could address a wide range of issues, including boundary disputes and trade. A briefing note prepared by the Department of Foreign Affairs and

International Trade stated: "Canada is of the strong view that a forum is needed to promote cooperation and concerted action and to bring political focus to addressing the urgent issues affecting the circumpolar North. *These issues go beyond those related to the protection of the environment*" (emphasis added)[38] The Americans quickly let it be known, however, that they would support an Arctic Council only if it focused solely on environmental concerns and could not deal with any security-related issues. The final agreement, which included a footnote that stated "[t]he Arctic Council should not deal with matters related to military security,"[39] clearly showed that the Americans had been successful. The Council was directed to incorporate the work of the AEPS by assuming control over the working groups and to build on the work of the Working Group on Sustainable Development by creating a sustainable development program.

The Americans were opposed to the Council's developing an independent bureaucracy and raising revenue sources of its own. As a result, Canada abandoned its efforts to give the Council a permanent secretariat with its own operating budget. Instead, the Council chair would rotate on a two-year basis among the eight Arctic states, and the state acting as the chair would also provide the secretariat costs. Additionally, the working groups would draw only on the resources that each state would volunteer. Canada and the United States also disagreed on the meaning of sustainable development within the Council. The Americans believed that Canadian efforts to establish a second tier within the Council, to focus on sustainable development, were meant to separate conservation from sustainability. The Americans took the position that these were the same and that creating an artificial division would interfere with the Council's work. Canada maintained, however, that it was necessary to be sensitive to the needs of the northern peoples, and that meant not only conserving the resources but using them in a sustainable manner. The difference between the two can be traced to the role of traditional hunting and fishing. The Canadian government strongly supports the right of northern peoples to engage in traditional hunting and to sell the results in the southern economy. The U.S. opposition to this view is expressed in its Marine Mammal Protection Act, which bans the trade in marine mammals. Then-president Bill Clinton specifically stated that: "I have further instructed the Department of State to oppose Canadian efforts to address trade in marine mammal products within the Arctic Council.... [I have instructed Congress] to withhold consideration of any Canadian requests for waivers to the existing moratorium on the importation of seals and/or seal products into the United States."[40]

The United Stares also opposes Canada's giving Inuit hunters permission to kill a small number of bowhead whales. Following the granting of permission in 1996, the U.S. State Department threatened to impose sanctions on Canada in accordance with the Pelly Amendment to the Fishermen's Protective Act. Though the sanctions were not implemented, their mere threat demonstrates continuing Canada–U.S. differences on this issue. There is a certain irony in the U.S. government's having granted permission to the Inupait of Alaska to hunt 204 bowhead whales during a four-year period commencing in 1997.[41] The United States rationalizes its contradictory position by stating that, unlike Canada, the United States is a member of the International Whaling Commission and, as such, its decision is in harmony with existing international regimes, while Canada's decision to allow its northern peoples to hunt whales is not. The net effect of the U.S. position is that the Council cannot discuss the issue of selling products gathered by traditional means – in other words, it cannot discuss the U.S. ban on the sale of these goods.

In summer 1996, the United States and Canada reached agreement despite these serious differences, and the Arctic Council was formally created on September 19, 1996, in Ottawa. Following the practices of the AEPS, the Council was composed of the eight Arctic states and the three permanent participants; three more have since joined the body – the Aleuts International Association, the Athabaskan Council, and the Gwich'in Council International. The Arctic Council has responsibility for the AEPS working groups and meets at the ministerial level every two years to ensure the progress of its various initiatives. There is no permanent secretariat; rather, member states volunteer to act as chair for two years and to assume responsibility for the coordination of activities and provide the necessary resources to fulfill these activities. Canada took the first turn as chair, with the United States following from 1998 to 2000. The Americans focused on local issues pertaining to the state of Alaska, and brought forward projects such as tele-medicine and other actions geared towards local communities in the North.

The Council has developed several new initiatives dealing with environmental challenges since it was established, particularly after the release of a 1997 study on the Arctic environment by the Arctic Monitoring and Assessment Programme, a group within the Council.[42] At its first ministerial meeting, in Iqaluit in September 1998, the Council initiated an Action Plan to Eliminate Pollution in the Arctic; another major project, the Arctic Climate Impact Assessment (ACIA) has also been completed.[43] One of the great ironies is that, while U.S. political leaders attempted to minimize ACIA's policy ramifications, Americans actually provided much of the leadership that led to this report's success. The multi-year, multidisciplinary project provided a clear understanding of the impact of climate change on the Arctic. The exhaustive scientific report was one of the study's most important contributions. More important, the public attention the report received was instrumental in making the Arctic the "canary in the coalmine" when it came to monitoring climate change.

The report, and the effort that went into it, reflected an interesting dichotomy about U.S. policy. On the one hand, an American, Robert Correll, led the entire study, organizing the research and producing the published papers. American researchers also conducted and led much of the actual research on which the report was based. There is little doubt that, without the American input, the report would not have been as thorough and detailed as it was. On the other hand, U.S. political leaders fought against the report's policy ramifications. Originally, the study was to have been disseminated in three reports: a scientific report based on peer-reviewed studies of the impact of climate change on the Arctic, a relatively short executive report summarizing the scientific findings and supported by graphics, and a set of policy recommendations to rectify the problems discovered by the science. The first two reports were released to extensive worldwide media attention. U.S. officials ultimately were successful, however, in watering down the policy recommendations, as they were concerned that these might run contrary to the Bush administration's position on climate change – in particular, its position on carbon emission reductions. While the Americans played a critical role in the report's development, they then prevented an international response to the problems their own scientists played a critical role in uncovering.

In its 2009 Arctic Policy, the United States reaffirmed its position that, while the Arctic Council plays an important role in the governance of the Arctic region, the United States still opposes any efforts to strengthen the Council's powers: "It is the position of the United States that the Arctic Council should remain a high-level forum devoted to issues within its current mandate and not be transformed into a formal international organization particularly one with assessed contributions."[44] At the same time, however,

U.S. policy does acknowledge that it might be possible to "update" the structure of the Council. What exactly this means needs to be further developed at future Arctic Council meetings.

The Obama administration has demonstrated its support of the Arctic Council through the active and strong leadership of Secretary of State Hillary Clinton. She is the first Secretary of State to attend an Arctic Council ministerial meeting when she attended the 7th Ministerial meeting in Nuuk, Greenland.[45] Previously, the Americans had sent substantially lower level officials as their senior arctic official. She made it clear that the United States also now sees the Arctic Council as becoming one of the key decision-making international body in the region.[46]

At the same time, the United States has agreed to several initiatives that are strengthening the Council and are in direct opposition to earlier American positions. First, they have agreed and applauded the formation of a permanent secretariat to be based in Norway.[47] Second, the United States played a leading role in the creation of a Search and Rescue Treaty that was negotiated under the responsibility of the Arctic Council.[48] Clinton has gone on to now call for the development of a treaty to address oil spills in the region. All of these actions demonstrate that the United States has moved well beyond its original opposition that it had demonstrated against the establishment of the Arctic Council.

The United Nations Convention on the Law of the Sea

The United Nations Convention on the Law of the Sea (UNCLOS) is the third major multilateral action that is reshaping the Arctic. This international treaty, negotiated between 1973 and 1982, codifies existing international maritime law and creates new international law. The Convention is one of the most sweeping international agreements created to date. The U.S. history with the Convention, which came into force in 1996, has been interesting. Successive U.S. administrations, including those of presidents Nixon, Ford, and Carter, supported the treaty's development because its U.S. negotiators were successful in protecting core U.S. interests. Just as the Convention was completed in 1981, however, the newly elected Reagan administration reviewed the treaty and decided that, unlike the previous Carter administration, it could not accept it because of its opposition to Part XI, which would have given the developing world a share of the ocean resources of the high seas beyond national control. The Reagan administration argued that this section would place an unfair burden on U.S. industries if deep-sea mining were to occur – that U.S. companies would be made to share a portion of their profit and technology with the developing world. Given the need for the United States to accept the treaty, the international community went back to the drawing board and gutted the offending section of the treaty, which calmed the Reagan administration's objections on that issue.

Yet, the United States still has not accepted UNCLOS – there still remain a sufficient number of Republican senators in Congress who view the treaty as an affront to U.S. interests to continue to assure its passage remains blocked. Recent gains by Democrats may make U.S. accession to the treaty more likely – certainly, the 2009 Arctic Policy explicitly makes the point that it is in the United States' interest to join UNCLOS, specifically calling for the U.S. government to "[c]ontinue to seek advice and consent of the United States Senate to accede to the 1982 Law of the Sea Convention."[49]

The Convention affects the Arctic in several ways. The most important is through article 76, which allows a state to extend control of its seabed and subsoil adjacent to its coasts beyond its existing 200-nautical-mile exclusive economic zone (EEZ) if it can show that it has a continental shelf. It is possible that Canada, Greenland (Denmark), Russia, and the United States all have the right to do so in the Arctic. Currently, Canada, Russia, and Denmark are engaged in scientific research to determine if they have a northern extension of their continental shelf. The United States began to address this question with research of its own in 2001 and in cooperation with Canada in the fall of 2008.[50] The problem the United States has to contend with is that, by not being party to the Convention, it is unable to submit a claim to the appropriate UN body (the Commission on the Limits of the Continental Shelf) for verification. The other Arctic states appear willing to engage the Americans on this issue, as evidenced by their inclusion in a meeting in Ilulissat, Greenland, in May 2008 with the other Arctic continental shelf claimants. How long the Americans will be included in these discussions is unknown, but the United States cannot submit its claim to the UN until it accedes to the Convention.[51] The effect of the Americans as a non-party on any overlap with Canadian and Russian Arctic continental shelf claims is also unknown. This is one of those cases where most senior U.S. leaders know they must act but have not figured out how to get beyond the Senate.

The Obama administration, like all those before it, has been a strong supporter of accession to the treaty. At her Senate hearings to confirm her as Obama's Secretary of State Hillary Clinton noted that one of her main priorities would be to accede to the treaty.[52] During his first term, Obama made the ratification of the newest Strategic Arms Reduction Treaty (START) his priority. However once this was successfully ratified by the Senate, he attempted to have UNCLOS ratified by the senate. Senate Foreign Relations Committee Chairman John Kerry attempted to bring the treaty to a vote in the summer of 2012. However, in July of that year he received a letter from 34 Republican Senators that they would not support the treaty, thereby preventing the necessary 2/3 majority necessary.[53] Thus, like all Presidents before him, he was stopped by a determined group of Republican senators. It remains to be seen if this will now change into the second term of the Obama administration.

Boundary disputes regarding the continental shelf are not the only such issues the Americans face in the Arctic. They also have an ongoing maritime boundary issue with Canada over the Beaufort Sea, and they disagree with both Canada and Russia over the status of the Northwest Passage and Northern Sea Route. Another issue, which had been thought resolved, may be arising over the maritime boundary between the Bering Strait and the Beaufort Sea. The Bering Sea maritime border case between the United States and the USSR/Russia was supposed to have been resolved in 1990, when the two countries agreed on a boundary. However, while the U.S. Senate has given its approval, the Russian Duma refuses to do so because of the impact of the boundary agreement on control of the region's resources.[54] Some U.S. senators and Alaska state officials have expressed concern over the status of several islands on the Russian side of the boundary, although the State Department has publicly stated the issue is closed.[55]

The issue of the so-called donut hole is more problematic for the United States and Russia. As a result of the geography of the U.S. and Russian coastlines, within their 200-mile EEZs, a section of the Bering Sea is outside their control – that is, considered to be the high seas. Japan, Taiwan, South Korea, and Poland all send large trawlers into this area, seriously depleting the fishing industry in the entire region.[56] Efforts to reach agreement among all these states have been limited, and there is ongoing fear that the entire eco-system could soon collapse. It is unclear how to resolve the situation.

Impact on Canada

The Beaufort Sea dispute centers on how the United States and Canada divide their territorial seas and the EEZ. Based on differing interpretations of an 1825 treaty between the UK and Russia, the United States draws the boundary at a 90° angle to the coastline, while Canada extends the land boundary as its maritime boundary. This difference has created a disputed zone of 6,250 square miles, resembling a triangle, segments of which both countries have offered for lease to private companies – Canada did so in the 1970s, and the United States continues to do so now. Off the record, some officials suggest that the two sides have unofficially agreed not to accept any bids, but it is not possible to confirm this. The U.S. Geological Survey suggests there is a high probability that gas fields exist in the disputed zone and a lower probability that oil fields exist.

This particular dispute could easily escalate. Any suggestion that Canada "surrender" part of its maritime claim undoubtedly would cause an outcry among Canadians, regardless of the merits of the case, and any issue that involves the apparent loss of Canadian Arctic sovereignty to the United States – even technically a boundary dispute – would be difficult for any Canadian government to handle. A U.S. government that was perceived to compromise U.S. energy security also would face domestic difficulties.

The U.S. disagreement with Canada (and Russia) about the Northwest Passage and the Northern Sea Route is based on its view that both waterways are international straits, meaning that foreign vessels – including warships – need not ask the coastal state, whether that be Russia or Canada, for permission to transit. Moreover, the United States takes the position, first developed in the late 1960s, that all vessels have the right to travel in the mode they normally use – so that, for example, submarines should be able to remain submerged during transit.[57] To this end, the United States has attempted to send vessels through both waterways – in 1967, for example, it sent two Coast Guard icebreakers, *Edisto* and *East Wind*, on a circum-arctic navigational voyage, but the Soviets refused passage to the U.S. vessels, and threatened to use force if necessary. The Americans backed down and canceled the trip, but only after posting a diplomatic protest. Then there was the voyage of the SS *Manhattan* in 1969 and 1970, which was noted above.

The United States bases its position on the principle of freedom of navigation.[58] Its primary concern is that any sign of its accepting the Canadian (or Russian) position would encourage other states, such as Iran in the Strait of

Hormuz, to assert greater national control over waters that are now considered international under law. At the same time, the United States does seem to place the Northwest Passage in a different category, having agreed – in the 1988 Arctic Water Cooperation Agreement – to ask Canada's consent before sending Coast Guard icebreakers through the Northwest Passage. American willingness to negotiate the agreement shows their willingness to grant Canada special attention. The impetus for the agreement came from the close relationship between then-prime minister Brian Mulroney and then-president Ronald Reagan, who directly ordered the U.S. State Department to negotiate the deal. The agreement continues to work well.

Concerns over climate change, however, are prompting speculation about the future viability of international shipping through the Northwest Passage, which could reignite disputes between Canada and the United States. It is unclear what would happen if a vessel attempted to go through the passage without asking Canada's permission. Would the United States keep quiet and let Canada deal with the crisis, or would it feel compelled to restate its position, and, if so, how forcefully should this be done? Some Canadian commentators suggest that U.S. security requirements in the post-9/11 world probably would lead them to remain silent. Canadian Arctic expert Franklyn Griffiths argues that the United States recognizes it is in its security interests for Canada to retain control over the Northwest Passage.[59] Even some U.S. commentators – such as former U.S. ambassador to Canada, Paul Cellucci, and U.S. Council on Foreign Relations Fellow Scott Borgerson – have suggested that, if Canada increased its defense capability in the North, the United States might look the other way in the event of a challenge to Canada's claim on the Northwest Passage.[60] The official U.S. position, as stated by President Bush as recently as 2007, is that the two sides "agree to disagree" and that the United States continues to view the passage as an international strait.[61] Thus, it is hard to know what will occur. A very strong Canadian response should be expected if the United States were to restate its opposition, which undoubtedly would hurt Canada–U.S. Arctic cooperation just when it increasingly would be needed.

The 2009 Arctic Region Policy has made this issue somewhat more difficult to resolve. At one time, it seemed likely that Canada and the United States could have quietly settled on a joint management program similar to that overseeing the St. Lawrence Seaway.[62] However, the 2009 policy makes it clear that the protection of "freedom of navigation" remains an American vital interest: "Freedom of the seas is a top national priority. The Northwest

Passage is a strait used for international navigation, and Northern Sea Route includes strait used for international navigation; the regime of transit passage applies to passage through those straits. Preserving the rights and duties relating to navigation and overflights in the Arctic region supports these rights throughout the world, including through strategic straits."[63]

The fact that these waters could be used for the shipment of Alaskan oil and gas in the new types of ice-strengthened tankers currently under construction by Asian shipbuilders adds economic pressure on this position. The explicitness of the U.S. position means that it is now unlikely that Canadian and U.S. officials will be able to find the "wiggle room" necessary to create the gentlemen's agreement that many had felt was possible, even given the developing relationship between Prime Minister Harper and President Obama. The 2009 Arctic Region Policy does accept the creation of "specific Arctic Waterway regimes" but makes clear that these must be developed with "international standards," not through unilateral action.[64] Thus, in the U.S. view, Canada cannot act unilaterally to develop laws governing maritime passage through the Northwest Passage.

4. U.S. Arctic Security Issues

The 2009 Arctic Region Policy reaffirms the high priority the United States places on security issues, particularly the importance of maintaining a military presence in the region. Throughout the 1990s, the United States retained a large number of troops in Alaska and have enhanced the Arctic's strategic importance by locating one of two missile defense interceptor bases at Fort Greely, Alaska. The U.S. Army maintains three bases (Forts Greely, Wainwright, and Richardson), and so does the Air Force (Eielson, Elmendorf, and Eareckson). The Coast Guard has Air Stations at Kodiak and Sitka and maintains safety offices in Anchorage, Juneau, and Valdez. Official figures are now hard to obtain, but estimated forces total slightly over 25,000.

The United States has closed some Alaska bases, including a naval base on Adak that had more than 6,000 personnel at the end of the Cold War.[65] Fort Greely was to have been closed by 2001, but the order was rescinded when it was decided to site a missile defense system at the base. The United States also maintained three fighter wings of F-15s (approximately 22 aircraft per wing) for air sovereignty flights. These began to be replaced by the

USAF's most modern fighter – the F-22 in 2007. Approximately 40 aircraft (out of the existing fleet of 182 aircraft) are now based with the 90th Fighter Squadron and the 525th Fighter Squadron of 3rd Wing.[66] During the 1990s, American fighters simply practiced flying to maintain their proficiency, but the patrols gained renewed importance following 9/11. Then in August 2007, the Russians announced the resumption of their long-range Arctic patrols. The U.S. F-15s and now F-22s are now called upon to intercept any Russian aircraft that are deemed to come "too close" to U.S. airspace.[67]

The number of subsurface voyages the Americans made throughout the 1990s is unknown. A core task of the U.S. submarine force during the Cold War was to track and prepare to engage Soviet submarines under the Arctic ice. With the end of the Cold War and the near collapse of the Soviet/Russian submarine force, the United States assumed that the importance of this task had greatly diminished. Indeed, the composition of its current submarine force reflects the U.S. perception that the Arctic is not of high strategic importance, although the U.S. Navy is known still to deploy a submarine in Arctic waters at least once a year.[68]

Another challenge Canada faces is the Arctic Region Policy's explicit regard of the Northwest Passage as an international strait in its assertion that "[p]reserving the rights and duties relating to navigation and overflights in the Arctic region supports our ability to exercise these rights throughout the world, including through strategic straits."[69] If this U.S. view ultimately prevailed, anyone, including the Russians, would have the right to fly their military aircraft over the waters of the Northwest Passage – clearly, such a right would not be in the security interests of either Canada or the United States.

If the Americans are serious about increasing their surface fleet presence and increasing the number of icebreakers, they will have continue to cooperate with Canadian security forces. Given the region's lack of infrastructure, any extended deployment would have to be a cooperative venture in any case. The Canadian Navy and Coast Guard have excellent operational relations with their U.S. counterparts, which should aid future efforts at cooperation in the region. Facilitating this interaction would be an increase in Canadian capability, which is slowly underway with the construction of Arctic Offshore Patrol Vessels and at least one new icebreaker. The U.S. Coast Guard is already assisting Canada to map its northern continental shelf.

One area that remains a question mark for Canada–U.S. security relations is that of missile defense. The United States has already placed one of two operational land-based anti-missile sites very near the Alaska–Yukon boarder. Canada, through a decision of the Paul Martin government, chose not to participate in the U.S. program, which raises the question of what this decision will mean as the Americans continue to develop their system.

Finally, the transit of U.S. submarines through the Northwest Passage remains an issue for Canada. If the passage were deemed an international strait, all countries would have the right to sail their nuclear-powered submarines submerged through these waters without notifying Canada. Canada argues that it "allows" U.S. submarines to do this in the name of common security, under the terms of either NORAD or NATO, but whenever a U.S. submarine is forced to show itself in these waters, the Canadian government risks facing substantial criticism from the media and the general public and an irritation of Canada–U.S. relations.

Thus, in general, increased U.S. and Canadian military presence in the North probably will lead to a further strengthening of operational relations between the two counties. But the U.S. insistence that the Northwest Passage is an international strait could have significant security costs for both states in the region.

Coming Challenges for U.S. Arctic Policy

Where does this leave the United States? U.S. action in the Arctic has significant core themes, within which numerous issues need to be addressed.

The first theme is that U.S. Arctic policy has two main thrusts: energy and security. The oil and gas in and around Alaska are seen as the primary means of increasing the domestic percentage of U.S. oil and gas supplies. Significant obstacles remain, however, before these resources can be developed. Although the indicators are promising, the location and quantity of these resources will remain unknown until exploratory drilling occurs. Several companies are now willing to begin the search but have hit up against the second core obstacle: political and public opposition. There is no clear consensus within the United States on the desirability of bringing these resources on line. There are strong opinions on both sides of the issue. While many Americans see the expected new supply as a means of providing both energy security and economic benefits, many others are afraid that any such development could cause major damage to the northern environment. As a result, political, legal, and public debates continue on this issue, and it is by no means clear how the United States will proceed.

The second theme is the unilateral focus that the United States places on its interactions with its Arctic neighbors. With the end of the Cold War, the Arctic region diminished in importance as the core strategic theater in the event of war. While several Arctic nations viewed this as an opportunity to improve international cooperation in the region, the U.S. response has been that of a very reluctant participant. The Americans have shown no interest in playing a leadership role in developing new cooperative instruments in the region. Instead, they have preferred to deal with issues on a bilateral basis or to simply ignore the issues facing the Arctic. Only in the very recent period under the Obama administrations have there been some signs that this may be changing. The United States has begun to treat the Arctic Council much more seriously, However the ongoing toxic relationship between the Democrats and the Republicans continue to limit American desires to cooperate more fully.

The United States will need to reconnect with the Arctic, however, given the developing situation. The triple forces of climate change, resource development, and geopolitical changes are now combining to make the Arctic a much more active region in the world. To a large degree, the Americans have been able to focus on local issues in Alaska and ignore the larger international issues because few international players could make it to the Arctic. There was little international activity even throughout the 1990s. So, for what does the United States now need to prepare?

Despite the U.S. government's reluctance to agree to a set of solutions or responses to climate change, U.S. scientists have been instrumental in showing that climate change is fundamentally changing the Arctic. The ice is melting and entire eco-systems are being transformed. This will have a direct impact on several economic interests, including oil and gas development, fishing, tourism, and shipping, to name only a few. Developing these resources will further facilitate change in the Arctic by drawing more international players to the region. In turn, Arctic nations will then increasingly have to improve their own ability to act in the Arctic, which will then serve to increase interaction between the Arctic states and the international actors. All of these factors feed into each other to accelerate the processes at play.

Climate change will transform how oil and gas resources are developed and transferred to market. Climate change is decreasing the amount of ice, but not eliminating it. Any offshore developments will need to deal with the impact of more open water (for example, in the form of more severe storms or higher waves). They will also need to address increasing variability in ice conditions. As the ice melts, producing larger areas of open water, it will be increasingly difficult to determine the position of the remaining ice. Offshore platforms will need to be built to handle more intensive wave action and increasingly mobile ice flows. Moreover, any effort to develop onshore sources of oil and gas will have to deal with an increasingly fragile land surface as the permafrost begins to melt. This is already causing problems with existing infrastructure. Any new systems – especially pipelines – will have to deal with the challenges that climate change brings.

This will also complicate the task of getting the product to market. New solutions are being developed outside North America: the Russians, Finns, and South Koreans are all now engaged in the design and construction of systems that can operate in an increasingly volatile Arctic Ocean. Samsung Heavy Industry in South Korea is building specially designed oil tankers that can operate in both ice-covered and ice-free waters. The Russians are in the process of designing and building new ice and open water platforms that can be anchored in Arctic waters. They reportedly have spent upwards of $44 billion on a system to exploit one of the world's largest gas fields (Stokman) in the Barents Sea, which is expected to come into production by the end of the decade even in the face of the current depressed market for gas. Obviously, U.S. industry has the ability to replicate all of this technology, but the Russians and Asian countries already have a substantial lead in many areas.

Although this chapter has not examined issues surrounding the Alaskan fisheries, climate change is already beginning to shift traditional habitats. No one really has a good understanding of what this ultimately will do to the existing bio-systems. Some species may flourish, but in all probability others will suffer. This means that the existing fishing industry will need to adjust. In some instances, this adjustment may require ceasing operations or at least downsizing. In fact, the Americans have already acted on a report by the U.S. North Pacific Fishery Management Council that had recommended a moratorium on commercial fishing as new stock move into the region.[70]

As the ice melts, tourism is paying increasing attention to the North. Southern Alaskan waters are already experiencing an increase in cruise ship traffic. This will soon create a host of new challenges and opportunities. While increasing tourism will provide new jobs and economic opportunities in the regions visited by these ships, concern is growing that their owners are beginning to push the boundaries of operating in a safe manner. While the ice is retreating, it can still sink ships. The cruise vessel *Explorer*, which was sunk due to damage caused by an ice pack in Antarctica, was a seasoned Arctic vessel; less experienced vessels are clearly at greater risk.[71] The Americans will be increasingly hard pressed to monitor their activity and to respond to accidents.

The United States has also reduced its icebreaking capabilities, having added just one new vessel to its existing small fleet since the early 1980s. As of 2008, there were only three icebreakers. However, only one is operational – the Healy. The two older icebreakers are both out of operations. The Polar Star is now completing an extensive refit and is expected back in service in December 2012. The Polar Sea experienced "an unexpected engine casualty" in June 2010. The Coast Guard placed the vessel in inactive status on October 14 2011 and is expected to decommission it at the end of 2012.[72]

In an era of intense debates concerning the building of new navy vessels, U.S. Coast Guard requirements tend to be completely overlooked. The diverse roles icebreakers play only make it more difficult to determine whose budget should pay for new ships. Both the Coast Guard and the National Science Foundation have shared responsibility for the maintenance of the vessels. However, this relationship has proven to be cumbersome. Some senior U.S. military leaders, becoming aware of the increasing accessibility of the Arctic, are calling for a recapitalization of the icebreaking fleet.[73] The former Commandant of the Coast Guard, Admiral Thad Allen, repeatedly called for the construction of new icebreakers: "All I know is, there is water where it didn't used to be, and I'm responsible for dealing with that.… Given the 8 or 10 years it would take to build even one icebreaker, … I think we're at a crisis point on making a decision."[74]

The Coast Guard was able to finally receive approval for $8 million for the design of a new icebreaker for fiscal year 2013. It then plans to commence building in FY 2014 for completion in 2017 for a total cost of $860 million.[75] However, this funding like all other large scale capital projects may be cut due to the current fiscal political crisis facing the United States. At the time of writing, it is not known if it was cut to avoid the "fiscal cliff" of 2012–13.[76]

The decision, if and when it comes, will be one of the most expensive the Americans will make pertaining to the Arctic. If the United States intends to maintain icebreaking capability when the demand for it increases, however, it will need to make a decision soon. At the same time, pressure is mounting to add icebreakers to the increasing U.S. military presence in the Arctic as more international actors begin to arrive in the region.

Impact on Canada

As the United States build its military capabilities in the Arctic, Canada faces a number of interesting challenges. First, it needs to reassess several of its cooperative military arrangements with the United States. The 2009 U.S. Arctic Region Policy stresses national security as that country's first priority in the region, but it is interesting to note that, although the document specifically names several international bodies, it fails to mention the one bilateral agreement that is instrumental to U.S. Arctic aerospace security: NORAD. While its mandate has been expanded to include all aerospace regions, NORAD has always focused on the North. In the face of renewed Russian northern bomber patrols, it is clear that there will continue to be a need for bilateral cooperation. From a Canadian perspective, it is interesting to observe that, although the Arctic Region Policy does not hesitate to list the disputes that exist between Canada and the United Nations, it makes no mention of this clear indication of successful cooperation.

The final economic issue the United States must address concerns the prospect of international shipping as the ice recedes. The current debate is whether such traffic will go through the Northwest Passage, the Northern Sea Route, or over the North Pole itself. The answer to this debate depends on the manner in which the ice melts, the time frame during which this occurs, and the new types of ship that are being designed and built. But any shipping that attempts to use the Arctic as a shorter route will have to pass through the Bering Strait. Thus, the United States will be at the front door of the new shipping route no matter what Arctic route is used.

This position poses numerous challenges for the Americans. Given their treatment of the issue of the TAPS tankers, they fully understand the need for ship construction and safety standards that exceed existing international standards. At the same time, they will have to coordinate this understanding with their position regarding international straits in the Arctic. Currently, only U.S. ships transport Alaskan oil through a set of convoluted policies that are throwbacks to the protectionist era of the 1920s. Consequently, the Americans can ensure that those U.S. ships adhere to their strict regulations concerning environmental and safety standards. These policies cannot ensure, however, that the international ships that will come through the Bering Strait have been built and are operated to the best environmental standards.

The Americans will also need to deal with the geopolitical reality that they share the strait with Russia. It should also be noted that an active environmentalist movement in the United States will act to ensure that the environment in and around the Bering Sea and Strait is protected, even if the U.S. government wants to ignore the issue.

Ultimately, U.S. policymakers need to address the changing geopolitical environment in the Arctic. The race by the Arctic states to determine their respective Arctic continental shelves is leading some observers to be concerned that this is the start of an Arctic resources rush.[77] The United States' Arctic neighbors are all beginning to rebuild their military and coast guard abilities in order to operate in the North, and to take more assertive – even aggressive – tones in the Arctic.[78] As a result, the United States will need to pay much closer attention to the region.

5. The Direction Ahead

America can no longer ignore Arctic issues. It has to deal with the main issues of resource development and relations with their Arctic neighbors in a much more comprehensive fashion than ever before. The costs of business as usual are too high. The Arctic is changing, and if the United States is to meet this challenge and gain the benefits, it must think ahead and it must think creatively. So what does it need to do?

1. The United States needs to develop its Arctic policy in a multidimensional, multidisciplinary fashion. Everything is connected in the Arctic. The United States cannot think of security as separate from the environment, and that these are separate from the economy. This can be difficult for any government to keep in mind, but it is absolutely necessary that the Americans understand the interconnectedness of issues in the Arctic.

2. U.S. leaders need to recognize that the age of the Arctic is dawning. There is no doubt that other issues, such as Iraq,

Afghanistan, Iran or the economy will continue to dominate the United States' attention, but it cannot ignore the North.

3. The key issues the United States will face are resource development and international relations. The coming political battles over the issue of energy development will dominate U.S. Arctic discourse for the next decade. The Americans must decide how this will be done, and this will require the participation of all interested parties in a dialogue about what this means. Oil and gas companies will have to engage in a frank and open discussion with the environment and northern aboriginal organizations. If the decision is made not to develop the northern energy sources, then let the U.S. government close further discussion on the matter so that these companies can avoid wasting their resources in the North. On the other hand, if development is to occur, it must be done in accordance with the highest environmental standards. This will entail considerable expense, and all parties involved in the process will have to be completely open about what is required and how it will be paid for.

4. Northerners should be consulted in any policies the U.S. government adopts for the North. They must not be harmed by, but must benefit from, the decisions that are reached. The Arctic is home to many Americans, some whose ancestors have lived there since time immemorial. Any U.S. policy must always have a human face.

5. The United States must abandon its unilateral (perhaps even *isolationist*) tendencies when dealing with its neighbors. It must build on the new attitude introduced by the Obama administration. It must accede to the United Nations Convention on the Law of the Sea. It was never in the American interest to sit on the sidelines; it definitely makes no sense in terms of the Arctic. The United States needs to think in multilateral policy terms. Until the end of the Cold War, U.S. leaders recognized that U.S. national interests were protected and promoted by adherence to multilateralism. After efforts to "go it alone," U.S. leaders again realize the

value of multilateralism. The developing challenges in the Arctic are multidimensional and do not stop at the borders of each Arctic state. They require solutions that are not unilateral.

6. The United States also needs to recognize the special relationship it shares with Canada in the North. The United States' core interests are very similar to Canada's – the protection of the North from all manner of threat, environmental to traditional, and the development of the North's resources through the best environmental practices in a manner that directly benefits all North American northerners.

These issues must be addressed now, as the Arctic is undergoing massive transformation. The U.S. government knows what it needs to do in the Arctic. Is it prepared to act?

Notes

1 Originally published in The School of Public Policy: SPP Briefing Papers Focus on the United States 2, no. 2 (2009): 1–26. Focus on the United States is a collection of papers resulting from an initiative of the Institute for United States Policy Research within The School of Public Policy (at the University of Calgary) and the Canada Institute of the Woodrow Wilson International Center for Scholars. The intention of this ongoing collaboration is to cast light on critical issues pertaining to Canada–U.S. relations.

2 United States, White House, Office of the Press Secretary, National Security Presidential Directive/NSPD 66; Homeland Security Presidential Directive/HSPD 25 – Subject: Arctic Region (Washington, D.C.: January 9, 2009); http://www.fas.org/irp/offdocs/nspd/nspd-66.htm. Hereafter referred to as Arctic Region Policy.

3 United States Department of State, "Fact Sheet: U.S. Arctic Policy," U.S. Department of State Dispatch (Washington, D.C., December 26, 1994).

4 Arctic Region Policy, 2.

5 United States Department of State, "Fact Sheet," 1.

6 Arctic Region Policy, 2.

7 United States Department of State, "Fact Sheet," 1.

8 There are also important fisheries issues, particularly surrounding the crab fisheries, but space limitations preclude a detailed examination of these issues here.

9 See, for example, CBCNews, "Shell to Halt Offshore Drilling in Alaska," July 21, 2007; http://www.cbsnews.com/stories/2007/07/21/business/main3084842.shtml?source=RSSattr=Business_3084842.

See also M. Lynne Corn, Bernard A. Gelb, and Pamela Baldwin, Arctic National Wildlife Refuge (ANWR): New Directions in the 110th Congress – CRS Report for Congress (Washington, D.C.: Congressional Research Service, February 8, 2007).

10 Yereth Rosen, "Shell delays Alaska drilling plan due to legal dispute," *Reuters*, June 21, 2008; http://uk.reuters.com/article/businessIndustry/idUKN2020246220080621.

11 Kim Murphy, "Appeals court rules against Arctic drilling plan," *Los Angeles Times*, November 21, 2008, A-26; http://articles.latimes.com/2008/nov/21/nation/na-arctic-drilling21.

12 Campbell Robertson and Clifford Krauss "Gulf Spill is the Largest of its Kind, Scientists Say," *New York Times*, August 2, 2010; http://www.nytimes.com/2010/08/03/us/03spill.html?_r=2&fta=y&.

13 U.S. Department of the Interior, Press Release – "Interior issues Directive to Guide Safe, Six-Month Moratorium on Deepwater Drilling," May 30, 2010; http://www.doi.gov/news/pressreleases/Interior-Issues-Directive-to-Guide-Safe-Six-Month-Moratorium-on-Deepwater-Drilling.cfm.

14 *Popular Mechanics*, "Everything you Need to Know about Shell Oil and Arctic Offshore Drilling in Alaska," September 14, 2012; http://www.popularmechanics.com/science/energy/coal-oil-gas/everything-you-need-to-know-about-shell-oil-and-arctic-offshore-drilling-in-alaska-10720112.

15 Margaret Croin Fisk, "Alaska Claims I Suit U.S. Government Improperly Banned Off-Coast Drilling," *Bloomberg*, September 9, 2010; http://www.bloomberg.com/news/2010-09-09/u-s-improperly-banned-drilling-off-alaska-coast-state-alleges-in-lawsuit.html.

16 *Popular Mechanics*.

17 CBCNews, "Shell suspends Alaska Offshore Oil Drilling for 2012," September 17, 2012; http://www.cbc.ca/news/business/story/2012/09/17/shell-alaska-oil.html.

18 Sean Cocerham and Kyle Hopkins, "Alaska Has Plenty to Ponder with Second Obama Term," *Kansas City Star*, November 8, 2012; http://www.mcclatchydc.com/2012/11/08/174184/alaska-has-plenty-to-ponder-with.html.

19 See, for example, the website of Arctic Power – the Arctic National Wildlife Refuge; http://www.anwr.org/.

20 See the website of Defenders of Wildlife; http://www.defenders.org/arctic-national-wildlife-refuge.

21 International Energy Agency *World Energy Outlook – 2012: Executive Summary* (Paris: International Energy Agency, 2012): 1–2; http://www.iea.org/Textbase/npsum/weo2012sum.pdf.

22 The land-based estimate is from United States Geological Survey, Economics of 1998 U.S. Geological Surveys of 1002 Area Regional Assessment: An Economic Update, Report 2005-1359 (Washington, D.C.: USGS, 2005); it is hard to find a published source for the offshore prediction.

23 Oil-Price.Net, "Crude Oil and Commodity Prices," November 18, 2012; http://www.oil-price.net/.

24 U.S. Energy Information Administration, "Projected Alaska North Slope Oil Production at Risk beyond 2025 if Oil Prices Drop Sharply," *Today in Energy*, September 14, 2012; http://www.eia.gov/todayinenergy/detail.cfm?id=7970.

25 See Kenneth J. Bird, Ronald R. Charpentier, Donald L. Gautier (CARA Project Chief), David W. Houseknecht, Timothy R. Klett, Janet K. Pitman, Thomas E. Moore, Christopher J. Schenk, Marilyn E. Tennyson, and Craig J. Wandrey, "Circum-Arctic Resource Appraisal; Estimates of Undiscovered Oil and Gas North of the Arctic Circle," U.S. Geological Survey Fact Sheet 2008-3049 (Washington, D.C.: USGS, 2008); http://pubs.usgs.gov/fs/2008/3049/.

26 See United States, Department of the Interior, Minerals Management Service,

Alaska Region, "Leasing Information – September 16, 2008" (Washington, D.C.).

27 United States, Department of the Interior, Minerals Management Service, Alaska Region, "Regional Director Update," August 11, 2008 (Washington, D.C.).

28 Alyeska Pipeline Service Company, "Trans Alaska Pipeline System" (Anchorage, AK: APSC, 2008); http://www.alyeska-pipe.com/.

29 Washington State, Department of Ecology, Pacific States/British Columbia Oil Spill Task Force Prevention Project, "TAPS Trade Tankers Present and Future" (Olympia, WA, April 3, 2008); http://www.oilspilltaskforce.org/docs/project_reports/2010_TAPS_Trade_Tanker_Report.pdf.

30 See United States, National Oceanic and Atmospheric Administration, Office of Response and Restoration, "Response to the Exxon Valdez Spill" (Washington, D.C., July 14, 2008); http://response.restoration.noaa.gov/oil-and-chemical-spills/significant-incidents/exxon-valdez-oil-spill/response-exxon-valdez.html.

31 The legislation is commonly known as the Jones Act after its sponsor, Senator Wesley Jones; its correct name is the Merchant Marine Act, 1920.

32 See Larry Kumins, West Coast and Alaska Oil Exports, CRS Report for Congress RS22142 (Washington, D.C.: United States, Congressional Research Service, May 6, 2005); http://www.ipmall.info/hosted_resources/crs/RS22142_050506.pdf.

33 CBCNews, "Keystone XL protesters amassing in Washington," November 18, 2012; http://www.cbc.ca/news/business/story/2012/11/18/keystone-xl-protest-washington.html.

34 Arctic Region Policy, 5, 8.

35 See Kristian Åtland, "Mikhail Gorbachev, the Murmansk Initiative, and the Desecuritization of Interstate Relations in the Arctic," Cooperation and Conflict 43, no. 3 (2008): 289–311.

36 The Inuit are often still referred to as "Eskimos" in the United States, a term not of Inuit origin but that of other Aboriginal groups to explain the people who lived beyond the tree line to European explorers. The self-identified term "Inuit" means "our people."

37 For the best overview of the U.S. position, see Evan Bloom, "Establishment of the Arctic Council," American Journal of International Law 93, no. 3 (1999): 712–22.

38 Canada, Department of Foreign Affairs and International Trade, "Canada's Proposal to Establish an Arctic Council of the Eight Arctic Nations," (Ottawa, April 20, 1995), 1.

39 Declaration on the Establishment of the Arctic Council (Ottawa, September 19, 1996). The inclusion of a "footnote" in an international agreement is unique.

40 President Bill Clinton, "Letter to the Congress of the United States," February 10, 1997.

41 See Canada, House of Commons, Standing Committee on Foreign Affairs and International Trade, Canada and the Circumpolar World: Meeting the Challenges of Cooperation into the Twenty-First Century (Ottawa, 1997), 212.

42 Arctic Monitoring and Assessment Programme, Report on the Status of the Arctic Environment (Oslo, Norway: AMAP, 1997).

43 See Arctic Council, "Arctic Council Action Plan to Eliminate Pollution of the Arctic" (Barrow, AK, October 13, 2000); Arctic Climate Impact Assessment, "Mission Statement" (presented at the Fourth Arctic Council Ministerial Meeting, Reykjavik, November 24, 2004); http://www.acia.uaf.edu/pages/mission.html.

44 Arctic Region Policy, 4.

45 U.S. Department of State, Bureau of International Information, "State Department on Conclusion of Arctic Council Ministerial," IIP Digital, May 12, 2011; http://iipdigital.usembassy.gov/st/english/texttr

ans/2011/05/20110512171128su0.1273921.
html#axzz2CbKhX2mO.

46 UPI.com, "Clinton: Arctic Council
a Decision-Maker," May 13, 2011;
http://www.upi.com/Top_News/
World-News/2011/05/13/Clinton-
Arctic-Council-a-decision-maker/
UPI-90971305305724/.

47 Arctic.info, "Clinton: The Arctic Council
should be the principal body to resolve
issues in the Arctic," June 4, 2012; http://
www.arctic-info.com/News/Page/
clinton--the-arctic-council-should-be-the-
principal-body-to-resolve-issues-in-the-
arctic.

48 CBCNews North, "Arctic Council Leaders
Sign Rescue Treaty," May 12, 2011;
http://www.cbc.ca/news/canada/north/
story/2011/05/12/arctic-council-greenland.
html.

49 *Arctic Region Policy*, 4.

50 United States, Department of State,
Bureau of Oceans and Environmental
and Scientific Affairs, "U.S. Extended
Continental Shelf Project" (Washington,
D.C.); http://2001-2009.state.gov/g/oes/
continentalshelf/index.htm.

51 See Denmark, Ministry of Foreign
Affairs, "Conference in Ilulissat, Greenland: Landmark Political Declaration
on the Future of the Arctic," May 28,
2008; http://fnnewyork.um.dk/en/
statements/newsdisplaypage.aspx?news-
id=3d153209-5740-4b81-ba8b-f89cd-
39ca4fc.

52 Council on Foreign Relations "Transcript
of Hillary Clinton's Confirmation
Hearing," *Essential Documents*,
January 13, 2009; http://www.cfr.org/
us-election-2008/transcript-hillary-
clintons-confirmation-hearing/
p18225.

53 Matt Cover, "GOP Senators Sink Law of the
Sra Treaty: 'This Threat to Sovereignty',"
CNSNews.com, July 16, 2012; http://
cnsnews.com/news/article/gop-senators-
sink-law-sea-treaty-threat-sovereignty.

54 See Alex Oude Elferink, "Arctic Maritime
Delimitation: The Preponderance of
Similarities with Other Regions," in *The
Law of the Sea in the Polar Oceans: Issues
of Maritime Delimitation and Jurisdiction*,
edited by Don Rothwell and Alex Oude
Elferink (Dordrecht: Kluwer, 2001), 182–83.

55 United States, Department of State, Bureau
of European and Eurasian Affairs, "Status
of Wrangel and Other Arctic Islands," Fact
Sheet (Washington, D.C.), May 20, 2003;
http://www.state.gov/p/eur/rls/fs/128740.
htm.

56 James Broadus and Raphael Vartanov,
*Environmental Security: Shared U.S. and
Russian Perspectives* (Woods Hole, MA:
Woods Hole Oceanographic Institute,
2002), 60–61.

57 See United States, Department of State,
Bureau of Oceans and Environmental and
Scientific Affairs, Limits in the Seas no
112: United States Responses to Excessive
Maritime Claims (Washington, D.C.:
Office of Ocean Affairs, Bureau of Oceans
and Environmental and Scientific Affairs,
March 9, 1992), 72–74; http://www.state.
gov/documents/organization/58381.pdf.

58 United States, Department of State,
"Washington, D.C., 20520, March 12,
1970, Information Memorandum for Mr.
Kissinger – The White House, Subject:
Imminent Canadian Legislation on the
Arctic," *Foreign Relations*, 1969–76, vol.
E-1, Documents on Global Issues, 1969–72
(Washington, D.C.: Department of State,
Office of the Historian); http://2001-2009.
state.gov/r/pa/ho/frus/nixon/e1/53180.htm.

59 Franklyn Griffiths, "Beyond Sovereignty:
Governing the Northwest Passage as
though It Was an International Strait," *CIC
– Foreign Policy for Canada's Tomorrow*
(Toronto: Canadian International Council,
July 2008).

60 Randy Boswell, "Simulated talks show
possible solution for Arctic dispute,"
National Post, February 19, 2008.

61 Associated Press, "Bush seeks to bolster
security and economic partnerships

with Canada, Mexico," *International Herald Tribune*, August 19, 2007; http://www.southcoasttoday.com/apps/pbcs.dll/article?AID=/20070821/NEWS/708210377/-1/rss01.

62 See Brian Flemming, *Canada–U.S. Relations in the Arctic: A Neighbourly Proposal* (Calgary: Canadian Defence and Foreign Affairs Institute, December 2008).

63 *Arctic Region Policy*, 3.

64 Ibid., 7.

65 Elmendorf Air Force Base, "Military History in Alaska 1867–2000," factsheet; http://www.jber.af.mil/library/factsheets/factsheet.asp?fsID=5304.

66 U.S. Air Force, "Elmendorf welcomes F-22 Raptor," August 8, 2007; http://www.af.mil/news/story.asp?id=123063874.

67 See Russian News and Information Service, "Russian strategic bombers fly routine patrols over the Arctic," September 6, 2007; http://en.rian.ru/russia/20080609/109606915.html.

68 The Seawolf class submarine, which was supposed to replace the Los Angeles class, is reported to have excellent under-ice capabilities – one, the USS *Connecticut*, has been seen at the North Pole. The class was deemed too expensive for the new security environment when the Cold War ended, however, and only three were built. The Los Angeles class is now being replaced by the Virginia class, which some sources have suggested does not have good under-ice capabilities. It is certainly the case that all U.S. submarines reported in the Arctic are either Los Angeles or Seawolf class boats.

69 *Arctic Region Policy*, 3.

70 Randy Boswell, "Arctic fishing ban places pressures on Canada," *Canada.com*, February 15, 2009; http://www.climateark.org/shared/reader/welcome.aspx?linkid=118536.

71 Colin Woodard, "Questions swirl around the sinking of the MV Explorer," *Christian Science Monitor*, December 3, 2007; http://www.csmonitor.com/2007/1203/p04s01-wogi.html.

72 Ronald O'Rourke, "Coast Guard Icebreaker Modernization: Background, Issues, and Options for Congress," *CRS Report for Congress*, RL 34391(Washington, D.C.: Congressional Research Service, September 11, 2008), 3-4; http://fas.org/sgp/crs/weapons/RL34391.pdf.

73 See National Research Council, Committee on the Assessment of U.S. Coast Guard Polar Icebreaker Roles and Future Needs, *Polar Icebreakers in a Changing World: An Assessment in a Changing World* (Washington, D.C.: National Academics Press, 2007).

74 Quoted in Andrew Revkin, "A push to increase icebreakers in the Arctic," *New York Times*, August 18, 2008; http://www.nytimes.com/2008/08/17/world/europe/17arctic.html.

75 O'Rourke, "Coast Guard Polar Icebreaker Modernization," 19.

76 Seth Andre Myers, "On Thin Ice in the Arctic," *Los Angeles Times*, November 16, 2012; http://articles.latimes.com/2012/nov/16/opinion/la-oe-myers-arctic-20121116.

77 Scott Borgerson, "Arctic Meltdown," *Foreign Affairs* 87, no. 2 (March/April 2008): 63–77.

78 For Canada's actions, see Rob Huebert, "Canada and the Changing International Arctic: At the Crossroads of Cooperation and Conflict" (Montreal: Institute for Research on Public Policy, 2008); http://www.irpp.org/books/archive/AOTS4/huebert.pdf. See also Russian News and Information Service, "Russia must protect its Arctic interests – Security Council" (October 1, 2008); http://en.rian.ru/russia/20081001/117375528.html; BarentsObserver.com, "Russia is not a threat to Norway" (September 19, 2008); http://barentsobserver.com/en/node/21371, "Is Norway putting relations with Russia in jeopardy?" (August 18, 2008); http://barentsobserver.com/en/node/21613.

11. U.S. Defense Policy and the North: The Emergent Arctic Power[1]

Barry Scott Zellen

As the Arctic continues to thaw, and with its thaw to integrate with the world ocean and the maritime economy that unites the world, the challenge of how best to organize the defense of the High North, increasingly recognized as a strategic interest of the United States and its allies has been discussed by American defense officials and their allied counterparts. Since the end of World War II, America's defense efforts worldwide have long been organized into distinct regional or functional Unified Combatant Commands (UCCs). All UCCs are commanded by either a four-star general or an admiral, known as Combatant Commanders or CCDRs, formerly CINCs, and are joint commands integrating at least two of the services. Every year, the Defense Department updates its Unified Command Plan (UCP) when it may modify the AORs and command assignments. In 2008, there were ten UCCs, six defined by their regional AOR and four by their specific functionality; the regional UCCs are Africa Command (AFRICOM), Central Command (CENTCOM), European Command (EUCOM), Pacific Command (PACOM), Northern Command (NORTHCOM), and Southern Command (SOUTHCOM), while the functional UCCs are Joint Forces Command (JFCOM), Special Operations Command (SOCOM), Strategic Command (STRATCOM), and Transportation Command (TRANSCOM).[2]

UCCs evolve over time, responding to changes in the strategic landscape; the very first, in fact, was established in 1946 by President Truman and reflected the strategic contours of the post-war environment, with an Alaskan Command, Atlantic Fleet, Caribbean Command, European Command, Far East Command, Northeast Command, and Pacific Command. Each new conflict is perceived, and operationalized, to some degree through the regional lens of its UCC, limiting cross-command efficiencies, and, more importantly, a cross-command flow of ideas and historical knowledge that could contribute to the development of doctrine and promote the diffusion of tactical and strategic insights gained during conflicts past and present. A particular challenge of Arctic defense and security is the geographical centrality of the Arctic basin to the world ocean – right at the geostrategic crossroads of the northern hemisphere, where both the Pacific and the Atlantic, as well as the North American and Eurasian landmasses, all come together. The Arctic basin, as a consequence of the geograpgical convergence at the top of the world, overlaps the Area of Operations (AO) of three of America's regional commands: the U.S. Northern Command (USNORTHCOM), Pacific Command (USPACOM), and European Command (USEUCOM). Yet, while enclosed by the high North Pacific region, the high North Atlantic, and the northern coast and offshore islands of high North America, Arctic history has not affected each defense sector equally, and consideration of the historical context will help to illuminate the quest for the appropriate balance of UCCs for meeting the challenges of Arctic defense and security in the coming years.

As noted on the Defense Department website, the Unified Command Plan is "a key strategic document that establishes the missions, responsibilities, and geographic areas of responsibility for commanders of combatant commands," and "[e]very two years, the Chairman of the Joint Chiefs of Staff is required to review the missions, responsibilities, and geographical boundaries of each combatant command and recommend to the President, through the Secretary of Defense, any changes that may be necessary."[3] Accordingly, "UCP 2011, signed by President Obama on April 6, 2011, assigns several new missions to the combatant commanders," among which was included: "Shifting AOR boundaries in the Arctic region to leverage long-standing relationships and improve unity of effort," and "Giving U.S. Northern Command responsibility to advocate for Arctic capabilities."[4] Before the 2011 changes, the world map of UCPs showed command overlap in Greenland and the high North Atlantic between NORTHCOM and EUCOM, and similar overlap in Alaska between NORTHCOM and PACOM. Now, Greenland falls squarely in EUCOM's domain and Alaska in NORTHCOM.

Clarifying the boundaries marking the AO's for NORTHCOM and EUCOM appears, at first glance, to be a constructive step toward resolving ambiguities with regard to defense responsibilities in the High North; but the solution obscures what remains in fact an important and continuing ambiguity of the region, where East literally meets West, and where Pacific and Atlantic waters converge. Alaska is as much a part of the North Pacific region as it is the Arctic, and its defense has long been central, not just to North America, but also to the stability of the North Pacific. And Greenland, while tied by sovereign possession with Denmark and thus part of the diplomatic-strategic architecture of Europe, has been as important to the defense of North America, not only providing an historic stepping stone during the early historical colonization by Vikings in medieval times, but centuries later providing the same potential path of conquest to the Nazis and an important line of defense against the growing Soviet threat.

Formalizing Alaska as part of NORTHCOM's AO is logical on one level, since it is responsible for the defense of North America, of which Alaska is a sovereign component – though ironically, the North American Arctic remains the most secure part of the Far North, thanks in large measure to the sparse population, extreme isolation, and still unpredictable ice conditions of Canada's vast northern archipelago. Alaska stands in marked contrast to the Canadian Arctic region, having been the most recent area in North America to come under direct external military assault, which transformed the once colonial backwater into an active war zone during World War II. PACOM – which is responsible for securing the Pacific, and which until recently included Alaska in the high North Pacific and thus incorporated the World War II-era Alaska Command into its AO – also made logical sense, since PACOM's mission included the defense of a region hotly contested by Japan in World War II and later threatened by the rising Soviet fleet in the Cold War, a mission comparable to elsewhere in the Pacific – and which suggests that it remains a logical command for coordinating the defense of the Arctic, particularly in light of China's rise as a maritime trading power, and increasing, a blue water naval power, all the more so given Beijing's growing interest in the Arctic. While Japan made a dramatic but in the end tenuous grab in its militarist past for the high North Pacific, gaining possession of the Kuriles, southern Sakhalin, and, during the opening shots of World War II, the outer Aleutians as well, Tokyo's far northern reign was brief, and currently its ambitions are primarily defensive in nature.[5]

Japan is no longer really a great power in the high North Pacific, owing to the defensive mission of the JMSDF – but with some 110 major warships it remains an important strategtic partner, particularly with regard to countering China's increasing naval power. China has increased its Arctic activities, while at the same time expanding its naval aspirations and capabilities from brown to blue water, but its primary far northern ambition appears most likely to establish a secure, and dramatically shortened, direct trade route to Europe, and to benefit from the increasing trade in Arctic natural resources that were formerly inaccessible, and these economic interests would favor a less aggressive position than Japan took during World War II, which viewed the region's resources less collaboratively and eyed the High North primarily for strategic defense of its home islands and as a tactical diversion for America's fleet during the Battle of Midway.[6]

With China's assertion of greater naval dominance of the South China Sea precipitating a robust balancing reaction by its neighbors in partnership with the USN, it is unlikely that Beijing will be able to assert naval predominance over the high North Pacific like Japan did in the first half of the twentieth century. And while Beijing will compete aggressively for resources, it will likely do so as a member of the world economy, and not as an external disruptor like Tokyo did in earlier times.[7] China may seek to explore the Arctic, and in so doing to demonstrate that it has become a great power with global capabilities – but it is not likely to threaten the security of the Arctic. Indeed, on November 22, 2010, the China National Petroleum Corporation entered into an agreement with Sovcomflot about shipping along the Northern Sea Route, which was signed with much fanfare by Sovcomflot CEO Sergey Frank and the President of CNPC, Jiang Jiemin in Saint Petersburg – suggesting China's prudence and practical preference for increasing its energy security will likely trump the perquisites of achieving greater power recognition in the manner embraced by Tokyo a generation earlier.[8] Two months earlier, the *Barents Observer* had reported in an article titled "Iceland Invites China to Arctic Shipping" on increasing maritime relations between China and Iceland: "Icelandic President Ólafur Ragnar Grímsson told Norwegian broadcaster NRK that relations with China has picked up pace after the financial crisis shattered the island's national economy in 2008," and "said that the Chinese positions in the cooperation have been 'constructive, balanced, positive and definitely not aggressive.'"[9]

Framing Arctic defense and security through a Pacific lens thus has a certain logic, given that the industrialized trading states of Northeast Asia have a strong economic interest in the emerging trade routes across the top of the world,[10] and that China, America's next most likely peer competitor, eyes the Arctic through a Pacific lens – something Tokyo did a generation earlier. But widespread usage of northern shipping lanes still remains a long way off – even if some tentative seasonal use is already being made of the Northern Sea Route, the Arctic Bridge between Murmansk and Churchill, and the famed Northwest Passage.[11] As one Arctic geographer recently reminded me, there's always going to be winter – and, with winter, the ice will return. Winter's recurring presence will thus continue to limit the integration of the Arctic and the North Pacific, at least for now.

So even as Northeast Asia's populous industrial states eye the thawing Arctic, they view the region primarily as a gateway to European markets and as a new source of natural resources for their expanding economies – and less a target for military expansion. With Northeast Asian states thinking primarily in terms of trade, and of a thawing Arctic as an emergent trade route and source of new raw materials for its growing industrial economies, they are unlikely to pose a strategic threat to the region or to its security. Consequently, the Russian bear stands alone as the primary Arctic power whose current intentions and capabilities could potentially conflict with those of the West.[12]

Just as strong a case – if not in fact stronger – can be made for EUCOM's suitability as a regional command for the defense of the Arctic, since, for the time being, the most probable threat to northern security emanates, not from China, whose interests in the region are largely of an economic nature, but from the bolder, resource-enriched, and diplomatically resurgent Russia, whose symbolic 2007 polar flag-planting on the deep sea floor made international headlines and provided notice to the world that Russia was prepared to draw a line in the ice and to strongly defend its northern national interests.[13] Geography also sides with the European Command, since Russia owns by far the largest sector of Arctic coast, and, by quirk of geography, the shallowest and most resource-accessible Arctic continental shelf. So as the Arctic thaws, Russia will have greater access to a greater share of the Arctic's long-hidden offshore resource wealth than any other Arctic state and will thus have much reason for a strong defense of its northern onshore and offshore domain.[14]

Recent history also is on the side of the Arctic being viewed as part of EUCOM's AO, as the longest recent conflict in Arctic waters was, not the relatively brief battle for the Aleutians, but the much longer Battle of the Atlantic, and, later, the implementation of the 1986 Maritime Strategy at the Cold War's end viewed the Arctic's undersea domain as primarily a route to contain then-Soviet Russia's fleet in its home waters, before it could menace North America.[15] For these reasons, the key to a secure Arctic will remain tied to the fate of Europe and the ambitions of its largest state: Russia.

Arctic waters came into play during the six-year Battle of the Atlantic from 1939 to 1945, considered by many to be the longest continuous military campaign of World War II. Efforts to assert command of the seas, especially vital to ensure Britain's survival as an independent country, but also important for resupply efforts of our wartime allies including Soviet Russia, and German efforts to deny North Atlantic waters to us, resulted in an ongoing naval clash between allied and axis sea power.[16] There were a total of seventy-eight Arctic convoys that resupplied the northern ports of Arkhangelsk and Murmansk under the protective escort of the U.S. Navy, Royal Navy, and Royal Canadian Navy – enabling some 1,400 ships to deliver Lend-Lease supplies to the Soviet Union. Ever since the long Battle of the Atlantic, the high North Atlantic and Arctic waters have been viewed through the lens of the Atlantic alliance, and as essential to the stability of the North Atlantic.

It was Greenland's vulnerability to external aggression that brought American military power to the island, a year after Denmark was invaded and occupied by Nazi Germany on April 9, 1940. After Denmark had fallen, the Germans eyed Greenland as their first stage of an invasion route of mainland North America via the Gulf of St. Lawrence through to Upper Canada along the Great Lakes – much the way Britain did during the War of 1812. The vulnerability of Greenland resulted in America extending defense protection on behalf of the Danish government in exile, which continued after the war through the entire Cold War era as Soviet naval power grew. Had the Germans gained possession of Greenland, it could have put their fleet in striking distance of Newfoundland, enabling a two-pronged attack of strategic British territories. Guaranteeing Greenlandic security was viewed as a necessity to ensure the independence of Britain. Then, had Britain fallen, keeping the Germans out of Greenland, Newfoundland, and inevitably Canada would have been harder – and America's northeast maritime and land frontiers would have been highly vulnerable, much as the Aleutians proved in the face of aggressive use of Japanese naval power.

According to a statement from the U.S. Department of State issued on April 10, 1941, one day after the United States and Denmark entered into a defense agreement for Greenland, "during the summer of 1940 German activity on the eastern coast of Greenland became apparent," when "three ships proceeding from Norwegian territory under German occupation arrived off the coast of Greenland," and then "in the late fall of 1940, air reconnaissance appeared over East Greenland under circumstances making it plain that there had been continued activity in that region."[17] And on March 21, 1941, "a German bomber flew over the eastern coast of Greenland and on the following day another German war plane likewise reconnoitered the same territory. Under these circumstances it appeared that further steps for the defense of Greenland were necessary to bring Greenland within the system of hemispheric defense envisaged by the Act of Habana."[18] So on April 9, 1941, an agreement "between the Secretary of State, acting on behalf of the Government of the United States of America, and the Danish Minister, Henrik de Kauffmann, acting on behalf of His Majesty the King of Denmark in his capacity as sovereign of Greenland" was agreed to, granting "to the United States the right to locate and construct airplane landing fields and facilities for the defense of Greenland and for the defense of the American Continent" – but only "after explicitly recognizing the Danish sovereignty over Greenland."[19] The agreement recognized that "as a result of the present European war there is danger that Greenland may be converted into a point of aggression against nations of the American Continent, and accept[ed] the responsibility on behalf of the United States of assisting Greenland in the maintenance of its present status."[20] The United States asserted it had "no thought in mind save that of assuring the safety of Greenland and the rest of the American Continent, and Greenland's continuance under Danish sovereignty."[21]

Early in the Cold War, a new external threat to Greenland and to North America arose, not from the decisively defeated and now divided Germany, but from the former wartime partner, the Soviet Union. On April 27, 1951, a new treaty was signed, the "Defense of Greenland: Agreement between the United States and the Kingdom of Denmark."[22] Article I of the 1951 treaty affirmed that both countries, "in order to promote stability and well-being in the North Atlantic Treaty area by uniting their efforts for collective defense

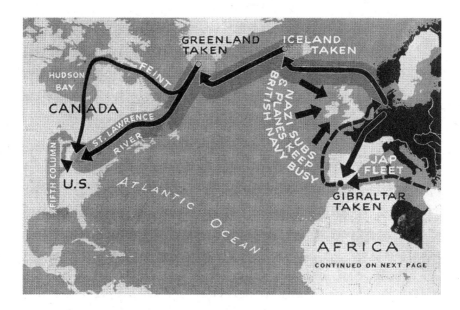

Fig. 1. This map, from the March 2, 1942, issue of *Life* magazine, details an 'alternate-historical' Nazi invasion of America imagined to have taken place shortly after the attack on Pearl Harbor. A discussion on the website BigThink.com (http://bigthink.com/ideas/26571) notes the above map depicts a "classic invasion down St. Lawrence and Hudson valleys. Germans could readily bomb Chicago, Detroit, Akron and rampage through Midwest. Big catch is getting past British Fleet. On all maps, black arrow alone means a feint; when combined with gray band, it means full invasion." The real-life efforts of the U.S. Coast Guard's Greenland Patrol are described in E. M. Van Duzer, "Watch over Greenland," in the April 1945 edition of *Popular Mechanics* 83, no. 4: 65–69, 156, 158.

and for the preservation of peace and security and for the development of their collective capacity to resist armed attack, will each take such measures as are necessary or appropriate to carry out expeditiously their respective and joint responsibilities in Greenland, in accordance with NATO plans."[23] This treaty would remain in place for more than half a century.

On August 10, 2004, Denmark, Greenland, and the United States updated their 1951 defense agreement, when "after two years of negotiations, all three parties – the U.S. on one side, and Denmark/Greenland on the other – reached consensus on the terms of the treaty. The United States was granted permission to upgrade Greenland's Thule Radar Station as part of the American Missile Defense (MS) program. The agreement itself implicitly recognized former Danish colony Greenland as an equal partner with influence over its own foreign affairs."[24] Among the most notable changes in the treaty's language was the emphasis on "partnership with Greenland," the inclusion of Greenland as a party to the treaty, and the evident spirit of equality among these three parties. According to Greenland's minister for Foreign Affairs, Josef Motzfeldt, "For us at home, this date marks the day that Greenland took a decisive step toward equality and responsibility on par with other countries of the world, and away from the indignity and indifference of the colonial era. By entering this agreement complex, Greenland has taken an active step toward increased foreign policy independence."[25] Colin Powell, then serving as the U.S. Secretary of State, echoed Motzfeldt's sentiment, adding that "it is important to demonstrate that Greenland is a full-fledged member of this partnership. And the best way of showing that is by being on hand today."[26]

Whoever Holds Iceland Holds the World

It was not just Greenland and its security that would be vital to the defense of the West. As important was Iceland. One could modify Billy Mitchell's well-known geopolitical maxim on Alaska from the 1930s – "I believe that, in the future, he who holds Alaska will hold the world, and I think it is the most important strategic place in the world"[27] – and apply it to the high North Atlantic – at least with regard to European and North American security. In this case, he who holds Greenland *and* Iceland seems destined to command the North Atlantic.

Indeed, novelist Tom Clancy imagined Iceland becoming the strategic pivot in a future conventional battle for the North Atlantic between NATO and the Soviet Union; the role of the G-I-UK gap throughout the Cold War, for both Soviet and NATO naval strategy, was indeed central – though ultimately untested by war in contrast to Clancy's fictional imaginings. Ironically, it was Clancy's conception of Iceland as a strategic pivot that would influence President Ronald Reagan on the eve of the almost history but in the end unsuccessful Reykjavik Summit with Soviet Premier Mikhail Gorbachev, where Gorbachev's bold proposal to rid the world of nuclear weapons was rebuffed because it would require a mutual commitment not to develop a strategic missile defense such as envisioned by Reagan's Strategic Defense Initiative, the cherished dream of Reagan known to many as Star Wars. As recounted in the December 8, 1986, edition of *Time*, "The phrase 'Reagan is not a detail man' is a mantra among Reaganites and suggests that he sees the big picture, that 'details' are for smaller minds. Yet such detachment can prove dangerous. In preparation for the Iceland summit, Reagan did not study the history and nuances of America's arms-control strategies; instead he practiced ways to sell Gorbachev on SDI. To get himself into the right frame of mind, he read Tom Clancy's *Red Storm Rising*, a potboiler about a non-nuclear war between NATO and the Soviet bloc."[28]

The Maritime Strategy of 1986 would likewise recognize the Arctic and the high North Atlantic as important areas for forward operations to contain the projection of Soviet naval power; critics feared it would destabilize deterrence but in the end it helped reassure Europe that Soviet power was far less potent than Moscow wanted people to believe. And in terms of economic potential, the commercial and strategic sea lanes of the North Atlantic, the vast North Sea oil fields, and the bountiful fisheries in the high North Atlantic – which almost led alliance members Iceland and the UK to come to blows during their 'Cod Wars' from the 1950s to the 1970s[29] – all illustrate the strategic-economic importance of the high North Atlantic as a bridge connecting Europe and North America.

As the Arctic thaws, North Atlantic fisheries,[30] natural resource extraction efforts,[31] and sea lanes will edge further north into Arctic seas,[32] eventually facilitating the emergence of an Asia-Europe-North America sea bridge some predict will be a modern-day silk road[33] – but the fundamental strategic relationship will remain the same. Consequently, it may continue to make sense to view the Arctic, as it becomes increasingly navigable and economically integrated, as an extension of the North Atlantic – since in addition to its historical linkages to the Euro-Atlantic community, the Arctic basin is only semi-enclosed, with its opening flowing into the North Atlantic, while in the Pacific it encounters a physical barrier, with only the narrow and shallow Bering Strait connecting the two. With an Arctic thaw, the Northeast Asian trading states will find a shorter and quicker direct route to markets in Europe and North America, but because of the narrowness (85 km) and shallowness (55 meters on average) of the Bering Strait,[34] they will not find as ready an opportunity to expand its naval influence into a sea still dominated by NATO and Russia.

The longer- term potential of trans-Arctic shipping, increased usage of the Northwest Passage, and the Northern Sea Route, while promising, has a long way to go before being viable – the Koreans, Chinese, and Japanese are eyeing shorter and safe shipping lanes to Europe over the top and the Koreans have taken the lead with regard to commissioning a new generation of ice-hardened tankers, though the Russians still dominate when it comes to heavy icebreakers.[35] While connecting Northeast Asian markets to Europe through an Arctic maritime bridge is compelling, there will always be winter and with winter, new ice will form in the Arctic basin, limiting the year-round viability of such sea routes – so it is unlikely that we will see the center of gravity tip entirely toward the Pacific, particularly given the extraordinarily close and enduring transatlantic relationships that have been forged across centuries of trade, wartime and peacetime alliances, and the much less united strategic environment in Northeast Asia. As transpolar shipping becomes more frequent, however, we may find reason for PACOM and EUCOM to conduct joint operations in the Arctic, perhaps formalizing the current regional command overlaps into a new, cross-regional sub-unified command, not unlike the new U.S. CYBERCOM that is subordinate to STRATCOM but which takes ownership of the distinct and emergent defense challenges of the information domain.

Even with Asian states eyeing Arctic trade routes, the North Atlantic still features prominently in most of their plans, most notably as the end destination for their marine exports or the starting point for their imports. Iceland could well become a primary trans-shipment hub for Asian cargo ships, positioning the high North Atlantic to remain of critical strategic importance. That may be one reason why Moscow was first to step up with an offer of neighborly assistance to bail out Iceland when its economy collapsed,[36] hoping perhaps to nudge Iceland a bit out of the western camp and help Moscow expand its influence in the high North Atlantic, counterbalancing the Scandinavian states that share maritime borders with Russia and which have historically contained its naval influence. As Konstantin Rozhnov reported on BBC:

> When Iceland announced it was seeking a $6bn (£4bn) loan from Russia to help rescue its crisis-ravaged economy, some in the NATO alliance, of which Iceland is a member, took fright. They suspected that Russia was acting to further its geopolitical interests in the region in the guise of a white knight. Reports of Russia seeking – or even securing – rights to Icelandic fisheries, energy and metal sectors, as well as in tourism, poured fuel on these fears. Russia has denied any political interest in its dealing with crisis-hit Iceland, but even some Russian media outlets have expressed scepticism, publishing caustic headlines such as "Ready to buy Iceland for good money." "If Russia becomes the country which saves the Icelandic economy, Russia could also end up securing an extended level of power in the North Atlantic," BarentsObserver website said in an editorial.[37]

This would not be the first time that Iceland looked east instead of west when in need; during its third Cod War with Britain in 1976, Iceland's government had sought to acquire U.S. Asheville class gunboats, but when its effort was thwarted by the U.S. government, it considered Soviet Mirka class frigates as an alternative.

The Inuit Dimension

Beyond Iceland, if Greenland were to become estranged from the West, and ultimately pursued an unfriendly secession from Denmark and ended up hostile to western interests, Moscow may find yet another friendly island-state open to courtship, and that would certainly favor its strategic position, putting pressure on the West and its command of the high North Atlantic. But for the moment, its independence movement is a friendly one, with Denmark's blessing – but that could always change if the cost/benefit calculation of Danish sovereignty over Greenland is re-assessed in light of the global thaw.[38] Going forward, the United States and its NATO allies might be wise to cultivate warmer relations with all the microstates and territories of the high North Atlantic and Arctic. Alaska and Iceland have especially close political ties, so this could be a good foundation, leveraging the warm relations state leaders in Alaska have fostered with Iceland's government.

Fostering a closer diplomatic relationship with Greenland is also under consideration, with its eventual independence anticipated. Consider a November 2007 State Department cable leaked by Wikileaks.org that observes "Greenland is on a clear track toward independence, which could come more quickly than most outside the Kingdom of Denmark realize…. With Greenlandic independence glinting on the horizon, the U.S. has a unique opportunity to shape the circumstances in which an independent nation may emerge. We have real security and growing economic interests in Greenland, for which existing Joint and Permanent Committee mechanisms … may no longer be sufficient. American commercial investments, our continuing strategic military presence, and new high-level scientific and political interest in Greenland argue for establishing a small and seasonal American Presence Post in Greenland's capital as soon as practicable."[39] The cable discusses the "High Stakes for the U.S. in Greenland," and argues that the "time is now to begin investing in a flexible, low-cost, official U.S. presence in Greenland" that "would allow us to advance our strategic and commercial agenda directly and to shape the image of the U.S. in Greenland as never before. For now, we can offer Greenland an American perspective. Down the road, we must be prepared for the day when we welcome a new and independent neighbor, one that will be a true partner within the transatlantic community of the 21st century."[40]

Like Iceland, Greenland could well be the key to a stable Arctic; no one at this stage can predict with accuracy where the sentiment and loyalties of an independent Greenland will lie. If the festering tensions between Europe and Canada's Inuit is any indication, there's much need for some fence-mending. Embracing the Inuit and their seal-hunting traditions would also go far to reduce tensions between the Inuit and the Europeans who oppose seal hunting and the fur trade generally, despite their long history of fur empires which, ironically, fostered their economic colonization of much of North America – from the strategic trading post at old Fort Niagara where the destiny of the continent was determined two and a half centuries ago, to the Hudson's Bay posts scattered across Rupert's Land, integrating the political economies of

Europe with the High North for the first time in human history.[41] More concerted confidence-building measures (CBMs) could help to ensure that the interests of the Inuit, and of the modern states that jointly assert sovereignty over their homeland, remain aligned.

This might in turn help thaw relations between the Inuit of Greenland as well as between Canada and the EU, helping to solidify transatlantic relations and to thereby boost regional security. During February's meeting of G7 finance ministers in the Canadian Arctic, Nunavut leaders generously hosted their international visitors with a taste of northern cuisine, including a staple of their subsistence diet: seal meat. As Andrew Clark reported in *The Guardian*, "None of the visiting ministers chose to attend a feast on Saturday night, laid on by the local Inuit community, at which raw seal was on the menu. Canada's Jim Flaherty was left to chow down on some seal meat alone."[42] Indeed, the refusal of the European G7 finance ministers to dine with the Inuit, and their very undiplomatic decision to disrespect Inuit hospitality in Nunavut's capital city by refusing to attend a feast held in their honor by the Inuit, was certainly not Europe's best moment. The opportunity to restore a climate of mutual friendship and trust may, with proper attention, still be with us; but that will take a more strenuous, and respectful, effort by the Europeans to mend fences with the still-disappointed Inuit.[43] This is perhaps why Secretary of State Clinton recently rebuked her Canadian counterparts for their exclusion of indigenous northerners from an A5 conference on the future of the Arctic, calling upon her peers to provide the Inuit with a seat at the table.[44]

The Inuit may be few in number, but they control many local economic and political levers, and their interests are now fully backed by Ottawa – their partner in land claims, self-government, and northern development.[45] Resolving lingering tensions between Europe and the Inuit is a necessary step to ensure the security of the High North, as greater issues are now in play that could affect the destiny of nations more than one people's views of another's dietary preferences. It wouldn't take much diplomatic savvy for the Russian bear to seize the opportunity and break bread with the Inuit over tasty slabs of whale and seal meat, hoping to forever drive a wedge between the people of the Arctic and the European states whose security will increasingly be tied to fate of the Arctic. Secretary Clinton's overture to the Inuit was thus a well-timed and diplomatically pre-emptive move to ensure the West doesn't lose the North on her watch.[46]

The Russian Bear

Russian activities in its sector of the Arctic generally focus on its vast, re-source-rich, and uniquely shallow continental shelf – which it smartly wants the world to recognize as its own extended continental shelf, and which un-der UNCLOS will likely be considered largely Russian and not high seas.[47] Its 2007 diplomatic stagecraft beneath the North Pole was less a grab for the polar seabed and more an assertion that there is a *Russian side* of the Arctic.[48] Moscow would very likely welcome the selection of the North Pole as the boundary point as it was in the Cold War, but the UN's Commission on the Limits of the Continental Shelf (CLCS) and the International Seabed Authority (ISA) may, once all the claims are filed and adjudicated, find that Canada's extended continental shelf extends past the pole onto what Moscow views as *its* side, depending in part on what the United States, Canada, and Russia can prove are continental shelf extensions.[49] But it may also find that Russia's extended continental shelf extends to what many in the West per-ceive as *our* side of the Arctic. As University of Calgary political scientist and leading Arctic expert Rob Huebert explained to *Up Here* magazine: "Russia's claim to the North Pole would give them an advantage. 'The North Pole is not the geographical centre between Russia, Alaska, Greenland and Canada; it's in fact further in towards the Russian coast. So claiming it would give them an advantage.' Still, Huebert says the Russians won't be able to claim the entire region to exploit as it sees fit. 'My guess is we'll see a complete division of the Arctic Ocean – except for two very clear depressions that are not part of a continental shelf,' Huebert says. 'Everyone would have a sector, like the Mediterranean or the North Sea.'"[50]

The primary Arctic tension – other than that between its indigenous peoples and the broad group of *southerners* who assert sovereign claim to the High North – is over offshore boundaries, and here the main fault line remains between Russia, on the one hand, and the West (Canada, the United States, and its European allies), on the other, even as political tensions thaw between old rivals. The United States and Canada are cooperating more closely even without agreeing fully on their Beaufort Sea boundary dispute or the status of the Northwest Passage; and the rhetorically muscular dispute between Ottawa and the Danes over Hans Island seems mostly for domes-tic play on both sides.[51] While in April 2010 Russia and its Cold War rival Norway buried the hatchet and resolved their long-simmering disagreements

over their offshore boundary line, easing the way forward to the joint development of the bountiful offshore petroleum resources in the hitherto contested waters, we should not presume that it will always be smooth sailing
ahead.[52] Economic collaboration can, and throughout history has, yielded
to nationalist rivalries and even war between trading partners. In the end,
the old East–West rivalry, with its millennial endurance, may well eventually
resurface, much as autopilot switches on during inclement weather, and this
reinforces the notion that the Arctic as a region, and a potential theater of
conflict, fits logically into EUCOM's AO and its continuing mission of securing Europe from external threat.[53]

Russian interests in the vast Eurasian Arctic are largely defined by its
exploitation and development of the enormous natural resource wealth both
along and beneath its northern shores, and rehabilitating its all-but-aban-
doned Northern Sea Route, which, during the immediate post-Cold War era,
lay largely abandoned (particularly off the shores of Eastern Siberia) but which
has lately enjoyed Moscow's recommitment to bring its vast treasure chest of
northern resources to market.[54] With its extensive, shallow, and increasingly
accessible Arctic continental shelf chock full of petroleum resources in exploitable quantities, Russia has much to gain from an Arctic thaw. But by
virtue of the strategic importance of this natural resource wealth to Russia's
economic resurgence, this also provides ample motivation for Moscow to ensure an adequate defense of its northern domain. It can no longer count on
nature to defend its northern flank with a 'great wall' of ice, and this could
result in rising security tensions along the old East–West faultline.[55] Just as
Canadians have a powerful emotional attachment to their northern frontier,
Russians view their Arctic lands and seas as an extension of their heartland
– which for them has been and remains their key to their survival, militarily
and economically. The intensity of this attachment, and the strategic importance of the heartland to Russian geopolitics, which saved the Russian nation from Napoleon's armies as it did from Hitler's, combine to define a vital
national interest for Moscow. This means that Russia, more than the other
littoral Arctic states, is more inclined to fully utilize its Arctic assets – even
though the post-Soviet economic collapse led to a decade-long abandonment
of much of its centrally subsidized mega-projects in the vast and now rusting
Russian Arctic, as well as its maritime infrastructure along its Northern Sea
Route. But in recent years, with higher commodity prices changing the cal-
culus, Moscow has reversed course, and there is now a growing commitment

to a fuller utilization of its Arctic resources, and a growing awareness that Russia's destiny, and a critical source of its future wealth, is tied to its fate in the North.[56]

Already there has been a restoration of Arctic naval, land, and air exercises to show the world that Moscow is serious about its Arctic ambitions, though these may be viewed as largely defensive in nature.[57] Along its borders, where the defensive nature of its regional military deployments could appear to be more menacing, this could lead to a re-emergence of historic tensions with its neighbors, especially after Moscow's smackdown of Georgia, as symbolic an act as its North Pole flag planting with greater muscularity, one that caught the attention of its many neighbors, particularly in the former Soviet satellite states, who united in their critique of the re-awakened bear. After Georgia, there could be little doubt that Russia would aggressively defend its Arctic interests if Moscow felt they were threatened.[58]

Still raw is Russia's loss of empire – first with its 1867 sale of Alaska to the United States, which many in Russia still feel was nothing short of wholesale theft, a transaction whose history remains clouded by distrust. The Russian-America Company was shuttered by Moscow after decades of sacrifice and investment by its explorers, who risked much to explore and colonize the high North Pacific, leaving many Russians perplexed by the abandonment of Alaska.[59] Some Russian ultra-nationalists, such as the infamous Vladimir V. Zhirinovsky, include a still-Russian Alaska on their national maps, though this may be largely symbolic and not necessarily a reflection of their true military ambitions.[60] In our own time, with the Soviet collapse, Russia became even smaller and more vulnerable with the loss of its Central European, Central Asian, and Baltic empire; its remaining Arctic lands and seas would thus be especially highly valued as a sacred and inseparable part of Mother Russia – a key to its future and one of the last sources of pride and hope that it has left. With new French warships on the way, and more heavy icebreakers than all of its neighbors combined, Russia might well emerge the predominant military power in the High North.

While Russia was at the table at Ilulissat in 2008 and pledged to support international law and the UNCLOS mechanism,[61] one must wonder what Moscow would do if the world community sided with Canada or Denmark in terms of continental shelf extensions at Russia's expense. While Moscow has resolved its border dispute with Norway, a welcome sign of a more collaborative Russia, sentiments and political winds can change. On the other hand, the Arctic, just as Gorbachev proposed in the 1980s,[62] could become a compelling testing ground for a new relationship between Russia and the West, and perhaps – if cooperation trumps competition over time – a path toward eventual NATO membership. But if competition trumps cooperation in the end, the Arctic may become one of the first regions in which a newly assertive Russia confronts the West. That's one more reason why EUCOM will invariably be drawn into the increasingly salient and ever-challenging mission of securing the Arctic.

Ultimately, if you look at which countries are Arctic nations, the *coastal* nations include Russia, Norway, Denmark/Greenland, Iceland – though its territory is nearly all subarctic, with the exception of diminutive Grimsey Island (which straddles the Arctic Circle, its northern waters reach well to the north), Canada, and the United States; and the *noncoastal* Arctic states include Finland and Sweden. Most are European, and the non-European Arctic states are NATO members with close historical, cultural, and strategic links to Europe. Only Russia's sparsely populated Far East, Alaska's equally sparsely settled southern coasts, and Canada's far western province of British Columbia, abut Pacific waters. Increasingly, transatlantic relations and the security of the West, and the continuing integration of the economies of the industrialized Far East with those of the West, will depend upon ensuring the security of the Arctic – suggesting that EUCOM may be the right command, in the right place, to play a key role on Arctic defense efforts. EUCOM – like the Arctic – enjoys an intimate proximity to Russia that ensures their fates will remain tied together for the years that lie immediately ahead. Proximity to an awakening Russian bear, and experience in taming its more aggressive instincts, will be an important key to a secure and peaceful North. While it can always be hoped that the bear can be tamed, enticed to join the West as a friend and partner, one must always be prepared for its more aggressive instincts to return. EUCOM, whose mission has been to defend the West from the darkest days of the Cold War through the glorious transformation to the post-Cold War era, has the experience to do both.

Until April 2011, all three commands shared some responsibility for the defense of the Arctic; as *Associated Press* correspondent Dan Elliot observed, "Previously, that responsibility was shared by the U.S. Northern, Pacific and European commands."[63] But now, this division has been both formalized and clarified – with NORTHCOM and EUCOM dividing the responsibility for the defense of the Arctic but PACOM being left out of the mix. *Stars and*

Stripes reporter John Vandiver noted that "U.S. Northern Command's area of responsibility was expanded earlier this year to include the North Pole and the Bering Strait," while "U.S. European Command's area was extended to include the water space of the Laptev and Eastern Siberian seas north of Russia. While NORTHCOM will be the lead advocate for Arctic issues within the Defense Department, EUCOM will manage military relationships with other Arctic nations in Europe."[64]

Vandiver added that at the headquarters of both NORTHCOM and EUCOM "officials have launched a review of the assets that will be required in the region in the years ahead," and he noted that "Col. Daniel Neuffer, the lead officer for Arctic issues at EUCOM, said the review will look at the Arctic from a long-term perspective," and cited Neuffer as saying: "What capabilities will we need 30 years from now? That's the assessment we're going through.... I think for Russian sustained growth, they will continue to need to harvest more natural resources. But nobody wants a conflict, because you can't extract anything if you're ducking bullets. In the Arctic, I think, cooler heads will probably prevail."[65]

But if they don't – a big uncertainty that our warfighters must be prepared to face – a more inclusive command structure might prove necessary, one that draws on PACOM for its expertise and capabilities from defending the high North Pacific, containing China's naval expansion, and its long and important legacy securing America's Pacific frontiers during the Cold War era and into the new, more chaotic, post-Cold War world. EUCOM is important, indeed critical, to the defense of the North; NORTHCOM, too, will find a central place. With an ascendant China on its historic rise, even if its ambitions are for the moment primarily commercial, the prospect of Beijing aspiring to greater geostrategic recognition as a great power, perhaps even a superpower whose reach extends far beyond the South China Sea into the global maritime commons that include the Arctic basin, cannot be discounted.

That's precisely what happened seventy years earlier, when an ascendant Tokyo's aspirations were similarly overlooked in the years that preceded World War II – until Japan's sudden, and unforeseen, assaults, not only upon Pearl Harbor, but also on Alaska's outer Aleutian Islands, shattered the calm – attacks that had been predicted with uncanny precision by noted air theorist Billy Mitchell more than a decade before they took place, but whose wise counsel was ignored at great peril and ultimately very high cost in blood and treasure.[66]

Notes

1 Originally published as "Cold Front on a Warming Arctic," *Proceedings* 137/5/1299 (May 2011): 44–49. Reprinted with permission from Proceedings: ©2011, U.S. Naval Institute/www.usni.org.

2 For full details, see: "Unified Command Plan," U.S. Department of Defense website; http://www.defense.gov/home/features/2009/0109_unifiedcommand/.

3 Ibid.

4 Ibid.

5 For more on Alaska in World War II, see: John Haile Cloe, *The Aleutian Warriors: A History of the 11th Air Force and Fleet Air Wing 4* (Missoula, MT: Pictorial Histories Publishing, 1990); Stan Cohen, *The Forgotten War: A Pictorial History of World War II in Alaska and Northwestern Canada* (Missoula, Montana: Pictorial Histories Publishing, 1981); Brian Garfield, *The Thousand-Mile War: World War II in Alaska and the Aleutians* (New York: Doubleday, 1969, and Fairbanks: University of Alaska Press, 1995); Otis Hays, *Alaska's Hidden Wars: Secret Campaigns on the North Pacific Rim* (Fairbanks: University of Alaska Press, 2004); Galen Roger Perras, *Stepping Stones to Nowhere: The Aleutian Islands, Alaska, and American Military Strategy, 1867–1945* (Vancouver: UBC Press, 2003).

6 For more in China's Arctic aspirations, see: Krista Mahr, "Does China Have an Eye on the Arctic?" Ecocentric Blog, *Time.com*, May 17, 2011; http://ecocentric.blogs.time.com/2011/05/17/does-china-have-an-eye-on-the-arctic/#ixzz1OMew4Ges; Gordon G. Chang, "China's Arctic Play," *The Diplomat*, March 9, 2010; http://the-diplomat.com/2010/03/09/china%E2%80%99s-arctic-play/; Joseph Spears, "China and the Arctic: The Awakening Snow Dragon," *China Brief* 9, no. 6, Jamestown Foundation, March 18, 2009; http://www.

jamestown.org/programs/chinabrief/single/?tx_ttnews[tt_news]=34725&tx_ttnews[backPid]=25&cHash=1c22119d7c.

7 See: Daniel Ten Kate, "China Reassures Its Neighbors after Clashes over Claims in South China Sea," *Bloomberg*, June 4, 2011; http://www.bloomberg.com/news/2011-06-05/china-reassures-its-neighbors-after-clashes-over-claims-in-south-china-sea.html; John Pomfret, "Beijing claims 'indisputable sovereignty' over South China Sea," *Washington Post*, July 31, 2010; http://www.washingtonpost.com/wp-dyn/content/article/2010/07/30/AR2010073005664.html.

8 See "China's new foothold on Northern Sea Route," *BarentsObserver.com*, November 26, 2010; http://barentsobserver.com/en/sections/business/iceland-invites-china-arctic-shipping and "Sovcomflot Group and China National Petroleum Corporation become strategic partners," Sovcomflot press release, November 22, 2010; http://www.sovcomflot.ru/npage.aspx?did=75963.

9 See: "Iceland invites China to Arctic shipping," *BarentsObserver.com*, September 22, 2010; http://barentsobserver.com/en/sections/business/iceland-invites-china-arctic-shipping.

10 On other Asian interest, see Jen Moon, "Revolution in Global Shipping Traffic: The Northern Sea Route," *Arirang: Korea's Global TV*, November 16, 2010; http://www.arirang.co.kr/News/News_View.asp?q=109124&code=Ne2&category=2; Shigeki Toriumi, "The Potential of the Northern Sea Route," *Chuo* Online, February 28, 2010; http://www.yomiuri.co.jp/adv/chuo/dy/opinion/20110228.htm.

11 Jan Husdal, "The Final Frontier: The Northern Sea Route," *Husdal.com*, May 22, 2011; http://www.husdal.com/2011/05/22/the-final-frontier-the-northern-sea-route/#ixzz1ON4uNQfS. A review article of

Halvor Schøyena and Svein Bråthenb, "The Northern Sea Route versus the Suez Canal: Cases from Bulk Shipping," *Journal of Transport Geography* 19, no. 4 (July 2011): 977–83; http://www.sciencedirect.com/science/article/pii/S096669231100024X. Also see: "More oil and ore along Northern Sea Route," *BarentsObserver.com*, February 11, 2011; http://barentsobserver.com/en/sections/norway/more-oil-and-ore-along-northern-sea-route.

12 "Russian Arctic brigade on border to Norway already in 2011," *BarentsObserver.com*, May 19, 2011; http://barentsobserver.com/en/topics/russian-arctic-brigade-border-norway-already-2011; also see, Олег Владыкин, "Заполярные планы Минобороны: Арктическую бригаду в Печенге собираются развернуть в текущем году," *Nezavisimaya Gazeta*, May 18, 2011; http://www.ng.ru/nvo/2011-05-18/1_minoborony.html.

13 See: "Russian Sub Plants Flag at North Pole: Tass," *Reuters*, August 2, 2007; http://www.reuters.com/article/2007/08/02/us-russia-arctic-flag-idUSL0286134520070802; Mike Eckel, "Russia Defends North Pole Flag-Planting," *Associated Press*, August 8, 2007; http://www.washingtonpost.com/wp-dyn/content/article/2007/08/07/AR2007080701554.html; Klaus Dodds, "Flag Planting and Finger Pointing: The Law of the Sea, the Arctic, and the Political Geographies of the Outer Continental Shelf," *Political Geography* 30 (2010): 1–11; http://royalholloway.academia.edu/KlausDodds/Papers/170877/Flag_planting_and_finger_pointing_The_Law_of_the_Sea_the_Arctic_and_the_political_geographies_of_the_outer_continental_shelf; CTV News Staff, "Canada, Russia Locked in Dispute over Arctic Border," *CTV.ca*, September 16, 2010; http://edmonton.ctv.ca/servlet/an/local/CTVNews/20100916/arctic-resources-100916/20100916/?hub=EdmontonHome.

14 See: "Outer Limits of the Continental Shelf beyond 200 Nautical Miles from the Baselines: Submission by the Russian Federation," Commission on the Limits of the Continental Shelf (CLCS), Updated June 30, 2009; http://www.un.org/depts/los/clcs_new/submissions_files/submission_rus.htm.

15 See: John B. Hattendorf, *The Evolution of the U.S. Navy's Maritime Strategy, 1977–1986* (Newport, RI: Naval War College Press, 1989); http://www.usnwc.edu/Publications/Naval-War-College-Press/Newport-Papers/Documents/19-pdf.aspx; Colin S. Gray, *Maritime Strategy, Geopolitics, and the Defense of the West* (New York: National Strategy Information Center, 1986); John J. Mearsheimer, "A Strategic Misstep: The Maritime Strategy and Deterrence in Europe," *International Security* 11, no. 2 (1986): 3–57.

16 See: "The Battle of the Atlantic," *The Times*; http://www.timesonline.co.uk/tol/system/topicRoot/The_Battle_of_the_Atlantic/; and Andrew Williams, *The Battle of the Atlantic: Hitler's Gray Wolves of the Sea and the Allies Desperate Struggle to Defeat Them* (New York: Basic Books, 2003); Admiral Kuznetsov, "The Northern Sea Route," *Memoirs of Wartime Minister of the Navy* (Moscow: Progress 1990), trans. Vladimir Krivoshchekov; http://admiral.centro.ru/memor00.htm; Dudley Pope, *73 North: The Battle of the Barents Sea* (London: Weidenfeld & Nicolson, 1958); Richard Woodman, *Arctic Convoys: 1941–1945* (Barnsley, UK: Pen and Sword Books, 2007).

17 "Statement by the Department of State on the U. S.–Danish Agreement on Greenland, April 10, 1941," U.S. Department of State, Publication 1983, *Peace and War: United States Foreign Policy, 1931–1941* (Washington, D.C.: U. S., Government Printing Office, 1943), 641–47.

18 Ibid.

19 Ibid.

20 Ibid.

21 Ibid.

22 See: *Defense of Greenland: Agreement between the United States and the Kingdom of Denmark*, April 27, 1951. Online at: http://avalon.law.yale.edu/20th_century/den001.asp. Signed in Copenhagen in duplicate in the English and Danish languages, both texts being equally authentic, this twenty-seventh day of April, 1951, by the undersigned duly authorized representatives of the Government of the United States of America and the Government of the Kingdom of Denmark.

23 Article I, *Defense of Greenland: Agreement between the United States and the Kingdom of Denmark*, April 27, 1951.

24 "History Made in Southern Greenland," Archives 2003–2004, Denmark.dk. Online at: http://www.denmark.dk/en/servicemenu/News/FocusOn/Archives2003-2004/HistoryMadeInSouthernGreenland.htm.

25 Ibid.

26 Ibid.

27 See: Barry Scott Zellen, *Arctic Doom, Arctic Boom: The Geopolitics of Climate Change in the Arctic* (Santa Barbara, CA: Praeger, 2009), 167; John Haile Cloe and Michael F. Monaghan, *Top Cover for America: The Air Force in Alaska, 1920–1983* (Anchorage: Anchorage Chapter–Air Force Association, 1984), 21; Claus-M Naske and Herman E. Slotnick, *Alaska: A History of the 49th State* (Norman: University of Oklahoma Press, 1994), 122.

28 Richard Stengel, Laurence I. Barrett, and Barrett Seaman, "How Reagan Stays Out of Touch," *Time*, December 8, 1986; http://www.time.com/time/magazine/article/0,9171,963023,00.html#ixzz1OT4DShys.

29 The "Cod Wars" placed Iceland's NATO membership and access to the strategic air base at Keflavik in jeopardy, with three distinct engagements that included deployment of British war ships to defend its fishing fleet from Iceland's use of net cutters, and which resulted in some ramming of vessels as well as some warning shots fired during the periods of September 1958 to November 1958; September 1972 to November 1973; and November 1975 to May 1976. Hannes Jonsson, *Friends in Conflict: The Anglo-Icelandic Cod Wars and the Law of the Sea* (London: Hurst & Co., 1982); "The High Seas: Now, the Cod Peace," *Time*, June 14, 1976; Hugh Clayton, "Dispute with Iceland Means Dearer Fish this Weekend," *The Times*, November 28, 1975, 6.

30 See: Kieran Mulvaney, "A New Fisheries Frontier in the Arctic," *Discovery News*, May 25, 2011; http://news.discovery.com/earth/a-new-fisheries-frontier-in-the-arctic-110525.html; The PEW Environment Group, "Oceans North International," *OceansNorth.org*; http://www.oceansnorth.org/faq.

31 Ironically, as coastal areas become more accessible, interior regions will become less so – potentially offsetting the benefits of a thaw in terms of net economic effects. As reported in *Reuters*, "Global warming will likely open up coastal areas in the Arctic to development but close vast regions of the northern interior to forestry and mining by mid-century as ice and frozen soil under temporary winter roads melt, researchers said.... The Arctic is increasingly a region of deep strategic importance to the United States, Russia and China for its undiscovered resource riches and the potential for new shipping lanes. The U.S. Geological Survey says that 25 per cent of the world's undiscovered oil and natural gas lies in the Arctic. But the warming also will likely melt so-called 'ice roads,' the temporary winter roads developers now use to access far inland northern resources such as timber, diamonds and minerals, according to a study published on Sunday in the journal Nature Climate Change.... The ice roads, made famous by the History Channel show 'Ice Road Truckers,' are constructed on frozen ground, rivers, lakes and swampy areas using compacted snow and ice. They cost only about 2 to 4 per cent of what permanent land roads would cost, making resource extraction

more cost effective in these remote areas."
Timothy Gardner, "Ice Melt to Close Off
Arctic's Interior Riches: Study" *Reuters*,
May 30, 2011; http://www.reuters.com/
article/2011/05/31/us-arctic-warming-
roads-idUSTRE74S1UF20110531.

32 "Terra Daily: Arctic Summer Sea Lanes
Open by 2015 Forecasts ONR," *SpaceDaily.
com*, February 14, 2002; http://www.
spacedaily.com/news/arctic-02a.html; Jill
Burke, "Brainstorming the Bering Strait
bottleneck," *AlaskaDispatch*, May 12, 2011;
http://www.alaskadispatch.com/article/
brainstorming-bering-strait-bottleneck.

33 Joe Friesen, "Russian Ship Crosses
'Arctic bridge' to Manitoba," *Globe and
Mail*, October 18, 2007; http://www.
theglobeandmail.com/news/national/
russian-ship-crosses-arctic-bridge-to-
manitoba/article1084466/. As Friesen
reported, "Michael Berk, a research fellow
at the Canadian Institute of International
Affairs, a non-profit think tank, said
Churchill could become the terminus of a
new silk road linking Eurasia and North
America. 'As ice continues to melt, this is
potentially the shortest route connecting
North America to Eurasia,' Mr. Berk said.
'If we expand and connect Churchill with
Murmansk, an ice-free, year-round port,
we're talking about creating a bridge that
will link North American markets with
increasingly important Eurasian markets.
It's also the closest route for transporting
goods from Asia to the Midwestern United
States directly, bypassing the bottlenecks
of congested ports in the Pacific. When one
starts to think about these issues combined,
the opportunity is tremendous.'"

34 Rebecca Woodgate, Knut Aagaard, Tom
Weingartner, Terry Whitledge, and Igor
Lavrenov, "Bering Strait: Pacific Gateway to
the Arctic," http://psc.apl.washington.edu/
HLD/Bstrait/bstrait.html#Basics.

35 Heather Exner-Pirot, "Eye on the Arctic:
How fast will Arctic shipping grow?,"
AlaskaDispatch April 11, 2011; http://www.
alaskadispatch.com/article/how-fast-will-
arctic-shipping-grow?page=0,0&sms_

ss=email&at_xt=4da728db4b8300df,0.
As Exner-Pirot writes, "South Korea, by
contrast, is interested in the economic
benefit of Arctic shipping, as it hosts the
largest ship building yards in the world.
Samsung Heavy Industries have developed
a double-acting vessel that has the same
open sea characteristics as other ships in its
class combined with the breaking capacity
of an icebreaker, cutting through up to 1.5
metres of ice. While the bow is shaped for
regular sailing, the stern is designed for
ice-breaking with the ship turned around
when there is heavy ice and the stern used
as the bow. South Korean industry (and,
incidentally, its subsidiaries in Finland)
thus has a vested economic interest in the
development of a trans-Arctic shipping
route and industry." Also see "Alaska Beat:
Korean gas execs explore Arctic LNG
shipping plan, in Canada," *AlaskaDispatch*,
April 20, 2011; http://www.alaskadispatch.
com/article/korean-gas-execs-explore-
arctic-lng-shipping-plan-canada.

36 Rowena Mason, "Financial Crisis:
Iceland gets €4bn Russian loan as banks
collapse," *The Telegraph*, October 7, 2008;
http://www.telegraph.co.uk/finance/
financialcrisis/3151148/Financial-
Crisis-Iceland-gets-4bn-Russian-
loan-as-banks-collapse.html; also see
Konstantin Rozhnov, "Russia's role in
rescuing Iceland," *BBC News*, November
13, 2008; http://news.bbc.co.uk/2/hi/
business/7720614.stm.

37 Rozhnov, "Russia's role in rescuing
Iceland."

38 Telegraph Foreign Staff and Agencies in
Nuuk, "Greenland Takes Step toward
Independence from Denmark," *The
Telegraph*, June 21, 2009; http://www.
telegraph.co.uk/news/worldnews/europe/
greenland/5594140/Greenland-takes-step-
toward-independence-from-Denmark.
html; Marianne Stigset, "Greenland
Bets on Oil, Metals, Cows as Ticket to
Independence," *Bloomberg*, May 12, 2011;
http://www.bloomberg.com/news/2011-
05-11/greenland-bets-on-oil-metals-cows-

as-ticket-to-independence.html; Shaun Walker, "Revealed: The Secret Battle for the Riches of the Arctic: Leaked cables show how nations are carving up pristine wilderness," *The Independent*, May 13, 2011; http://www.independent.co.uk/environment/climate-change/revealed-the-secret-battle-for-the-riches-of-the-arctic-2283229.html; Marianne Stigset, "Greenland Bets on Oil, Metals, Cows as Ticket to Independence," *Bloomberg*, May 12, 2011; http://www.bloomberg.com/news/2011-05-11/greenland-bets-on-oil-metals-cows-as-ticket-to-independence.html.

39 "Shaping Greenland's Future," Cable 07COPENHAGEN1010, *Wikileaks.org*, November 2007; http://wikileaks.org/cable/2007/11/07COPENHAGEN1010.html.

40 Ibid.

41 See: John R. Bockstoce, *Furs and Frontiers in the Far North: The Contest among Native and Foreign Nations for the Bering Strait Fur Trade* (New Haven, CT: Yale University Press, 2009), and Richard Clarke Davis, ed., *Rupert's Land: A Cultural Tapestry* (Waterloo: Wilfrid Laurier University Press, 1988). Also see Barry Zellen, "Cold Front: Hillary, Ottawa, and the Inuit: A Year after the Inuit Re-Assert their Sovereignty, Washington Takes Their Side," *Journal of Military and Strategic Studies* 12, no. 3 (2010): 5–11.

42 Andrew Clark, "Mervyn King goes dog sledding but all avoid seal meat at G7 summit in Canada," *The Guardian*, February 8, 2010; http://www.guardian.co.uk/business/andrew-clark-on-america/2010/feb/08/canada-alistairdarling.

43 Bill Curry, "G7 visitors take a pass on 'country food' feast," *Globe and Mail*, February 6, 2010; http://www.theglobeandmail.com/news/politics/ottawa-notebook/g7-visitors-take-a-pass-on-country-food-feast/article1458974/.

44 Barry Zellen, "Cold Front: Hillary, Ottawa, and the Inuit: A Year after the Inuit Re-Assert their Sovereignty, Washington Takes Their Side," *Journal of Military and Strategic Studies* 12, no. 3 (2010): 5–11.

45 Barry Zellen, *On Thin Ice: The Inuit, the State and the Challenge of Arctic Sovereignty* (Lanham, MD: Lexington, 2009).

46 Zellen, "Cold Front".

47 Husdal, "The Final Frontier: The Northern Sea Route." A review article of Halvor Schøyena and Svein Bråthenb, "The Northern Sea Route versus the Suez Canal: Cases from Bulk Shipping," *Journal of Transport Geography* 19, no. 4 (2011): 977–83; http://www.sciencedirect.com/science/article/pii/S096669231100024X. Also see: "More oil and ore along Northern Sea Route," *BarentsObserver.com*, February 11, 2011; http://barentsobserver.com/en/sections/norway/more-oil-and-ore-along-northern-sea-route.

48 See: "Russian Sub Plants Flag at North Pole: Tass" ; Eckel, "Russia Defends North Pole Flag-Planting"; Dodds, "Flag Planting and Finger Pointing"; http://royalholloway.academia.edu/KlausDodds/Papers/170877/Flag_planting_and_finger_pointing_The_Law_of_the_Sea_the_Arctic_and_the_political_geographies_of_the_outer_continental_shelf; CTV News Staff, "Canada, Russia Locked in Dispute over Arctic Border," *CTV.ca*, September 16, 2010; http://edmonton.ctv.ca/servlet/an/local/CTVNews/20100916/arctic-resources-100916/20100916/?hub=EdmontonHome.

49 See: "Russian Sub Plants Flag at North Pole: Tass"; Eckel, "Russia Defends North Pole Flag-Planting"; Dodds, "Flag Planting and Finger Pointing; http://royalholloway.academia.edu/KlausDodds/Papers/170877/Flag_planting_and_finger_pointing_The_Law_of_the_Sea_the_Arctic_and_the_political_geographies_of_the_outer_continental_shelf; CTV News Staff, "Canada, Russia Locked in Dispute Over Arctic Border," *CTV.ca*, September 16, 2010; http://edmonton.ctv.

ca/servlet/an/local/CTVNews/20100916/ arctic-resources-100916/20100916/?hub=E dmontonHome. Also see: "Outer limits of the continental shelf beyond 200 nautical miles from the baselines: Submission by the Russian Federation," Commission on the Limits of the Continental Shelf (CLCS), Updated June 30, 2009; http://www.un.org/ depts/los/clcs_new/submissions_files/ submission_rus.htm.

50 Graham Chandler, "Pole Position," *Up Here*, December 18, 2007; http://www. uphere.ca/node/177.

51 See: Yereth Rosen, "U. S.–Canadian mission set to map Arctic seafloor," *Reuters*, August 1, 2010; http://www.reuters.com/ article/2010/08/01/us-usa-canada-arctic-idUSTRE6700SP20100801. As close neighbors with a long, complex but largely pacific history of bilateral relations (with perhaps the War of 1812, domestic Canadian tensions during World War II and the early Cold War over a largely unrestricted U.S. military operating within Canada's sovereign boundaries, reciprocal tensions in the United States in response to Canadian support of America's Vietnam War resistors finding sanctuary from conscription, and a variety of protracted trade disputes as notable exceptions), Canada and the United States have learned to cooperate on many issues while nonetheless continuing to disagree with each other on various issues of policy – so it is no surprise this continues in the Arctic. As the Arctic Governance Project has noted, the 1988 Canada–U.S. Arctic Cooperation Agreement is a case in point, in that it "allows for practical cooperation regarding matters relating to the Northwest Passage while affirming that the two countries agree to disagree about the status of the passage under applicable international law. It demonstrates a capacity to collaborate in functional terms without resolving legal differences." See: "The Canada–U.S. Arctic Cooperation Agreement," The Arctic Governance Project; http://arcticgovernance.custompublish.com/the-canada-us-arctic-cooperation-agreement.4668242-142904.html.

On the long dispute between Canada and Denmark over Hans Island, see: "Canada and Denmark to share Hans Island? 37-year dispute over one-kilometre square rock may be coming to an end," *Maclean's*, November 9, 2010; http://www2.macleans. ca/2010/11/09/canada-and-denmark-to-share-hans-island/. Also see this interesting exchange of letters in the *Ottawa Citizen*: David Anido, "Greenland is an important neighbour," *Ottawa Citizen*, May 14, 2011; http://www2.canada.com/ottawacitizen/ views/story.html?id=ffe612ab-9184-444b -b295-294e558e6870, and: Peter Juel Thiis Knudsen, "Strong arm not wanted in Arctic," *Ottawa Citizen*, May 18, 2011. On the general issue of boundary disputes between Canada and its Arctic neighbors, and their domestic political roots, see: John Ivison, "How to keep a cool head in the Arctic," *National Post*, March 30, 2010; http://oped. ca/National-Post/john-ivison-how-to-keep-a-cool-head-in-the-arctic/.

52 Luke Harding, "Russia and Norway resolve Arctic border dispute: Treaty allows for new oil and gas exploration and settles 40-year row over Barents Sea," *The Guardian*, September 15, 2010; http://www.guardian. co.uk/world/2010/sep/15/russia-norway-arctic-border-dispute; and "Russia, Norway border agreement opens Arctic up to exploration," *New Europe*, September 19, 2010; http://www.neurope.eu/article/ russia-norway-border-agreement-opens-arctic-exploration.

53 On the renewal of Cold War-like tensions between Russia and the West, see: M. K. Bhadrakumar, "U.S. Breathes Life into a New Cold War," *Asia Times Online*, June 7, 2011; http://www.atimes.com/atimes/ Central_Asia/MF07Ag01.html.

54 As described on a Northern Sea Route website (http://northern-sea-route.co.tv/), "After the breakup of the Soviet Union in the early 1990s, commercial navigation in the Siberian Arctic went into decline. More or less regular shipping is to be found only from Murmansk to Dudinka in the west and between Vladivostok and Pevek in the

east. Ports between Dudinka and Pevek see virtually no shipping. Logashkino and Nordvik were abandoned and are now ghost towns. Renewed interest led to several demonstration voyage[s] in 1997" – as described by Lawson W. Brigham: "The Northern Sea Route, 1997," *Polar Record* 34 (1998): 219–24. In the years since, interest in, and use of, the route has been steadily rising.

55 See Halford J. Mackinder, "The Round World and the Winning of the Peace," *Foreign Affairs* 21, no. 4 (1943): 595–605. Also see Barry Zellen, *Arctic Doom, Arctic Boom* and Caitlyn L. Antrim, "The Next Geographical Pivot: The Russian Arctic in the Twenty-first Century," *Naval War College Review* 63, no. 3 (2010): 14–37; http://www.usnwc.edu/getattachment/ f8217b41-afd2-4649-8378-7b6c8a7e61d2/ The-Next-Geographical-Pivot--The-Russian-Arctic-in.aspx.

56 See: Lawson W. Brigham, "Russia Opens Its Maritime Arctic," *Proceedings*, May 2011, and Antrim, "The Next Geographical Pivot."

57 "Russia outlines Arctic force plan," *BBC News*, March 27, 2009; http://news.bbc. co.uk/2/hi/7967973.stm; "Moscow to deploy more forces in Arctic," *Russia Today* (*RT.com*), March 30, 2011; http://rt.com/ politics/moscow-deploy-forces-arctic/.

58 See: Dan Shapley, "Global Warming, the Arctic Thaw and the New Cold War: Why Russia's Incursion into Georgia Bodes Ill for the Climate," *The Daily Green*, August 18, 2008; http://www.thedailygreen.com/ environmental-news/blogs/shapley/arctic-thaw-47081802, and Robert Coalson, "A Year After Russia-Georgia War – A New Reality, But Old Relations," *Radio Free Europe/Radio Liberty* (*RFE/RL*), August 5, 2009; http://www.rferl.org/content/A_ Year_After_RussiaGeorgia_War__A_ New_Reality_But_Old_Relations/1793048. html.

59 For details on the final years of Russian America, see Anatole G. Mazour, "The Prelude to Russia's Departure from

America," *Pacific Historical Review* 10, no. 3 (1941): 311–19; and Frank A. Golder, "The Purchase of Alaska," *American Historical Review* 25 (1920): 411–25; Victor J. Farrar, *The Annexation of Russian America to the United States* (Washington, D.C.: W. F. Roberts, 1937).

60 Vladimir Solovyov and Elena Klepikova, *Zhirinovsky: Russian Fascism and the Making of a Dictator* (New York: Perseus, 1995); Timothy Egan, "The World; Alaskans Don't Want to Be Anyone's Siberia," *New York Times*, December 19, 1993; http://www.nytimes.com/1993/12/19/ weekinreview/the-world-alaskans-don-t-want-to-be-anyone-s-siberia.html; David McHugh, "Zhirinovsky Snubs Court Date Again," *The Moscow Times*, December 18, 1997; http://www.themoscowtimes.com/ news/article/zhirinovsky-snubs-court-date-again/296373.html; "Zhirinovsky Beat: At Home with Russia's Top Ultranationalist," *Time*, February 28, 1994; http://www.time.com/time/magazine/ article/0,9171,980254,00.html. As Timothy Egan wrote in the *New York Times*, "the 49th state is not exactly warming to the idea of taking this a step further. So it is saying no, thanks, to Vladimir V. Zhirinovsky, the right-wing extremist who stunned the world with his strong showing in elections in Russia on Sunday, and who in the past has suggested that Alaska be reclaimed by his country.... Whether Mr. Zhirinovsky is serious about restoring Alaska to what was once imperial Russia remained unclear after his press conference last week. But his party emblem offers a clue; it includes a map of the czarist empire embracing everything from Finland to Alaska."

61 See: The Ilulissat Declaration, Arctic Ocean Conference, Ilulissat, Greenland, May 27–29, 2008; http://www.oceanlaw.org/ downloads/arctic/Ilulissat_Declaration. pdf.

62 Mikhail Gorbachev, Speech in Murmansk at the Ceremonial Meeting on the Occasion of the Presentation of the Order of Lenin

and the Gold Star to the City of Murmansk, Murmansk, Russia, October 1, 1987; http://www.barentsinfo.fi/docs/Gorbachev_speech.pdf. Also see: Kristian Åtland, "Mikhail Gorbachev, the Murmansk Initiative, and the Desecuritization of Interstate Relations in the Arctic," *Cooperation and Conflict* 43, no. 3 (2008): 289–311.

63 Dan Elliot, "AP Interview: NORAD Commanders Say Melting Ice and Energy Development Will Make Arctic Busier," *Associated Press*, May 7, 2011.

64 John Vandiver, "Arctic Pact may Herald Cooperation in Region," *Stars and Stripes*, May 13, 2011; http://www.stripes.com/news/arctic-pact-may-herald-cooperation-in-region-1.143488.

65 Ibid.

66 As noted on the web page of the National Museum of the U.S. Air Force, in 1924, "Mitchell made an inspection tour of the Pacific and the Far East, after which he made his famous prediction that the Japanese would attack Pearl Harbor on a Sunday morning." As further noted, "During World War II, some of Billy Mitchell's warning came through, none more so than his famous prediction of war with Japan. In an official report submitted after his trip around the Pacific Ocean in 1924, Mitchell warned that Japan's expansionism would lead to conflict with the United States, and he foretold how a war would start. He stated that the war would begin with a surprise attack by Japanese forces on Pearl Harbor, Hawaii, in conjunction with an assault on the Philippines. 'Attack will be launched as follows: Bombardment, attack to be made on Ford Island (in Pearl Harbor) at 7:30 a.m.... Attack to be made on Clark Field (Philippines) at 10:40 a.m.' On December 7, 1941, the Japanese attacked Pearl Harbor at 7:55 a.m. and Clark Field just hours later." See: "Brig. Gen. William 'Billy' Mitchell," NationalMuseum.af.mil, February 11, 2010; http://www.nationalmuseum.af.mil/factsheets/factsheet.asp?id=739.

Russia

12. Mirror Images? Canada, Russia, and the Circumpolar World[1]

P. Whitney Lackenbauer

The United States of America, Norway, Denmark and Canada are conducting a united and coordinated policy of barring Russia from the riches of the shelf. It is quite obvious that much of this doesn't coincide with economic, geopolitical and defense interests of Russia, and constitutes a systemic threat to its national security.

> Russian Security Council Secretary Nikolai Patrushev,
> *Rossiiskaya Gazeta*, March 30, 2009

Canada takes its responsibility for its Arctic lands and water seriously and "this is why we react so strongly when other nations like Russia engage in exercises and other activities that appear to challenge our security in the North ... [and] push the envelope when it comes to Canada's Arctic.... The Canadian Forces have a real role to play in defending our sovereignty in the North."

> Hon. Lawrence Cannon
> to the Economic Club of Canada, November 20, 2009

The Arctic is a topic of growing geostrategic importance. Climate change, resource issues, undefined continental shelf boundaries, potential maritime transportation routes, and security issues now factor significantly into the domestic and foreign policy agendas of the five Arctic littoral states. The region has also attracted the attention of non-Arctic states and organizations, some of which assert the need to protect the Arctic "global commons" from excessive national claims and allegedly covet Arctic resources. Whether these geopolitical dynamics constitute an inherently conflictual "Arctic race" or a mutually beneficial "polar saga" unfolding according to international law is hotly debated.

Both Canada and Russia have extensive jurisdictions and sovereign rights in the Arctic and see the Arctic as their frontier of destiny. The region plays a central role in their national identities. Both countries intertwine sovereignty issues with strong rhetoric asserting their status as "Arctic powers" and have promised to invest in new military capabilities to defend their jurisdictions. Fortunately, for all the attention that hard-line rhetoric generates in the media and in academic debate, it is only one part of a more complex picture.

Nevertheless, scholars like Rob Huebert point to Russia as Canada's foremost adversary in the circumpolar world.[2] If Americans have constituted the primary threat to Canadian sovereignty, the Russians have been re-cast in the familiar Cold War role of the primary security threat. Russia, after all, has been the most determined Arctic player. Its domestic and foreign policy has repeatedly emphasized the region's importance, particularly since Putin's second presidential term, and assertive rhetoric about protecting national interests has been followed up by actions seeking to enhance Russia's position in the region. A new Arctic strategy released in September 2008 described the region as Russia's main base for natural resources in the twenty-first century. Considering Russia's dependency on these resources and its concerns that Western interests are diverging from their own, that the U.S. still intends to "keep Russia down," and that the Western military presence in the Arctic reflects anti-Russian strategic agendas,[3] "realists" like Huebert and Scott Borgerson interpret the Russian approach as confrontational and destabilizing. Does this "hard security" discourse portend an "Arctic arms race"[4] and a new Cold War in the region?

The key audience for confrontational rhetoric is domestic. In its official policy and statements on the High North, Russia follows a pragmatic line and pursues its territorial claims in compliance with international law. Leaders dismiss foreign criticisms that they are flexing their muscles to extend their claims beyond their legal entitlement. The prevailing *international message* that Russia seeks to project is that it will abide by international law – but that it will not be pushed around by neighbors who might encroach on its Arctic jurisdiction.[5] This mixed messaging is disconcerting to Canadian observers who see Russia as belligerent and aggressive. Ironically, our own discourse and positions are strikingly similar. On the one hand, the Harper government adopts provocative rhetoric, proclaiming that it will "stand up for Canada," that we must "use it or lose it" (presuming that there is a polar race), and promoting Canada as an Arctic and energy "superpower." It has adopted a sovereignty-security framework as a pretext to invest in Canadian Forces (CF) capabilities and extend jurisdictional controls. Canada's messaging and actions are sending the same signals as Russia's. Even Minister of Foreign Affairs Lawrence Cannon's speeches, which emphasize and promote circumpolar cooperation, also assert the need to defend against outside challenges – specifically Russian activities that purportedly "push the envelope" and "challenge" Canadian sovereignty and security. These alleged threats are mobilized to affirm that the Canadian Forces have a "real role" to play in defending our northern sovereignty.[6] Like much of the government's rhetoric, however, the precise nature of this role, and the nature of the Russian threat, remains ambiguous.

This chapter reflects upon how Canada reads – and *constructs* – Russian actions and intentions in the Arctic.[7] Do the countries see the strategic situation in fundamentally different ways? Are Canada and Russia on an Arctic collision course, or are we regional actors with shared interests and opportunities for expanded cooperation? As critical as Canadian politicians, journalists, and academic "purveyors of polar peril" (to borrow Franklyn Griffiths' phrase) are of Russia's rhetoric and behavior in the Arctic, Canada is actually mirroring it. Politicians in both countries use this dynamic to justify investments in national defense. If this "saber-rattling" is carefully staged and does not inhibit dialog and cooperation on issues of common interest, this theater may actually serve the short-term military interests of both countries. But the long-term goal of a stable and secure circumpolar world, where each Arctic littoral state enjoys its sovereign rights, must not be lost in hyperbolic rhetoric geared toward domestic audiences for political gain.

The Role of the Arctic in National Mythologies

The Arctic factors heavily into both Russian and Canadian national mythologies. Although Russia's approach to the North was sporadic from the era of Ivan the Terrible in the mid-sixteenth century to the early twentieth century, dreamers like scholar Mikhail Lomonosov proclaimed that "it is in Siberia and the waters of the Arctic that Russia's might well begin to grow." Russia's sale of Alaska to the United States in 1867 ended the dream of a great Russian-American fur empire, and war and revolution stymied development and exploration in the Arctic until 1920. The new Bolshevik government set its sights on the untapped economic potential of the Arctic, historian John McCannon observes, and its "conquest of the North" campaign in the 1930s "helped to hold the Soviet nation together during an era of great stress and strain in a way that simple coercion could not have done." The Arctic culture of the high Stalinist period, which wedded the "enigmatic mystique" of the North Pole with ideas of industrial and technological prowess, made the Russian Arctic "one of the most visible and appealing elements in a cultural environment already saturated with attempts to make every deed seem epic and grand."[8] Echoes of this patriotic propaganda resonate with current Russian political rhetoric, which also combines iconic imagery of heroic exploration, resource wealth, and military muscle-flexing to try to build consensus about the need to defend this strategic frontier.

Canada inherited its Arctic Archipelago from Great Britain in 1880 but governed its northern territories in a "fit of absence of mind" – to borrow Louis St. Laurent's apt characterization – until after the Second World War. The primary impetus for development was the Cold War, which placed the Arctic at the center of superpower geopolitics and American security agendas in conflict with Canada's sovereignty. The United States largely dictated the pace of "military modernization," which had had profound socio-economic, cultural, and environmental impacts on the North.[9] Civilian projects were more tentative. Prime Minister John Diefenbaker's bold "Northern Vision," unveiled in February 1958, was a national economic development strategy at its core. It was only partially realized before he lost his political focus.[10] Despite land claim agreements and new governance systems, the Arctic has remained an unfulfilled political and economic opportunity ever since.

The "sovietization" of the Russian North yielded more deliberate economic development. Closed industrial cities, as well as infamous gulags, joined military bases along the northern frontier by the 1940s, but they did not reflect a coherent strategic plan for the Russian Arctic. "From the 1940s through the end of the Soviet era in the early 1990s, expansion in the North continued to be haphazard, plagued perpetually by shortcomings and disorganization," McCannon summarized. Resource development and the improper disposal of radioactive material led to environmental degradation, and the collapse of the Soviet economy left Arctic communities in miserable conditions.[11] While countries such as Canada talks about the Arctic as a potential resource base for the future, Russia has been exploiting its riches for decades. Nevertheless, both countries share a sense of northern destiny that drives political, economic, and popular interest in "their" Arctic.

The Future Arctic: Polar Race or Polar Saga?

Development scenarios frame issues and influence priorities. In 2008, the Global Business Network published a framework to analyze plausible futures for Arctic marine navigation. The horizontal axis describes the degree of relative governance stability within and beyond the region, while the vertical axis describes the level of demand for resources and trade. This yields four scenarios. Neither "Polar Lows" nor "Polar Preserve" would bring the economic development that the Russian and Canadian governments desire. An "Arctic Race" envisions intense competition for resources and a corresponding willingness for states to violate rules and take unilateral action to defend their national interests. In this scenario, shared interests are few and unreliable, and rapid climate change will fuel a resource feeding frenzy in an anarchic region.[12] By contrast, the "Arctic Saga" scenario anticipates "business pragmatism that balances global collaboration and compromise with successful development of the resources of the Arctic" in a manner that "includes concern for the preservation of Arctic ecosystems and cultures."[13]

By the early 1990s, Russia and Canada seemed to be moving towards an Arctic saga. Mikhael Gorbachev's landmark Murmansk speech in October 1987 called for the Arctic to become a "zone of peace." Although Western commentators treated the Russian policy initiatives with scepticism, the potential de-securitization of the region opened up opportunities for political, economic, and environmental agendas previously subordinated to national security interests. In Canada, the Mulroney government shifted from a strong

MORE DEMAND

Arctic Race
High demand and unstable governance set the stage for a "no holds barred" rush for Arctic wealth and resources.

TRADE &

Arctic Saga
High demand and stable governance lead to a healthy rate of development that includes concern for the preservation of Arctic ecosystems and cultures.

UNSTABLE & AD HOC

GOVERNANCE

STABLE & RULES-BASED

Polar Lows
Low demand and unstable governance bring a murky and underdeveloped future for the Arctic.

RESOURCES

Polar Preserve
Low demand and stable governance slow development in the regions when introducing an extensive eco-preserve with stringent "no shipping zones".

LESS DEMAND

Fig. 1. Future Arctic scenarios matrix by the Global Business Network (GBN) for the Protection of the Arctic Marine Environment working group of the Arctic Council (2008). Source: Arctic Council.

sovereignty and military emphasis after the 1985 *Polar Sea* voyage to propose, in 1989, an international Arctic Council predicated on circumpolar coop- eration. Prominent commentators suggested that circumpolar cooperation would allay Western concerns about post-Soviet aspirations in the Arctic. "It would be no small accomplishment for Canada to bring Russia onto the world stage in its first multilateral negotiation since the formation of the Soviet Union," Franklyn Griffiths argued. "All the better if the purpose of the negotiation is to create a new instrument for civility and indeed civilized behavior in relations between Arctic states, between these states and their aboriginal peoples, and in the way southern majorities treat their vulnerable northern environment."[14] Tom Axworthy agreed: "As Arctic neighbours and as the biggest members of the circumpolar North, Canada and Russia share many common interests and problems. We must do what we can to encourage Russian democracy and oppose the resurgence of ultra-nationalist and autocratic forces there. The creation of an Arctic Council will be a modest but real recognition that Russia has joined the democratic community of nations."[15]

Canada–Russia relations in the Arctic began to thaw. In 1992, Mulroney and Yeltsin issued a Declaration of Friendship and Cooperation, then a formal Arctic Cooperation Agreement. In the absence of a sovereignty or security crisis, Ottawa had space to accommodate broader interpretations of security with environmental, cultural, and human dimensions. After 1993, the Chrétien Liberals continued to promote a message of diplomacy, governance, and long-term human capacity-building. In 2000, *The Northern Dimension of Canada's Foreign Policy* (NDFP) set four objectives for circumpolar engagement. Traditional security threats were notably absent. One of the NDFP's key priorities was working with Russia to address northern challenges such as cleaning up Cold War environmental legacies and funding Russian indigenous peoples' participation in the Arctic Council. "Perhaps more than any other country," the NDFP declared, "Canada is uniquely positioned to build a strategic partnership with Russia for development of the Arctic."[16]

Over the last decade, the language and emphasis has changed. Although no country challenged Canadian sovereignty directly in the late 1990s, Colonel Pierre Leblanc, the commander of Canadian Forces Northern Area (now Joint Task Force North), began to doubt Canada's military capability to deal with this possibility. Rob Huebert embraced the cause and tirelessly promoted his Canadian "sovereignty on thinning ice" thesis: climate change would invite foreign attempts to undermine our control over and ownership of our Arctic.[17] Disputes with Denmark over Hans Island and the United States over the Beaufort Sea and Northwest Passage were held up as prime examples of conflicts with our circumpolar neighbors. By coupling these "sovereignty" issues with the uncertainty surrounding climate change, commentators demanded a stronger Canadian Forces *presence* to address new sovereignty, security, and safety issues in a rapidly changing and allegedly volatile Arctic world.

The debate over sovereignty remained largely academic until it intersected with more popular perceptions about competition for Arctic resources. Record lows in the extent of summer sea ice, combined with record high oil prices and uncertainty over maritime boundaries (pushed to the fore by the Russian underwater flag-planting at the North Pole), conspired to drive Arctic issues to the forefront of international politics in 2007. The U.S. Geological Survey (USGS) estimated that the region holds 13 per cent of the undiscovered oil and 30 per cent of the undiscovered natural gas in the world. Commentators held up the absence of an Antarctic-like treaty and the U.S. failure to ratify the UN Convention on the Law of the Sea (UNCLOS) as evidence that the region lacked stable governance. In the popular imagination, the Arctic remained a vast *terra nullius*. Canada had allegedly fallen behind in a "race for resources," and nationalists demanded urgent action to defend its final frontier from outside aggressors. A similar message gained traction in Russia, conflating identity politics, national interests, the delimitation of the continental shelf, energy security, mineral resources, and security and control over Arctic jurisdictions.

A Race for Resources – or Sensible Northern Economic Development?

Russian authorities, mirroring views commonly expressed in Canada, emphasize the decisive role that the Arctic will play in their country's economic development and global competitiveness. According to President Dmitri Medvedev, the Arctic provides 20 per cent of Russian GDP and 22 per cent of Russian exports. Intense interest in the oil and gas reserves in the region has been fueled by the Russian economy's heavy reliance on energy extraction, of which the Arctic's share – particularly the resources of the continental shelf – is expected to grow. The USGS report expected that more than 60 per cent of the undiscovered oil and gas reserves in the Arctic will be on Russian territory or within its exclusive economic zone (EEZ). Strategic reserves of metals and minerals like copper, cobalt, nickel, gold, and diamonds add to Russia's high stakes in Arctic resource development.[18]

Russia's ultimate objective is to transform the Arctic into its "foremost strategic base for natural resources" by 2020, and the Russian Security Council has assured "serious economic support" to implement the government's Arctic policy. As a corollary, Russia intends to develop the Northern Sea Route (NSR) as a wholly integrated "national transportation route" connecting Europe and Asia by 2015. This will require modern harbors, new icebreakers, air support, and enhanced search and rescue capabilities. Prospects for development under current economic circumstances are poor, however, and experts warn that long-term sustainable growth in Russia can be achieved only with comprehensive structural reforms. Furthermore, the financial downturn and relatively low energy prices have affected investments and slowed the pace of hydrocarbon development in the Arctic.[19]

Although these considerations complicate the actual implementation of Russia's Arctic strategy, President Dmitry Medvedev told his security council in March 2010 that Russia must be prepared to defend its country's resources. "Regrettably, we have seen attempts to limit Russia's access to the exploration and development of the Arctic mineral resources," he said. "That's absolutely inadmissible from the legal viewpoint and unfair given our nation's geographical location and history."[20] These alleged "attempts to limit" are not specified but the bogeyman of outside encroachment feeds domestic anxiety. Russians are concerned about the legal process of defining the outer limits of their extended continental shelf (beyond 200 nautical miles), but Moscow is strident that the partition of the Arctic will be carried out entirely within the framework of international law. UNCLOS defines the rights and responsibilities of states in using the oceans and lays out a process for determining maritime boundaries. Littoral countries are therefore mapping the Arctic to determine the extent of their claims. Russia filed its extended continental shelf claim in 2001, but the Commission on the Limits of the Continental Shelf (CLCS) told Russia to resubmit its claim before its scientific data could be considered conclusive. Accordingly, Russia is engaged in further research to bolster its claim, which includes the Lomonosov and Mendeleev ridges crossing the central Arctic Ocean.

Whereas Russia has exploited Arctic resources for decades, Canadian political rhetoric continues to promote the High Arctic as "the land of tomorrow" – a *potential* resource frontier that could melt away from Canada's control along with the sea ice. This message has been broadcast in throne speeches and government proclamations in the past four years. Prime Minister Harper proclaimed in July 2007: "Just as the new Confederation looked to securing the Western shore, Canada must now look north to the next frontier – the vast expanse of the Arctic.... More and more, as global commerce routes chart a path to Canada's North – and as the oil, gas and minerals of this frontier become more valuable – northern resource development will grow ever more critical to our nation. I've said before that the North is poised to take a much bigger role in Canada."[21]

The following year, the Canadian government pledged to invest $100 million over five years to map resources in the North, streamline regulatory processes so that economic development can proceed, and improve northern housing, amongst other announcements. Huebert observed "that this was one of the largest budget allocations for northern expenditures in Canadian history."[22]

The government's "use it or lose it" mantra serves as a justification for Canada to assert control over its Arctic lands and waters. In terms of the extended continental shelf, Canadian commentators often paint the Russians (along with the U.S. and the Danes) as challengers to Canada's claim, spreading popular misconceptions about the process and alleging that the Arctic is a "lawless frontier." Canada ratified UNCLOS in 2003 and has ten years to submit evidence for its extended continental shelf. The 2004 federal budget announced $69 million for seabed surveying and mapping, and the government allocated another $20 million in 2007 to complete the research by the deadline. Critics suggest that Canada lacks the icebreaking capacity to meet this timeline, while government officials insist that Canada will submit its claims to the CLCS on schedule.

What is the real cause for alarm? Are Russian interests antithetical to Canada's? Initial Canadian concerns about Russia related to continental shelf claims, particularly the Lomonosov Ridge, which Canada also claims as an extension of its continental shelf. This *potential* dispute (Canada has not submitted its claim) took on heightened profile when the Russian *Arktika* expedition planted a titanium flag on the seabed at the North Pole in July 2007. "The Arctic is Russian," the bombastic Russian Duma politician and explorer Artur Chilingarov proclaimed. "We must prove the North Pole is an extension of the Russian continental shelf." Although the Russian Foreign Minister later dismissed this as a "publicity stunt" that the Kremlin had not approved, the world was quick to react. Then Canadian Foreign Affairs Minister Peter MacKay was adamant that this "show by Russia" posed "no threat to Canadian sovereignty in the Arctic" in legal terms. "This isn't the 15th century," he quipped. "You can't go around the world and just plant flags and say 'We're claiming this territory.'"[23] Accordingly, many Canadian politicians and journalists held up Chilingarov's action as a quintessential example of Russian belligerence, one that highlighted an abject disregard for due process and international law.

While these events received significant attention in the press, this narrative was not echoed in official bilateral statements, all of which emphasized cooperation, collaboration, and shared interests. In July 2006, Prime Minister Harper and President Putin issued a joint policy statement reaffirming that the countries are "neighbours in the vastness of the North and we share a deep commitment to the welfare of our Arctic communities." Through partnership in the Arctic Council and bilateral channels, the countries pledged to "continue to work together toward sound and sustainable Northern development, balancing environmental protection with economic prosperity."[24] In December 2007, Harper and Prime Minister Viktor Zubkov pledged to cooperate on Arctic economic opportunities, search and rescue, marine pollution control, and mapping of their respective continental shelves. Both countries agreed on the need for science to support their claims.[25] The following May, the declaration of the Arctic littoral states (the "Arctic five") at the Ministerial Conference in Ilulissat, Greenland, reaffirmed that all would adhere to the "extensive international legal framework" that applied to the Arctic Ocean. The declaration reinforced that the Arctic was not a lawless frontier, and sovereignties were compatible under international law. Rather than anticipating an Arctic race or arbitration by force of arms, the Ilulissat declaration promised "the orderly settlement of any possible overlapping claims."[26]

This line of argument resonates with both Canadian and Russian policy statements that promote circumpolar cooperation. The Russian Arctic strategy, approved in September 2008, prioritizes maintaining the Arctic "as an area of peace and cooperation." Russian ambassador-at-large Anton Vasilyev, a high-ranking participant in the Arctic Council, insists that "media assessments of possible aggression in the Arctic, even a third world war, are seen as extremely alarmist and provocative: In my opinion, there are no grounds for such alarmism."[27] Foreign Affairs Minister Cannon began to articulate a similar position in his Whitehorse speech on March 11, 2009, when he acknowledged that geological research and international law – not military clout – would resolve boundary disputes. His statement emphasized collaboration and cooperation. "The depth and complexity of the challenges facing the Arctic are significant, and we recognize the importance of addressing many of these issues by working with our neighbours – through the Arctic Council, other multilateral institutions and our bilateral partnerships,"

Cannon expressed. "Strong Canadian leadership in the Arctic will continue to facilitate good international governance in the region."[28] Canada's long-awaited northern strategy, released that July, reaffirmed that the process for determining Canada's continental shelf, "while lengthy, is not adversarial and is not a race." Indeed, bilateral relations with Russia on trade, transportation, environmental protection, and indigenous issues were cast in positive terms.[29]

Potential Conflict in the Arctic

A parallel discourse, however, continues to suggest that the circumpolar Arctic is volatile. Huebert insists that Moscow's political strategy is "an iron fist in a velvet glove," pointing to Russia's "escalatory" military activities in the North and around the world: the war in Chechnya, strategic bomber flights in the Arctic, missile test-firings near the North Pole, nuclear submarine cruises in the region, and commitments to expand land force activities.[30] Russia's bold military re-modernization plans appear to be part of Putin's ambitious agenda to correct the devastating state of its armed forces after the end of the Cold War. Are these events evidence that the Russian bear has emerged from its post-Cold War hibernation, seeking to re-assert its power and anticipating an Arctic conflict?

In 2001, the Russian government endorsed an Arctic policy document linking all types of activities in the region to national security and defense interests. Russia's Northern Fleet, the largest and most powerful component of its navy, is based on the Kola Peninsula. With the weakening of Russia's conventional forces, nuclear deterrence (and particularly sea-based nuclear forces) has grown in importance and assumed a high priority in military modernization efforts. At the same time, political scientist Katarzyna Zysk observes, "old patterns in Russian approaches to security in the High North are visible in the way other actors in the region are viewed through lenses of a classical *Realpolitik*." Russian elites continue to view the United States and NATO as threats to Russian security and perceive a "broad anti-Russian agenda among America and its allies, aimed at undermining Russia's positions in the region." The West's growing interest in the Arctic feeds suspicions that rival powers may seek to constrain and even dispossess Russia of its rights.[31] "If we do not take action now, we will lose precious time," Secretary of the Russian Security Council Nikolai Patrushev warned in 2008, "and later in the future it will be simply too late – they will drive us away from here."[32] This Russian logic is remarkably similar to the "use it or lose it" message emanating from Canada.

Although Russian statements do not anticipate a large-scale military confrontation in the region, strategic documents raise the possibility that international competition could result in small-scale confrontations related to energy resources. Accordingly, Russian authorities emphasize that a reliable military presence is essential to secure national interests. The Russian Ministry of Defense announced in July 2008 that the navy would become more active in Arctic waters, and senior officials insisted that military exercises would prepare Russian troops for combat missions if they were needed to protect the nation's claims to the continental shelf. Despite this harsh Russian rhetoric, Zysk concludes, it is unlikely that Russia would push for military confrontation in the Arctic. Demonstrations of military force would work against the normal legal resolution of Russia's claim to its extended continental shelf, and geography dictates that Russia has the most to gain if the process unfolds according to international law. Furthermore, "one of the region's biggest assets as a promising site for energy exploration and maritime transportation is stability," Zysk observes. "As the report to the WEU Assembly on High North policies stated in November 2008, given the economic importance of the Arctic to Russia it is likely that leaders will avoid actions that might undermine the region's long-term stability and security."[33]

Canadian reactions to Russian activities would suggest a different reading of the Russian threat. Are renewed Russian military overflights and the July 2008 decision to send warships into Arctic waters (for the first time in decades) indications of nefarious intentions? The flight of two Russian military aircraft close to Canadian airspace on the eve of President Barak Obama's visit to Canada in February 2009 is a prime example. National Defence Minister Peter McKay explained that two CF-18 fighters were scrambled to intercept the Russian aircraft and "send a strong signal that they [the Russians] should back off and stay out of our airspace." Prime Minister Harper echoed that: "I have expressed at various times the deep concern our government has with increasingly aggressive Russian actions around the globe and Russian intrusion into our airspace. We will defend our airspace."[34]

To Russian spokespersons, this tough talk seemed misplaced. News agencies in Russia reported that "the statements from Canada's defence ministry are perplexing to say the least and cannot be called anything other than a farce."[35] Dmitry Trofimov, the head of the Russian embassy's political section in Ottawa, insisted that there was no intrusion on Canadian national airspace or sovereignty and "from the point of international law, nothing happened, absolutely nothing." The countries adjacent to the flight path had received advanced notification, and this scheduled air patrol flight did not deviate from similar NATO practices just beyond Russian airspace.[36] Georgiy Mamedov, the Russian ambassador to Canada, confessed that he had "a hard time explaining this bizarre outburst to Moscow."[37]

The tough rhetoric persists. Canadian politicians reacted sharply when Russia stated its intention to drop paratroopers at the North Pole in the spring of 2010. While a Russian embassy spokesman insisted that the mission was a "solely symbolic" event aimed at celebrating the sixtieth anniversary of a Cold War achievement by two Soviet scientists, Defence Minister MacKay was emphatic that Canada was going to "protect our sovereign territory. We're always going to meet any challenge to that territorial sovereignty, and I can assure you any country that is approaching Canadian airspace, approaching Canadian territory, will be met by Canadians." The language was peculiar, given that the Russians had expressed no intention of encroaching on Canadian "territory."[38] Similar rhetoric about "standing up for Canada" followed the CF-18 interception of Russian *Tu-95 Bear* bombers off the east coast of Canada in July 2010, once again outside of Canadian airspace. Journalists and military analysts immediately tied the issue to Arctic sovereignty and security, casting the Russians in the familiar role of provocateurs attempting to violate Canada's jurisdiction.

Ironically, while Canadian politicians and commentators have been quick to accuse the Russians of militarizing the Arctic agenda, the tempo of Canada's military activities has increased significantly over the last decade, matched by major commitments to invest in northern defenses. The Canadian navy resumed Arctic operations in 2002, and the military initiated enhanced sovereignty operations to remote parts of its archipelago that same year. These exercises are now carried out annually. Sovereignty and security has become intertwined in political rhetoric and strategic documents, beginning with the Liberal government's *Defence Policy Statement* (2005) and the Conservatives' *Canada First Defence Strategy* (2008) and *Northern Strategy* (2009). Internationally, Canada finds itself cast in the unfamiliar role of a catalyst for militarizing the region, staging "Cold War-style exercises" just like the Russians.[39]

The North was a key component of the Conservatives' 2005 election platform, which played on the idea of an Arctic sovereignty "crisis" demanding decisive action. Stephen Harper indicated during his election campaign that Canada would acquire the military capabilities necessary to defend its sovereignty against external threats: "The single most important duty of the federal government is to defend and protect our national sovereignty.... It's time to act to defend Canadian sovereignty. A Conservative government will make the military investments needed to secure our borders. You don't defend national sovereignty with flags, cheap election rhetoric, and advertising campaigns. You need forces on the ground, ships in the sea, and proper surveillance. And that will be the Conservative approach."[40] His political message emphasized the need for Canadian action with a particular emphasis on conventional military forces, differentiating his government from the Liberals whom he believed had swung the pendulum too far towards diplomacy and human development. Harper was going to swing it back towards defense and resource development and enforce Canada's sovereign rights.

Since assuming office in 2006, Harper has made the CF the centerpiece of his government's "use it or lose it" approach to the Arctic. This fits within the *Canada First Defence Strategy* vision that pledges to defend Canada's "vast territory and three ocean areas" through increased defense spending and larger forces.[41] Naval patrols, over-flights, effective surveillance capabilities, and boots on the ground are identified as tools that Canada will use to defend its northern claims. A spate of commitments to invest in military capabilities – from Arctic patrol vessels to new military units – reinforces the Harper government's emphasis on "hard security" rather than "human security" like its predecessors. The prime minister explained on February 23, 2007: "We believe that Canadians are excited about the government asserting Canada's control and sovereignty in the Arctic. We believe that's one of the big reasons why Canadians are excited and support our plan to rebuild the Canadian Forces. I think it's practically and symbolically hugely important, much more important than the dollars spent. And I'm hoping that years from now, Canada's Arctic sovereignty, military and otherwise, will be, frankly, a major legacy of this government."[42] The logic holds that Canadians are interested in Arctic sovereignty, which makes it a useful issue to generate voter support for defense. This formulation offers little political incentive to downplay the probability of military conflict in the Arctic.

The Harper government, like the Russians, is trying to project an image of northern resolve. Ironically, both countries accuse the other of militarizing the Arctic agenda. This may represent a classic case of the liberal security dilemma – states misperceive each other's intentions and, in striving to be defensively secure, others perceive their actions as threatening. On the other hand, this may be a simple case of political theater in the high Arctic, staged by politicians on both sides of the Arctic Ocean to convince their domestic constituencies that they are protecting vital national interests – yet another convenient pretext to justify major investments in defense.

Canada–Russia Cooperation

In an April 2009 plea for "why the bear and the beaver should make nice together," Carleton University political scientist Piotr Dutkiewicz lamented that, while the United States had declared its intention to "press the reset button" and enhance its working relationship with Russia, and the European Union was talking with Moscow about energy, security, environmental, and economic interests, Canada's government was "resurrect[ing] Cold War phantoms and scar[ing] children with tales of Russian bombers and reincarnated KGB troops storming Ottawa from the Arctic." Ottawa had dropped its Russian programs through the Canadian International Development Agency and cut its "only viable student and academic mobility program that permitted Russians and Canadians to collaborate in areas ranging from Arctic research to NGO co-operation." Fortunately, the Canadian business community remained "ahead of its political leadership in understanding the Canada–Russia opportunity" and bilateral trade continued to grow.[43]

If the probability of a Russia–Canada confrontation over Arctic boundaries and resources is remote, what shared interests might political leadership in both countries seek to pursue collaboratively? The idea of an "Arctic bridge" linking Eurasian and North American markets certainly remains attractive as a means to promote trade in natural resources and agricultural produce. In 2007, for example, the first inbound shipment of fertilizer from northwestern Russia arrived in Churchill, Manitoba, and both countries have emphasized plans to expand and diversify the shipments using this route.

More generally, safe and competitive maritime traffic through Arctic waters will require addressing significant gaps in marine governance and research, as demonstrated by groundings of fuel supply and passenger vessels in the Northwest Passage in 2010. Both countries continue to work through international organizations (particularly the IMO) to support a mandatory polar code, harmonize safety and pollution regulations, and develop a cooperative Arctic Search and Rescue instrument with the other Arctic states through the Arctic Council.

Canada can also find solace in the fact that Russia is the only Arctic littoral state that does not officially challenge its position on the legal status of the Northwest Passage. Indeed, Canada stands to learn from Russia's experience in managing their Northern Shipping Route. Most careful commentators note that the NSR will be a more attractive option for commercial vessels interested in Arctic transit over the next few decades, and Canada is advantageously positioned to study scientific research and implementation issues related to polar transits, including navigational requirements, pollution standards, emergency facilities, and fees.[44] These "lessons learned" will help Canada devise its own management regime when its archipelagic waters become attractive and economically viable for commercial transit traffic.

Russian spokespersons have also indicated that the countries should work cooperatively to "freeze out" non-Arctic states who may seek to encroach on their sovereign rights. "Those like Canada and Russia who have access to [the] Arctic ... they seem to have a better understanding of how to do it collectively," Sergey Petrov, the acting chief of the Russian embassy in Ottawa, told reporters in July 2009. "But there's some outside players [later identified as the European Union and its members] that want to be involved, and they're putting some oil on the flame of this issue." He reiterated that it was not in the interests of Canada or Russia to involve states that did not border the Arctic Ocean in establishing extended continental shelf boundaries and other UNCLOS-related matters.[45] In this regard, the March 2010 meeting of the Arctic-Five in Chelsea, Quebec – which the U.S. and Canadian media criticized for not including Iceland, Sweden, Finland, or the permanent participants – was applauded in the Russian media. Containing the state-centered dialog on issues related to national jurisdictions and resources may be appropriate until continental shelf claims are settled. This does not undermine the Arctic Council, as critics allege, as long as the agenda is confined to boundaries and sovereign rights under UNCLOS.

Canada and Russia can reiterate the message to the Arctic community that they have shared interests in a stable, secure, and sustainable circumpolar world. As mentioned earlier, working with Russia to address its northern challenges was a key component of the Liberal government's *Northern Dimension of Canada's Foreign Policy*. This is echoed in Conservative government actions, such as the 2007 Joint Statement on Canada–Russia Economic Cooperation and the Memorandum of Understanding between the Ministry of Regional Development of the Russian Federation and the Department of Indian Affairs and Northern Development concerning cooperation on aboriginal and northern development.[46] Canada and Russia should continue to reaffirm their bilateral agreements on cooperation in the Arctic and the North,[47] based on their continuing desire for partnership to serve the interests of northerners. Priority areas should remain economic development, Arctic contaminants, Aboriginal issues, resource development, geology, tourism, and health. The governments should facilitate continued contact between government representatives, aboriginal organizations, other NGOs, scientists, and business associations and firms. INAC's Circumpolar Liaison Directorate should remain the lead federal coordinator for implementation of this agreement. Canadian Inuit groups have been strong proponents of the Russian Association of Indigenous Peoples of the North (RAIPON), encouraging Canada to help their Aboriginal peoples tackle environment development challenges and supporting Aboriginal representation at the national and international levels.[48] Although modest technical assistance initiatives designed to share best practices (such as the Institutional Building for Northern Aboriginal Peoples in Russia program, which is continuing under a modest northern development stream, and the Canada–Russia Northern Development Partnership Program funded by the Canadian International Development Agency) may not enjoy a strong political or media profile, Russians perceive them as constructive initiatives and they contribute to regional and local Aboriginal entrepreneurship, as well as improved regional governance systems.[49]

"Russia's Arctic opening is a huge challenge with tremendous strategic, commercial, and environmental ramifications," Charles Emmerson recently summarized in *Foreign Policy*. "It is also an opportunity do things right."[50] The same conclusion can be drawn about Canada, offering possibilities for stronger bilateral cooperation. Despite both countries' commitments to resource development, balancing economic prosperity with environmental protection and improved living conditions for northern peoples remain significant challenges. Fortunately, for all the high-level political and media talk of conflict, bilateral relations at the working group level remain positive.[51] The prospects for enhanced partnerships on policy areas of common concern are strong, despite strong rhetoric from each country accusing the other of militarizing the Arctic agenda and destabilizing the region.

Conclusions

In late April 2010, Canada's Chief of the Maritime Staff, Admiral Dean McFadden, explained that the Canadian Forces do not anticipate an armed standoff over Arctic resources. Economic interests should not lead to the militarization of the North, he emphasized, and the real challenges relate to safety and security – an environmental spill, search and rescue, and climate change causing distress to communities. The role of the Canadian Forces is to support other government departments, not to lead Canada's charge in a military showdown.[52] This reassuring message is more frequently echoed at the political level. For example, Minister Cannon told a Moscow audience on September 15, 2010, that Canada "look[s] forward to working with our Arctic partners to advance shared priorities and to address common challenges to fulfill our vision of the Arctic as a region of stability, where Arctic states work to foster sustainable development, as well as to exercise enlightened stewardship for those at the heart of our Arctic foreign policy – Northerners."[53]

International newspaper commentators suggest that the world is not registering these rational and reasonable messages. Timothy Bancroft-Hinchey's article in *Pravda* is an extreme example: "What does Prime Minister Stephen Harper have in common with the Canadian Minister of Defence? He shares a sinister, hypocritical and belligerent discourse bordering on the lunatic fringe of the international community.... From Canada, Russia has become used to seeing and hearing positions of sheer arrogance, unadulterated insolence and provocative intrusion.... What these statements hide is Canada's nervousness at the fact that international law backs up Russia's claim to a hefty slice of the Arctic and that international law will favour Russia in delineating the new Arctic boundaries."[54] Is Canada belligerent, even lunatic, megalomaniacal, arrogant, insolent, provocative, and insecure about its claims? Ironically, this harsh characterization of Canada is a mirror image of the way that some muckraking journalists in the Western world characterize talk about Russia.

Sovereignty and security are compatible in the circumpolar world. So is cooperation and competition. The dance between Canada and Russia over Arctic issues, rich in mixed messaging, can serve the complex political interests of both parties if it is carefully choreographed. Both governments have indicated their desires to revitalize their military forces. This requires national will, and Russian and Canadian politicians are tapping into identity politics associated with the Arctic to justify investments in military capabilities for defense of sovereignty. In this sense, rhetorical jousting serves political interests in both countries, and the primary audiences are domestic.

It is shared interests in, and commitments to, international law that make this a safe political dance. Both countries can point to one another as provocateurs with relative certainty that neither will use force to undermine the other's sovereign rights in the region. There is little likelihood that the continental shelf delimitation process will lead to military intimidation or confrontation. (The 2010 Russia–Norway agreement in the Barents Sea sets the standard for peaceful resolution of contentious issues.[55]) The downside is that this political theater could inhibit cooperation between two Arctic states that share many common interests in the region. Given geographical realities, both countries have the most to gain from an orderly process that creates a stable environment for resource development and safe shipping through Arctic waters. They also have common interests in ensuring that non-Arctic littoral states and organizations do not encroach on resource rights or jurisdictions to which Canada and Russia are entitled under international law.

Both nations' Arctic policy documents assert their status as leading Arctic powers, but rhetorical and material investments in "hard security" must be situated within broader Arctic discourses and policies. It is unlikely that Canada and Russia will be close friends, given historical mistrust, geopolitical interests in other parts of the world, and lingering questions about their respective motives. This does not preclude opportunities for bilateral and multilateral cooperation in the Arctic. The challenge is cutting through the mixed messaging emanating from government officials. Careful stage-managing might continue to produce political theater that sustains national will to implement military plans, but it could also reinforce broader Arctic strategies that balance defense, diplomacy, and development for Canada and Russia alike.

Notes

1 An earlier version of this chapter was published in *International Journal* 65, no. 4 (2010): 879–97. Reprinted with permission of the Canadian International Council.

2 Rob Huebert, "Welcome to a new era of Arctic security," *Globe and Mail*, August 24, 2010.

3 Katarzyna Zysk, "Russia and the High North: Security and Defence Perspectives," in *Security Prospects in the High North: Geostrategic Thaw or Freeze?*, edited by S. G. Holtsmark and B. A. Smith-Windsor (Rome: NATO College, 2009), 102, and "Geopolitics In the Arctic: The Russian Security Perspective," *Climate of Opinion: The Stockholm Network's Energy and Environment Update no. 12 – The Arctic* (March 2009).

4 See, for example, Rob Huebert, *The Newly Emerging Arctic Security Environment* (Calgary: Canadian Defence and Foreign Affairs Institute, 2010); Scott Borgerson, "Arctic Meltdown: The Economic and Security Implications of Global Warming," *Foreign Affairs* 87, no. 2 (March/April 2008): 63–77.

5 Zysk, "Russia and the High North," 106.

6 Address by Minister Cannon to the Economic Club of Canada, "The Global Economy and Canada's Response," No. 2009/58, Toronto, Ontario, November 23, 2009.

7 The author thanks Jennifer Arthur, Rob Huebert, Stéphane Roussel, Ron Wallace, and Katarzyna Zysk for their valuable comments on an earlier version, first published in *International Journal* 65, no. 4 (2010): 879–97 (reprinted with permission of the Canadian International Council), as well as the ArcticNet project on The Emerging Arctic Security Environment for research support.

8 John McCannon, *Red Arctic: Polar Exploration and the Myth of the North*

in the Soviet Union, 1932–1939 (Oxford: Oxford University Press, 1998), 8–9, *passim*.

9 See, for example, P. Whitney Lackenbauer and Matthew Farish, "The Cold War on Canadian Soil: Militarizing a Northern Environment," *Environmental History* 12, no. 3 (2007): 920–50.

10 Philip Isard, "Northern Vision: Northern Development during the Diefenbaker Era." MA thesis, University of Waterloo, 2010.

11 McCannon, *Red Arctic*, 177. See also Antrim, "Next Geographical Pivot," 21; Robert Conquest, *The Great Terror: A Reassessment* (Oxford: Oxford University Press, 1990).

12 Borgerson, "Arctic Meltdown," 71.

13 Global Business Network, "The Future of Arctic Marine Navigation in Mid-Century," scenario narratives produced for the Protection of the Arctic Marine Environment (PAME) working group, May 2008.

14 "Let's invite Yeltsin to join our club," *Toronto Star*, November 6, 1991.

15 "Rallying around the North Pole," *Globe and Mail*, November 13, 1992.

16 DFAIT, *The Northern Dimension of Canada's Foreign Policy* (Ottawa: DFAIT, 2000), 16.

17 See, for example, Huebert, "Climate Change and Canadian Sovereignty in the Northwest Passage," *Isuma* 2, no. 4 (2002): 86–94, and "The Shipping News Part II: How Canada's Arctic Sovereignty Is on Thinning Ice," *International Journal* 58, no. 3 (2003): 295–308. Franklyn Griffiths offers the contrary viewpoint in "The Shipping News: Canada's Arctic Sovereignty Not on Thinning Ice," *International Journal* 53, no. 2 (2003): 257–82, and "Pathetic Fallacy: That Canada's Arctic Sovereignty Is on

Thinning Ice," *Canadian Foreign Policy* 11, no. 3 (2004): 1–16.

18 Katarzyna Zysk, "Russia's Arctic Strategy: Ambitions and Constraints," *Joint Force Quarterly* (April 2010): 105; "Circumpolar Resource Appraisal: Estimates of Undiscovered Oil and Gas North of the Arctic Circle," USGS Fact Sheet 2008-3049 (Washington, D.C.: U.S. Geological Survey, 2008). See also Caitlyn Antrim, "The Next Geographical Pivot: The Russian Arctic in the Twenty-first Century," *Naval War College Review* 63, no. 3 (2010): 19, and Oleg Alexandrov, "Labyrinths of Arctic Policy," *Russia in Global Affairs* 7, no. 3 (2009): 110.

19 Zysk, "Russia's Arctic Strategy," 105.

20 Quoted in CBC News, "Canada–Russia Arctic tensions rise," March 17, 2010.

21 PMO, "Prime Minister Stephen Harper announces new Arctic offshore patrol ships," July 9, 2007.

22 Rob Huebert, "Canada and the Changing International Arctic: At the Crossroads of Cooperation and Conflict" (Institute for Research on Public Policy, 2008), 23. http://www.irpp.org/books/archive/AOTS4/huebert.pdf.

23 Quoted in "Russias plant flag in Arctic seabed," *Ottawa Citizen,* August 3, 2007.

24 Joint Policy Statement by Prime Minister Stephen Harper and President of the Russian Federation Vladimir Putin on Canada–Russia Relations, Saint Petersburg, July 15, 2006.

25 DFAIT, "Russian PM's Official Visit to Canada, November 28–29, 2007," Joint Statement on Canada–Russia Economic Cooperation.

26 Ilulissat Declaration, adopted at the Arctic Ocean Conference hosted by the Government of Denmark and attended by the representatives of the five costal states bordering on the Arctic Ocean (Canada, Denmark, Norway, the Russian Federation, and the United States) held at Ilulissat, Greenland, May 27–29, 2008.

27 "Russia says media reports on possible Arctic conflict 'alarmist,'" *RIA Novosti,* October 22, 2008.

28 Notes for an Address by the Honourable Lawrence Cannon, Minister of Foreign Affairs, on Canada's Arctic Foreign Policy, Whitehorse, March 11, 2009. Cannon also insisted the same month that Canada "won't be bullied" by Russia after the Kremlin released a military strategy emphasizing the importance of the Arctic. Philip Authier, "Canada won't be bullied by Russia: Cannon," *Montreal Gazette,* March 27, 2009.

29 *Canada's Northern Strategy: Our North, Our Heritage, Our Future* (Ottawa: Minister of Public Works and Government Services Canada, 2009), 12, 34.

30 Quoted in Randy Boswell, "Polar posturing: Canada, Russia tensions in Arctic part politics, experts say," *Calgary Herald,* October 19, 2009. Also, see R. Wallace, Op-Ed Review. Canadian Defence and Foreign Affairs Institute: *Canada's Re-Emerging Arctic Imperative: The Iron Fist in an Arctic Mitt?* http://www.cdfai.org/PDF/R.%20Wallace%20op-ed%20on%20Huebert%20Arctic%20paper.pdf. 20 March 2010.

31 Zysk, "Geopolitics In the Arctic." See also Antrim, "Next Geographical Pivot," 19.

32 Quoted in Zysk, "Russia and the High North," 118.

33 Zysk, "Geopolitics in the Arctic," 9.

34 Quoted in Allan Woods, "'Back off and stay out of our airspace,' Russia," *Toronto Star,* February 28, 2009.

35 Mike Blanchfield, "Harper warns Russians after two bombers intercepted," *National Post,* February 28, 2009.

36 Meagan Fitzpatrick, "Russian bombers did not breach Canadian airspace: Diplomat," *Canwest News Service,* March 23, 2009.

37 David Pugliese and Gerard O'Dwyer, "Canada, Russia Build Arctic Forces," *DefenseNews,* April 6, 2009.

38 See Randy Boswell, "Russia surprised by ice reaction to Arctic jump," *National Post*, August 4, 2009. The Russians could have noted that Canada had sent paratroopers to the Pole in 1974 and planted flags without claiming Canadian sovereignty. In the end, the Russians did not conduct the exercise.

39 Lawson W. Brigham, "Think Again: The Arctic," *Foreign Policy*, no. 181 (September/October 2010): 72.

40 Steven Harper, "Harper Stands Up for Arctic Sovereignty," address in Ottawa, December 22, 2005.

41 Prime Minister's Office (PMO), "PM unveils Canada First Defence Strategy," May 12, 2008.

42 Quoted in Kathleen Harris, "Laying claim to Canada's internal waters," *Toronto Sun*, February 23, 2007.

43 Piotr Dutkiewicz, "Why the bear and the beaver should make nice together," *Globe and Mail*, April 23, 2009.

44 See, for example, Arctic Marine Shipping Assessment *2009 Report*; Mariport Group, *Canadian Arctic Shipping Assessment: Main Report*, prepared for Transport Canada (June 2007), 132, 137; Marine and Environmental Law Institute, Dalhousie Law School, *Governance of Arctic Marine Shipping* (2008), 66–67.

45 Campbell Clark, "Russia proposes Arctic détente," *Globe and Mail*, July 1, 2009.

46 DFAIT, "Joint Statement on Canada–Russia Economic Cooperation," November 28–29, 2007; http://www.cbern.ca/cms/One.aspx?portalId=625751&pageId=9815452.

47 Agreement between the Government of Canada and the Government of the Russian Federation on Cooperation in the Arctic and the North, E100317 – Canada Treaty Series 1992. no. 18.

48 ICC (Canada). *Project Description: Institutional Building for Northern Aboriginal Peoples in Russia (INRIPP-2)* (2008); Gary N. Wilson, "Inuit Diplomacy in the Circumpolar North," *Canadian Foreign Policy* 13, no. 3 (2007): 72–73.

49 See, for example: Embassy of the Russian Federation in Canada, press release, "Russia-Canada Cooperation in the Arctic," March 11, 2009. In February 2010, Chuck Strahl, the Minister of Indian Affairs and Northern Development, signed a new work plan with the Honorable Viktor Fyodorovich Basargin, Minister of Regional Development of the Russian Federation, to implement concrete activities under the 2007 Memorandum of Understanding through the exchange of best practices in the preservation of Aboriginal languages; building capacity for local public administration; sharing tools for Aboriginal policy research; and the promotion of public private partnerships. Indian and Northern Affairs Canada, News Release 2-3317, "Canada and Russia Working Jointly for the Well-Being of the Aboriginal Peoples of the Arctic," February 12, 2010.

50 Charles Emmerson, "Russia's Arctic Opening," *Foreign Policy* online edition (March 30, 2011); http://www.foreignpolicy.com/articles/2011/03/30/russias_arctic_opening?page=0,0.

51 Dutkiewicz, "Why the bear and the beaver should make nice together"; DFAIT, "Terms of Reference and Vision Statement of the Canada–Russia Intergovernmental Economic Commission Arctic and North Working Group," last updated March 10, 2011; http://www.international.gc.ca/polar-polaire/anwg-gtan.aspx?lang=en&view=d.

52 VAdm Dean McFadden, speaking notes, "The Evolution of Arctic Security and Defense Policies: Cooperative or Confrontational," Center for Strategic and International Studies Conference, Washington, D.C., April 28, 2010.

53 Address by Minister Cannon to Diplomatic Academy of the Russian Ministry of Foreign Affairs on Canada's Arctic Foreign Policy, Speech No. 2010/70, Moscow, Russia, September 15, 2010.

54 Timothy Bancroft-Hinchey, "Climate Change, the Arctic and Russia's National Security," *Pravda*, March 25, 2010; http://

english.pravda.ru/russia/politics/25-03-2010/112732-climate_russia-0/.

55 In April 2010, Russia and Norway resolved a forty-year disagreement over the division of the Barents Sea. To optimists, this agreement signaled the appropriateness of efforts to promote a secure, stable region characterized by international cooperation and responsible resource exploration. Cajoling Canada to take note of this landmark resolution, Sergei Lavorv and Jonas Gahr Støre (the Russian and Norweigan foreign ministers respectively) noted that "the Law of the Sea provided a framework that allowed us to overcome the zero-sum logic of competition and replace it with a process focused on finding a win-win solution. We hope that the agreement will inspire other countries in their attempts to resolve their maritime disputes, in the High North and elsewhere, in a way that avoids conflict and strengthens international co-operation." Sergei Lavrov and Jonas Gahr Støre, "Canada, take note: Here's how to resolve maritime disputes," *Globe and Mail*, September 21, 2010.

13. Russia's Arctic Strategy: Ambitions and Restraints[1]

Katarzyna Zysk

In recent years, the Arctic region has emerged as an issue in world affairs. Both challenges and opportunities from rapidly changing climatic conditions in the region have contributed to give the Arctic a place on the domestic and foreign policy agendas of many key countries and organizations.

Russia stands out as one of the most determined Arctic players. A focus on the region features increasingly in Russian domestic and foreign policy discourse, particularly since Vladimir Putin's second presidential term. The importance of the Arctic to Russia, on the one hand, and growing international interest, on the other, has fueled Russia's determination to make its role as a central Arctic nation eminently clear by political, economic, and military means. In September 2008, Moscow endorsed *Fundamentals of State Policy of the Russian Federation in the Arctic for the Period up to 2020 and Beyond*, which was aimed at preserving Russia s role as a "leading Arctic power."[2] The adoption of the document has further highlighted the country's increased interest in the region.

This chapter addresses elements of Russia's plans for the Arctic in terms of economic policy and legal and military issues and devotes particular attention to the differences between the current Russian approach to security in the region and the attitudes presented in the previous Arctic strategy adopted in 2001.[3] Subsequently, it examines the geopolitical context of the Russian Arctic policies and sheds light on the country's foreign policy rhetoric and its impact on the regional security environment. Finally, it assesses prospects for implementation of the Russian policy objectives and draws implications of the findings for regional security.[4]

Background

The Arctic policy document was published in March 2009, six months after it was signed. In contrast with the widespread media coverage that Russian activity in the Arctic was getting only a few months before, the document was posted by the authorities without further notice and publicity, and it was immediately filed in the archives section of the Russian Security Council website. Unlike the previous Arctic policy document of 2001, it refers sparingly to Russia's hard security interests and plans in the region. It also abstains from the assertive, belligerent rhetoric frequently used by Moscow in Vladimir Putin's last years of the second presidential term (2007–08).

The Russian authorities have ambitions to address one of the biggest challenges in the country's approach toward the vast northern regions – the lack of a coherent strategy. Despite attempts to revive the state policy, its objectives, formulated in 2001, were not carried out with sufficient assiduity, something Russian politicians admit themselves.[5] Can this new document make a difference?

The fundamentals of the Arctic policy were designed under the auspices of the influential Russian Security Council, whose permanent members include the most important centers of power, such as the president, prime minister, ministers of interior, foreign affairs, and defense, and the directors of the Federal Security Service of the Russian Federation (*Federal'naya sluzhba bezopasnosti Rossiyskoy Federatsii*, or FSB) and the Foreign Intelligence Service. In drafting the document, most of the ministries and other parts of the executive and legislative branch responsible for various aspects of the policies in the region have been involved, supported by leading experts and academics. The version of the document presented to the public sheds light on how the Russian authorities think about the Arctic and reflects areas of particular interest and aspirations rather than presenting a consistent strategy to pursue objectives consciously and systematically over time.

The document gives certain general policy guidelines; the final shape of the Russian Arctic policies, however, will depend on detailed programs formulated in the appropriate ministries and governmental agencies on the basis of the document and subsequently on their implementation – or lack thereof. As experience with the previous ambitious plans shows, achieving the goals may take longer than scheduled, if they are achieved at all. That said, for a number of reasons, the Russian approach to the Arctic today is compared to the previous period. Among them are is the acknowledgment of the rapid changes in Arctic natural environment and warming of the climate, opening the region for a potentially sharply increased Russian and foreign human activity. This requires necessary preparations in order to seize new opportunities on the one hand, and, on the other, prepare to meet new threats that emerge alongside.

Economic Development

The Russian leadership clearly emphasizes the importance of the Arctic to the country's wealth and competitiveness on global markets as a major source of revenue, mainly from production of energy. As much as 20 per cent of Russia's gross domestic product (GDP) and 22 per cent of the total Russian export is generated north of the Arctic Circle.[6] The region's economic promise lies primarily in its rich natural resources and its potential as an attractive maritime transit passageway. The ultimate objective of the state policy is to transform the Arctic into "Russia's foremost strategic base for natural resources" by 2020.[7]

The Arctic is clearly vital to Russia's relevance in world affairs as well. The role of energy reserves in strengthening the country's position and influence on the international stage has been emphasized in the national security strategy up to 2020 that was adopted in May 2009. According to Russian sources, up to 90 per cent of the hydrocarbon reserves found on the entire Russian continental shelf is in the Arctic, with 66.5 per cent located in its western part, in the Barents and Kara Seas.[8] The project for Russia's energy strategy up to 2030 points out that resources located in the Arctic seas and in the Russian northern regions could compensate for dwindling deposits in existing fields based in Western Siberia, where a sharp decline in oil and gas production is expected in the next twenty years.[9] Consequently, one of the main goals of the Arctic policies is to increase extraction of the natural resources in the region.[10]

In September 2008, the Russian Security Council gave assurances that the government had earmarked "serious economic support" for implementation of the Arctic policy goals. However, prospects for developing the region under current economic circumstances are poor.[11] The Russian Ministry of Economic Development and Trade announced that the Russian GDP dropped 10.1 per cent in the first six months of 2009. The World Bank assessed that Russia experienced in 2009 "larger-than-expected losses in output and employment, and a sharp rise in poverty." Although the Russian economy might grow 3.2 per cent in 2010, experts warn that long-term sustainable growth can be achieved only with the introduction of comprehensive structural reforms, including diversification of the economy.[12]

The financial downturn and relatively low energy prices have affected investments in the Arctic and slow the pace of development of the petroleum industry in the region. One of the biggest offshore gas fields in the world, the Shtokman in the Eastern Barents Sea and Prirazlomnoe oil field in the Pechora Sea, are to be Russia's first Arctic offshore fields in production. Due to a dramatic drop in exports and revenues, Gazprom suffered serious losses and accordingly cut its investment plans for 2010 by about 50 per cent. In July 2009, the company officially confirmed that it was delaying the launch of Shtokman. Gazprom's partner in this project, French Total, stated in October 2009 that Shtokman simply would not be profitable with the current gas prices.[13] Apart from the price of energy, solutions to unprecedented technological challenges connected to extraction in the harsh climatic conditions and tremendous distances to onshore infrastructure and markets will be other major factors in deciding the development of the energy industry in the region.

One of Russia's fundamental goals in the Arctic is the development of the Northern Sea Route (NSR) as a central transportation link in maritime connections between Europe and Asia. The NSR cuts transit distances by thousands of miles, making it an attractive alternative to traditional trade routes. The importance of the NSR has been highlighted in a range of Russian strategic documents, which point to a "sharply increasing role" of the NSR in connection with the future growing extraction of the Arctic's natural reserves.[14] Russia perceives this shipping channel as the sole means of transportation for the important industries located in Russian coastal and insular Arctic regions.

By 2015, Russia aims to have established and developed an infrastructure and system of management of communications for the NSR to secure

Euro-Asiatic transit. The expected increase in Russian petroleum activity will lead to a sharp boost in the level of shipping through the NSR westward, mainly from the Barents and Kara Seas. Some Russian forecasts expect that the cargo flowing through the NSR may reach a volume of 5 to 6 million tons, and increase to 13 to 15 million tons by 2015. For comparison, at its peak in 1987, the transport volume through the NSR reached 7 million tons, while in the 1990s it diminished gradually to a relatively stable 1.5 to 2 million tons.[15]

Russia is interested in attracting interest of international shipping companies for the NSR. However, despite the fact that this route may be shorter, a number of factors such as drifting ice, extreme temperatures, polar night, as well as poorly mapped waters, could slow navigation and lengthen transit time, especially under difficult weather conditions. The NSR may thus not necessarily result in fuel, emissions, and manpower savings. The ships will also have reduced cargo-carrying capacity because some of the Arctic straits are shallow. Nor can the ships be larger than the icebreakers that they will need to escort them through the ice at times. The ships will also be more expensive as they have to be strengthened to withstand ice. Together with higher insurance premiums consonant to the higher risk of sailing in the Arctic waters, this will increase the transport costs. Shipowners and operators may also be discouraged by an inability to establish year-long operations since it will be impossible to predict exactly when and for how long the passages will be open.

Nevertheless, despite this host of technical and not the least economic factors, a few Russian and international shipping companies decided to try out the NSR. In 2009, and in particular in 2010, they successfully carried gas condensate, oil, and iron, and other commodities along this channel. The number of cargo ships to sail along the NSR doubled in 2011, together with the cargo tonnage compared to the previous year.[16]

To meet the requirements of the increased economic activity in the Arctic and to ensure restructuring of the volume of maritime freight, Russia recognizes as a prerequisite the development of modern harbors with appropriate infrastructures and the acquisition of new nuclear-powered icebreakers together with assets for an air support and rescue fleet.[17] Although Russia still has the world's largest and most powerful icebreaker fleet, limited maintenance and construction capacity has caused general deterioration since the 1990s. The seven active (and world's only) nuclear-powered icebreakers constructed in the 1970s and 1980s are aging quickly, and all except one will be decommissioned by 2020.[18] Viacheslav Ruksha, head of Atomflot, which manages the icebreakers, warned that Russia will face a "collapse" of these capacities in 2016–17 if a new generation nuclear-powered icebreaker is not ready by that time.[19]

The Russian authorities have taken steps to address the problem and charged the State Nuclear Energy Corporation (Rosatom) with development of a long-term plan for construction of new vessels. Rosatom's director, Sergei Kirienko, argues that Russia has to build at least three to four third-generation icebreakers in the next few years to maintain the country's potential in the Arctic.[20] The first was due to be launched in 2010 but was postponed due to lack of funding.[21] The government plans to finance the new construction partly with resources obtained from privatization of the state-owned maritime shipping company, Sovcomflot, to be conducted in the coming years.[22] However, given that it takes five to six years to build an icebreaker, with the current pace of rejuvenating the fleet, Russia's capacity to support its economic activities in the region is likely to be reduced by 2020, making implementation of the Arctic strategy less realistic.

Legal Questions

Closely intertwined with the importance of the Arctic to Russia are the country's efforts to settle the outer limits of the continental shelf in the region beyond two hundred nautical miles, noted in the Arctic document as a top priority to be accomplished in the period 2011–15.[23] In this context, the government is clear that the partition of the Arctic will be carried out entirely within the framework of international law.

Russia filed its first request with the United Nations Commission on the Limits of the Continental Shelf in 2001, but the board demanded more evidence. Consequently, Moscow attaches importance to scientific research in the region (geological, geophysical, cartographical, hydrographical, and other) since the results will play a decisive role in the accomplishment of the legal process.[24] On the basis of the research, Russia intends to develop a competitive economic activity within extraction and transportation of energy resources in the region.

Unlike the 2001 strategy, the Russian government highlights in the new Arctic document its longstanding position on the legal status of the NSR, thus reflecting its expected increasing significance. The document states that the NSR is a "national transportation route" under Russia's jurisdiction. Navigation via this sailing channel is to be carried out in compliance with Russian laws and the country's international agreements. In the federal statute of July 31, 1998, the NSR is defined as "a historically existing national unified transport route of the Russian Federation in the Arctic." It includes navigation via straits within and between the Russian Arctic archipelagos, including the Vilkitski, Shokalski, Dmitri Laptev, and Sannikov Straits. Russia labels these straits as part of its internal waters.

The Russian claim to jurisdiction over the NSR is based on article 234 of the UN Convention on the Law of the Sea. The article "gives coastal states the right to unilaterally adopt and enforce non-discriminatory laws and environmental regulations in their Exclusive Economic Zones (EEZs) where ice coverage and particularly severe climate conditions cause exceptional hazards to navigation, and where pollution could cause major harm to the ecological balance."[25] According to the Russian regulations, all vessels intending to enter the NSR should give advance notification to Russian authorities and submit an application for guiding, which implies paying a fee for using the route.

The question of the legal status of the NSR complicates the fact that it is not a single shipping channel but a series of different shipping lanes stretching between 2,200 and 2,900 nautical miles, depending on ice conditions.[26] According to Russian experts, "the integral nature of the NSR as a transport route is not affected by the fact that individual portions of it, at one time or another, may pass outside boundaries of internal waters, territorial waters and EEZ, i.e., it may pass into the high seas."[27] The NSR may thus include sea lanes running beyond Russia's EEZ as long as part of the voyage includes waters under undisputed Russian jurisdiction.

Other important actors in the region may regard the Russian interpretation as somewhat controversial – particularly the United States, which considers the straits of the NSR as international and thus subject to the right of transit passage. This position was confirmed in the U.S. Arctic region policy document adopted in January 2009.[28] On different occasions, Russia has warned that attempts by other countries to change the NSR's legal status and transform it into an international transit corridor would be in conflict with Russia's national interests. As the importance and value of this transport channel are likely to increase in the future, the question of its legal status may become a matter of contention.

Military Issues

The Russian authorities highlight the need to make necessary preparations for the security challenges that may derive from the expected increase in economic and other activities in the Arctic. Hence, they devote much attention to development of search and rescue capabilities, surveillance, and navigation systems to provide safety for and control of the economic, military, and ecological activities.[29] One of the goals of the Russian policy is the creation of a comprehensive security system by 2015, including early warning, prevention, and crisis management capabilities. Russia also emphasizes a need for cooperation with other Arctic countries and defines strengthening efforts to establish a unified regional search and rescue system as a strategic priority.[30]

Russia stresses the importance of a continued military presence as essential for securing national interests in the Arctic, although Russia's defense policy in the region is discussed in the Arctic document only in vestigial form.[31] The document vaguely states that Russia needs to maintain a "necessary combat potential" in the North and reveals plans to establish special Arctic military formations to protect the country's national interests "in various military and political situations."[32] The Russian authorities, however, underscore that the main purpose of such military preparations is to combat terrorism at sea, smuggling, illegal migration, and unsustainable use of aquatic biological resources. Hence, the FSB is to play a central role in protecting national security interests in the region. A strong emphasis has been put on the development of a coastal defense infrastructure and advanced technological capabilities, including satellites and radars. In September 2009, the FSB announced that Arctic formations were established in borderguard units in Arkhangelsk and Murmansk and were patrolling along the NSR for the first time in many years.

The document has thus to some extent confirmed information released by representatives of the Russian Ministry of Defense in mid-2008 concerning adjustments being made to the combat plans and military organization of the three military districts bordering the Arctic: Leningrad, Siberian, and Far Eastern (reorganized in 2010 into the West, Central, and East Strategic Commands) – to incorporate additional missions in the northern regions.[33] In March 2011, the Commander of the Russian Ground Forces, General Aleksander Postnikov, confirmed that one of the central military goals defined in the Arctic policy document is being implemented. Postnikov informed the

Committee on Defense and Security of the Council of the Federation that an Arctic brigade will be established in Pechenga, close to borders with Norway and Finland.[34] Russian military and political leaders have argued that defense of national interests from the northwest strategic direction has become more relevant and have pointed also at other existing motivations behind such military preparations. They have noted the international attention to the military potential and energy resources of the Arctic as factors calling for an immediate strengthening of Russia's positions in order to secure the region.[35] That said, any radical strengthening of Russian military posture in the region is unlikely in the near future for a number of reasons, including resource deficiencies, slow pace of introduction of new material and lack of sound justification by immediate security needs. The ambition to reorganize the 200th motorized infantry brigade in Pechenga into the Arctic brigade has been thus postponed to 2015.[36]

Russia's approach to Arctic affairs has been of two minds, based on a combination of deterrence and assurance, and thus sometimes confusing and difficult to interpret. Self-assertive and occasionally aggressive rhetoric has alternated with more conciliatory signals and practical compliance with international law. The tone of the Arctic document is moderate and stands in contrast to the harsh language previously used by Russian high-ranking officials, concerning various activities in the region, in particular in the military field. It not only refrains from belligerent language but also omits issues that could be contentious or alarming. Apart from the few vague indications concerning military plans, references to the hard security sphere in the region are absent. The Russian authorities clearly highlight the importance of bilateral and multilateral cooperation in the region and the need to strengthen good relations with neighboring countries, in particular the "Arctic five."[37]

The difference in approach to hard security in the Arctic is striking in comparison with the 2001 Arctic document, where issues of military security were understood in terms of zero-sum game and classical *Realpolitik*, assuming that states, particularly great powers, are in principle mutually hostile and competitive. The document stated that "all kinds of activity in the northern regions are in the highest degree connected to providing of national security." It urged steps to "actively counter strengthening of military infrastructure and enlargement of military activities" in the region by other countries and actors.[38] The document underlined the military strategic importance of the region to Russia's defense and pointed out that almost 20,000 kilometers of the state border were in the Arctic Ocean and its protection and defense imposed particular problems.[39]

Security of the border remains prominent in the new Arctic document. However, it approaches these issues in relation to soft security challenges, with the discussion of the hard security sphere being nearly absent. Despite this change of tone, the region has retained its special importance to Russia in a more traditional definition of security. The military strategic importance of the Northwest with its direct and easy access to the world's oceans has paradoxically been strengthened since the Cold War due to the geopolitical changes that limited Russia's access to the Baltic and the Black seas. The Arctic is still an important home base and a suitable operational area for the Russian navy, in particular for its most powerful part, the Northern Fleet and the sea-based component of the Russian nuclear triad. The nuclear deterrent has maintained the key role in Russia's military strategy, strengthened by its weakness in conventional forces. Its continued importance has been corroborated by the priority given to modernization of the Russian nuclear arsenals, including the building of eight fourth-generation *Borei*-class ballistic missile submarines and and six nuclear-powered attack submarines planned to be completed by 2015.

Russia's intensifying of naval and air activity in the Arctic has taken place simultaneously with its increased and global focus on the region's energy potential. At the same time, in particular since Putin's second presidential term, the armed forces have been given an enhanced role in Russia's efforts to return to the world stage as a major player. The resumption of strategic bomber flights along the Norwegian coast and in the Pacific in 2007 and the presence of the Northern Fleet in the Arctic in 2008, similarly to other parts of the Russian Navy in different parts of the world, have been visible expressions of this trend. The increased activity has been partly an outcome of a systematic increase in defense funding and military training after a long period of stagnation. However, Russian authorities have at least initially connected symbolic and political significance to the intensified military activity, which was accompanied by an assertive rhetoric.

In the Russian assessment, there is no imminent threat of direct aggression against Russian territory or a large-scale military confrontation in the region. Nonetheless, Russia does not rule out the possibility of competition for hydrocarbon reserves developing into small-scale tensions involving use of military power. Dwindling global petroleum and gas resources have been defined as a security concern in the 2009 National Security Strategy. The document asserts that, in a long-term perspective, international policy will focus on access to energy resources, including in the major regions such the continental shelf in the Barents Sea and other parts of the Arctic, in addition to the Middle East, the Caspian Sea, and Central Asia (article 11). The document maintains that it cannot be excluded that problems related to the competitive struggle for dwindling resources worldwide may be solved with the use of military force, although the statement is made without pointing at the Arctic or any of the other aforementioned regions (article 12).[40] Nevertheless, a conviction that the contest for natural reserves may in the future pose a threat to Russia has been widespread, among others, in military circles. For instance, the General Staff in June 2009 described the "struggle for energy resources in the Arctic" as one the most important challenges and argued that the region should be included in the new revised European security architecture.[41] Although Russian military activity in the Arctic has received less publicity and attention in the official rhetoric since 2009, it has not become less important. Russia has maintained the military activity at a relatively high level (compared to the previous period of stagnation). It included large-scale military exercises of all components of the Russian armed forces, trained also in demanding polar conditions. One of such exercises, the Ladoga–2009, which involved all units of the Leningrad Military District and some units of the Siberian Military District, interior troops, borderguards, and the Northern and Baltic fleets. In compliance with the Russian threat perception, one of the training scenarios included protection of oil and gas installations in northwest Russia.[42]

Among Russia's military plans, which once realized could increase its striking power in the Arctic, is a major naval build-up aimed at strengthening blue-water capabilities, including, among others, several aircraft carrier groups, twenty new multipurpose corvettes (*Steregushchii* class), and twenty frigates (*Admiral S. Gorshkov* class). With few exceptions, however, these plans so far are only ambitions. Despite the clearly increased military activity and improved combat potential of the armed forces, these developments should be seen against the background of a still weak military. The pace of modernization has been slow, although a radical characteristic of military reforms being implemented, aimed at moving away from a mass mobilization army to a permanent readiness brigade model, reveals a new quality in the Russian approach. Much of these plans will depend on development in the Russian economy and the leadership's ability to transform and modernize it.[43]

Geopolitics

As the example of the Russian Arctic security policy discourse has shown, in particular in the years 2007–08, the manner in which communication transpires matters and has the force to shape the reality. The sometimes tough Russian talk and behavior, including not only verbal statements but also military posturing, have attained one of its goals and reminded the world that Russia remains a key factor for political developments in the Arctic region. On the other hand, responses from the world have shown that this strategy has had the potential to harm rather than promote Russia's interests abroad.

One of the outcomes of the Russian policy has been to strengthen the international focus on military security in the Arctic. The occasionally aggressive Russian rhetoric has lowered the threshold of sensitivity in other states toward Russia's moves in the hard security sphere and has raised, particularly in polar states, the question of their own military presence and preparedness in the region – an outcome that Russia can hardly see as being in its interest. The perception of Russia as a potentially unpredictable player and security concern has been strengthened by the experience of the Russo-Georgian war in August 2008, which triggered security assessments in a range of countries. One example is that even the few modest sentences in the Arctic policy document concerning Russia's military plans immediately spurred speculation about "militarization" of the region. Russian authorities have repeatedly rebuffed such accusations and have given assurances that Moscow would regulate Arctic issues through negotiations and with respect for the rules of international law.

Canada has been among the most vocal states in articulating its intentions to upgrade its military capabilities with regard to tasks in the Arctic. Commenting on the ground-sea-air joint Operation Nanook, Defence Minister Peter MacKay stated that the operation was intended "to very clearly send a message, and to announce with authority, that we intend to use the Arctic … and that our presence there is going to continue to expand."[44] The intention to strengthen military capabilities in the Arctic has also been signaled in Denmark. A defense plan for the period 2010–14 approved in June 2009 envisages establishment of an Arctic military command structure and task force.

One of Russia's major foreign policy objectives in recent years has aimed at limiting the presence of the North Atlantic Treaty Organization (NATO) in the proximity of Russia's borders included in the Arctic. But the outcome in the region has been quite the opposite. As stated in October 2009 by NATO Supreme Allied Commander Europe Admiral James Stavridis, the Russian "assertive conduct in the Arctic and a muscle-flexing" were among the factors "grabbing the attention of increasingly wary NATO leaders."[45] He described the High North as an area of growing strategic concern.

The sometimes assertive responses from the other Arctic states stimulate Russia's counter-responses and strengthen the rationale for an increased military presence. Such mutually reinforcing dynamics may in the longer term lead to a stronger militarization of the region, potentially creating new sources of tensions. Russian authorities have repeatedly expressed their discontent with the focus on hard security in the Arctic and warned against its militarization, indicating measures it might take to address the challenges implied by such developments. According to Chief of the General Staff Nikolai Makarov, those measures would be reflected in assignments given to the Northern and Pacific Fleets and the sea-based strategic nuclear deterrent.[46]

The adjustments in the Russian Arctic rhetoric – less publicity for the military posturing and stronger emphasis on conciliatory positions – provide better ground for closer cooperation and facilitate diplomatic progress. Focus on common interests and areas where parties involved need each other can be a way of improving international relations in the region. One of the areas where international cooperation is welcomed by Russia (and is unavoidable in order to address challenges emerging in the hostile and highly vulnerable natural environment) is marine safety, search and rescue, and crisis management. None of the Arctic countries has the complete spectrum of assets needed to cover the whole geographic area and respond on their own to asymmetrical and soft security challenges. Apart from being necessary, such cooperation has a strong confidence-building potential, still in shortage in the region as the recent military and security dynamics have shown.

Tentative Conclusions

While it is still too early to assess whether the increased Russian focus on the Arctic translates into a more coherent approach and what chance the Arctic policy objectives have of being implemented, it has become clear that the already announced delays, mainly due to financial constraints, will make it difficult if not impossible to achieve the strategic goals in the indicated timeframe.

In a long-term perspective, the widely expected growing global demand for gas and oil, combined with dwindling reserves in existing fields, may argue for exploration of new deposits in the North and offshore. Climate change will most probably continue, opening the Arctic to increased economic and industrial activity. Together with their geopolitical implications, these developments argue for Russia's continued efforts to strengthen its presence, in accordance with reasoning expressed by Deputy Prime Minister Sergei Ivanov: "If we do not develop the Arctic, it will be developed without us."[47] Nonetheless, expecting the vision of the Russian Arctic as a thriving economic hub for energy production and transpolar maritime transit to come true by 2020 may be too optimistic. The Arctic document has confirmed what Russian leaders have reiterated with increasing intensity: the region's importance, first and foremost in economic and security dimensions. One conclusion to be drawn from the ambitious economic projects is that Russia, for purely material reasons, has an interest in maintaining the region as an area of international cooperation and in preserving its most important asset as the country's future economic engine – its stability.

At the same time, the growing importance of the Arctic both to Russia and the world is generating new driving forces for the Russian military presence. As economic activities increase, Russia will need to protect the significant assets that it is placing in the region. Thus, its military presence is likely to increase further in the future. Russia's continued reliance on the nuclear deterrent, together with the focus on enhancing global naval power projection capabilities, indicates that the military strategic importance of the Arctic will remain high for the foreseeable future.

Notes

1 Reprinted, with permission, from *Joint Force Quarterly* 57, no. 2 (2010): 103–10.

2 *Osnovy gosudarstvennoi politiki Rossiiskoi Federatsii v Arktike na period do 2020 goda i dal'neyshuyu perspektivu*, September 18, 2008, accessed at the home page of the Security Council of the Russian Federation, http://www.scrf.gov.ru. Hereinafter *Osnovy*, 2008.

3 *Osnovy gosudarstvennoi politiki Rossiskoi Federatsii v Arktike*, June 14, 2001. Hereinafter *Osnovy*, 2001.

4 This article was first published in *Joint Force Quarterly* (*JFQ*) 57, no. 2 (2010): 103–110, and was written as part of the Geopolitics in the High North research program funded by the Research Council of Norway. Reprinted with permission of the author and the publisher of *JFQ*, NDU Press.

5 The problem was analyzed by the Russian State Council's working group and came under scrutiny at the highest political level in 2004.

6 Dmitrii Medvedev, speech at Meeting of the Russian Security Council on Protecting Russia's National Interests in the Arctic, September 17, 2008; http://eng.kremlin.ru.

7 *Osnovy*, 2008.

8 *Osnovy*, 2001.

9 *Energeticheskaya strategiya Rossii na period do 2030 goda*, November 13, 2009; http://www.energystrategy.ru.

10 *Osnovy*, 2008.

11 For statistics and analysis of major trends in world economic developments in the first part of 2009, see *OECD Economic Outlook*, no. 85 (June 2009); http://www.oecd.org.

12 World Bank, *Russian Economic Report no. 20: From Rebound to Recovery?*; http://www.worldbank.org.

13 N. J. Watson, "Total says Shtokman uneconomic at today's gas prices," *Petroleum Economist*, October 2009.

14 See, for instance, "Russia's transport strategy up to 2030," and "The concept for a long-term socioeconomic development for the period up to 2020." The documents (in Russian) are available at http://www.government.ru.

15 Quoted in Claes Lykke Ragner, "The Northern Sea Route" ("*Den norra sjövägen*"), in *Barents – ett gränsland i Norden*, ed. Torsten Hallberg (Stockholm: Arena Norden, 2008).

16 For an overview of the maritime shipping activity, see: "More oil and ore along Northern Sea Route," *Barents Observer*, February 11, 2011; "Preparing for next year's Northern Sea Route season," *Barents Observer*, October 20, 2010.

17 *Osnovy*, 2008.

18 For further information, see an analysis by Oleg Bukharin, "Russia's Nuclear Icebreaker Fleet," *Science and Global Security* 14 (2006): 25–31.

19 "Russia could lose its nuclear icebreaker fleet in 2016–2017 – Atomflot," *Interfax*, October 2009.

20 "Krienko otsenil atomnyi ledokol 3–go pokolenia na 17 mlrd rublei," *Rosbalt Biznes*, April 21, 2009, http://www.rosbalt.ru.

21 "Atomflot' rasschityvaet chto novye ledokoly nachnyt stroit v 2011 godu," *RIA novosti*, October 17, 2009.

22 "Privatization of Sovcomflot to finance icebreakers," *Barents Observer*, January 3, 2011.

23 *Osnovy*, 2008.

24 Ibid.

25 Quoted in Lykke Ragner, "The Northern Sea Route."

26 The Russian definitions of the Northern Sea Route are explored also in Willy Østreng, "Historical and Geographical Context of the Northern Sea Route," in *The Natural and Societal Challenges of the Northern Sea Route. a Reference Work*, ed. Willy Østreng (Dordrecht: Kluwer Academic, 1999).

27 A. L. Kolodkin and M. E. Volosov, "The Legal Regime of the Soviet Arctic: Major Issues," *Marine Policy* 14 (1990): 163–67.

28 The National Security Presidential Directive and Homeland Security Presidential Directive, Arctic region policy, The White House, January 9, 2009; http://georgewbush-whitehouse. archives.gov.

29 *Osnovy*, 2008.

30 Ibid.

31 For a broader discussion of Russia's defense policy in the Arctic, see K. Zysk, "Military Aspects of Russia's Policy: Hard Power and Natural Resources," in *Arctic Circumpolar Security in an Age of Climate Change*, ed. James Kraska, 85–106 (Cambridge: Cambridge University Press, 2011).

32 *Osnovy*, 2008.

33 Yurii Ivanov, Press Office of the Russian MoD, quoted in Tatiana Abramova, "Vymysly i pravda ob arkticheskom spetsnaze," *Murmanskii vestnik*, July 1, 2008; "Russia's New Arctic Force to Focus on Border Protection," *RIA novosti*, March 30, 2009.

34 Viktor Myasnikov, "Sukhopytnye voiska raznei stepeni i tyazhelosti," *Nezavisimaya gazeta*, March 16, 2011.

35 See for instance the statement by Gen. Postnikov, ibid.; An interview with N. Patrushev in a TV program on the Russian Security Council's meeting on Franz Joseph Land in September 2008, "Sovbez v serdce Arktiki," The Russian state TV channel *Vesti Nedeli*, September 14, 2008, http://www.vesti7.ru.

36 "Pervaya arkticheskaya brigada budet sozdana v 2015 godu – glavkom CV," *RIA novosti* February 21, 2012.

37 *Osnovy*, 2001.

38 *Osnovy*, 2001.

39 Ibid.

40 *Strategiya natsional'noi bezopasnosti Rossiiskoi Federatsii na period do 2020 goda*. The documents are available at the website of the SCRF; http://www.scrf.gov. ru/documents/18/33.html.

41 Quoted in Olga Kolesnichenko, "Arktika – prioritet rossiiskoi vneshnei polityki," *VPK. Voenno-promyshlennyi kurier*, August 26, 2009.

42 "Military drills in Nord Stream waters," *Barents Observer*, August 20, 2009; *RIA novosti*, August 18, 2009.

43 For an analysis of the current state and development prospects of the Russian Navy see K. Zysk, "Russia's Naval Ambitions: Driving Forces and Constraints," in: *Twenty-First Century Seapower: Cooperation and Conflict at Sea*, Routledge 2012, pp. 112–35.

44 Randy Boswell, "Canada to conduct anti-sub exercises in Arctic," *Times Colonist*, August 8, 2009.

45 John Vandiver, "NATO Commander Sees Arctic Seabed as Cooperative Zone," *Stars and Stripes*, October 10, 2009.

46 Quoted in "Rossiiskii VMF syadet na khvost' korablyami NATO v Arktike," *Izvestiya*, February 24, 2009.

47 See Alexander Balyberdin, "Arctic in the system of priorities for maritime activities," *Military Parade*, no. 4 (2009): 40–50.

14. Russia Opens Its Maritime Arctic[1]

Lawson W. Brigham

As use of the Russian Arctic coastal seas expands and commercial interests drive marine transportation along the Northern Sea Route, the region is linked increasingly to the rest of the planet. Natural-resource developments in these northern onshore and offshore areas are closely tied to the future of the Russian Federation, as higher global commodity prices spur exploration and new investments in Russia's Arctic infrastructure. The nation has developed a program for strategic development of the region, in recent pronouncements promoting Arctic cooperation as a central theme. Diplomatic developments and marine operations during 2010 have also aroused worldwide attention to this formerly remote and closed region of the Soviet era.

Barents Sea Agreement

After forty years of negotiating, Norway and Russia announced in April 2010 that a preliminary agreement had been reached on maritime delimitation and cooperation in the Barents Sea and Arctic Ocean.[2] The differences in boundary lines between the two Arctic states in the Barents Sea (and by extension north into the Arctic Ocean) had remained problematic, but broad Norwegian–Russian fisheries cooperation in the region has existed since 1975. Recent pressures for expanded oil and gas exploration in and near the disputed areas made the lack of a boundary agreement more vexing.

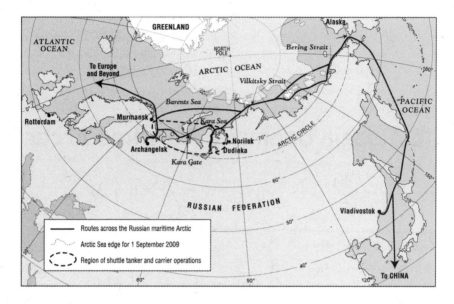

FIG. 1. ICE-CAPABLE RUSSIAN AS WELL AS FOREIGN-FLAG SHIPS MAY SOON BE MAKING
GREATER USE OF THE NEW SUMMER MARITIME TRADE ROUTE.

The new treaty concerning "Maritime Delimitation and Cooperation in the Barents Sea and the Arctic Ocean" was signed September 15, 2010, in Murmansk by Russian and Norwegian foreign ministers Sergey Lavrov and Jonas Gahr Støre. It is historic in several ways. Not only does it establish a stable and secure Arctic boundary, it also includes detailed annexes addressing fisheries and trans-boundary hydrocarbon deposits. Both nations noted the importance of close Arctic fisheries cooperation and agreed that the Norwegian–Russian Joint Fisheries Commission will continue to handle the negotiation of total allowable catches and quotas, while considering measures such as monitoring and control related to jointly managed fish stocks.

Annex II addresses the complicated issue of a hydrocarbon deposit extending across the new boundary. A joint operating agreement will now be required to explore and exploit, as a single unit, any trans-boundary deposit. Norway and Russia also agreed to establish a joint commission for consultations, exchange of information, and as a means of resolving issues.

The culmination of this significant accord, once it has been ratified by the two parliaments, will strengthen Norwegian–Russian cooperation in a key Arctic maritime region and remove a longstanding, disputed area from Arctic state concern. For the Russian Federation and Norway, this agreement provides a framework of cooperation and a stable political environment in which the Barents Sea's continental-shelf hydrocarbon resources can be increasingly exploited. The treaty also provides a unique and workable model for further circumpolar cooperation.

Trans-Arctic Voyages and Shuttle Operations

The Northern Sea Route, defined in Russian federal law as the set of waterways from Kara Gate (southern tip of Novaya Zemlya) to the Bering Strait, does not include the Barents Sea. The navigation season of 2010 for this route was notable, not for total tonnage carried or number of ships, but for several experimental trans-Arctic voyages involving diverse ship types. Four of the voyages took place during the summer, when sea ice is at its minimum in August and September; the fifth was a historic east-to-west escort of an ice-breaking offshore vessel in December.

Sovcomflot's ice-class tanker SCF *Baltica* (Liberian flag) completed a voyage carrying gas condensate from Murmansk to Ningbo, China, in twenty-two days; a reduced draft and slower speeds were necessary through the shallow straits of the New Siberian islands.[3] SCF *Baltica* is the first tanker of more than 100,000 deadweight tons to sail the Northern Sea Route, testing its viability for high tonnage. Also testing the route was the *Nordic Barents* (Hong Kong flag), an ice-class bulk carrier, on a voyage with iron ore from Kirkenes, Norway, to China. This was the first foreign-flag ship to carry cargo from one non-Russian port to another through Russian Arctic waters.[4] The route has the potential to link northern European mines to markets in China, Japan, Korea, and other Pacific nations.

In a similar voyage, Norilsk Nickel's icebreaking carrier *Monchegorsk* sailed from Murmansk and Dudinka along the Northern Sea Route east to Shanghai.[5] However, the key difference in comparison with other full transits was that this one was conducted by an ice-capable commercial ship sailing the length of the route without icebreaker escort. With a change in federal regulations, such independent sailings could become more common during the short summer navigation season.

Two 2010 voyages were unique. On August 28, the passenger ferry *Georg Ots* departed St. Petersburg for Murmansk and a subsequent voyage under nuclear icebreaker escort along the Northern Sea Route, arriving in Anadyr, Chukota, on September 26. The ferry reached its new homeport of Vladivostok in October, for use during the 2012 Asian-Pacific Cooperation Summit and future local operations.[6] More challenging was the December 16–26 escort by the nuclear icebreaker *Rossiya* of the icebreaking offshore vessel *Tor Viking* from the Bering Strait to the northern tip of Novaya Zemlya across the Northern Sea Route.[7] This successful voyage indicates the sailing season may be extended for passage of ice-capable ships under close escort.

Arctic shuttle operations are the key to efficient marine transportation of natural resources in the Barents and Kara seas, encompassing the western end of the Russian maritime Arctic. Two innovative systems are fully developed and operate year-round. A five-ship Arctic icebreaking carrier fleet carries nickel plate from Dudinka on the Yenisey River to Murmansk; this fleet is owned and operated by Norilsk Nickel, the mining complex in western Siberia, and year-round navigation has been maintained since 1979.

A three-ship icebreaking tanker operation services the offshore oil terminal at Varandey in the Pechora Sea (southeast corner of the Barents Sea). The three Panamax-size shuttle tankers can annually deliver nearly 12 million tons of oil to a floating tank farm in Murmansk.[8] The terminal and marine shuttle system represent a prime example of Arctic globalization: the Russian company Lukoil teamed with the American firm ConocoPhillips for investment and development of the offshore terminal; the tankers were built in Korea by Samsung Heavy Industries using Finnish icebreaking technology; and the ships are operated by Sovcomflot.

A third shuttle system came into full operation in 2011; a two-ship fleet began delivering oil to Murmansk from the Prirazlomnoye offshore oil production platform in the Pechora Sea.[9] Both tanker shuttle fleets have significant potential to provide year-round service to other projects and thereby optimize regional marine operations.

China and Finland Alliances

As hydrocarbon exploration and transportation development of the Russian maritime Arctic have rapidly evolved, Russia has been quick to forge strategic commercial alliances with China, as well as Finland and other western companies. Early in the operation of the Varandey terminal, Lukoil signed an agreement with Sinopec (China Petroleum and Chemical Corporation) to supply 3 million tons of oil to China.[10]

Sovcomflot Group reported on November 22, 2010, that it had signed a long-term agreement with China National Petroleum Corporation regarding seaborne carriage of hydrocarbons from the Arctic to China. The cooperative agreement envisions using the Northern Sea Route, not only for moving oil and gas from Russia's developing offshore, but also for trans-Arctic shipments in the summer navigation season. It includes a provision for Sovcomflot to assist in the training of Chinese mariners in Arctic navigation.[11]

A new venture was created between Russian and Finnish commercial interests in December 2010. STX Finland Oy and the United Shipbuilding Corporation (composed of 42 shipyards in Russia) formed a joint venture that will focus on Arctic shipbuilding technology. The newly named Arctech Helsinki Shipyard Oy will build specialized icebreaking vessels for key operators throughout the Russian maritime Arctic, and likely also for foreign buyers.[12]

Arctic Hub and Infrastructure

The ice-free port of Murmansk has long been viewed as a critical economic component of the Russian maritime Arctic. Recent reports in Russia confirm a strategy to fully develop Murmansk as the major oil, gas, and container port, as well as a transportation hub for the entire Russian Arctic. Tax and customs benefits from a new port economic zone will facilitate investment, as Murmansk is increasingly tied to offshore development in the Barents Sea.[13] Companies such as BP, for its potential Kara Sea venture, and others such as Gazprom, planning the offshore Shtokman gas field, look to establish bases for Arctic operations (including response and emergency services) in Murmansk.

Northern Sea Route headquarters of the western sector may be moved from Dikson, on the remote Kara Sea coast, to Murmansk. As well, it is clear that new port and construction activities along the Russian Arctic will be serviced from a modern hub in Murmansk. More new marine infrastructure has been planned. New Arctic rescue centers, Russian-built satellite systems

Fig. 2. The nuclear icebreaker *Rossiya* escorted the *Tor Viking* across the Northern Sea Route from 16 to 26 December 2010, indicating a potential extension of the sailing season for ice-capable ships under close escort. Russian nuclear icebreakers would be used for escorting convoys, scientific expeditions, and summer sealift. (Photo: RIA Novosti)

for the North, and a new Arctic research vessel were all discussed in 2010 by several federal ministries. Some of this critical Arctic infrastructure may come about through investment by public-private partnerships, including foreign capital.

The Russian nuclear-powered icebreaker fleet under the state-owned Atomflot (part of Rosatom) is a legacy of the Soviet Union but retains near iconic status in the Russian North and the polar world. There are plans to modernize the fleet by building dual-draft ships that can operate along the coastal waters of the Northern Sea Route and in the Siberian estuaries and rivers. It is apparent that shuttle fleets in the Barents and Kara seas do not intend to operate with icebreaker support or in convoys. However, the nuclear icebreakers would be used to escort Russian and foreign ships along the Northern Sea Route during extended navigation seasons and to conduct scientific expeditions, support Arctic oil and gas offshore development, and support summer sealift to Arctic communities. Most certainly the nuclear icebreakers remain a visible and tangible presence of the Russian Federation in the Arctic Ocean.

State Policy and International Cooperation

Russian President Dmitry Medvedev approved a new Arctic policy statement on September 18, 2008, titled "The Foundations of the Russian Federation's State Policy in the Arctic until 2020." This document outlines the strategic priorities for the Russian Federation in the Arctic, noting unique features of the region including low population, remoteness from major industrial centers, a large natural-resource base, and dependence on supplies from other regions in Russia. One of the critical points is that Russia intends to use its Arctic regions as a "strategic resource base."

For the maritime world, the policy mentions use of the Northern Sea Route as a national, integrated "transport-communications system" in the Arctic, specifically an "active coast guard system" in the Russian Arctic under the direction of the Federal Security Service. Important for the Arctic states, the document notes Russia's interest in enhancing cooperation with other national coast guards in the areas of terrorism on the high seas, prevention of illegal immigration and smuggling, and protection of marine living resources. Russia, Norway, and the United States already cooperate in these pursuits, but more can be expected as marine activities expand throughout the Arctic Ocean.

On September 22–23, 2010, the Russian Geographical Society held a key conference in Moscow that focused on the importance of international cooperation. Appropriately called "The Arctic: Territory of Dialogue," this forum gave prominence to the roles of indigenous people, the need to protect the environment, the vast storehouse of Arctic resources to be developed, and the need to affirm the region as a "zone of peace and cooperation." Prime Minister Vladimir Putin addressed the conference in a wide-ranging speech, noting that 70 per cent of the country is located in northern latitudes, and that the issues of Arctic development are high on Russia's national agenda. He mentioned the importance of the Arctic Council to the "integration" of ideas and concepts.[14]

Fig. 3. In September 2010, Prime Minister Vladimir Putin spoke at the conference "The Arctic: Territory of Dialogue," focusing on indigenous people, the environment, natural resources, and the area as a "zone of peace and cooperation." Here, Putin inspects models of two Sovcomflot ice tankers, accompanied by chief company executive Sergei Frank (left) and shipyard director Vladimir Aleksandrov. (Photo: RIA Novosti)

Overall Implications

The Russian Federation is embarking on a long-term strategy to link its Arctic region economically to the rest of the globe. The drivers are clearly the development of natural resources and timely export of domestic production. The facilitators are innovative marine transportation systems that can move cargoes of hydrocarbons and hard minerals both westbound (year-round) and eastbound (summer season) along the top of Eurasia.

There will be opportunities for ice-capable, foreign-flag ships to gain access to Russian Arctic waters, as illustrated by recent operations in summers 2009 through 2012. For example, bulk carriers could increasingly link northern

European mines to Pacific ports during summer seasons of navigation. And foreign-flag ice-class tankers could compete with modern Russian-owned fleets of advanced carriers for this potential summer maritime trade route, especially linking China to Russian Arctic oil and gas.

For safety and security reasons, Russia is sure to manage tightly the opening of its Arctic waters to maritime trade. Similarly, the capabilities of its borderguard of the Federal Security Service will be enhanced for Arctic operations. There have been no announced changes in the regulations along the Northern Sea Route for mandatory icebreaker escort in certain straits, despite Norilsk Nickel's *Monchegorsk* full passage without escort in 2010. Commercial ships without ice classification have not yet sailed along the eastern reaches of the route.

Changes could come soon, with legislative action from the State Duma. All this new activity will require improved environmental observations, new marine charts, traffic monitoring, enforcement capability, and control measures. We are witnessing the cautious evolution of an Arctic region from a once-closed security bastion to a vast marine area more open for use and, potentially, integrated with the global economy.

Notes

1 Reprinted, with permission, from *Proceedings* 137, no. 5 (2011): 1299. http://www.usni.org/magazines/ proceedings/2011-05/russia-opens-its-maritime-arctic. Copyright 2010, U.S. Naval Institute.

2 Press release, September 15, 2010, Office of the Prime Minister, Norway; http://www. regjeringen.no/en/dep/smk/press-center/ Press-releases/2010/treaty.html?id=614254.

3 Press release, September 9, 2010, SCF (Sovcomflot) Group, Russia's largest shipping company (state owned); http:// www.scf-group.com.

4 Joint press release, August 20, 2010, Nordic Bulk Carrier A/S and Tschudi Shipping Company A/S.

5 Press report, November 16, 2010, Norilsk Nickel, on the return of its carrier *Monchegorsk* to the port of Dudinka on the Yenisey River from Shanghai; http://www. nornik.ru/en/press/news/3101/.

6 Reported in *MB News* (*Murmansk Business News*), September 29, 2010; and *BarentsObserver.com*, September 30, 2010.

7 Voyage details provided by the Swedish shipping firm TransAtlantic, operator of *Tor Viking*, January 2011.

8 Oil and Gas Eurasia, "First Shipment of Oil from the Varandey Terminal," June 10, 2008; http:// www.oilandgaseurasia.com/news/ lukoil-starts-oil-export-varandey-terminal.

9 Oil and Gas Eurasia, "Double Acting Tankers for the Prirazlomnoye Project," November 2010; http://www.oilandgaseurasia.com/tech_trend/double-acting-tanker-set-pechora-sea-debut-first-two-new-arctic-double-acting-shuttle.

10 Reuters, Moscow, June 16, 2009, from a Lukoil report.

11 Press release, November 22, 2010, Sovcomflot Group.

12 Press release, December 10, 2010, STX Finland and United Shipbuilding Corporation, agreement signed in St. Petersburg.

13 "Planned Seaport Would Turn Murmansk into Major Hub," *St. Petersburg Times*, October 5, 2010.

14 Address to the international forum, "The Arctic: Territory of Dialogue," September 22, 2010, official site of the prime minister of the Russian Federation; http://www.arcticgovernance.org/prime-minister-vladimir-putin-addresses-the-international-forum-the-arctic-territory-of-dialogue.4823958-142902.html.

15. Regional Security and Prosperity: The U.S.–Russia Reset in the Antimeridianal Arctic

Caitlyn Antrim

It has been over two decades since the breakup of the Soviet Union and the declaration by President George H. W. Bush that a "new world order" would rise to replace the East versus West orientation of the Cold War era. Slow in coming and evolving along the way, this new approach is seen in the security strategies and policies of both the United States and Russia. This new order retains the military security components of the past but increases emphasis on interests in sovereignty and border security, economic prosperity, and international cooperation.

This new approach is particularly well suited to the Arctic Ocean, where changes in climate, advances in technology and growing demands for energy are opening a region that in the twentieth century had little role other than as a buffer zone between east and west, a frigid laboratory for scientific research and a hidden realm of nuclear deterrence. Cooperation, respect for sovereign rights, sustainable development, environmental protection, and respect for native culture all a part of a new definition of security that promotes peaceful uses of the Arctic.

As security perspectives have evolved, the United States and Russia have emphasized a need to change their relationship from contention to cooperation, represented by the concept of a "reset" in U.S.–Russian affairs. Much

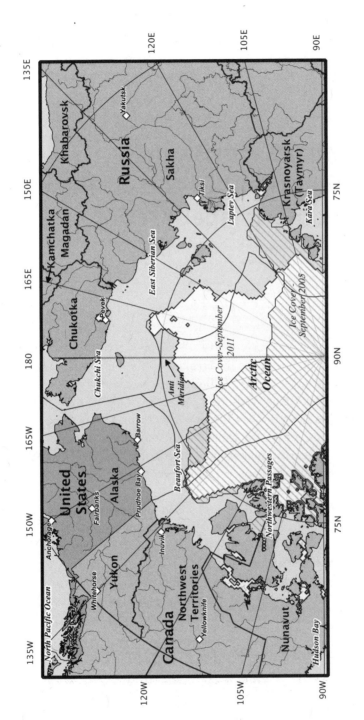

THE ANTIMERIDIANAL ARCTIC

15. REGIONAL SECURITY AND PROSPERITY

work has been undertaken in the three years since the initial U.S.–Russia joint action plan in July 2009, including the establishment of the U.S.–Russia Bilateral Presidential Commission in October 2009 as the mechanism for pursuing the reset in relations.[1] The Commission, with its seventeen bilateral working groups, has a broad agenda, but visible results seem mainly focused on arms control and other great power issues, with notable success in the approval of the "New START" agreement on strategic weapons.

The effort has a distinct government-to-government approach, but the effects of a "reset" that is primarily limited to the two federal governments may last only as long as the leaders of both countries find it politically beneficial. A more lasting reset would require change at the level of the people of each country, not just the current leaders. Grounding the evolution of the U.S.–Russia relationship in the populations, businesses, civil society organizations, and sub-national governance bodies across the vast Eurasian state would help ensure that the turn toward cooperation is vulnerable to another change in the capitals of either country.[2]

While Russia and the United States each have their own particular interests in the Arctic, their national security and sustainable development policies are strikingly similar. Under the umbrella of the new concepts of national security, the United States and Russia, neighbors across the Bering Strait, have the opportunity to put into practice a partnership that would promote the interests of both nations and cement a reset of relationships between the people of the Russian Far East and Alaska that will be deeper and more stable than the relations between capitals.

Arctic Change and Changing Geopolitics

Geography may not be "destiny," but for geopolitical analysts it is the first place to look to understand issues of international politics. Lack of awareness of arctic geography and the extent of change in the Arctic has been a critical weakness of many analysts and commentators who have jumped to conclusions about the potential for conflict while underplaying opportunities for collaboration as the Arctic becomes increasingly accessible.

The "Antimeridianal Arctic" is the area that spans the Arctic region across the Anti-Meridian – 180 degrees directly opposite the Prime Meridian. It includes territory north of Alaska and the Far East Federal District of Russia.

In Alaska, it includes the oil-rich North Slope, the Brooks Range, and the Yukon River. The land is home to native people and Alaska residents. At sea, it includes the Bering Strait, the Beaufort, Chukchi, East Siberian, and Laptev seas and part of the central Arctic Ocean. While the Bering Strait divides the two countries, it is also an area of common interests in maritime commerce and safety, environment, and culture.

The waters are home to fish and marine mammals, and the seabed to the north is projected to have extensive, though as-yet undiscovered, oil resources. Russia's territory includes Chukotka and the northern borderlands of the Sakha Republic, including the mouth of the great Lena River, the gateway to a watershed of 2.5 million square kilometers that reaches to the southern border of Russia. Along its northern coast, Russia has a string of aging ports, airfields and mineral production facilities, a legacy of the Cold War that has eroded over the two decades since the end of the Soviet Union and is only now being redeveloped.

Recent changes in the Arctic have been the source of both excitement and alarm. The opening of Russia's Northern Sea Route in 2008 to foreign shipping and several commercial transits of the Northwest Passage led to predictions of a growth of commercial shipping that would take advantage of shortened trade routes between Europe and the Far East, saving thousands of miles and many days at sea. Forecasts of potentially large, though as yet undiscovered, oil and gas reserves under the Arctic continental shelf have focused attention on issues of sovereignty, security, and sustainability throughout the region.

Changes in the Arctic may be addressed in four categories: technical, economic, climatic, and legal:

- *Technological Advances and the Arctic*: Technology to conquer the Arctic ice made gradual but consistent advances throughout the twentieth century. Reinforced bows and hulls gave way to steel ships with hulls specially designed to break through ice. Nuclear reactors were introduced to provide the power and endurance for icebreakers to patrol the length of Russia's Arctic coast. The introduction of the azimuth pod and dual-acting hull designs led to the construction of commercial cargo ships and tankers able to operate without icebreaker assistance. These advances were followed by new technologies for development of oil and gas deposits in deep water and polar conditions.

- *Economic Change*: In the later decades of the twentieth century, rising energy demands in western Europe led to partnerships linking resource production in the Soviet Union with markets in Europe that broke the economic isolation of the USSR that had followed World War II. The breakup of the Soviet Union further increased European access to Russian energy resources. This led to acceptance in Europe that Russian resources not only diversified energy supplies but opened new sales and investment opportunities for the West. Oil on Alaska's North Slope and natural gas in Russia's northwest highlighted the Arctic as a world-class energy resource. The 2008 estimate by the U.S. Geological Survey that perhaps a quarter of the world's undiscovered hydrocarbon resources may be found in the Arctic further increased interest in the potential contribution of resources of the Russian Arctic to European markets and to markets in east Asia and the Americas.

- *Changes in Climate*: The increased accessibility of the Arctic in recent years has also resulted from cumulative changes in climate over the past three decades. Over that time, winter ice cover has declined by nearly 10 per cent. Summertime observations in 2007 revealed the area of ice cover reduced by one third from its 1979–2000 average. In 2008, the sea routes transiting both the Russian and Canadian arctic were, for the first time, simultaneously declared ice-free, even if only for a short period. These changes are projected to continue for decades to come. In its 2008 report to the Intergovernmental Panel on Climate Change (IPCC), Russia's Hydrometeorological Service projected that by 2040 winter temperatures could increase along the Arctic coast by about four degrees centigrade and by two to three degrees in the summer.[3] Such increases will moderate the severity of winters and lengthen ice-free periods on rivers and coasts. Over several decades, this will change plant life in the region, with forests moving further north and extended growing periods in the south. It is geopolitically significant that climate change and global warming will increase the accessibility of the heartland of Russia and connect it to the rest of the world. It is important to recognize that climate change will bring costs as well. Melting permafrost will undermine roads and buildings in the north and frozen rivers that serve as winter ice roads will be increasingly less available.

- *Changes in the Legal Regime*: In 1926, the Soviet Union proposed a sectoral division of the Arctic with lines drawn from the North Pole to the eastern and western extremes of its northern coast that proclaimed that all land area within the sector was the sovereign territory of the Soviet Union.[4] Due to the inaccessibility of the Arctic, the proposal had little impact. It was not until the Third United Nations Conference on the Law of the Sea considered the limits of national jurisdiction at sea that global agreement on the extent and limits of national jurisdiction at sea was reached. The 1982 United Nations Convention on the Law of the Sea (UNCLOS) codified new rules to establish the extent of coastal states' offshore jurisdiction. In 1990 the United States and the Soviet Union concluded a treaty delineating their common maritime boundary in the Pacific and Arctic oceans. Russia joined the Convention in 1997 and accepted the its definition of sovereignty in the Arctic, including a twelve-nautical-mile territorial sea and a two hundred-mile Exclusive Economic Zone (EEZ) off its coast and islands in the Arctic Ocean.[5] The Convention also provided a detailed definition of the continental shelf that held out the prospect of encompassing much of the seabed within the region of the 1926 sectoral claim. The establishment of the Arctic Council in 1996 added a new forum for cooperation on sustainable development among Arctic states. While the founding documents specifically excluded "security" from the purview of the Council, the evolution of the concept of national security into areas of prosperity and cooperation may slowly bring these aspects of national security into the scope of the Arctic Council.

National Security in the Twenty-first Century

In the two decades since the end of the Cold War and the break-up of the Soviet Union, both the United States and the Russian Federation have developed new concepts of national security that better reflect the complexity and interconnections of the modern international order.

The importance of the Arctic in modern Russia's security is best noted by recognizing that Russia's Arctic watershed encompasses 13 million square kilometers or three quarters of the land area of Russia and an area larger than any other country save Russia itself. The Lena, the Yenesei, and the Ob river systems are each comparable to the entire Mississippi River system in the United States. While these rivers have been largely limited to internal communications due to near year-around ice in their northern reaches, the prospect of increased river access to the Northern Sea Route is a game-changing concept in the development of the watershed and the conversion of Russia from a 'heartland' to a maritime state.

Geography also defines America's arctic security interests. In contrast to Russia's vast arctic watershed, Alaska's arctic coast is a much narrower coastal plain bordered to the south by the Brooks Range. The arctic coast lacks major rivers and bays that are suitable as harbors for large ships. The major river of northern Alaska, the Yukon, flows from Canada south of the Brooks Range and reaches the north Pacific south of the Bering Strait. The coastal plain and continental shelf are well endowed with oil, and recent research suggests that the continental shelf extends perhaps 650 nautical miles or more northward along the Chukchi Plateau with indications of possible hydrocarbon deposits.[6] Maritime traffic between the Arctic and the Pacific Ocean must pass through either the U.S. or Russian sides of the Bering Strait where increased traffic may over-stress existing navigational aids and vessel tracking systems.

Security Policies of the United States

In the past five years, the United States published a new national security strategy and a maritime security strategy. Recently, the themes of both strategies were consolidated and extended in a paper presented at the Woodrow Wilson International Center for Scholars.[7] Together, these publications identify the current framework and direction of U.S. security policy as it guides the country's arctic policy.

The U.S. National Security Strategy

The 2010 U.S. national security strategy views security in four aspects:[8]

- *Security*: Security interests span from the management of weapons of mass destruction and control of their dissemination to protection of borders and the homeland from violation and attack. This encompasses traditional views of security based on military and diplomatic capability, emphasizes the maintenance of alliances and creation of new partnerships and addresses new threats such as cyber-attacks.

- *Prosperity*: Interests in prosperity focus on building the domestic base to support traditional security programs and to ensure that the domestic economic base of society remains strong. Strengthening human capital through education, supporting future competitiveness through science, technology and innovation, maintaining balance in development, and ensuring development is sustainable are the core aspects of prosperity for national security.

- *Values*: U.S. interests in values provide a focus for strengthening democracy and promoting respect for individuals and cultures. Supporting the rights of individuals and movements to be heard, protecting human rights, fighting corruption, and fostering transparency are all aspects of strengthening U.S. security through the promotion of public participation in governance in foreign countries. Values supported by the United States of relevance to the Arctic include respect for rights of indigenous people, promotion of roles of civil society, and application of the principles of the 1992 Rio Declaration on Environment and Development.

- *International order*: Extending beyond bilateral relationships and alliances with like-minded states, the U.S. strategy views a strong international order supported by capable international institutions as important to U.S. security. In substantive areas, U.S. interests in the international order include safeguarding the global commons and promoting

national interests in the Arctic through regional cooperation and international organizations.

U.S. national security policy has a special position for Russia in all four of its
aspects. Russia's role was singled out in the 2010 National Security Strategy
as follows:

> We seek to build a stable, substantive, multidimensional relation-
> ship with Russia, based on mutual interests. The United States
> has an interest in a strong, peaceful, and prosperous Russia that
> respects international norms. As the two nations possessing the
> majority of the world's nuclear weapons, we are working together
> to advance nonproliferation, both by reducing our nuclear arse-
> nals and by cooperating to ensure that other countries meet their
> international commitments to reducing the spread of nuclear
> weapons around the world. We will seek greater partnership with
> Russia in confronting violent extremism, especially in Afghani-
> stan. We also will seek new trade and investment arrangements
> for increasing the prosperity of our peoples. We support efforts
> within Russia to promote the rule of law, accountable government,
> and universal values. While actively seeking Russia's cooperation
> to act as a responsible partner in Europe and Asia, we will support
> the sovereignty and territorial integrity of Russia's neighbors.[9]

A Cooperative Strategy for Twenty-first Century Seapower

As a maritime nation, U.S. policy toward the ocean commons is part of the
bedrock of its security policy:

> We must work together to ensure the constant flow of commerce,
> facilitate safe and secure air travel, and prevent disruptions to
> critical communications. We must also safeguard the sea, air, and
> space domains from those who would deny access or use them for
> hostile purposes. This includes keeping strategic straits and vital
> sea lanes open, improving the early detection of emerging mar-
> itime threats, denying adversaries hostile use of the air domain,
> and ensuring the responsible use of space. As one key effort in the

sea domain, for example, we will pursue ratification of the United
Nations Convention on the Law of the Sea.[10]

The strategy issued by America's sea services (the Navy, Marine Corps and
Coast Guard) in 2007 begins with the premise that "the security, prosperity
and vital interests of the United States are best served by fostering a peaceful global system comprised of interdependent networks of trade, finance,
information, law, people and governance."[11] The strategy recognizes that
major disruptions, whether from war, conflict, or natural disaster, threaten
both U.S. security and global prosperity. As such, it is important, not only
to be able to fight and win wars and to prevent wars altogether, but also to
respond to natural disasters and other non-military crises. The strategy posits
that "maritime forces will be employed to build confidence and trust among
nations through collective security efforts that focus on common threats and
mutual interests in an open, multi-polar world."[12]

Maritime security, humanitarian assistance, and disaster response
are recognized in the 2007 Cooperative Strategy for Twenty-first Century
Seapower as areas ripe for international cooperation. The Cooperative Strategy
moves beyond traditional cooperation among military allies to developing relationships among sea services worldwide to support collaboration and joint
activities through agreements such as the Proliferation Security Initiative
and global and regional initiatives such as the multinational anti-piracy patrols operating off the coast of Somalia under the authority Security Council
resolutions.

The "Mr. Y" Paper

This expanded view of national and maritime security is new and still evolving. The trend of a more expansive definition of national security developed
in the National Security Strategy and the Cooperative Strategy was explored
further by two officers on the staff of the Joint Chiefs of Staff who recently
published an article that elaborated on the broadening concept of American
national security.[13] Writing under the pseudonym "Mr. Y" in order to emphasize that the views were those of the authors, the two officers continued
to develop the emerging themes of the National Security Strategy and the
Cooperative Strategy for Twenty-first Century Seapower.

The "Mr. *Y*" paper puts additional emphasis on economic issues as an element of national security, with focus on three key factors: *Human Capital*: focus on the health, education, and social support structure for American workers; *Sustainable Security*: Involve all relevant departments and agencies in national security policies in a "whole of government" approach; and *Natural Resources*: Invest in natural resources management to address supplies in a period of growing world demand.

U.S. Policies in the Arctic

The 2010 U.S. National Security Strategy addresses American security interests in the Arctic in a single concise paragraph:

> *Arctic Interests*: The United States is an Arctic Nation with broad and fundamental interests in the Arctic region, where we seek to meet our national security needs, protect the environment, responsibly manage resources, account for indigenous communities, support scientific research, and strengthen international cooperation on a wide range of issues.[14]

U.S. policy towards the Arctic was the subject of a major review in 2008 and 2009, leading to the adoption of a significantly revised and expanded policy adopted at the end of the Bush Administration. This policy was continued by the incoming Obama administration and expanded by President Obama in the summer of 2010 as part of a new national oceans policy.

U.S. arctic policy is given more depth in the 2009 NSC Decision Memorandum on Arctic Policy adopted at the end of the Bush Administration and continued by the Obama administration.[15] According to this document, it is the policy of the United States to:

- Meet national security and homeland security needs relevant to the Arctic region;

- Protect the Arctic environment and conserve its biological resources;

- Ensure that natural resource management and economic development in the region are environmentally sustainable;

- Strengthen institutions for cooperation among the eight Arctic nations (the United States, Canada, Denmark, Finland, Iceland, Norway, the Russian Federation, and Sweden);

- Involve the Arctic's indigenous communities in decisions that affect them; and

- Enhance scientific monitoring and research into local, regional, and global environmental issues.

U.S. arctic policy identifies eight specific topics for attention that can be grouped into three overarching interests:

Security and Sovereignty

1. *National Security and Homeland Security* interests in the Arctic focus on the protection of U.S. territory and resources, maintenance of border security, and enforcement of domestic laws and regulations on vessels and other maritime activities.

2. *Sovereignty* issues lie in the definition of the outer limit of the extended continental shelf and in the delineation of boundaries with Russia and Canada. This includes promoting Russian ratification of the 1990 Maritime Boundary Agreement, resolution of claims in the Beaufort Sea, and the division of the extended continental shelf north of the U.S.–Canada land boundary.

Prosperity

3. *Arctic Maritime Transportation* interests in the Arctic include assurance of access for ships to the waters north of Alaska and the development of harbors and port facilities to support development and commerce. This further entails establishment of additional navigational aids and new capabilities for search and rescue, emergency environmental response, and regulation and enforcement.

4. *Ecosystem Management and Spatial Planning* for marine activities is the mechanism for addressing U.S. uses of the oceans and coasts to achieve national policy goals. The final recommendations of the U.S. Ocean Policy Task Force in 2010 endorse ecosystem management as the process for evaluation

of ocean activities and interactions and the use of marine spatial planning as the tool for conducting these evaluations.

5. *Environment and Conservation of Natural Resources* are primary considerations of the ocean policy recommendations. In implementing a precautionary approach to the oceans, U.S. policy emphasizes caution in expanding human activity in a region such as the Arctic until sufficient information is gathered and assessed to guide and regulate activities to protect the environment and conserve resources. Examples of this include the moratorium placed on exploitation of living resources in the EEZ north of Alaska and review of the potential impact of exploratory drilling in the Chukchi Sea, particularly in light of the unexpected marine disaster of the Deepwater Horizon in the Gulf of Mexico in 2010.

6. *Economic development* interests begin with the development of onshore and offshore hydrocarbon deposits, including exploration and assessment activities as well as oil and gas production activities at sea. Interest in commercial fishing in the Arctic is likely to increase as fish stocks migrate to the warming waters north of the Bering Strait. As energy and living resource exploitation develops, onshore development will increase as well, bringing with it increased need for food and supplies, housing, health services, port facilities, and other infrastructure to support human habitation on or near the Alaskan arctic coast. Caution is a significant factor in U.S. offshore energy policy, but the Administration has committed to support exploratory drilling in the Chukchi and Beaufort seas, and federal efforts will be made to gather scientific information and public views in advance of deciding whether to advance to commercial exploitation in the Arctic Ocean.[16] While recognizing special issues of the region, U.S. Arctic policy will be guided by national and global level policies. Energy development in the Arctic will y emphasizes caution in expanding human activity in a region such as the Arctic until sufficient information is gathered and assessed to guide and regulate activities to protect the environment and conserve resources. Examples of this include the moratorium placed on exploitation of living resources in the EEZ north of Alaska and review of the potential ibe subject to regulatory policies of the Bureau of Ocean Energy Management. Regulation and Enforcement, policy will be developed and management will be implemented through marine spatial planning techniques, fisheries management will be eventually be guided by regional fisheries councils, and arctic conservation policies will be a subset of national policies. Because of the criticality of the provisions of UNCLOS

on international straits, the U.S. position on the Northwest Passage will remain rooted in the position that the passage is an international strait and will be guided by the national interest in freedom to pass through international straits worldwide rather than accept a compromise of a limited recognition of Canadian claims of internal water status of the passage.

International Cooperation

7. *International Governance* in the Arctic is supported from the bi-lateral level to the global. The United States engages bilaterally with Russia and Canada on arctic issues. With Russia, the navies and coast guards of the two countries conduct joint exercises and even support joint fishery enforcement activities. Matters of nuclear forces are primarily limited to bilateral interactions. At the regional level, the United States recognizes the Arctic Council as the primary forum for discussion of issues of environment and development. At the global level, the United States recognizes the role of the International Maritime Organization in establishing rules and guidelines applicable in the arctic and elsewhere. It also recognizes the role of the International Whaling Commission in protecting marine mammals. The United States is party to the 1995 UN Fish Stocks agreement that defines the role of regional fisheries organizations and can guide the eventual establishment of a fishery management council for the Antimeridianal Arctic.

8. *Promoting International Scientific Cooperation* has been a foreign policy interest in the Arctic since the first International Polar Year in 1882–83. President Reagan's Ocean Policy Proclamation of 1983 specifically recognized the right of states to conduct scientific research at sea and specifically noted that the United States would not exercise the right to block research in its EEZ as permitted by the LOS Convention. International scientific cooperation is facilitated through the International Oceanographic Commission.

U.S. National Oceans Policy

In the 2010 *National Policy for Stewardship of the Ocean, our Coasts, and the Great Lakes*, emphasis is given to maintaining the health and resiliency of the ocean and coasts, incorporating science and knowledge into policy-making, promoting sustainable, safe, and productive access to, and uses of, the oceans, coasts, and the Great Lakes.[17] Development of living or mineral resources is not specifically addressed. National priorities for the oceans emphasize information, ecosystem management and spatial planning, and coordination among all levels of government, native peoples, and the international community. One of the "National Priority Objectives" specifically addresses the Arctic:

> *Changing Conditions in the Arctic*: Address environmental stewardship needs in the Arctic ocean and adjacent coastal areas in the face of climate-induced and other environmental changes.[18]

The 2010 National Oceans Policy emphasizes information, sustainability, coordination, ecosystem management and marine spatial planning, U.S. energy policy, and other ocean activities. Raw materials found in the Arctic can provide a basis for economic development both regionally and as a nation. While the United States has an interest in arctic hydrocarbon development, such development is subject to an environmental sustainability criteria. Similarly, fishery development in the Arctic is guided by a conservation criterion. This reflects a growing incorporation of conservation and environmental protection interests into the prosperity aspect of national security.

Russia's National Security Strategy

Russia's current National Security Strategy, most recently revised and issued in 2009, identifies three long-term national interests:

- Enhancing the competitiveness of the national economy;
- Ensuring the inviolability of the constitutional order, territorial integrity, and sovereignty of the Russian Federation;
- Transforming the Russian Federation into a world power that seeks to maintain strategic stability and a mutually beneficial partnership in a multipolar world.[19]

While national defense, government, and public safety are important priorities, the security strategy recognizes that its interests cannot be secured by traditional military and border forces alone. It goes on to say that the Russian Federation's policy is to ensure the country's national security and advance its security policy priorities by focusing on priorities for sustainable development:[20]

- Improving the quality of life of Russian citizens by ensuring personal safety, as well as high standards of livelihood;

- Economic growth, which is achieved primarily through the development of national innovation systems and investment in human capital;

- Science, technology, education, health and culture, which develop by strengthening the role of the state and improve public-private partnership;

- Ecology of living systems and environmental management, the maintenance of which is achieved through balanced use and development of advanced technology and purposeful reproduction of natural-resource potential of the country; and

- Strategic stability and equal strategic partnership, which is strengthened through the active participation of Russia in the development of a multipolar model of world order.

Russia's Security and Policy in the Arctic

Over two-thirds of Russia's ocean coastline is found in the Arctic. Until recently, that appeared to be more of an item of curiosity than a fact of significance to Russia's interests and policies. During World War II, Murmansk has served as the arctic terminus of the North Atlantic shipping route through which supplies could be shipped from the United States to support the war effort on the Eastern Front. During the Cold War, Russia's Arctic coast was primarily an aerial frontier, with bases watching for incursions from the West and ports and airfields from which strategic forces could be deployed in times of tension. Ice breakers and ice-reinforced cargo ships traveled the coastline to supply bases and carry strategic materials from the mines of the North to the production facilities and rail lines of the Kola Peninsula near Murmansk and Archangel.

Russia's vision of the Arctic has gone through several revisions since the latter years of the Soviet Union. The most significant change began under Michael Gorbachev, the USSR's last secretary general. As part of Gorbachev's effort to reduce international tension, he proposed that the Arctic should be a zone of peace and cooperation and even suggested that the strategic waterway of the North – the Northern Sea Route – could be opened to foreign shipping.[21] Gorbachev's Arctic vision was derailed by the collapse of the Soviet Union and the changes wrought during the presidency of Boris Yeltsin. Although the Northern Sea Route was declared open to foreign shipping in 1991, the route fell into disuse and disrepair. The reduction of the military threat from the United States removed the state imperative of maintaining the strategic forces and defenses along the Arctic coast while rapid privatization of state assets decimated the Russian-flag shipping fleet. Annual shipping on the Northern Sea Route dropped from almost 6.6 million tons in 1987 to about 2.0 million tons in 1998.[22]

As traffic on the NSR declined, so too did the facilities strung across the North that supported traffic on the route. By the time Yeltsin left office in 1999, the Northern Sea Route and Russia's capacity to use it were at their lowest ebb since the NSR was established in the 1930s. Much as western geostrategists had assumed for more than a century, Russia became nearly isolated from its northern frontier. As Moscow and St. Petersburg increasingly became the focal points of Russian government, economics, and culture at the beginning of the twenty-first century, Russia was in danger of being relegated to the role as Europe's eastern frontier. But while the concentration of power and wealth in the two major cities would continue, political, economic, resource, technology, and climate changes would soon begin to reverse the vision for Russia's Arctic.

Vladimir Putin became prime minister in 1999 and president in 2000, and with him came a number of changes that reflected a greater role for the central government. This was particularly true in the case of the Arctic. There should have been no surprise in the turn of policy, given that President Putin's 1999 PhD dissertation was titled "Mineral and Raw Material Resources and the Development Strategy for the Russian Economy."[23] As president, Putin quickly became the chief advocate for northern resource development and rehabilitation of the Northern Sea Route. Within a decade, a series of formal strategies would change the role of the Arctic from a forgotten fortress to a new source of national strength for Russia. This was formalized when an Arctic security strategy was endorsed by President Dmitry Medvedev in 2008.[24] In this strategy, the basic national interests of the Russian Federation in the Arctic are:

- Use of the Arctic zone of the Russian Federation as a strategic resource base of the Russian Federation to deal with the socio-economic development;

- Preservation of the Arctic as a zone of peace and cooperation;

- Conservation of unique ecosystems of the Arctic; and

- Use the Northern Sea Route as a national integrated transport communications in the Arctic, the Russian Federation[25]

The strategy also identified six primary policy objectives:

1. Socio-economic development, including application of advanced technology for production, modernization of the transportation and fisheries sectors, and improved quality of life for indigenous people and other arctic residents;

2. Defense and protection of the state border in the Arctic, including collaboration with other arctic states in delimiting the outer limits of Russian jurisdiction in the Arctic;

3. Preserving and protecting the natural environment of the Arctic, including cross-border cooperation for conservation of the natural environment;

4. Creating a unified information space in the Russian Arctic utilizing information and communications technologies;

5. Ensuring an adequate level of basic and applied research to support security, life-support, and production activities in the Arctic climate;

6. Ensuring an international regime of bilateral and multilateral cooperation between Russia and other arctic states, increasing

the involvement of public institutions and organizations in international arctic forums, and ensuring that the northern sea routes are managed in conformity with international treaties.

These objectives were taken further in Russia's draft "Development Strategy for the Arctic Zone to 2020,"[26] which was discussed at the Moscow conference "The Arctic: Territory of Dialog" in September 2010 and released in draft form by the Ministry for Regional Development in 2011. The theme of the draft strategy has been summarized by Dr. Alexander Pelyasov as "Knowledge, Presence, Innovation."[27] The strategy implements these three elements with its emphasis on gathering information about the Arctic and developing new understanding, strengthening human capital through education, improved work and living conditions and use of the internet and satellite communications to strengthen society in the Far North, and developing and implementing new technologies, including alternative energy systems, to the problems of living and working in the harsh arctic environment.

Opportunities for a Joint Arctic Strategy

Russia and the United States are both "Arctic Nations," but they differ in the degree to which the Arctic is integrated into their national vision. With objectives established by their respective national security policies, both the United States and Russia approach their Arctic policies guided by sustainable development concepts integrated into ocean and regional development policies, but emphasis differs based on their geography, climate, resources, culture, and national and local interests and policies.

Russia's draft development strategy for the Arctic encompasses several key points that are part of the U.S. national security strategy and are highlighted in the "Mr. Y" paper:

- The U.S. security interest in the development of human capital is matched by the arctic development strategy's focus on developing human capital in the Arctic, including education, health, and quality of life;

- The U.S. focus on enhancing science, technology, and innovation can be paired with the focus on the need to apply knowledge, understanding, and innovation to Russia's arctic development;

- A U.S. strategy to develop natural resources in response to growing U.S. needs is matched by Russia's commitment to develop its natural resources in the Arctic.

Contrasting National Approaches

Russia and the United States share the general themes of security and sovereignty, prosperity through sustainable development, and governance through cooperation and collaboration. In practice, however, there remain differences in emphasis that affect the potential for collaboration in managing the Arctic.

In sovereignty and security, both states have agreed to respect the provisions of the Law of the Sea Convention for determining the limits of national jurisdiction. This is hampered, however, by the failure to date for the United States to ratify the LOS Convention and Russia to ratify the U.S.–Russian maritime boundary delimitation treaty.

Both countries are still developing their own balance between environmental protection and economic development. While these are largely domestic matters, differences in national policies that affect trans-boundary fisheries, protection of marine mammals, and effects of development on the marine environmental may lead to disagreement and political conflict. Russia's policies see the Arctic first as a strategic resource warehouse that can kickstart development while U.S. policies approach Arctic resources with a high degree of caution and unresolved conflict between development and environment.

Russia and the United States both support bilateral coordination and cooperation and regional cooperation through the Arctic Council, but there are likely to be different perspectives of the roles of local, national, and global interests in developing and implementing security, sustainable development, and governance policies for the Arctic. When interests coincide, the potential benefit of cooperation can be high, as demonstrated by the successful negotiation of a binding agreement among Arctic Council members for search and rescue in the Arctic Ocean.

In both countries, however, Arctic policy is driven by internal interests at the national level. Bilateral cooperation is already conducted by the navies and coast guards stationed in the Pacific and Arctic oceans. Only to a lesser degree do regional and local governments, civil society, and native people have a say in policy. These other groups generally lack the resources to pursue their different agendas on their own and are limited to working around the edges of federal policy. U.S. environmental NGOs may collaborate with Russian counterparts. Communication among native people of the two countries has been facilitated by the lifting of visa requirements for crossing the U.S.–Russian border and efforts are underway to obtain a reciprocal extension of the duration of visa for other travelers.

Toward An Antimeridianal Arctic Partnership

The official policies of the United States and Russia demonstrate that the two nations share interests and approaches in the Arctic in the areas of security and sovereignty, prosperity, the environment, and international and regional cooperation. These shared interests provide the basis for increased collaboration and partnership. While they have different perspectives and emphasis, both nations place high emphasis on safe navigation, development of domestic sources of energy, management and conservation of living resources, protection of the marine environment, inclusion of native people in developing and implementing Arctic policies, and adherence to the principles of state sovereignty and regional cooperation specified in the UN Convention on the Law of the Sea and the Rio Declaration of the UN Conference on Environment and Development.

The interests of Russia and the United States are particularly aligned in the areas of border and boundary delimitation and in homeland security. Approaches differ significantly in regard to the balance between economic development and environmental protection and conservation, but the general approach based on sustainable development is shared. Both endorse multilateral approaches, including regional cooperation though the Arctic Council and broader cooperation through functional international organizations, notably the International Maritime Organization.

Prosperity and environment, the constituent components of sustainable development, address aspects of each nation's new view of national security. Maritime transportation in the Arctic is a core aspect of both country's policies. For Russia, the development of the Northern Sea Route across Arctic Asia as a national transportation corridor is a primary interest. For the United States, safe transportation and security in the maritime domain are likewise primary security interests that contribute to security and prosperity aspects of the national interest.

While relations at the national level have ebbed and flowed according to relations between capitals, there is a history of regional and local cooperation that dates back to the beginning of the "glasnost" era. Led by early academic cooperation and exchanges, cultural exchanges followed, as did state-level negotiations and cooperation on international fishery policy in the Bering Sea. As Governor of Alaska, Wally Hickel made extensive efforts to build connections with the regional and provincial governments of the Russian Far East. Cities in Alaska and Russia have established "sister city" relationships.[28]

The United States and Russia share a long maritime boundary and at their closest approach their shores are less than two and a half miles apart. Over the past three decades, there have been many scientific, cultural, and resource interchanges between Alaska and the Russian Far East at the state/federal district, city, and organization levels. Native people in Alaska and the Russian Far East share roots of language and culture that reach deep into pre-history. Far from their respective capitals, the people of Alaska and the Russian Far East have developed their own low-key relationships, mostly outside of the awareness of policymakers in their capitals.

An Agenda for Reset and Partnership in the Antimeridianal Arctic

The common interests in security, prosperity, and cooperation in the Arctic give rise to a promising opportunity to make the reset of relations between the United States and Russia more robust and durable. Here is a twelve-point program for an Arctic Regional Partnership that focuses on the three core areas of interest to both the United States and Russia: security, prosperity and cooperation:

Security and Sovereignty

Shared interests in protecting sovereignty and maintaining security in the northern Pacific Ocean have led the United States and Russia to develop pragmatic relationships to facilitate collaboration on matters of search and rescue, communications, regulatory enforcement, and traffic monitoring in the Bering Strait region. Out of the public eye, working relationships in ocean use and management under international law that have been a model of cooperation in the north Pacific should be extended northward to the Antimeridianal Arctic:

1. *Reinforce the rule of law*: First, Russia and the United States need to take the lead in strengthening the rule of law in the Arctic. Russia should finally ratify the 1990 maritime boundary agreement with the United States and the United States should accede to the UN Convention on the Law of the Sea. A firm commitment to a common understanding of the Law of the Sea Convention will help Arctic states to resolve issues among themselves and to implement policies and regulations governing Arctic use that will be accepted by non-Arctic states seeking to transit the Arctic, exploit its resources, and conduct marine scientific research.

2. *Cooperate in strategic force activities in the Arctic*: As long as the United States and Russia maintain strategic nuclear weapons, these forces will be deployed in the Arctic, primarily under the polar ice and high in the atmosphere. Effective deterrence depends on continued demonstration of response capability, but such demonstration can be achieved while also maintaining communication and enacting confidence-building measures regarding operations, intelligence, and interaction between offensive and defensive systems.

3. *Enhance military cooperation and plan for emergency response*: Improve the capability of all Arctic states to respond to natural disasters and man-made crises. Increased activity in the Arctic need not require each Arctic state to maintain a full spectrum of ships, aircraft, satellites, and observation stations or emergency supplies. Shared awareness of assets,

joint planning, and training in combined operations would benefit all users of the Arctic in providing combined aid and assistance. Successful implementation of the Search and Rescue agreement adopted in Nuuk in May 2011 will demonstrate the potential for further cooperation.

4. *Maritime safety and regulation of activities*: The Arctic states, with Russia and the United States in the lead, should collaborate to ensure safety at sea in line with national and international regulations, from implementation of the search and rescue agreement to response to major disasters at sea, such as vessel damage and oil spills. Leadership by the Arctic states in the International Maritime Organization can help avoid different, perhaps conflicting, national design specifications and operating regulations for trans-arctic shipping, and collaboration on regional fisheries management can lead to sustainable fisheries rather than over-exploitation. Agreement between Russia and the United States on traffic separation and monitoring in the Bering Strait is an important step in addressing safety and security in the Arctic to the benefit of both countries as well as other nations whose ships enter the Arctic for commercial or scientific purposes. Cooperation in communication, GPS, and observation satellite coverage can reduce the cost, widen the coverage, and speed the availability of these services to Arctic users.

Prosperity and Sustainable Development

The Antimeridianal Arctic is already a resource base for the United States and a part of the national transportation infrastructure of the Russian Arctic. Increasingly, both energy and fishery resources will lead the expansion of civilian interests in economic development, protection of the environment, conservation of resources, and support for Arctic residents and peoples. Proximity suggests that people, businesses, and organizations of both the United States and Russia will have increasing opportunities to collaborate in pursuing sustainable development, but this will require considerable effort to lay the groundwork for cooperation:

5. *Sustainable development and integrated planning.* Both the United States and the Russian Federation have included the concept of spatial planning as a tool for balanced development in the Arctic. Policy-making based on concepts of ecosystem and watershed management and spatial planning, both in the marine environment and on shore, is still in development. This should be topic of collaboration in which planners and policymakers further develop the concepts and learn lessons from one another.

6. *Improved business and investment environment.* Trans-border business opportunities should be fostered, but this will require improvements in commercial law and practice. Joint business opportunities will need special attention and oversight in order to develop a fair and predictable environment for trade and investment with processes to resolve conflict and enforce agreements. Codes of business practices, training in cultural differences, effective remedies for disputes, support for investment and other policies to promote U.S.–Russian business activities in the Arctic need support and oversight at both the national and regional level (state level in the United States, district and federal subject level in Russia). Federal ministries should establish policies that allow local governments to reduce barriers to cross-border business arrangements.

7. *Regional, local, and indigenous people's interests.* U.S. and Russian interests can benefit from collaboration below the national level. The State of Alaska, the Russian Far Eastern Federal District, and Russian provincial governments on the Arctic and Pacific coasts have much to gain from collaboration, communication, and educational exchanges. Polices on issues such as distance education, public health in remote areas, and renewable energy in the Far North and support for cross-border travel and communication among indigenous people need to be given greater support.

8. *Conservation and environmental protection.* Designation of protected areas, development of guidelines for oil and gas

development, implementation of procedures for rapid response to environmental emergencies, and guidelines and regulations for marine shipping and structures should be approached as a matter of joint interest. Non-governmental organizations should participate in the identification of areas of concern, proposal of protection measures, and local participation in policy development and implementation. U.S. and Russia coordination in these areas can foster agreement within the Arctic Council.

Regional Cooperation

The primary focus for Arctic governance of both the United States and Russia is regional, primarily thorough the Arctic Council. However, common interests can support bilateral collaboration in joint initiatives and in the application of collaborative tools for ocean governance that can then be further expanded to the entire region. Recognizing that interest in the Antimeridianal Arctic is not limited to just the United States and Russia, such collaborative activities will need to be conducted in cooperation with both the Arctic Council members and the more distant parties that have interests and rights in Arctic waters, as well as with indigenous people who have their own interests in maintaining and developing their way of life through traditional activities and through new trade and economic development opportunities made possible by a warming Arctic. These parties must be involved in all Arctic management activities that touch their substantive interests, not just in the Arctic Council, but in other organizations and agreements that address Arctic issues:

9. *Oversight of Arctic activities and policies*: The Arctic Council should serve as the principal forum for discussion of Arctic issues related to sustainable development, even when specific actions are conducted under State authority or oversight of other organizations (for example, the negotiation of Arctic ship design codes in the IMO). Border issues, including boundary delimitation, customs and immigration, vessel inspection, and regulatory enforcement should be regularly

discussed bilaterally by diplomatic and coast guard officials and reported upon periodically to the Arctic Council.

10. *Arctic domain awareness and foresight*: Support for maritime security, resource management, and marine environmental protection should be enhanced by collaborative collection, assessment, and dissemination of accurate and up-to-date information regarding human activities and ocean, ice, and climate data. Joint observation of the maritime domain, identification and tracking of ships and aircraft, particularly those of non-Arctic states, will be needed to maximize the effectiveness of the limited monitoring assets available in the Arctic. This information can be supplemented with reports from Arctic Council working groups, national reports, and other contributions to support a joint assessment and foresight capability within the Arctic Council that can integrate information and analyses from diverse sources to support issue identification and policy development by Council members.

11. *Arctic science*: Conduct of Arctic research by all interested parties and sharing of results should be promoted, especially in areas of sustainable development and climate-change mitigation. Coastal states should facilitate approval of foreign scientific research within their EEZs, promoting collaboration and ensuring sharing of data and findings. Multilateral polar science programs should be fostered and given access to non-security, non-commercial data from national sources.

12. *Increase cross-border cooperation by sub-national actors*: As interest and activities in the Antimeridianal Arctic increase, there will be greater interest in Alaska, the Far East Federal District and its sub-units, private enterprises, NGOs, and native peoples' groups. This needs to be facilitated with cross-border communication, increased ease of travel, improvement of commercial codes and dispute resolution systems, and transparency of regional and local governance.

Conclusion

Since the summer of 2009, the United States has followed a policy of a "reset" in U.S.–Russian relations. This policy has focused on high-profile great power issues epitomized by the successful conclusion of the "New START" treaty in late 2010. However, the reset has largely focused on intergovernmental activities and relations between the two national capitals. As such, the durability of the reset may be only as long-lasting as the current leadership of the two nations.

Broader and more lasting results may be achieved when the local populations and the regional governments of both countries are engaged in relations between the two countries. Alaska and the Russian Far East, adjacent on their shared maritime border and far from the federal power centers, can provide a complementary form of reset that reaches deeper into the social fabric of both countries, building familiarity, and addressing day-to-day issues of cooperation in government regulation, development, and environmental management. Such a reset can build upon regional connections and partnerships to address issues of environment and development and can work in partnership with federal agencies, particularly the U.S. Coast Guard, and Federal Security Service's Coastal Border Guard, in creating the maritime infrastructure to support regional commerce and collaborative regulatory enforcement. Increased regional collaboration and trans-border commerce can be facilitated by national ministries but needs active involvement and leadership by state and regional government as well.

Policy for the Antimeridianal Arctic is not the exclusive provence of the United States and Russia, but as the nations that bear responsibility for maritime safety, whose citizens are best placed to exploit arctic resources and to be affected by failures to manage resources well, they need to be the leaders in developing policy for the region. While they cannot manage the region in isolation from other arctic states and more distant states that have interests in the Arctic, they are the natural geopolitical leaders of the region. Together they can build on their common interests to ensure that the Antimeridianal Arctic truly becomes a region of peace and prosperity.

Notes

1 U.S. Department of State, *Fact Sheet: Bilateral Presidential Commission*, July 6, 2009; accessed at http://www.whitehouse. gov/the_press_office/FACT-SHEET-US-Russia-Bilateral-Presidential-Commission/ on December 20, 2012.

2 Deana Arsenian and Andrey Kortunov, "The U.S. and Russia: Reinventing a Relationship," *World Politics Review*, December 1, 2010; accessed at http://www. worldpoliticsreview.com/articles/7195/the-us-and-russia-reinventing-a-relationship.

3 Federal Service for Hydrometeorology and Environmental Monitoring (ROSHYDROMET), *Assessment Report on Climate Change and Its Consequences in the Russian Federation: General Summary* (Moscow: ROSHYDROMET, 2008), 13 (author's translation).

4 Timtchenko, Leonid, "The Arctic Sectoral Concept: Past and Present," *Arctic* 50, no. 1 (1997): 30.

5 As of July 2011, the United States has signed the 1994 Agreement on Implementation of part XI of the Law of the Sea Convention but not formally acceded to the Convention where Russia acceded to the Convention in 1997. The United States ratified the 1990 maritime Boundary Agreement but Russia has not, leaving the Agreement in force under executive agreement rather than by treaty.

6 Larry A. Mayer and Andrew A. Armstrong, "Cruise Report: U.S. Law of the Sea cruise to map the foot of the slope and 2500-m isobath of the U.S. Arctic Ocean margin," *CRUISE HEALY 1102 August 15 to September 28, 2011*. Center for Coastal and Ocean Mapping, University of New Hampshire. On page 8 of the cruise report, the authors note the possibility that the 2,500-meter isobath may be as far as 81 degrees north latitude. Accessed on May 22, 2012, at http://ccom.unh.edu/sites/ default/files/publications/Mayer_2011_ cruise_report_HEALY1102.pdf.

7 "Mr. *Y*" (CAPT Wayne Porter, USN and Col Mark Mykleby, USMC), *A National Strategic Narrative* (Washington, D.C.: Woodrow Wilson International Center for Scholars, 2011). The name "Mr. *Y*" was chosen in homage to George Keenan's 1947 classic article "The Sources of Soviet Conduct" that appeared in *Foreign Affairs* under the pseudonym "*X*."

8 United States of America, *National Security Strategy*, May 2010; accessed at http:// www.whitehouse.gov/sites/default/files/ rss_viewer/national_security_strategy.pdf.

9 Ibid., 44.

10 Ibid., 50.

11 United States Navy, United States Coast Guard and United States Marine Corps, *A Cooperative Strategy for 21st Century Seapower*, October 2007.

12 Ibid.

13 "Mr. *Y*" (CAPT Wayne Porter, USN and Col Mark Mykleby, USMC), *A National Strategic Narrative* (Washington, D.C.: Woodrow Wilson International Center for Scholars, 2011).

14 *United States National Security Strategy*, 2010, 49.

15 National Security Council, NSDM-66/ Homeland Security Presidential Directive, *United States Arctic Policy*, January 2009.

16 U.S. Department of the Interior Press Release, "Secretary Salazar Announces Comprehensive Strategy for Offshore Oil and Gas Development and Exploration," March 31, 2011; accessed at http://www. doi.gov/news/pressreleases/2010_03_31_ release.cfm?renderforprint=1&.

17 Interagency Ocean Policy Task Force, *Final Recommendations of the Ocean Policy Task Force*; accessed online on July

10, 2010, at http://www.whitehouse.gov/
files/documents/OPTF_FinalRecs.pdf.
The recommendations were adopted in an
executive order by President Obama on July
19, 2010, as part of the *National Policy for
the Stewardship of the Ocean, Coasts, and
Great Lakes.*

18 Ibid., 9.

19 *National Security Strategy of the Russian
Federation to 2020*, Presidential Decree No.
587, issued May 12, 2009. Translation by
the author.

20 Ibid.

21 Mikhail S. Gorbachev, speech on the
presentation of the Order of Lenin and the
Gold Star Medal to the city of Murmansk,
October 1, 1987, excerpted in Lawson W.
Brigham, ed., *The Soviet Maritime Arctic*
(Annapolis, MD: U.S. Naval Institute Press,
1991), 309.

22 Lawson W. Brigham, "Professional Notes:
Soviet Russian Polar Icebreakers: Changing
Fortunes," *U.S. Naval Institute Proceedings*,
January, 1999; accessed on May 22,
2012, at http://www.usni.org/magazines/
proceedings/1999-01/professional-notes.

23 A summary of the dissertation findings is
reported in an article by Vladimir Putin
titled "Минерально-Сырьевые Ресурсы
В Стратегии Развития Российской
Экономики" (Mineral Resources in a

Development Strategy for the Russian
Economy); accessed on May 22, 2012, at
http://rus-stat.ru/stat/1062000_2.pdf.

24 *Foundations of State Policy in the Arctic
of the Russian Federation for the Period
to 2020 and Beyond*, September 18, 2008
(author's translation, from the original,
"Основы государственной политики
Российской Федерации в Арктике на
период до 2020 года и дальнейшую
перспективу"); http://www.scrf.gov.ru/
documents/98.html.

25 Ibid.

26 Ministry of Regional Development, Russian
Federation, Draft *Development Strategy for
the Arctic Zone of the Russian Federation*;
accessed at the Ministry for Regional
Development website. The draft document
is no longer accessible at the site, but an
English translation is available from the
author.

27 Alexander Pelyasov, "The Development
Strategy of the Russian Arctic in 2020,"
presented at the conference "The Arctic:
Territory of Dialogue," Moscow, Russia,
September 23–24, 2010.

28 Alexander Dolitsky, "My Turn: U.S.–
Russian relations: The Alaska experience,"
Juneau Empire, October 13, 2008; accessed
on May 22, 2012, at http://juneauempire.
com/stories/101308/opi_343472537.shtml.

CONCLUDING OBSERVATIONS

16. Stability and Security in a Post-Arctic World: Toward a Convergence of Indigenous, State, and Global Interests at the Top of the World[1]

Barry Scott Zellen

Over the centuries, interest in the Arctic and the commercial and strategic potential of its sea lanes and natural resources has been persistent, from the fur-trading empires of Rupert's Land and Russian America to our own time – but climatic conditions prevented the region's full potential from being achieved before now, holding back its development, and limiting its contribution to the world economy, making it neither a rimland or a heartland but something that more closely resembles what geopolitical theorist Mackinder called *Lenaland*[2] – named for the isolated Lena river valley in Russia and which captured the unique geostrategic insularity of the Far North, which made it possible for the Cold War's two armed and often hostile superpowers to come face to face along their long ice curtain with very little risk of war, in great contrast to the Central Front in the once-divided Germany where a million men stood armed and ready for war for a generation. This long isolation dates back before the dawn of man and accounts for the region's unique fauna, like the polar bear and beluga whale, blending into an environment defined by ice and snow for millennia. What long defined the region's biological evolution also shaped its geopolitical stability and limited mankind's otherwise heavy footprint.

But all this now looks to be changing, or least the prospect of such a change has tipped from the implausible to the possible – as a result of the rapid warming of the Arctic climate and the measurably accelerated summer ice melts, catching even the most alarmist of ice scientists off guard three years ago with summer ice minimums hitting new lows several decades earlier than anyone had imagined possible.[3] This put the region in play strategically for the first time since the Cold War's end as the renewed promise of unlocking the Arctic's full potential and the simultaneous global natural resource rush stimulated interest in the region among numerous stakeholders, many of whom had otherwise been content to ignore the polar region throughout the 1990s.[4]

A Post-Arctic World? Time Again for 'Thinking About the Unthinkable'

During the Cold War, with the threat of nuclear apocalypse hanging over all of our heads, several bold strategic theorists sought to "think about the unthinkable," and prepare for all potential scenarios that might unfold in this new dangerous world that greeted us on the morning after Hiroshima. Herman Kahn, the former RAND analyst and founder of the Hudson Institute, was amongst this era's most colorful and controversial thinkers, becoming, according to some observers, the template for the character of Dr. Strangelove in the popular Kubrick dark comedy.[5] Kahn is famous for his *Thinking About the Unthinkable*, which was one of the first explicit attempts to resist political correctness in "defense of thinking" – even about frightening and dangerous things like thermonuclear warfare. His earlier magnum opus, *On Thermonuclear War*, made him a celebrity and was one of the sources of the more apocalyptic elements of *Dr. Strangelove*'s unique conceptual vocabulary, like 'doomsday machines' and 'mine-shaft gaps.' What, one might reasonably ask, does Herman Kahn and the literature of nuclear warfare have to do with the Arctic sovereignty? Quite a lot: from our need to think about some pretty unthinkable things like a potential (though now somewhat less imminent) collapse of the polar ice pack and the possible end of a frozen

Arctic, to a near-term increase in Arctic shipping, resource development, urbanization, industrialization, and even the ultra-long-term possibility of re-forestation – as well, with the potential destabilization of the permafrost and warming of the polar sea, the more worrisome specter of catastrophic methane dumps inducing rapid temperature increases with the potential of outpacing evolution's adaptive capability, which as Al Gore famously noted in *An Inconvenient Truth*, could mean the end of life itself.[6] These are all worrisome, potentially catastrophic, phenomena, no different than the issues faced in the nuclear age in terms of the underlying risks to mankind and our planet, if the more pessimistic scenarios involving a cascade of worsening feedback cycles such as massive methane dumps into the atmosphere, or the end of our oceans' ability to serve dutifully as carbon sinks, or even the hyper-acidification of the seas wiping out the bottom of the food change and invariably causing extinction to all of us who reside higher up the chain. With the stakes of climate change so high, in the Arctic and around the world; and with the clash between the optimists (who critics think of as denialists or flat-earthers) and pessimists (who since Climategate have been laying low) every bit as intense as that witnessed during the Cold War's doctrinal debates, a look at some metaphors and scenarios for our age makes as much sense as it did for Kahn and the other strategic thinkers of the Cold War.

During the Cold War there were two dominant and competing schools of strategic thought that emerged to manage the unique opportunities and challenges presented by nuclear weapons and their spread. One was Bernard Brodie's "absolute weapon" concept, which sought to maintain stability by balancing mutual fear of apocalypse, known as MAD or Mutual Assured Destruction, or what some described as the Balance of Terror.[7] Then there was Kahn's response, more in style than in doctrine since his ideas and Brodie's evolved largely in sync – which was to imagine nuclear warfighting at every level from localized nuclear wars to a general, total war, with all levels not only considered survivable but also winnable. Their core differentiator was less theoretical or doctrinal, and more emotional: one was guardedly optimistic about the prognosis for an enduring peace predicated upon deterrence, while the other was much more optimistic about a positive outcome of a nuclear war, and our ability to both survive and win one, in the event deterrence failed.

With the Arctic, we have a similar divergence between optimists and pessimists: some like Canadian author and dedicated Arctic journalist Ed

Struzik have postulated that what we think of as the Arctic is actually coming to an end, and that we now stand at what might very well be the threshold of what I've been calling the "Post-Arctic" world. Struzik referred to the "End of Arctic," which was more elegant and ominous, a phrase he introduced in the early 1990s and still uses to describe our historical and geopolitical moment. The Arctic Ocean and its increasingly active basin will of course still be there – more obviously so as the ice retreats. But its currently dominant characteristics are changing rapidly – in particular the massive, permanent, continent-sized barrier of multi-year ice that sits atop the pole, which could in time disappear and has certainly shown a capacity to retreat further and faster than anticipated, presenting us with something of a strategic surprise that suggests further surprises could arise. As the ice pack retreats, the polar barrier that marked the very "ends of the Earth," or what was long ago called "Ultima Thule" has the potential to become something of a trans-polar crossroad, or what mapmakers long ago imagined to be the "Midnight Sea," and already shipping companies are testing routes across the top of the world linking Northeast Asian ports with their counterparts in Europe, and Russian ports with their counterparts in Canada, in anticipation of new sea lanes becoming a feature of the maritime world.

What Rob Huebert and Brooks Yeager called a "New Sea" in their January 2008 World Wildlife Fund Report will eventually emerge if summer warming trends are sustained (and if decelerations of the ice-melts prove to be only temporary), with huge geopolitical consequences.[8] What was once the "ends of the Earth" now has the potential to become its new center, a literal "*medi*-ter-ranean." Many are worried about these consequences; Ed Struzik, in his 1992 *Equinox Magazine* article titled appropriately enough "The End of Arctic," predicted a world without a frozen Arctic;[9] and more recently, of course, is Al Gore's "Inconvenient Truth"[10] thesis (which experienced something of a melt-down on the eve of Climategate when he exaggerated Wieslav Maslowski's predictions of an ice-free Arctic (Maslowski was thinking *seasonally,* and Gore was thinking *messianically*) which echoed Struzik's earlier argument that we are witnessing the end of a unique part of the Earth's heritage.[11] Gore went further, suggesting a potential global catastrophe that threatens to end most life on our planet. But even if such an apocalyptic end does not result from climate change, Arctic peoples and their governments will have to contend with the impacts of shifting wildlife migration patterns, coastal erosion, and permafrost thaws that jeopardize much northern infrastructure. And even new opportunities such as increased trans-polar shipping will bring new risks and challenges, especially as multi-year ice breaks up and drifts south into the emergent sea lanes, requiring much investment and infrastructure development to ensure adequate safety, search and rescue, environmental cleanup, and marine service capabilities are in place.

There are also some optimists who see us standing at the start of a new era, much like Francis Fukuyama viewed the end of the Cold War as a symphonic Hegelian finale called the "End of History,"[12] and the dawn of a new era of hope. This more optimistic viewpoint believes we're entering a new "Age of the Arctic," the title of the well-known book (and earlier *Foreign Policy* article by Oran Young from the winter 1985/86 edition[13]), or as described by the phrase made famous in 1973 by the late Walter Hickel, Alaska's very own philosopher-king – who not only helped endow the state of Alaska with the necessary land base to be viable (103 million acres), but who would later run the state as governor, serving two separate terms, and who also served in President Nixon's cabinet as interior secretary – that it's the dawn of the "Day of the Arctic."[14] One can look even further back, all the way to William H. Seward's 1853 "Destiny of America" speech that predicted the expansion of America "so that it shall greet the sun when he touches the Tropic, and when he sends his glancing rays towards the Polar circle."[15] Seward helped fulfill his prediction when he negotiated the purchase of Alaska from Russia in 1867 – though at the time he was much criticized for such reckless and shortsighted folly infamously known as Seward's Folly.

Whether you stand at a precipice before a tragic "End of the Arctic," or at the gateway to a promising "Day of the Arctic," depends ultimately on whether you approach the climate issue with hope or fear, and whether you anticipate great opportunity, or severe danger. I prefer to think of the coming era as the onset of the "Arctic Spring," a theme I present in my book, *Arctic Doom, Arctic Boom: The Geopolitics of Climate Change in the Arctic* – and which imagines a forthcoming period of great change that offers tremendous hope as well as risk, a view that is shared by many northerners who look to climate change with something of a "bring it on" mentality, seeing in the thaw a potential economic awakening. "Arctic Spring" has the potential to transform the Arctic basin much like Prague Spring promised to open up and integrate Czechoslovakia with the West, but which in the end was crushed for another generation. However, the hope expressed in 1968 was finally realized twenty years later when the Velvet Revolution succeeded in toppling the communist regime. As we think about this coming transformation, we should remember that this is a new (and as such unwritten) chapter of history – with the potential for new ideas and innovation.

Former Soviet premier Gorbachev had such a vision for the Arctic at the Cold War's end, expressed in October 1987 in his Murmansk Initiative,[16] which called for the Arctic to become a "Zone of Peace," and to lead the way forward to an end of the Cold War, a vision articulated by the Inuit as well and which showed a unique alignment of tribal, territorial, state, and international interests. But events quickly sped beyond Gorbachev's control with the fall of the Berlin Wall, and the cascading swarms of people-power more speedily integrating East and West than his imaginative Arctic diplomatic efforts. But the idea was a good one, and perhaps worth revisiting. At Ilulissat in May 2008, a similar vision of an Arctic united and governed by international law was asserted; it remains to be seen if this vision ultimately triumphs, but, as Lawson Brigham has recently observed in *Foreign Policy*, the prognosis is good and even recent saber-rattling through military exercises and assertive policy statements has not created frictions "beyond the realm of diplomacy,"[17] or I might add, beyond the realm of optimism. It remains possible that the Arctic basin will become a new arena for cooperation between Russia and the West, much like Gorbachev foresaw at Murmansk before his empire collapsed internally, fostering an East-West unification along the Central Front and not the northern front as he had hoped.

But much depends on the evolution of political attitudes in all of the Arctic states, and whether the political climate warms along with the geophysical climate. It is notable that at the Ilulissat Summit in 2008, only the top foreign affairs officials of the Arctic rim states were invited – suggesting that even as they pledged to collaborate in their efforts to resolve future Arctic disputes, they have yet to fully integrate the input of the region's inhabitants, and in particular its indigenous peoples. This was noted by the Inuit leadership, who a year later issued their own Circumpolar Declaration on Arctic Sovereignty,[18] calling for their rightful, and central, place in determining its future and taking a baby-step forward toward a more robust assertion of sovereignty. In response to the emboldened Inuit response to their exclusion at Ilulissat, Secretary of State Clinton famously waded into the muskeg in March 2010, chastising her alliance partner, next-door neighbor to the north, and primary oil supplier, for excluding the Inuit and the non-rim Arctic states from the next meeting of the A5.[19]

It appears that more than the climate was heating up; with Secretary of State Clinton's diplomatic engagement on behalf of the Inuit, a tectonic shift in the diplomatic balance of power looked to be taking place, with sub-state indigenous groups like the Inuit now finding a sympathetic ear in the U.S. State Department, and values long localized at the tribal level now shared by powerful states, not unlike the alignment that nearly came into balance at Murmansk a generation ago. The next step is to continue to broaden the circle of stakeholders, so that the dynamic and creative efforts of the indigenous peoples of the region, and their many interests and perspectives, can increasingly shape the world's response to the changes taking place at the top of the world. With the new regional governing structures across the Arctic now fully integrating the Inuit, from the North Slope Borough to the increasingly autonomous island-province of Greenland, and settled land claims empowering indigenous peoples with huge tracts of lands and substantial economic resources across the North American Arctic, their participation is not only enabled, it is essential – as the internal and external dimensions of Arctic security come together at the top of our world.

The Inuit Political Odyssey: From Assimilation to Empowerment

Over the last half century, tremendous structural innovations have been made to the the political economy of Arctic North America, stretching from the Bering Sea to Baffin Bay, with the completion of a multigenerational process of negotiating comprehensive Aboriginal land claims treaties to resolve issues of land ownership, and to foster an enduring partnership between the indigenous peoples and the modern state through a variety of new institutions, including Aboriginal regional and community corporations, investment corporations, land administration agencies, a variety of tribe-state co-management boards, plus a complex patchwork of local, regional, and territorial governments created to give a voice to the Native interest. As a result of these changes, which I examine in my book, *Breaking the Ice* and its sequel, *On Thin Ice*, the Inuit and other Aboriginal northerners have become powerful stakeholders in the economic and political systems that govern the Arctic today, and also, importantly, the largest private land owners with direct control over some 10 per cent of North America's Arctic territories, and indirect influence over a far larger portion of the Arctic land mass.[20]The historical process, seen from Alaska to Nunatsiavut, has been by and large a two-step process. The first step was to address the land question, and to negotiate and, in most cases, implement land claims accords to bring clarity of title, helping to identify who owns which lands and to reconcile the competing interests of tribe and state and thereby open up (or, for sensitive ecosystems and traditional hunting lands, close off) the region to economic development with various mechanisms of co-management helping to keep native and state interests in balance. Once land claims were settled, the next step in the process of northern development has been the pursuit of new systems of Aboriginal self-governance, taking various forms and employing various structures over time (with greater powers becoming available as time went by, and earlier policies of assimilation being replaced by more contemporary policies promoting cultural and political renewal) – from the establishment of municipal or borough governments under existing constitutional law, as we saw in Alaska in the 1970s, to the creation newly empowered tribal councils governed by federal Indian law in Alaska and the NWT in the 1980s and 90s) or the negotiation of entirely new systems of governance – with the most ambitious being Nunavut, with their comprehensive land claim settlement in 1993 linked to the subsequent formation of a new territorial government in 1999, creating a complex and potentially powerful system of self-governance applying a public model to a predominantly indigenous region for de facto indigenous self-governance.

After Nunavut, the evolution toward more distinctly indigenous self-governing structures has continued, as reflected in the Labrador Inuit Land Claim of 2005 with the very first truly Inuit self-governing structure, whose governing principles were articulated in detail in the 2002 Labrador Inuit Constitution. More recently, in November 2008, the far-flung Danish province of Greenland held a referendum on evolving beyond their "home rule" system of autonomy toward formal state sovereignty and independence, which passed decisively – paving the way forward for the eventual emergence of a formally sovereign Arctic state with a majority Inuit population, with literally revolutionary (or devolutionary) implications for the rest of the Inuit homeland. In the years ahead, we may see even further advances in the process of Native empowerment toward increased autonomy and perhaps leading toward the Balkanization of the Arctic into independent (or at least more genuinely autonomous) political units.

Regardless of the jurisdiction, whether in Alaska or Arctic Canada, or beyond the shores of North America, indigenous peoples have shown tremendous ingenuity in their effort to build new systems for self-governance since the land claims movement took root in the 1960s, creatively adapting existing institutions or creating new ones when possible, lobbying for and negotiating to further advance their powers. Ideas and institutions for reconciling the interests of indigenous northerners and the modern state have evolved, following, broadly but with some exception (such as James Bay and Northern Quebec, due to the intensification of Quebec's hydro-electric power development activities in its northern reaches), a west-to-east arc across the North, becoming stronger with each new iteration and reversing many of the negative consequences of the colonial experience, and transforming the domestic balance of power to lean heavily in favor of tribal interests, particularly on social, environmental, and economic matters. This increasing shift in power has increased the capacity for the indigenous peoples of the North to confront the many social and economic challenges that remain in their communities, providing the tools necessary to face these broad social and economic challenges, to innovate new opportunities, and to grapple with the complex challenges (as well as potential opportunities) associated with climate change and a potential Arctic thaw.

Social conditions in Alaska and the Canadian Arctic have been described by many as a Fourth World, with Third World conditions exacerbated by climate, isolation, and limited infrastructure including a near absence of roads and rail networks – making seasonal ice roads and summer sea lifts an economic lifeline.[21] Communities are generally small, ranging from just a few dozen people to several hundred, with the larger administrative centers being home to just a few thousand people; their populations are predominantly indigenous, with subsistence hunting, fishing, and trapping still essential to their nutritional and cultural survival. Fuel costs are high, as are imported foods, making hunting and fishing all the more important. Economic opportunities have been limited, with natural resource development presenting one of the more enduring opportunities, from last century's Klondike gold rush to the oil boom of the 1970s, to the diamond rush of the 1990s, to the more recent rush for all manner of Arctic natural resources. Land claims have helped to ensure that when economic development does take place, local concerns and tribal interests are not overlooked, with indigenous leaders becoming governing partners in assessing environmental risk, mitigating impacts to traditional subsistence, and ensuring economic participation through jobs, training, and resource royalties. This can create deep rifts within the Native community, as tradition and modernity collide. But the new governing structures were designed in part to intermediate this collision, converting thesis and antithesis into a truly northern synthesis. The settlement of land claims and emergence of new structures of self-government have increased the role of indigenous peoples in the decisions made about the Arctic and its future. One dramatic illustration: in the 1970s, when the Mackenzie Valley Pipeline Inquiry was held by Justice Berger, the struggle was primarily between corporate interests and tribal interests, with the latter excluded from the decision-making of the former. During the more recent Mackenzie Gas Project, the Aboriginal Pipeline Group sat with the oil companies as an Aboriginally-owned equity partner; and the Joint Review Panel examining the environmental and social impacts of the proposed pipeline was empowered by the settled regional land claims, providing an indigenous perspective on both sides of the table – contributing to a slow pace but a unique review process with indigenous inputs at all levels.[22]

Alaska Native Claims: Starting the Process

When the Alaska Native Claims Settlement Act (ANCSA) was enacted in 1971, it aimed to quickly bring Alaska Natives into the modern economy and at the same time to clarify the limits of Aboriginal title, making it possible to fully develop the state's natural resources and in particular to build the trans-Alaska pipeline. Because its objectives were largely economic, its corporate model became its defining and most transformative characteristic – not without controversy, since the corporate model was viewed with some skepticism by indigenous leaders as a tool of assimilation, and there remains a continuing debate over the appropriateness of the corporate model to the indigenous North. ANCSA formally extinguished Aboriginal rights, title, and claims to traditional lands in the state, while formally transferring fee-simple title to 44 million acres – or some 12 per cent of the state's land base – to Alaska Natives, with $962.5 million in compensation for the lands ceded to the state, $500 million of which was to be derived from future oil royalties (as a result of which over half the "compensation" was to be derived from resources extracted from the Inupiat homeland – an irony not missed by Alaska

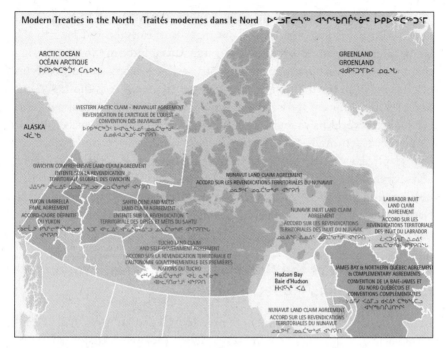

FIG. 1. Comprehensive land claims are now settled across the entire Arctic coast of Canada, from the 1984 Inuvialuit Final Agreement in the west to the 2005 Labrador Inuit (Nunatsiavut) Land Claim Agreement in the east.

Natives). ANCSA also created twelve regional Native corporations (and later a thirteenth for non-resident Alaska Natives), and over two hundred village corporations to manage these lands and financial resources.

These new corporate structures introduced a brand new language and culture, as well as a new system of managing lands and resources that seemed at variance with the traditional cultures of the region and their traditional subsistence economy. The early years of ANCSA were famously described by justice Thomas Berger as dragging Alaska Natives "kicking and screaming"[23] into the twentieth century, and many native corporations approached the brink of bankruptcy, forced to monetize their net operating losses in a last desperate bid to stay in business. A new cottage industry of northern investment, legal, and policy advisors emerged – sometimes to the benefit of their clients, but often not.

In addition to the *corporatization* of village Alaska, ANCSA's original design also had some structural flaws that also nearly proved fatal to the land claims experience, including a twenty-year moratorium in transferring shares in Native corporations to non-Natives, which many feared would inevitably result in the dilution of Native ownership, known as the *1991 Time Bomb*. While critics of the land claims process are correct to point out these original structural flaws and the assimilating pressures introduced by new corporate structures, the land claims model has nonetheless proved resilient and adaptive, as Native corporations matured and their boards, managers, and shareholders found ways to better balance traditional and modern values, learning from their crash course in capitalism as they went – so today the Native corporations represent a huge economic force in the state of Alaska.

The Inuvialuit of the Northwest Territories: Evolving the Land Claims Model

Across the border, the Inuvialuit of the Western Canadian Arctic had a front-row seat to ANCSA and were impressed by all the money that was flowing north, as well as the new corporate structures created and the sizeable land quantum formally transferred to Alaska Natives. But they also noted the continuing threat to indigenous culture and the lack of adequate protections of subsistence rights, traditional culture, and environmental protection and were determined to do better. So when they negotiated the 1984 Inuvialuit Final Agreement (IFA) in the late 1970s, the land claims model became significantly enhanced – in addition to creating new Native corporations, the IFA also made an equal institutional commitment to the preservation of Native culture and traditions, to preserve the land and the wildlife, and to empower, not just new corporate interests, but also traditional cultural interests as well, by creating new institutions of co-management and more powerful hunter and trapper committees. They also made sure all Inuvialuit became shareholders and that no non-Inuvialuit ever could, learning from the Alaskan experience. The Inuvialuit thus successfully modified the land claims concept so that its structure included a natural institutional balancing – not unlike our own balance of powers concept – that has enabled a greater commitment to cultural and environmental protections.

Their land claim entitled the 3,000 Inuvialuit living in six communities to 35,000 square miles of land; co-management of land and water use, wildlife, and environmental assessment; wildlife harvesting rights; financial compensation of $45 million in 1978 dollars, inflation-adjusted to $162 million, for lands ceded to Canada; and a share of government royalties for oil, gas, and mineral development on federal land; the formation of new national parks in their settlement area that further protect their land base from development, while allowing subsistence activities unhindered; and a commitment to meaningful economic participation in any development in their settlement area. This model has remained largely intact in later comprehensive land claims, showing a twenty-five-year endurance as a model for northern development. But one issue that was not yet on the table in the late 1970s and early 1980s when the Inuvialuit chose to pursue their own regional land claim (and thereby gain some control over the intense oil boom in their homeland) was the establishment of new institutions of Aboriginal self-government, something that the Inuit of the central and eastern Arctic (the future Nunavut territory) decided to wait for. The Inuvialuit felt they did not have the luxury of time given the frenetic pace of oil and gas exploration in their lands. But Nunavut remained more isolated, providing more time to rethink, and renegotiate, the land claims model.

Nunavut: Augmenting Land Claims with Regional Political Power

In the years separating the signing of the Inuvialuit land claim in 1984 and the signing of the Nunavut land claim in 1993, much progress was made on the political question, and an increasing respect for Aboriginal rights in Ottawa enabled the establishment of a new concept: reshaping political boundaries to correspond to a land-claims settlement area and establishing a new government to administer this region, augmenting the land claims with real political power. In 1993, with their signing of their historic accord, the Inuit of Nunavut were awarded $1.1 billion and title to 135,000 square miles of land, including 13,600 with subsurface rights, on top of various co-management boards, clearly defined rights protecting subsistence, and royalty sharing from resource development activities. Nunavut has a population of around 30,000 in twenty-eight communities spread out across over 770,000

square miles, or one fifth of Canada's land mass, including the High Arctic islands and the central-Arctic coastal mainland. While its population is tiny, its
jurisdiction is vast and its resource base potentially tremendous, and the sea
lanes that cross through the territory include the famed Northwest Passage.

The most striking innovation of the Nunavut claim was the way it was
formally linked to the division of the Northwest Territories and the formation
of a brand new territory, resulting in the 1999 birth of Nunavut. Nunavut has
now been up and running for well over a decade, gaining valuable but often
painful experience in self-governance – and thus showing many strains as it
struggles to confront some daunting social and economic challenges in one
of the most challenging geophysical environments imaginable. There have
also been intergovernmental frictions with Ottawa over implementation and
a growing perception of a crisis in Canada's youngest territory. But there is
still much reason for hope for the future; the roots of the problems facing
Nunavut go deep and are not likely to be quickly overcome, but the solutions
developed can now be Northern solutions, rooted in a deep understanding
of Northern social realities. Since its population is predominantly Inuit, a
public government can, at least for now, govern in an indigenous style – as
the principles of the Nunavut land claim and the governing power of the new
territorial government mutually reinforce one another. There is a long-term
risk the territory could become more like the Yukon, especially if a major
mineral strike results in a new mining center. But, for now, a public model
in an indigenous context is a creative way to bring about self-government by
other means.

After Nunavut: The Labrador Land Claim and the Dawn of Inuit Governance

Half a decade after Nunavut made headlines around the world, the final
Inuit land claim along the North American Arctic and Subarctic coast – the
Labrador Inuit (Nunatsiavut) Land Claims Agreement – was settled. It was
ratified in December 2004 and came into effect a year later, presenting a
new stage in the evolution of Inuit governance, making the two-step process
more of a one-step process, further redefining the limits of self-government
within a land settlement area – transcending the public model applied by the
Inuit of Nunavut and the Inupiat of the North Slope. The agreement created

the 28,000-square-mile Labrador Inuit Settlement Area with an adjoining 18,800-square-mile ocean zone extending as far as Canada's territorial waters. The settlement area includes 6,100 square miles of Labrador Inuit Lands, five predominantly Inuit communities, and 3,700 square miles set aside for the Torngat Mountains National Park Reserve (following a tradition established by prior Inuit land claims to create vast national parks in which subsistence was protected) – with the Inuit retaining special rights in each of these areas. The Government of Canada will pay the Labrador Inuit $140 million in 1997 dollars in compensation for lands ceded to the Crown.

Just as the formation of the Nunavut territory was the really cool innovation of the Nunavut land claim, the emergence of truly Inuit self-government is the hallmark of the Labrador claim. As described in section 17.2 of the claim, it "exhaustively sets out the law-making authorities and self-government rights of Inuit," with the newly created Nunatsiavut Government to be governed by the "fundamental law of Inuit" as enunciated by the 159-page 2002 Labrador Inuit Constitution. The constitution, among its many components, included an Inuit charter of human rights, recognized Inuit customary law and its application to "any matter within the jurisdiction and authority of the Nunatsiavut Government," and embraced laws to protect Inuit culture, language, and traditional knowledge. The Labrador Inuit Constitution created a blueprint of Inuit values and a pathway to the rapid formation of a truly Inuit system of government in a region that's adjacent to coastal waters of emergent strategic significance, with active commercial and subsistence fisheries, major strategic mineral deposits such as the Voisey's Bay project, and the prospect of much future economic potential. It also showed a new path toward Aboriginal self-government, one that did not require a secession like Nunavut but instead forged a regional sub-government within an existing province, but with unique governing principles.

A Path toward Sovereign Independence: Beyond the Land Claims Model

The Arctic land claims model, with its subsequent modifications, has become an inspiration to many, proof positive of what can be gained through a determined, forward-looking effort to rebalance and modernize the relationship between the indigenous people of the North and the modern state. As with any land reform effort, changes in land tenure can have a profound impact on the domestic balance of power, shifting, not just title to land, but the wealth created from that land, resulting in concentrations of economic power in the hands of a small indigenous population numbering in the thousands or tens of thousands. In Alaska and the Canadian Arctic, the Inuit have become owners of vast tracts of land, making them a landed elite with control over numerous economic and, increasingly, political levers. While not formally sovereign, they are poised to become influential stakeholders, partners in the consolidation of state sovereignty and in the economic development of the northern frontier. A comparable situation exists in the post-Ottoman Middle East, with extended tribal families and clans sitting at a powerful and lucrative nexus of land ownership, natural resource wealth, and political power. While northern Natives in Arctic North America are not in command of the ultimate levers of sovereign state power, such as military forces or national treasuries, they do have in their possession or within reach many tools of regional power, making them dominant regional elites. As the climate warms and the Arctic basin yields more natural resource wealth, the economic resources in their possession will also increase, and with that political influence.

In 2008, Greenland held a non-binding referendum on increasing the island's autonomy and eventually restoring its sovereign independence; it was approved decisively, showing how the desire to be self-governing is universal across the Arctic.[24] Denmark has shown a unique openness to the possibility of Greenland becoming formally independent (in contrast to the other Arctic states which attach great economic, strategic, and emotional/ideological significance to their Arctic territories), and if independence happens, it would mark perhaps the final stage in the process that began with ANCSA nearly half a century ago, with the full restoration of sovereignty to an Arctic nation. Other microstates are sovereign (even if unable to defend that sovereignty) – from the South Pacific to the city-states of Europe. So why not in the Arctic? What a sovereign Arctic state will look like, how it affirms traditional Native values and balances modernization with tradition, will be fascinating to observe. The risks are real; Iceland's economic collapse, Nunavut's persistent social challenges, the near-collapse of Alaska's Native corporations, are cautionary tales to consider.

Fostering a Tribe-State Partnership:
A Sea Change in America's Arctic Policy

In the closing hours of President George W. Bush's presidency, the White House issued the first new American Arctic policy since 1994 – a fascinating document full of multilateralism, pledging the United States to work with international, regional, local, and even tribal organizations that continued to provide a blueprint for the Obama Administration, and appears to have been written with the new era in mind. The collaborative spirit of the policy update was so unexpected that the initial response was largely one of denial, with media attention fixating on the few unilateral components relating to national and homeland security, but not on the dozens of other more collaborative dimensions. Those unsung affirmations of a multilateral Arctic future reflected a rather sophisticated awareness of the transformation of the Arctic and showed an appreciation of the increasing role of its indigenous peoples – marking a collaborative and multilateral conclusion to his highly controversial presidency.

A tectonic shift – toward greater collaboration with, and participation of, the numerous tribal, national, and international actors on the circumpolar stage – was evident in the first comprehensive re-articulation of U.S. national policy on the Arctic region since 1994.[25] Indeed, it is noteworthy that among the six policy objectives identified in Section III, Part A of National Security Presidential Directive 66/Homeland Security Presidential Directive 25 (NSPD-66/HSPD-25) – issued on January 9, 2009, in the final days of the Bush administration – were to "Strengthen institutions for cooperation among the eight Arctic nations" (objective 4) and to "Involve the Arctic's indigenous communities in decisions that affect them" (objective 5). This is historically significant and demonstrates both an increased awareness of, and respect for, the growing political and economic participation of the Arctic peoples in governing their own affairs, as well as a continued commitment to a collaborative, multilateral approach to solving the region's challenges. Also of significance: while the very first policy objective listed in Section III, Part A, is to "Meet national security and homeland security needs relevant to the Arctic region," a point that dominated initial news coverage and commentaries on the new Arctic policy, the second objective listed is to "Protect the Arctic environment and conserve its biological resources," while the third is to "Ensure that natural resource management and economic development in the region are environmentally sustainable," which will directly benefit the foundational pillars upon which the indigenous Arctic cultures depend for their cultural, nutritional, and economic survival. The sixth policy objective listed, to "Enhance scientific monitoring and research into local, regional, and global environmental issues," further reinforces America's renewed commitment to multilateralism at the top of the world, and to increasing its environmental knowledge at all levels, from the local to the global, during this time of Arctic transformation.

These important dimensions to the new U.S. Arctic policy were largely overlooked by many observers, in particular by the op-ed pages of several newspapers north of the border that emphasized the national security and unilateral dimensions of America's new Arctic policy. But somehow, the unprecedented level of collaboration that the White House embraced – with its top-level commitment to indigenous as well as global participation, and its refreshingly holistic approach to the region's environmental and ecological health as well as to continued scientific research in the interest of protecting this fragile domain – got overlooked in the first round of commentary, analysis, and opinion that greeted the release of the directive. Clarifying its policy, on 13 January 2009, the U.S. State Department provided a statement in response to a question at its daily press briefing in which it explained: "The new directive is the culmination of an extensive interagency review process undertaken in response to rapid changes taking place in the Arctic, the principal drivers of which are climate change, increasing human presence in the region, and the growing demand for Arctic energy deposits and other natural resources" and noted the "directive focuses on seven broad areas of Arctic policy."[26] The State Department also reiterated its commitment to Arctic cooperation, noting that "states safeguard their national security interests in numerous ways, some on their own, and some in cooperation with others. The United States wants to cooperate with other governments in the Arctic. The best way to address both the challenges and opportunities of the Arctic is through cooperation. Any U.S. action would respect international law."[27] This certainly does not suggest a go-it-alone attitude by the United States. Quite the contrary, it reflects an awakening to the increased participatory role of indigenous peoples, circumpolar neighbors, and international organizations in the management of the Arctic and the continued need for a multilateral approach to managing the Arctic's unique challenges in the years ahead. While the new policy does not reflect a change of perspective on the legal status of the Northwest Passage, or a softening in America's commitment to freedom of the seas, it does suggest a sea change is underway in its perception of, and sensitivity to, the numerous challenges mounting at the top of the world as the ice continues its retreat and the prospect of a post-Arctic world enters the realm of the possible. Most importantly, it shows a far greater sensitivity to the interests and perspectives of the indigenous peoples as well as America's Arctic neighbors, and a willingness to work together in a joint effort to resolve these challenges in the years ahead – so much so that America's Arctic policy remained unchanged under the Obama administration, with Secretary of State Clinton, as noted above, providing her vocal support to the Arctic's non-state peoples.

The Circumpolar Inuit Declaration: Reasserting Indigenous Sovereignty in the Arctic

On April 28, 2009, a delegation of Inuit leaders from Greenland, Canada, Alaska, and Russia presented a Circumpolar Inuit Declaration on Arctic Sovereignty[28] in Tromsø, Norway, where the Arctic Council was meeting. It represented the Inuit response to their exclusion at Ilulissat, and while it does not directly consider the many details presented in the new U.S. Arctic policy, it nonetheless illustrates that both the Inuit and the modern state are converging in their conceptualization of Arctic sovereignty, with both viewing it to be an increasingly collaborative and mutually reinforcing concept. The declaration emerges from the work of the first Inuit Leaders' Summit on November 6–7, 2008, in Kuujjuaq, Nunavik, in Northern Quebec, where they "gathered to address Arctic sovereignty" and "expressed unity in our concerns over Arctic sovereignty deliberations, examined the options for addressing these concerns, and strongly committed to developing a formal declaration on Arctic sovereignty."[29] There, the Inuit leaders "noted that the 2008 Ilulissat Declaration on Arctic sovereignty by ministers representing the five coastal Arctic states did not go far enough in affirming the rights Inuit have gained through international law, land claims and self-government processes."[30] In many ways, their declaration was their direct response to the foreign ministers of the Arctic states for their exclusion at Ilulissat, and it constructively redresses this exclusion and persuasively argues for their central role in determining the fate of the Arctic. As the ICC observed in a press release issued at this start of their effort in November 2008: "Sovereignty is a complex issue. It has a variety of overlapping elements, anchored in international law. But fundamentally it begins with the history and reality of Inuit use and occupation of Arctic lands and waters; that use and occupation is at the heart of any informed discussion of sovereignty in the Arctic. Arctic nation states must respect the rights and roles of Inuit in all international discussions and commitments dealing with the Arctic."[31]

The April 2009 declaration unveiled at Tromsø updates the Inuit policy on sovereignty in the Arctic and asserts that "central to our rights as a people is the right to self-determination," which "is our right to freely determine our political status, freely pursue our economic, social, cultural and linguistic development, and freely dispose of our natural wealth and resources. States are obligated to respect and promote the realization of our right to self-determination."[32] Section 2 of the declaration concerns the "Evolving Nature of Sovereignty in the Arctic," and notes sovereignty "has often been used to refer to the absolute and independent authority of a community or nation both internally and externally" but that it remains a "contested concept, however, and does not have a fixed meaning."[33] Further, the declaration notes, "Old ideas of sovereignty are breaking down as different governance models, such as the European Union, evolve," where "sovereignties overlap and are frequently divided within federations in creative ways to recognize the right of peoples."[34] Therefore, for the Inuit, "issues of sovereignty and sovereign rights must be examined and assessed in the context of our long history of struggle to gain recognition and respect as an Arctic indigenous people having the right to exercise self-determination over our lives, territories, cultures and languages."[35] The Inuit further note that "recognition and respect for our right to self-determination is developing at varying paces and in various forms in the Arctic states in which we live," and that:

> Following a referendum in November 2008, the areas of self-government in Greenland will expand greatly and, among other things, Greenlandic (Kalaallisut) will become Greenland's sole official language. In Canada, four land claims agreements are some of the key building blocks of Inuit rights; while there are conflicts over the implementation of these agreements, they remain of vital relevance to matters of self-determination and of sovereignty and sovereign rights. In Alaska, much work is needed to clarify

and implement the rights recognized in the Alaska Native Claims Settlement Act (ANCSA) and the Alaska National Interest Lands Conservation Act (ANILCA). In particular, subsistence hunting and self-government rights need to be fully respected and accommodated, and issues impeding their enjoyment and implementation need to be addressed and resolved. And in Chukotka, Russia, a very limited number of administrative processes have begun to secure recognition of Inuit rights. These developments will provide a foundation on which to construct future, creative governance arrangements tailored to diverse circumstances in states, regions and communities.[36]

The Circumpolar Inuit declaration observes that in "exercising our right to self-determination in the circumpolar Arctic, we continue to develop innovative and creative jurisdictional arrangements that will appropriately balance our rights and responsibilities as an indigenous people, the rights and responsibilities we share with other peoples who live among us, and the rights and responsibilities of states," and that in "seeking to exercise our rights in the Arctic, we continue to promote compromise and harmony with and among our neighbours."[37]

However, even though the Ilulissat Declaration pledged the Arctic rim states to "use international mechanisms and international law to resolve sovereignty disputes," thus far "in their discussions of Arctic sovereignty," the Arctic rim states "have not referenced existing international instruments that promote and protect the rights of indigenous peoples. They have also neglected to include Inuit in Arctic sovereignty discussions in a manner comparable to Arctic Council deliberations."[38] The Inuit declaration thus reminds us that the "inclusion of Inuit as active partners in all future deliberations on Arctic sovereignty will benefit both the Inuit community and the international community,"[39] and that "extensive involvement of Inuit in global, trans-national and indigenous politics requires the building of new partnerships with states for the protection and promotion of indigenous economies, cultures and traditions."[40] These partnerships, the declaration contends, "must acknowledge that industrial development of the natural resource wealth of the Arctic can proceed only insofar as it enhances the economic and social well-being of Inuit and safeguards our environmental security."

Anything less will be rejected by the Inuit, and, with their many settled land claims accords, regional and territorial governments, and numerous mechanisms of co-management and environmental regulation, proceeding without the full support of the Inuit might be surprisingly futile. That's why the Inuit have drawn a line in the tundra, and so vocally insisted that their exclusion from the table at Ilulissat must be redressed so that the future development of the Arctic is a truly joint effort, not just between the Arctic states, but between the states and the Inuit as well.

The Warming Earth and the New Sea: Onset of the Arctic Spring

But there is still reason for hope, as evident by the tremendous progress made since 1971. But the challenges are still substantial – and just as we approach the end of this long journey of Native empowerment, with the institutional transformation of the Arctic nearing completion, a new challenge emerges: that of rapid climate change. The visible evidence is overwhelming, as illustrated by the record ice melts (coming decades ahead of scientists' predictions), the greening of the tundra as southern flora migrate north, and the melting of permafrost (affecting northern infrastructure and releasing methane trapped below, which could accelerate the warming trend.) The geophysical landscape of the Arctic is in a rapid transition. While this presents new economic opportunities for the least-developed part of North America and promises to alleviate endemic poverty with new jobs and new sources of revenue for the emergent Inuit governments, there is still much uncertainty and risk – particularly to subsistence hunting that depends on predictable wildlife migration patterns and on stable winter ice and summer ground conditions. At risk are the indigenous cultures that have evolved along with the unique Arctic ecosystem and all its interconnected components. But all of the efforts to modernize the Arctic's political economy over these past forty years have empowered the indigenous people of the region to directly address, mitigate, and potentially resolve these new challenges, and to leverage the emerging economic opportunities – with a wide assortment of new tools and increasing levels of power. While that can't stop or even slow the warming, it can at least enable the peoples of the Arctic to contribute toward the creation of new solutions, as they rise to the new challenges of this era.

While many climate-change pessimists have concluded that the Earth system is heading into a profound climate crisis, and that action is required at a planetary level to prevent the coming tragedy caused by rapid climate change, a more optimistic few anticipate there will be far less severe consequences and perhaps even some positive ones. Though evidence of climate change has tipped from speculative to possible to probable, a debate on winners and losers of Arctic climate change is still worth having. Indeed, rather than focus on whether the Earth is warming or not; or whether the warming is anthropogenic or not, the fundamental question of whether climate change is *ipso facto* a crisis or merely one more challenge to adapt to is a question worthy of debate. Such a debate long seemed futile, given the degree to which the climate crisis camp had come to dominate the scientific and policy agendas, but just because there is a convergence of political correctness and political power does not mean such a debate should not be held. Political action has always been a Newtonian phenomenon, with the individual unit being us, people, whether individual actors or various aggregations into groups such as clans, tribes, sects, nations, states, corporations, and multilateral alliances and coalitions. But scientific knowledge, with all its complexity, from the macro to the micro, from the cosmic to the quantum, has been forced to recognize less black-and-white truths, such as those unveiled by the imaginative leaps of Einstein and Heisenberg, among others, who found that, at the quantum level, the world is riddled with ambiguity. And when scaled up to global systems, these ambiguities do not disappear but instead cast a long shadow of paradox, uncertainty, and nonlinearity.

Climate change is thus more complex (and inherently uncertain) than the elegant simplicity that is generally required for effective political mobilization for action – particularly at the planetary scale, which requires compelling moral argumentation to alter the trajectories of nations and thus change the very destiny of humankind. The underlying reality of climate change is thus as fertile a ground for complexity and uncertainty as the riddles of chaos theory, and the dualistic ambiguities of quantum theory. And yet the climate activists keep warning us in no uncertain terms that the sky is falling, as Vice President Al Gore told us when he accepted his Nobel Peace Prize in 2007 – though his words were more modest and less reified when he accepted his Oscar in Hollywood earlier in the year. But what if reality was less simple, and the future far from the predicted clarity presented in *An Inconvenient Truth*? It seems as if the climate-crisis movement has taken a page from the anti-nuclear movement of an earlier generation, which argued passionately that there cannot be any winners in nuclear war, and, as a consequence, we must bottle up the atomic genie that we had unleashed to defend our very freedom and step away from the nuclear chasm before we fall into its abyss and self-destruct – the theme echoed in the 1983 film *War Games* when the WOPR computer simulating atomic war, nicknamed Joshua, came to realize that in nuclear war there could be no winners. Like Joshua, the anti-nuclear activists had their cherished faith that we would all be losers in nuclear war, that the only solution was to step back from the brink and seek nuclear abolition.

But theirs was not the only point of view: closer to the strategic nerve-centers of the nuclear states emerged a diverse ecosystem of nuclear thinkers, strategists, and planners whose jobs involved figuring out how to do what the anti-nuclearists said was impossible: fighting and winning a nuclear war. Men like Herman Kahn dared to "think about the unthinkable," coming up with various proposals and ideas to mitigate the risks and dangers of nuclear war, from civil defense preparations to detailed war plans in case deterrence failed. The Cold War ended quickly, and with a whimper, before there was a strategic nuclear show-down, a climactic big bang to end the era – so we'll never know who was right or wrong. When it comes to climate change, its risks and dangers, and its opportunities as well, it is time again to "think about the unthinkable." We must confront once more the self-same duality, the persistent ambiguity, that reluctant riddle that remains unanswered: can there be both winners and losers of climate change? And in the case of the Arctic, still locked in an Ice Age that never truly ended, might the impacts of climate change in fact be positive? Indeed, what if trying to slow, stop, or reverse global warming prevented the Arctic's full integration into the world economy, its transformation from a frozen, under-populated desert region into a veritable oasis of life, ending the region's long isolation with its transformation from the very "ends of the Earth" to tomorrow's most central strategic crossroads? Indeed, what if life itself, an oasis of green, proliferated across the Arctic as it became increasingly habitable, its own indigenous peoples lifted out of the poverty borne of their isolation as they became reunited with mankind?

Already, mule and white-tailed deer have migrated north, joining the moose and caribou populations, and barrenground grizzlies have begun to show a liking for the Far North's warmer climes. While this will naturally create more competition between newly arrived species and those who have been there since time immemorial, this need not be considered an unnatural or even an unfortunate turn of events. The abundance of deer has not been viewed with alarm by local hunters, who find its meat quite palatable. And while polar bears and grizzlies could become fierce competitors in the battle to survive above the treeline, some forward-thinking members of both sub-species have shown a more collaborative instinct, a go-it-together approach that is yielding a brand new sub-species of hybrid "grolar" or "pizzly" bear. After all, scientists now think the polar bear evolved quite recently, perhaps as recently as 100,000 years ago – a mere blink in geological time, and its evolutionary journey may therefore just be getting under way. And though the great white bear may one day cease to exist in its current pure form, the polar bear's legacy will surely continue through the genetic mixing of evolution, as more and more hybrid bears emerge better able to survive in the post-Arctic world.

One important story often overlooked by climate change pessimists is that other half of the evolution story; not the extinction of species that did not make the cut, but the creation of those that did – as new genetic traits become strengths and not weaknesses. Life itself is a process of renewal and decay, extinction and species birth. Extinction may seem to be a terrible tragedy, nature's own version of the human crime of genocide, but the rise of new species better suited to an altered landscape is something altogether different. Mourn we may of those unique species that leave our earthly stage; but not of the process itself, the very competition to survive, for this is the story we must continue to tell, indeed to act out, as players on the earthly stage. As the predominant creature, ruling over most of the Earth's surface, we naturally want evolution to stand still, our time here to last forever. But this is not necessarily nature's way. Nor is it nature's way to pick sides, nor to keep one species alive at the expense of another's arrival. We all have our time, its beginning and its end. These are issues that we need to keep in mind and explore without passing judgment. So while Al Gore has rightfully earned his Nobel Prize for Peace for his heart-felt and hard-fought effort to stop man's silent war against the Earth, this does not mean his perspective is the *only* one to consider. From the Arctic perspective, Gore's logic would mean a perpetuation of an Ice Age that the rest of the world was content to see end. But with climate change also comes the promise that the frozen polar sea, so long a barrier to progress, may now become a channel of commerce, a sea lane of hope, uniting the world at its top, something many pragmatic Inuit leaders at the local and regional level embrace, knowing it means jobs for their people and growth for their communities. So while national and circumpolar Inuit leaders lobby heads of state and UN officials to stop global warming, and equate the melting ice with an assault on Inuit traditions, their perspective is not the only one: in the isolated Inuit villages where poverty remains persistent, a more pragmatic perspective has taken root, one that looks forward to the increased maritime trade, tourism, and natural resource development expected in a warmer Arctic.

In Greenland, the thawing of the Arctic is widely viewed to be an opportunity for that island-colony to become independent, with the promise of economic self-sufficiency. It is the promise of a post-Arctic world that inspires the people of Greenland, offering them not only a way out of endemic poverty but a path toward true independence; they took their first step along this road two years ago, voting overwhelmingly in favor of increased autonomy in a non-binding but closely watched referendum on November 25, 2008, with a decisive 75 per cent yes vote. By voting yes so decisively, the people of Greenland were casting their vote for hope in a warmer future. As reported in *Nunatsiaq News* on December 14, 2009, "Greenland wants to develop and gain financial independence from Denmark, which would require a doubling of its output of climate-warming greenhouse gas emissions, Greenland's premier Kuupik Kleist said during a news conference in Copenhagen."[41] Kleist explained that "Greenland has the right to pursue industrial development and offer its citizens more access to jobs, education, health care and independence – even if that means substantially increasing its production of climate-warming greenhouse gas emissions."[42] Greenlanders thus view the glacial retreats and earlier spring ice melts as an opportunity for growth and development, a view shared across much of the North.

And so it may be for all of the peoples of the Arctic. A post-Arctic world promises to put the North smack dab in the center of the world of commerce and geopolitics, as elegantly argued by Caitlyn L. Antrim in the summer edition of the *Naval War College Review*. The Far North will no longer be the "last frontier" or the "ends of the Earth." Some observers, especially Arctic visionaries like the late Walter Hickel, who served twice as governor of Alaska and also as U.S. Secretary of the Interior, believe the coming years promise to bring many positive changes to the Far North. For the polar regions, the warming of the Earth may bring a true Arctic Spring, for its people, indeed for all people – fostering our unity, increasing our security, decreasing the likelihood of conflict and war over natural resources in persistent trouble-spots like the Persian Gulf, and reducing the risks faced at strategic chokepoints along current international shipping lanes such as the canals of Panama and Suez and the pirate-infested waterways off Somalia and along the Strait of Malacca. As Gorbachev hoped a generation ago, a thawing of long-frozen circumpolar relations could go far to reduce Cold War tensions; in our current era, a geophysical warming could go even further to reduce international tensions as new economic opportunities encourage old adversaries to rethink the nature of their relationships, evident in the recent resolution of long-simmering border tensions between Russia and Norway, and in the renewed collaboration between the Canadian and U.S. coast guards in the High North, not to mention the historic reconciliation of tribe and state in the Far North that began with ANCSA a generation ago and which continues to this day.

We must therefore look beyond the question of whether the Earth is warming or not, or whether this warming is anthropogenic or not: the more salient question is whether Arctic climate change is by definition a crisis as it is so often portrayed far to the south – or if perhaps it may present a new and historic opportunity for the Arctic and its peoples. Indeed, the very real possibility exists that the people of the Arctic, and the Arctic states, could become the Earth's biggest winners of climate change – after they adapt to the new contours of the post-Arctic world and overcome its early challenges. Instead of a future defined by doom and gloom, we may soon witness a coming Arctic *boom*, and perhaps, in time, even a bountiful Arctic *bloom*. And that's change we can all believe in.

Whether we call it the "Day of the Arctic," as Walter Hickel did forty years ago, the "Age of the Arctic," as Oran Young, Ed Struzik, and others have done in the decades since, or the "Arctic Spring," as I do now, the strategic, diplomatic, economic and political opportunities ahead are indeed compelling – for the peoples of the Arctic as well as the states that assert sovereignty up to the North Pole, where all cartographic divisions created by man magically disappear into a single, convergent point.

Notes

1 This paper previously appeared in *Strategic Insights* 9, no. 2 (2010): 54–78; http://edocs.nps.edu/npspubs/institutional/newsletters/strategic%20insight/2010/ZellenB10.pdf.

2 Halford John Mackinder, *Democratic Ideals and Reality: A Study in the Politics of Reconstruction* (Washington, D.C.: NDU Press Defense Classic, 1996), 199.

3 See the Sea Ice News, National Snow and Ice Data Center website; http://nsidc.org/arcticseaicenews/.

4 See: Rob Huebert, "Renaissance in Canadian Arctic Security?" *Canadian Military Journal*, July 14, 2008; http://www.journal.forces.gc.ca/vo6/no4/doc/north-nord-eng.pdf; Rob Huebert, "Welcome to a new era of Arctic security," *Globe and Mail*, August 24, 2010; http://www.theglobeandmail.com/news/opinions/welcome-to-a-new-era-of-arctic-security/article1682704/; Lawson Brigham, "Think Again: The Arctic – Everyone wants a piece of the thawing far north. But that doesn't mean anarchy will reign at the top of the world," *Foreign Policy* 181 (September/October 2010): 70–74; http://www.foreignpolicy.com/articles/2010/08/16/think_again_the_arctic; Scott G. Borgerson, "Arctic Meltdown: The Economic and Security Implications of Global Warming," *Foreign Affairs* 87, no. 2 (March/April 2008): 63–77; http://www.foreignaffairs.com/articles/63222/scott-g-borgerson/arctic-meltdown; Alun Anderson, *After the Ice: Life, Death, and Geopolitics in the New Arctic* (Washington, D.C.: Smithsonian, 2009); and Barry S. Zellen, *Arctic Doom, Arctic Boom: The Geopolitics of Climate Change in the Arctic* (Westport, CT: Praeger, 2009).

5 See: Herman Kahn, *Thinking About the Unthinkable* (New York: Avon Library, 1966). Also see Kahn's *On Escalation* (Westport, CT: Praeger, 1965) and *On Thermonuclear War* (Princeton, NJ: Princeton University Press, 1960).

6 Albert Gore, *An Inconvenient Truth: The Planetary Emergency of Global Warming* (New York: Rodale Press, 2006).

7 See: Bernard Brodie, ed., *The Absolute Weapon: Atomic Power and World Order* (New York: Harcourt, Brace, 1946). Also see Brodie's *Strategy in the Missile Age* (Princeton, NJ: Princeton University Press, 1959); *War and Politics* (New York: Macmillan, 1973); and "The Development of Nuclear Strategy," *International Security* 2, no. 4 (1978): 65–83.

8 Rob Huebert and Brooks Yeager, *A New Sea: The Need for a Regional Agreement on Management and Conservation of the Arctic Marine Environment* (Oslo: World Wildlife Fund, 2008).

9 Ed Struzik, "The End of Arctic," *Equinox Magazine* 66 (November/December, 1992): 76–92.

10 Albert Gore, *An Inconvenient Truth: The Planetary Emergency of Global Warming* (New York: Rodale Press, 2006).

11 Hannah Devlin, Ben Webster, and Philippe Naughton, "Inconvenient truth for Al Gore as his North Pole sums don't add up," *Times Online*, December 15, 2009; http://feldt.wordpress.com/2009/12/16/inconvenient-truth-for-al-gore-as-his-north-pole-sums-dont-add-up/.

12 Ibid.

13 Francis Fukuyama, *The End of History and the Last Man* (New York: Free Press, 1992).

14 Walter J. Hickel, "The Day of the Arctic Has Come," *Reader's Digest* (June 1973): 133–36.

15 William H. Seward, "The destiny of America," Speech of William H. Seward at the dedication of Capital University, at Columbus, Ohio, September 14, 1853; http://international.loc.gov/

cgi-bin/query/h?intldl/mtfront:@OR(@
field(NUMBER+@band(mtfgc+1002))).

16 Kristian Åtland, "Mikhail Gorbachev,
the Murmansk Initiative, and the
Desecuritization of Interstate Relations in
the Arctic," *Cooperation and Conflict* 43,
no. 3 (2008): 289–311.

17 Lawson Brigham, "Think Again: The
Arctic – Everyone wants a piece of the
thawing far north. But that doesn't
mean anarchy will reign at the top of the
world," *Foreign Policy* 181 (September/
October 2010): 70–74; http://www.
foreignpolicy.com/articles/2010/08/16/
think_again_the_arctic.

18 Inuit Circumpolar Council, *Circumpolar
Inuit Declaration on Arctic Sovereignty*,
April 28, 2009; see also: Inuit Circumpolar
Council Press Release, "Arctic Sovereignty
Begins with Inuit: Circumpolar Inuit
Commit to Development of 'Inuit
Declaration on Sovereignty in the Arctic,'"
Ottawa, Ontario, November 10, 2008.

19 Barry S. Zellen, "Cold Front: Hillary,
Ottawa, and the Inuit," *Journal of Military
and Strategic Studies* 12, no. 3 (2010): 5–11.

20 Barry S. Zellen, *Breaking the Ice: From
Land Claims to Tribal Sovereignty in the
Arctic* (Lanham, MD: Lexington, 2008) and
*On Thin Ice: The Inuit, the State, and the
Challenge of Arctic Sovereignty* (Lanham,
MD: Lexington, 2009). The historical and
structural details of Inuit governance
and land claims accords presented in the
following pages present an overview of
the case studies presented in this work.
Also see Barry S. Zellen, "The Arctic Land
Claims Journey," *Tundra Telegraph*, April
6, 2010; and Richard Condon, "Canadian
Inuit Land Claims and Economic
Development," *Alaska Native News* 1, no.
10–12 (1983): 37; and *Alaska Native News* 1,
no. 12 (1983): 16–18, 40.

21 Sam Hall, *The Fourth World: Heritage of the
Arctic and Its Destruction* (London: Bodley
Head, 1987).

22 See the website of the Mackenzie Gas
Project at http://www.mackenziegasproject.

com/ and the Aboriginal Pipeline Group at
http://www.mvapg.com/. As described by
Aboriginal Pipeline Group chairman Fred
Carmichael, "Community consultations
on a proposal to bring Mackenzie Delta
natural gas to southern markets have begun
in the Northwest Territories. As a longtime
northerner, it reminds me of the Berger
Inquiry. But this time, northern Aboriginal
people are at the planning table. In a sense,
we are now wearing two hats. One hat
we wear identifies our traditional role as
guardians and stewards of the land. The
other hat represents our emerging role as
business opportunity developers."

23 See Thomas R. Berger, *Village Journey:
The Report of the Alaska Native Review
Commission* (New York: Hill and Wang,
1985).

24 Martin Fletcher, "Greenland referendum
offers break from links to Denmark," *Irish
Independent*, November 26, 2008; http://
www.independent.ie/world-news/europe/
greenland-referendum-offers-break-from-
links-to-denmark-1552692.html.

25 Barry S. Zellen, "Multilateral Legacy: A
Sea Change in America's Arctic Policy,"
Tundra Telegraph, March 22, 2010. The
full text of NSPD-66/HSPD-25 can be
found at http://www.fas.org/irp/offdocs/
nspd/nspd-66.htm. As cited by Andrew C.
Revkin in "Ice Retreat Prompts Bush Shift
in Arctic Policy," *New York Times*, January
13, 2009; http://dotearth.blogs.nytimes.
com/2009/01/13/in-parting-move-bush-
sets-arctic-priorities/.

26 As cited by Andrew C. Revkin in "Ice
Retreat Prompts Bush Shift in Arctic
Policy," *New York Times*, January 13,
2009; http://dotearth.blogs.nytimes.
com/2009/01/13/in-parting-move-bush-
sets-arctic-priorities/.

27 Ibid.

28 Inuit Circumpolar Council, *Circumpolar
Inuit Declaration on Arctic Sovereignty*,
April 28, 2009. Discussed in further detail
in Barry S. Zellen, "The Inuit, the State,
and the Battle for the Arctic," *Georgetown*

Journal of International Affairs 11, no. 1 (2010): 57–64.

29 Inuit Circumpolar Council, *Circumpolar Inuit Declaration on Arctic Sovereignty,* April 28, 2009, Section 4.1.

30 Ibid.

31 Inuit Circumpolar Council press release, "Arctic Sovereignty Begins with Inuit: Circumpolar Inuit Commit to Development of 'Inuit Declaration on Sovereignty in the Arctic,'" Ottawa, Ontario, November 10, 2008.

32 Inuit Circumpolar Council, *Circumpolar Inuit Declaration on Arctic Sovereignty,* Section 1.4.

33 Ibid., Section 2.1.

34 Ibid.

35 Ibid.,

36 Ibid., Section 2.2.

37 Ibid., Section 2.3.

38 Ibid., Section 3.6.

39 Ibid.

40 Ibid., Section 3.7.

41 Jane George, "Melting ice stats don't sway Greenland premier," *Nunatsiaq News*, December 14, 2009; http://www.nunatsiaqonline.ca/stories/article/9657_melting_ice_stats_dont_sway_greenland_premier/.

42 Ibid.

Afterword: Think Again – The Arctic[1]

Lawson W. Brigham

Everyone wants a piece of the thawing Far North. But that doesn't mean anarchy will reign at the top of the world.

"The Arctic Is Experiencing a Twenty-first-Century Gold Rush."

Wrong. In August 2007, a minisubmarine carrying Artur Chilingarov, a Russian parliamentarian and veteran explorer, descended into the ice-covered sea at the North Pole, extended its robotic arm, and planted a Russian flag on the seafloor. The world's reaction was swift, and in some cases furious. "This isn't the 15th century," fumed Peter MacKay, then Canada's minister of Foreign Affairs. "You can't go around the world and just plant flags and say, 'We're claiming this territory.'"

Maybe not, but many countries are looking at the Arctic today with fresh eyes. Because of climate change, the Arctic Ocean's summer ice cover is now half of what it was fifty years ago. In recent years, Russian and Canadian armed forces have staged Cold War-style exercises in the Far North, and in the summer of 2009 a pair of German merchant ships conducted voyages across the relatively ice-free waters of the Northeast Passage, the long-dreamed-of trade route from Europe to Asia. And maybe the only thing heating up faster than the Arctic Ocean is the hyperbole over what's under it. "Without U.S. leadership to help develop diplomatic solutions to competing claims and potential conflicts," scholar Scott G. Borgerson wrote in *Foreign Affairs* in 2008, "the region could erupt in an armed mad dash for its resources."

It could – but it won't. Anarchy does not reign at the top of the world; in fact, it's governed in a manner not unlike the rest of the planet. The region's land borders – shared by Canada, Denmark (which controls Greenland), Finland, Iceland, Norway, Russia, Sweden, and the United States – are all set and uncontested. Several maritime boundaries do remain under dispute, most notably those between Canada and the United States in the Beaufort Sea and between Canada and Denmark in Baffin Bay. But progress has been made recently in resolving even the thorniest disagreements: In April, after forty years of negotiating, Norway and Russia were able to forge an equitable deal for a new boundary in the Barents Sea, a continental-shelf area rich in fisheries and oil and gas reserves.

What about the part of the Arctic where sovereignty remains unresolved: the seafloor that Chilingarov tried to claim? Despite being covered with ice for much of the year, the Arctic Ocean is governed much like the rest of the world's oceans – by a maritime treaty that has been ratified by all the Arctic countries except the United States, which generally abides by its terms anyway.

Chilingarov's flag gambit was a clever bid for attention, but not much more than that. Although the resources of the Arctic seabed are likely to be partitioned among the five countries that could plausibly claim them, it won't be on a first-come-first-served basis. The world has learned a lot since the re-source and land grabs of earlier centuries; for the most part, the only scuffles over borders and oil fields today are in regions that are badly destabilized already.

"Climate Change Is Driving the Transformation of the Arctic."

Not entirely. In recent decades the Arctic's average temperature has risen almost twice as fast as the rest of the world's. Sea ice is retreating, Greenland's glaciers are melting, snow cover is decreasing, and permafrost is thawing. Some Arctic communities are literally washing away into the ocean. These are unprecedented changes, and they have had profound impacts on the culture and way of life of the Far North's 4 million people, and especially its 400,000 indigenous residents.

But the transformation in how humans use the Arctic hinterlands is be-ing driven as much by global economics and natural resource availability as it is by climate change. It is mostly the work of a few industries: natural resource development (think oil and gas, minerals, and timber), marine tourism (think cruise ships), and fishing.

Regional warming has had little effect, positive or negative, on Norway's and Russia's extraction plans, which have been driven by global prices of oil and gas. The cruise ship industry's newfound interest in the Arctic, particularly the voyages now running along Greenland's west coast, is in keeping with the expansion of tourism to once-remote destinations everywhere. Arctic voyages are lucrative, in demand, and relatively safe (pirates are few and far between in Baffin Bay). As for fishing, fleets and some fish populations are moving north as Arctic and sub-Arctic seas become warmer and more navigable. But the fleets are also there because fish stocks in more temperate waters have been badly overfished – and not necessarily just because of climate change.

"The Arctic Is a Vast Storehouse of Natural Resources."

True. The Arctic's resources may not be subject to an anarchic scramble, but that doesn't mean they aren't hugely valuable. The largest zinc mine on the planet, called Red Dog, is located in northwest Alaska. Across the Arctic in western Siberia is the massive Norilsk Nickel mining complex, the world's leading source of nickel and palladium and one of its largest copper producers. Canada's Baffin Island is home to one of the best undeveloped iron-ore deposits on Earth; European steel companies are already experimenting with ways to get the ore into their blast furnaces and envisioning a fleet of polar ore carriers that could deliver the mineral year-round. There are renewable resources, too: world-class fisheries in the Barents and Bering seas, and abundant fresh water elsewhere.

But the most valuable Arctic commodities, today and in the future, are likely to be oil and gas. In 2008 the U.S. Geological Survey released a report indicating that natural gas resources above the Arctic Circle could amount to 30 per cent of the world's undiscovered reserves; oil in the region was estimated at 13 per cent of the world's undiscovered supply. (Saudi Arabia, by comparison, has 21 per cent of the world's proven oil.)

Two Arctic states are already banking on the oil and gas reserves on their northern frontiers: Norway has developed the Snohvit gas field in the Barents Sea near the fishing-community-turned-industrial-port of Hammerfest and is shipping its output of liquefied natural gas to North America and Europe.

Russia has been similarly busy working the oil and gas fields of western Siberia and has recently started shipping oil from an offshore terminal in the Pechora Sea to Murmansk. But for the current global oversupply of natural gas, the giant Russian firm Gazprom would be making good on its longstanding plans to develop the Shtokman field in the eastern Barents Sea, one of the world's largest natural gas deposits. Greenland has also linked its economic and perhaps political future to offshore drilling, recently beginning work near Disko Island off its west coast.

Taken together, this means that the distant and once-economically unviable resources of the Far North will be linked to global markets more closely than ever before, playing an increasingly important role in the world economy. They constitute a new frontier of investment and industrialization and will add considerably to the fortunes of the countries that possess them. But these riches amount to an economic shot in the arm – not a fundamental game-changer – for the eight Arctic states, most of which are already major producers of oil, gas, and minerals. Arguably, the countries that stand to be most transformed by the Arctic resource boom aren't in the Arctic at all; they're emerging, resource-hungry economies such as China and India whose future development is likely to be fueled by the exports of the Far North.

"The Arctic Will Become a Shipping Superhighway."

Not so fast. As early as the fifteenth century, European monarchs and capitalists salivated over the idea of a navigable northern waterway that would allow them to reach the Pacific Ocean without a grueling sail around Africa or land crossing of Central Asia. Some in today's shipping industry are no less enamored of the prospect: By one (perhaps optimistic) estimate, bringing a container ship from Northern Europe to the West Coast of the United States via Canada's fabled Northwest Passage – whose deep-water route was ice-free for a few days during the summer of 2007 – could cut shipping costs 20 per cent. And the security challenges and threats (again, think pirates) would be minimal.

But just because ships will soon be able to traverse the Arctic doesn't mean many actually will. The Northwest Passage and the Northern Sea Route across the top of Russia have indeed been made navigable by climate change, but only for a few days or weeks a year. Although several climate models predict an ice-free Arctic Ocean for a brief period each summer as early as

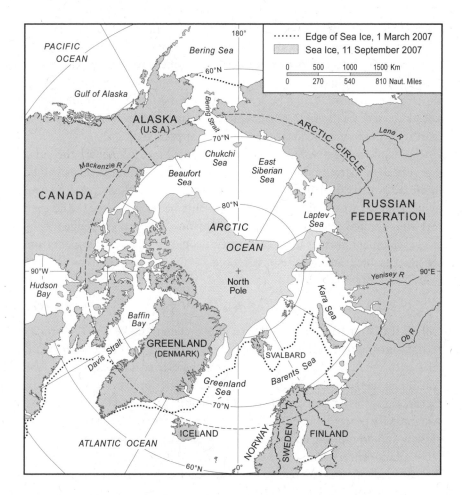

Fig. 1. See Ice Extent, 2007. Source: Lawson W. Brigham.

2030, they also project a mostly ice-clogged ocean in winter, spring, and fall through at least the end of the twenty-first century. No one predicts an ice-free Arctic Ocean throughout the year.

This means that an Arctic Ocean crossing, while theoretically possible, might be too difficult and costly to be worth the effort. The more ice along an Arctic navigation route, the slower the ship's speed, a factor that could easily negate the shorter distance gained by sailing across the top of the world.

Expensive polar-class ships – ice-breaking cargo carriers – would still be required for most operations. And many other economic details have yet to be filled in. The Arctic Marine Shipping Assessment released by the Arctic Council in 2009 found significant challenges and unanswered questions regarding the endeavor: Can it be economically viable as a global trade route if not conducted year-round? What are the risks assumed in Arctic navigation, and how will the marine insurance industry respond to them?

So, while modest volumes of cargo might be carried during the summers ahead, a majority of the Arctic voyages in the coming decades will be destinational: A ship sails north, performs an activity in the Arctic, and goes home. In other words, don't expect a new Panama or Suez Canal. And even this more limited activity will require adaptation. The real challenge will be the development of rules to protect Arctic people and the environment from the new marine traffic, wherever it's going.

"We Need a New Treaty to Govern the Arctic."

Not really. Do we need a new international system to make sure the Arctic's future is managed equitably and responsibly? That was what the seven countries with territorial claims on Earth's other polar region decided in 1959 when they set them aside to join five other countries in the Antarctic Treaty. Conceived at the height of the Cold War, the treaty reserved the uninhabited Antarctic for peaceful purposes, notably scientific research, banning military activity and prohibiting nuclear explosions and disposal of radioactive waste. Over a half-century later, it stands as a landmark of peaceful cooperation, demilitarization, and shared governance among the forty-seven countries that have signed.

It's highly unlikely, however, that the Arctic countries would ever agree to the same sort of comprehensive treaty for the North. All have huge economic stakes in the Arctic; some have centuries of sovereign claims to the region, and others still use its waterways for strategic purposes, even twenty years after the Cold War. And that's fine because we already have a diplomatic framework to deal with most of the Arctic: the UN Convention on the Law of the Sea. The treaty allows coastal states everywhere – not just those in the Arctic – to extend their seabed claims beyond their sovereign waters, but only after extensive scientific surveys and submissions of geologic data to the New York-based UN Commission on the Limits of the Continental

Shelf. It is a complex process, but an orderly one. And it isn't new: More than fifty claims have been submitted to the commission over the past decade. The International Maritime Organization, a UN agency, can also craft binding rules for shipping in the Arctic Ocean.

Then there's the Arctic Council, an intergovernmental forum (established in 1996) that brings the eight Arctic states to the table along with six indigenous groups (and other observers) to discuss environmental protection and sustainable development. The council is essentially toothless, at least in a legal sense: It's not bound by any treaties, and members have chosen not to deal with military and security issues, or even fisheries management. But it has nonetheless been a force for good, getting everyone in the habit of discussing the future of the region in a diplomatic setting. It has also conducted several pioneering assessments on climate change, oil and gas, and Arctic shipping. Look for it to take a more forceful role as Arctic relations become ever-more important. Already, it has a task force on search and rescue in the region, negotiating the first legally binding agreement among its members.

"Conflict Is Inevitable in the Arctic."

No, it isn't. The Arctic has been a geopolitical flashpoint before: During the Cold War, the United States and Soviet Union faced off directly in the region. But that was then. Today's Arctic is governed by eight developed states that arguably cooperate more than they have at any other period in history. International collaboration in scientific research, for instance, is at record levels in the Arctic today.

The looming Arctic resource boom doesn't threaten this stability – it reinforces it. States such as Norway and Russia have much to lose economically from Arctic conflict, as do the many non-Arctic countries and multinational corporations that will be among the eventual investors in, and consumers of, future Arctic ventures. No one is contesting anyone else's sovereignty in the region; in fact, the Arctic might one day play host to the emergence of a new sovereign state, Greenland, with the support and encouragement of Denmark, its long-time colonial ruler.

This isn't to say that saber-rattling hasn't happened and won't happen again in the future. Canada, Norway, and Russia have conducted military and naval operations in the region to showcase their capabilities and demonstrate their sovereignty. (The United States has been more modest in this regard, though the U.S. Navy last fall did release a "roadmap" for the Arctic, emphasizing the need for military readiness in the Far North.) NATO's role in the Arctic is uncertain and unfocused – five Arctic states are members, but three (Sweden, Finland, and Russia) are not – and the organization could go a long way toward reducing tension and building trust in the Arctic by promoting cooperation on matters of military security, law enforcement, and counter-terrorism there.

But none of this friction is beyond the realm of diplomacy. Even Chilingarov, the flag-wielding champion of Russian northern expansionism, understands the virtues of negotiation. When he met Chuck Strahl, Canada's minister of Northern Affairs, in June of 2010, the first thing he reportedly did was invite his would-be adversary to a conference in Moscow: "The Arctic: Territory of Dialogue" (held in September, 2010). The two countries' representatives have trumpeted their thawing relations in the Arctic, meeting regularly and even discussing plans to work together on mapping the seafloor where Chilingarov planted the Russian standard. The lesson is clear enough: The world has plenty of regions where serious conflict is a way of life already. Let's worry about them first.

Note

1 Reprinted and adapted (with permission of the publisher) from Lawson W. Brigham, "Think Again: The Arctic: Everyone wants a piece of the thawing far north. But that doesn't mean anarchy will reign at the top of the world," *Foreign Policy* 181 (September/October 2010): 70–74; http://www.foreignpolicy.com/articles/2010/08/16/think_again_the_arctic.

About the Contributing Authors

ALUN ANDERSON is the author of *After the Ice: Life, Death and Geopolitics in the New Arctic* and has traveled to many regions of the Arctic, including Greenland, Svalbard, Alaska, and the northern islands of Canada, as well as Antarctica. From 1992 to 2005 he was Editor-in-Chief and Publishing Director of the weekly magazine *New Scientist* and took the magazine from its home in London into the U.S. and international markets. Earlier, he was an Editor at the science journals *Nature* and then *Science* and lived in London, Tokyo, and Washington, D.C. Currently he writes articles for magazines around the world and helps manage a start-up business called *Xconomy. com*, which is based in Cambridge, Massachusetts, and brings together the innovation community of high-tech scientists and venture capitalists. Before becoming a journalist, he carried out research on how animals see the world, receiving a PhD from the University of Edinburgh and holding post-doctoral positions at the University of Oxford and Kyoto University in Japan. He is a member of the council of the Society for Experimental Biology, a trustee of the St. Andrews Prize for the Environment and is on the editorial board of Oxford University's magazine *Oxford Today*.

CAITLYN ANTRIM is the Executive Director of the *Rule of Law Committee for the Oceans*, a committee of experts in international law and policy for the oceans. On behalf of the Committee, she provides education and outreach regarding the UN Convention on the Law of the Sea and the benefits of the convention to U.S. and global interests. Ms. Antrim focuses on national and international issues related to oceanic, continental, and polar resources and to the national and international regimes that affect their development and conservation. She served as a Deputy U.S. Representative to the Third UN Conference on the Law of the Sea in 1982, an adviser to the president of the preparatory committee for the 1992 UN Conference on Environment and Development, Senior Analyst and Project Director at the Congressional Office of Technology Assessment, Policy Analyst in the U.S. Department of Commerce and an officer in the U.S. Navy. She has also directed major projects for the American Academy of Diplomacy and the American Academy of Arts and Sciences and served as a Project Officer at the National Academy of Sciences. Her publication topics range from resource, economic, and policy assessments of minerals on land and on the deep ocean floor to the theory of international regimes and international systems for dispute settlement. Her most recent publications address the geopolitics of a changing Arctic, particularly the effects of a more accessible arctic watershed on Russia's role in the world. Ms. Antrim conducted her undergraduate and graduate studies at the Massachusetts Institute of Technology, where she earned her BS in Mechanical Engineering and the professional degree of Environmental Engineer with her graduate research on the technology, economics, law, and policy affecting the development of the deep seabed mining industry. In addition to her academic credentials, she was designated a Distinguished Naval Graduate by the U.S. Navy for her work in the NROTC programs at MIT and Harvard University.

RASMUS GJEDSSØ BERTELSEN is a postdoctoral fellow at the Department of Learning and Philosophy at Aalborg University (Denmark). His field of research is International Relations, where he focuses on transnational flows of knowledge between the West and the Middle East and East Asia, as well as Arctic and North Atlantic studies. As a Danish political scientist who grew up in Iceland, he is deeply interested in the micro (proto) states of the North Atlantic, Iceland, Greenland, and Faroe Islands. How Iceland with a very small population and very harsh natural conditions has become one of the socio-economically most successful countries in the world is a passionate interest for Bertelsen. Equally, the independence politics and state formation of Iceland in the past and Greenland and the Faroe Islands in the present and future are key questions for him. Bertelsen is a former Nordplus student at the University of Iceland and intern in the Icelandic Ministry of Finances. He holds a PhD in International Relations from the University of Cambridge, where he started his North Atlantic research agenda inviting then Icelandic

Minister of Justice Björn Bjarnason to speak about North Atlantic security and thinking about Icelandic security after U.S. withdrawal from Keflavik. This activity and interest was continued as a research fellow at the Harvard Kennedy School of Government, bringing Björn Bjarnason to speak on security and Minister of Business and Dr. Gylfi Magnússon to speak on the financial crisis. Bertelsen continued these interests as JSPS Postdoc at United Nations University Institute of Advanced Studies and Tokyo Institute of Technology. He is active in the Association of Polar Early Career Scientists and has presented at the Northern Research Forum, the Arctic Science Summit Week, the International Polar Year Oslo Science Conference, the International Symposium on Arctic Research, the International Conference on Environmental Diplomacy and Security, and the International Polar Year From Knowledge to Action.

LAWSON W. BRIGHAM is Distinguished Professor of Geography and Arctic Policy at the University of Alaska Fairbanks and a senior fellow at the Institute of the North in Anchorage. From 2005 to 2009, he was chair of the Arctic Council's Arctic Marine Shipping Assessment and Vice Chair of the Council's working group on Protection of the Arctic Marine Environment. Dr. Brigham was a career U.S. Coast Guard officer serving from 1970 to 1995, retiring with the rank of Captain. He commanded four Coast Guard cutters, including a Great Lakes icebreaker and the polar icebreaker *Polar Sea*; he also served as Chief of Strategic Planning at Coast Guard Headquarters. He has participated in over fifteen Arctic and Antarctic expeditions, and during summer 1994, aboard *Polar Sea*, he crossed the Arctic Ocean for science with the Canadian Coast Guard icebreaker *Louis S. St-Laurent*. Dr. Brigham has been a research fellow at Woods Hole Oceanographic Institution, a faculty member of the U.S. Coast Guard Academy and the Naval Postgraduate School, and Alaska Office Director of the U.S. Arctic Research Commission. He is a graduate of the U.S. Coast Guard Academy (BS) and a distinguished graduate of the U.S. Naval War College, and he holds graduate degrees from Rensselaer Polytechnic Institute (MS) and the University of Cambridge (MPhil & PhD). His research interests have focused on the Russian maritime Arctic, Arctic climate change, marine transportation, Arctic futures, remote sensing of sea ice, and polar geopolitics. Captain Brigham was a 2008 signer of the American Geographical Society's Flier's and Explorer's Globe, the Society's historic globe that has been signed by more than 75 explorers of the twentieth century. This signing was in recognition of *Polar Sea*'s 1994 voyages, becoming the first ship in history to reach the extreme ends of the global ocean. He currently serves as a member of NOAA's U.S. federal Hydrographic Services Review Panel.

IAN G. BROSNAN is a PhD student in the Ocean Resources and Marine Ecosystems Program (Ecology and Evolutionary Biology) at Cornell University and is the recipient of a National Defense Science and Engineering Graduate Fellowship. His research interests include the application of advanced acoustic telemetry technology in marine fisheries ecology and the use of structured decision-making in marine policy. He received a master's in Marine Affairs from the University of Washington, where he studied governance and security in a changing Arctic and co-authored a report on the Arctic region for the National Assembly of Korea. His work has been published in the journals *Marine Policy* and *Ocean Development and International Law*. He is a former active-duty U.S. Coast Guard officer and served as the Commanding Officer of the Coast Guard Cutter COBIA and as a liaison to members of Congress. His awards include the Humanitarian Service Medal and the Coast Guard's Commendation Medal. He continues to serve in the Coast Guard Reserve as the Engineering Officer for Port Security Unit 305.

DANIEL CLAUSEN is a PhD candidate in International Relations at Florida International University. He is a graduate from the University of Miami with a BA in English and American Studies. He completed an MA degree in Strategic Studies from American Public University System–AMU. His current research focuses on the domestic political dynamics of Japanese defense policy, Japan's pursuit of human security, and the relationship between development aid and conflict. Throughout his research, Mr. Clausen has attempted to find new ways to explore complexity in social life and conflict. In particular, his most recent research attempts to conceptualize the role of policy entrepreneurs. He believes that policy entrepreneurs will be an important area of future inquiry because they demonstrate the limits and possibilities of available political resources and structures. He has presented research at conferences for the Peace Research Society, the International Studies Association, and the Guild of Independent Scholars. His prior research has appeared in *The Journal of Alternative Perspectives in the Social Sciences*, *The Electronic Journal of Contemporary Japanese Studies*, *Strategic Insights*, and *Asian Politics and Policy*.

LTJG MICHAEL CLAUSEN is a United States Coast Guard Officer, Lieutenant Junior Grade, with extensive experience in environmental management and pollution investigation. He is a graduate of Harvard University's extension program in Environmental Management and earned his master's degree in Organizational Management and his bachelor's degree in Sociology.

LASSI KALEVI HEININEN is a University Lecturer and Docent (Adjunct Professor) at University of Lapland, and Docent at University of Oulu, Finland. He is also Visiting Professor at University of Akureyri, Iceland; Adjunct Faculty at Frost Center for Canadian Studies, Trent University, Canada; Associate Researcher of the Center for Geopolitical Studies at the University of Quebec in Montreal; and Director of International Summer School in Karelia at Petrozavodsk State University, Russia. Dr. Heininen is regularly teaching abroad (Canada, Iceland, Latvia, Portugal, and Russia) and supervising PhD students from Finland and other Arctic countries. His research fields include IR, geopolitics, security studies, environmental politics, Russian studies, northern and arctic studies, and political history. He actively participates in international scientific conferences and workshops and organizes international seminars and forums with a new kind of design, such as Calotte Academy and Northern Research Forum's (NRF) Open Assemblies. He also acts as the chairman of the NRF Steering Committee. He is also constantly publishing, and among his more than 150 publications are his recent Arctic Strategies and Policies: Inventory & Comparative Study; "The End of the post-Cold War in the Arctic" at *Nordia Geographical Publications* Yearbook 2011; *Globalization and the Circumpolar North* (with C. Southcott); "Polar Regions – Comparing Arctic and Antarctic Border Debates" (with M. Zebich-Knos) in *Ashgate Research Companion to Border Studies*; and "Post-Cold War Arctic Geopolitics: Where are the Peoples and the Environment?" in *Arctic Geopolitics and Autonomy*.

NONG HONG is Associate Professor (Research) and Deputy Director at the Research Centre for Oceans Law and Policy, National Institute for South China Sea Studies (NISCSS). She received her PhD in Political Science from the University of Alberta, Canada, and held a postdoctoral fellowship with China Institute, University of Alberta. She was ITLOS-Nippon Fellow for International Dispute Settlement (2008–2009), visiting fellow at Center of Oceans Law and Policy, University of Virginia (2009), and visiting fellow at Max Planck Institute for Comparative Public Law and International Law (2007). Her research takes an interdisciplinary approach of international relations and international law, with focus on international relations and comparative politics in general; ocean governance in East Asia; law of the sea; international security, particularly on non-traditional security; and international dispute settlement/conflict resolution. Her most recent publications include *UNCLOS and Ocean Dispute Settlement: Law and Politics in the South China Sea* (Routledge, 2012); "The melting Arctic and its impact on China's maritime transport," in *Research in Transportation Economics* 35, no. 1 (May 2012), 50–57; "Chinese Perceptions of U.S. Engagement in the South China Sea," *China Brief* XI, no. 12 (July 1, 2011), 7–9; and "Charting a Maritime Security Cooperation Mechanism in the Indian Ocean: Sharing Responsibilities among Littoral States and User States," in *Strategic Analysis* 36, no. 3 (2012), 400–412.

ROB HUEBERT is Associate Professor in the Department of Political Science at the University of Calgary. He is also the Associate Director of the Centre for Military and Strategic Studies. He was a senior research fellow of the Canadian International Council and a fellow with Canadian Defence and Foreign Affairs Institute. In November 2010, he was appointed as a director to the Canadian Polar Commission. Dr. Huebert has taught at Memorial University, Dalhousie University, and the University of Manitoba. His area of research interests include: international relations, strategic studies, the law of the sea, maritime affairs, Canadian foreign and defense policy, and circumpolar relations. He publishes on the issue of Canadian Arctic Security, Maritime Security, and Canadian Defence. His work has appeared in *International Journal*; *Canadian Foreign Policy*; *Isuma-Canadian Journal of Policy Research* and *Canadian Military Journal*. He is co-editor of *Commercial Satellite Imagery and United Nations Peacekeeping* and *Breaking Ice: Canadian Integrated Ocean Management in the Canadian North*. His most recent book, written with Whitney Lackenbauer and Franklyn Griffiths, is *Canada and the Changing Arctic: Sovereignty, Security, and Stewardship*. He also comments on Canadian security and Arctic issues in both the Canadian and international media.

MAJ. HENRIK JEDIG JØRGENSEN presently serves as Desk Officer in the Strategic Competence Development Branch of the Chief of Defence Staff (*Forsvarschefen*) of the Royal Danish Armed Forces. . He previously served as XO, OMLT VI Shorabak, Combat Support Wing, and from February 20 to July 13, 2011, he underwent mission-specific training prior to deployment to Afghanistan, where he served through February 2012 in Helmand Province, as part of NATO's mission to train and mentor the Afghan National Army (ANA). In 2010, he was appointed Military Analyst at the Center for Military Studies at the University of Copenhagen, where he served as acting director from April 2010 through February 2011. In 2011, he earned his master's degree in War in the Modern World from King's College, University of London, with distinction. From April 2007 through January 2011, he was a Military Analyst at the Danish Institute for Military Studies. He served as Press Officer at Defence Command Denmark in 1998–99.

P. WHITNEY LACKENBAUER is Associate Professor and Chair of the Department of History at St. Jerome's University in the University of Waterloo, Canada. He is also a fellow with the Canadian Defence and Foreign Affairs Institute, the Arctic Institute of North America, and the Wilfrid Laurier Centre for Military and Strategic Disarmament Studies. His recent books include *The Canadian Rangers: A Living History, 1942–2012* (forthcoming 2013), *Canada's Rangers: Selected Stories, 1942–2012* (forthcoming 2012), *Canada and the Changing Arctic: Sovereignty, Security and Stewardship* (edited, 2011), *Canada and Arctic Sovereignty and Security: Historical Perspectives* (with Franklyn Griffiths and Rob Huebert, 2011), *A Commemorative History of Aboriginal People in the Canadian Military* (with Scott Sheffield and others, 2010), *The Canadian Forces and Arctic Sovereignty: Debating Roles, Interests, and Requirements, 1968–1974* (with Peter Kikkert, 2010), and *Arctic Front: Defending Canada in the Far North* (with Ken Coates, Bill Morrison, and Greg Poelzer, 2008) (winner of the 2009 Donner Prize for the best book on Canadian public policy). He was a Fulbright Fellow at Johns Hopkins University in 2010 and a Canadian International Council Research Fellow in 2008–09. Lackenbauer's current research includes histories of the Canada–U.S. Joint Arctic Weather Stations program, the Distant Early Warning (DEW) Line, Arctic sovereignty and security since the Second World War, and community-based histories in partnership with the Kitikmeot Heritage Society.

THOMAS M. LESCHINE is Director of the School of Marine and Environmental Affairs and Ben Rabinowitz Professor of the Human Dimensions of the Environment at the University of Washington, Seattle. He is also Adjunct Professor in the School of Aquatic and Fisheries Sciences. His research interests are in the areas of environmental decision-making, marine environmental protection and restoration, and marine pollution management and policy. He has served on numerous National Research Council panels and is currently Vice Chair of the NRC Marine Board. In Washington State, he serves on the Nearshore Science Team of the Puget Sound Nearshore Partnership and as a member of the Puget Sound Partnership's Science Panel. He was a member of the Washington State Pilotage Commission from 1992 to 1998, having earlier led the U.S. Coast Guard team that produced the Federal On-Scene Coordinator's Report following the 1989 *T/V Exxon Valdez* oil spill. Dr. Leschine received his PhD in mathematics from the University of Pittsburgh. His transition to a career in marine policy came by way of a postdoctoral fellowship in marine policy, and later as a Policy Associate, at the Woods Hole Oceanographic Institution in Woods Hole, Massachusetts.

JAMES MANICOM received a PhD from Flinders University in Adelaide, Australia, in October 2009. He recently completed a two-year SSHRC postdoctoral fellowship at the Balsillie School of International Affairs in Waterloo, Canada, and is now a Research Fellow in Global Security at the Centre for International Governance Innovation in Waterloo. His dissertation examined maritime boundary disputes between China and Japan and was funded by the Endeavour International Postgraduate Research Scholarship. He is currently affiliated with the Asian Institute in the Munk School of Global Affairs at the University of Toronto and is a member of the executive of the Toronto Branch of the Canadian International Council. His research interests include East Asian international relations and strategic studies, maritime security, energy security, nationalism, and territorial disputes – the latter three as they pertain to the Canadian Arctic. Manicom has taught at York University, the University of Waterloo, and Flinders University. He frequently lectures at the Canadian Forces College and has supervised research projects in their Master of Defence Studies program. He is a graduate of Mount Allison University in Sackville, New Brunswick. Manicom's published works have appeared in *Geopolitics, International Relations of the Asia- Pacific, The Journal of East Asian Studies, International Studies Perspectives, Pacific Affairs, The Pacific Review,* and *The*

Australian Journal of International Affairs. He has also contributed to *China Brief,* the *Globe and Mail* and the *Asian Wall Street Journal.*

EDWARD L. MILES is Virginia and Prentice Bloedel Professor (Emeritus) of Marine Studies and Public Affairs at the University of Washington and a former Director of the School of Marine Affairs. He remains an active member of the Climate Impacts Group engaged in research, particularly concerning the problem of ocean acidification. His fields of specialization are international science and technology policy; marine policy and ocean management; and the impacts of climate change at global and regional scales. He is a member of the National Academy of Sciences and the American Academy of Arts and Sciences and a Fellow of AAAS. He received his PhD in International Relations and Comparative Politics from the University of Denver in 1965.

THE HONORABLE MEAD TREADWELL is Lieutenant Governor of the State of Alaska. He was elected as Alaska's lieutenant governor in November 2010. A graduate of Yale University and the Harvard Business School, Treadwell brings a record of private and public sector success to his job as Lieutenant Governor and is recognized as one of the world's Arctic policy experts. Treadwell was appointed to the United States Arctic Research Commission by President George W. Bush in 2001 and was designated by the president as the commission's chair in 2006. Under his leadership, a new United States Arctic policy was developed and adopted by President Bush and is now being implemented by the current administration.

BARRY SCOTT ZELLEN is a specialist on arctic security, sovereignty, and self-governance at the Anchorage-based Institute of the North, where he is a Senior Fellow. He also serves on the board of the Arctic Research Consortium of the United States (ARCUS). He is author of numerous books, including *Breaking the Ice: From Land Claims to Tribal Sovereignty in the Arctic* (2008); *On Thin Ice: The Inuit, the State and the Challenge of Arctic Sovereignty* (2009); *Arctic Doom, Arctic Boom: The Geopolitics of Climate Change in the Arctic* (2009); the four-volume series, *The Realist Tradition in International Relations: Foundations of Western Order* (2011); *State of Doom: Bernard Brodie, the Bomb, and the Birth of the Bipolar World* (2011), *The Art of War in an Asymmetric World: Strategy for the Post-Cold War Era* (2012), and *State of Recovery: The Quest to Restore American Security after 9/11* (2013).

KATARZYNA ZYSK is Associate Professor at the Norwegian Institute for Defence Studies (NIDS)/the Norwegian Defence University College in Oslo. She also serves as a non-resident Research Fellow at the U.S. Naval War College, Center for Naval Warfare Studies (Strategic Research Department). Dr. Zysk is working on a post-doctoral research project on security in the Arctic, with special focus on Russia. The project is a part of the international research program *Geopolitics in the High North*, sponsored by the Norwegian Research Council and chaired by NIDS. Dr. Zysk has a background in both international history and international relations and specializes in security studies. She earned her PhD from Institute for International Relations (2006) and MA (2002) in history and international relations from Nicholas Copernicus University in Torun, Poland. Her recent publications include: "Military Aspects of Russia's Arctic Policies: Hard Power and Natural Resources," in *Arctic Circumpolar Security in an Age of Climate Change*, ed. J. Kraska (2011), and "Russia's Naval Ambitions: Driving Forces and Constraints," in *Emerging Naval Powers in the 21st Century – Cooperation and Conflict at Sea* (2012). Ongoing research projects include: Russian strategic culture and developments in the Russian armed forces; continuity and change in Russian and Norwegian foreign and security policies in the High North; maritime security in the Arctic; Russia in an Asian-centered world.

Index

Fort Greely, Alaska, 212
France, 22, 29, 104
freedom, 210–11, 320, 357
frontiers, 245, 258, 265
full independence, 175, 177–79
fur, 239, 250, 260, 339

G

gas, 25–27, 108–11, 193–200, 214–16, 370–72
geographical pivot, 277–78
geopolitics, 84–85, 247–48, 342–43
GIUK (Greenland-Iceland-United Kingdom), 174, 176
global climate change, 3, 76–78, 137
Global South, 63, 72, 78
globalization, 11, 51–52, 54–55, 136, 189
Gorbachev, Mikhail, 48, 236, 244, 261, 323, 344, 365
Gore, Al, 60, 341–42, 361, 363, 366
governance, 5, 39–41, 87, 89–92, 110
    regional, 334
Great Lakes, 232, 320
Greenland, 97–100, 159–64, 174–80, 232–33, 238–39
    Command, 184
    Home Rule, 165, 184
    referendum, 367
    independence, 86, 178, 239
    vulnerability, 232

H

Hans Island, 241, 263
hard power, 289, 292, 296
Harper, Stephen, 8, 104, 271, 275, 278–79
heartland, 242, 312–13, 339
helicopters, 166, 175, 177, 184
high Arctic, 44, 265, 272, 352
high North, 42–43, 51, 161, 229–30, 240–41
high North Atlantic, 157, 159, 228, 232, 235–39
High North Strategy, 85–86, 99
home rule, 86, 167–68, 174–75, 177
homeland security interests, 90, 318
Homeland Security Presidential Directive (HSPD), 25, 317, 355–56
hulls, 310
human activities, 37, 92, 136–37, 333
    expanding, 319
human capital, 314, 317, 322, 325
human rights, 171, 353
human security, 37, 45, 271
hydrocarbons, 106, 111, 118, 120, 122–23

I

ice, 17–18, 22, 215–18, 248–50, 366–70
ice roads, 248
ice-free Arctic, 9, 342
icebreakers, 3, 9–10, 33, 213, 217–18, 285–86, 302–3
Iceland, 25–27, 159–83, 230, 235–39, 248–49
    Air Defense System, 170
    Coast Guard, 171, 183
    Defense Agency, 170, 176
    government, 161, 170, 172, 238–39
    independence, 175
    Kingdom of Iceland, 167–68
    military, 170
    security policy, 168, 170
    waters, 171
Ilulissat, Greenland, 6, 20, 24, 26, 208, 243, 267, 344, 357, 360
Ilulissat Declaration, 107, 148–49, 267, 357, 359
inconvenient truth, 341–42, 361, 366
independence, 160–61, 163–64, 167, 178–81, 249–50
indigenous peoples, 45–51, 148–50, 344–48, 355–57
industrialization, 37, 40, 45–46, 341, 372
infrastructure, 14, 89, 91, 284–85, 301–2
initiatives, 11, 48, 138–39, 142, 150–51
innovation, 170, 314, 325–26, 344, 352
insecurity, 65, 141, 144
intentions, 103, 111, 270, 272, 292
interdict, 88, 92–93, 100
interests
    competing, 138, 140, 346
    mutual, 37, 259, 261, 267, 315–16
    tribal, 347–48
Intergovernmental Panel on Climate Change (IPCC), 42, 44, 59–60, 62, 311
international
    agreements, 41–42, 174, 207, 287
    cooperation, 49–50, 140–41, 293–94, 303, 316–17
    law, 258–59, 267, 275–76, 356–59
    order, 65, 314
    organizations, 31, 41, 107, 174, 177
    relations, 131–32, 190, 220
    security, 131–32, 160, 165
    standards, 31, 197–98, 212
International Maritime Organization (IMO), 5–7, 13, 31, 104
International Seabed Authority (ISA), 107, 241
International Union for Conservation of Nature (IUCN), 31, 41

R

radioactivity, 36, 38, 44–46, 51, 202
raucous Canadian reaction, 126
Reagan, Ronald, 236
Red Arctic, 277
regional
  commands, 228, 231, 237
  cooperation, 112, 315, 326–27, 332
  development, 279
reindeer, 44, 53
Research Council of Norway, 295
resource
  base, 303, 324, 330, 352
  curse, 67, 79
  development, 86–88, 92, 96, 219–20, 274
  distribution, 70, 73
  exploitation, 18, 86, 127, 173
  exploration, 85, 90
  scarcity, 58, 67, 69, 78–80, 132
  wealth, 65, 118–20, 122, 242, 354
resources, 67–68, 70, 105–7, 193–95, 214–15
  biological, 192–93, 288, 317, 355
  economic, 126, 345, 354
  mineral, 107, 264, 320, 336
  non-renewable, 68
  renewable, 68, 70, 371
  scarce, 68, 70
Revkin, Andrew C., 367
Reykjavik, Iceland, 54–55, 167, 182–83, 223
rhetoric, 127, 269–70, 292
rivers, 46, 302, 311, 313
Royal Canadian Navy, 232
Royal Danish Navy, 165–66, 168, 174–75, 177, 179
Russia, 241–45, 257–66, 281–88, 290–98, 320–31
  assertive, 244
  and Canada, 267, 272, 276, 311
  collaborative, 243
  eastern, 27
  and Georgia, 146, 252
  imperial, 252
  northwest, 272, 291
  and Norway, 25, 94, 110, 276, 280
  prosperous, 315
  resurgent, 231
Russian
  Arctic, 260–61, 281–82, 292–94, 300–305, 326
  bombers, 272, 278
  border, 327
  citizens, 322
  coast, 209, 241, 284
  democracy, 263
  Duma, 209

economy, 118, 264, 284, 291, 323
embassy, 270, 273
exports, 264
Far East, 309, 328, 331, 334
geopolitics, 242
interests, 144, 242, 331
jurisdiction, 287, 324
laws, 3, 287
leaders, 119, 283, 294
logic, 269
media, 26, 127, 238, 273
military, 104, 144, 269, 289–94
Ministry of Defense, 126, 269, 288, 296
Ministry of Economic Development and
  Trade, 284
Navy, 290, 296
North, 120, 260, 302, 376
Northern Fleet, 144
occupation, 123, 145
oil, 21, 300
reset, 307
security, 268
suspicion, 127
threat, 259, 269
ultra-nationalists, 243
waters, 25
Russian Association of Indigenous Peoples, 203,
  274
Russian-America Company, 5, 243, 260, 339
Russian Federation, 278–79, 303–4, 324
Russian Geographical Society, 303
Russian Security Council, 119, 127, 257, 264,
  295–96

S

Saami, 47, 49, 53
Safety of Life at Sea (SOLAS), 31–32
Scandinavian Arctic, 27
scarcity, 45, 59, 65–79, 142
sea ice, 1–3, 44, 95–96, 137
sea spaces, 160–61, 164–65, 168, 180–81
seal meat, 240, 250
Search and Rescue (SAR), 95, 138–39, 164–65,
  169–71, 329–30
security, 41–43, 52–55, 165–70, 178–84, 326–30
  capabilities, 166
  challenges, 61, 177, 288, 290, 293
  common, 214
  dilemma, 70–71
  environment, 61, 136, 151–52, 282
  food, 45, 59
  homeland, 60, 85, 191–92, 317, 355